Day-by-Day in Baseball History

For Beth and Jane.
May they each discover
their special place in history.

Day-by-Day in Baseball History

by Carl R. Moesche

McFarland & Company, Inc., Publishers
Jefferson, North Carolina, and London

Library of Congress Cataloguing-in-Publication Data

Moesche, Carl R., 1959–
    Day-by-day in baseball history / by Carl R. Moesche.
        p.   cm.
    Includes index.
    ISBN 0-7864-0886-3 (softcover : 50# alkaline paper) ∞
    1. Baseball — United States — History — Chronology.
    I. Title.
    GV863.A1 M62   2000
    796.375'0973 — dc21   00-44217

British Library Cataloguing data are available

Cover image © 2000 Photospin

Manufactured in the United States of America

*McFarland & Company, Inc., Publishers
    Box 611, Jefferson, North Carolina 28640
    www.mcfarlandpub.com*

Contents

Foreword

I'm glad Carl Moesche has finally written this book. I've been looking for it for years. As a compulsive baseball historian, it has always amazed me that there was no reliable, comprehensive source giving the full calendar of anniversaries in the only sport in which it is as easy to go backwards as it is forwards.

In 1976, the Society for American Baseball Research put out a small paperback volume which gave a few highlights on a day-to-day basis. A decade later, the first edition of *Total Baseball* included a similar "this date in baseball history" format. But other than that, the obvious marriage between the sport's past and the freshness of the newest calendar has been overlooked. Until now.

Did you realize that there have been six no-hitters thrown on the various September 20ths? That half of them were in the city of Chicago? Can you identify the Hall of Fame birth clusters? Do you know what was happening in baseball the day you were born? That the day former National League first baseman and executive Mike Jorgensen was born, Babe Ruth died? That Ken Griffey, Jr., hit his first Major League homer on his father's 39th birthday?

You will have to stop yourself from connecting the dots even more wildly. And this book is anything but a collection of obscurely interrelated trivia. Arranging the game's history on a calendar basis, rather than the more frequently used chronological one, allows the fan to cut across generations, to realize that what you're watching today didn't begin last week or last year or even last century, but is merely the latest chapter in a continuum of daily developments, evolutions, setbacks, beginnings, and endings, that stretches back to that first opening day, in the long-forgotten National Association, in 1871.

So this is that rarest of baseball "historical" works: one that simultaneously serves as a reference work and as a starting point for flights of fancy or the rigors of research. Moreover, it provides the historical context in which today's events can take on more meaning than just their passing relevance to the pennant races or the vagaries of an individual's career.

Please, then, open the pages and dwell in baseball's history. Watch the coincidences form, the patterns emerge, and the overlooked moments of import come alive. Oh, and do remember to count the 25 hall of famers for whom April 26th is particularly important.

Keith Olbermann • Spring 2000

Preface

From a historical sense, *Day-by-Day in Baseball History* is perhaps a reflection of ourselves as we realize the events and examine our place in time during the storied history of baseball. For the casual fan or the diehard enthusiast, it recreates the moments, both on and off the field, that touched our hearts and identified our generation.

Unlike other major sports in America, baseball follows no clock—and indeed it is timeless in every sense. It is played indoors and out, enduring changing weather conditions and relief pitchers alike. It has withstood several wars, the Great Depression, and many civil and social changes. It has adapted through times of discovery and technology, yet remains a simple game. It subtly reminds us that while oil, automobiles, and the Internet made this country great, baseball kept it going.

The fact that baseball has a life of its own was more and more apparent to me as I compiled the information in this book. As I cross-referenced and categorized, I found new significance in the events before me. The ironies and intricacies of the game's moments became innumerable. Is it mere coincidence that longtime teammates Hank Aaron and Eddie Mathews joined the 500-homer club on the same date? Or that the first base hit allowed by the great Walter Johnson was earned by the equally great Ty Cobb? That on the same date Casey Stengel passed away, Walter Alston decided to retire, just four games removed from season's end?

Special moments in baseball become the landmarks of memory. Remember when Babe Ruth opened Yankee Stadium? Remember Joe DiMaggio's 56-game hitting streak, Lou Gehrig Day, Jackie Robinson's historic breakthrough, Ted Williams' final at-bat, that one titanic swing from Hank Aaron, Cal Ripken's magical night in Baltimore?

For myself, the magical moment came one June afternoon in Milwaukee. I was a 16-year-old outfielder at Nicolet High School in Glendale, Wisconsin. On June 29, 1975, my childhood hero Willie Mays hit a three-run homer off Early Wynn in an old-timers game at Milwaukee's County Stadium. I was in the left field bleachers, and I caught the ball. The moment lasted only a few seconds, but it changed my life and inspired me to choose a career that would always keep me near the ballfield.

A portion of the proceeds from this book will go to the Jim "Catfish"

Hunter ALS Foundation. It is ironic yet somehow fitting that the events of two centuries reserve room for a Jim Hunter moment as the final entry.

Certainly to include all the events, names, and places that have etched themselves into baseball history would have been an enormous task, one too great for a single researcher or even a team of them. While I have included a great many birthdays, milestones, and record-setting performances, information on trades, awards, and player death dates have been confined to the more recognizable to the average fan.

In researching this book I had the pleasure of discovering libraries and publications coast to coast — from Lakeland, Florida, to Butte, Montana, to San Diego, California. My thanks to all those individuals who gave me invaluable help. Thanks, too, to family and friends who afforded me the time and the tidbits, and the encouragements to keep going through this seemingly endless project. Thanks to Keith Olbermann of Fox Sports, Commissioner Bud Selig, Tommy Lasorda of the Los Angeles Dodgers, and Rob Butcher of the Cincinnati Reds for their timely contributions.

Special thanks to Barb Kozuh, whose late inning magic made this project possible.

I hope you enjoy reading and discovering as much as I have enjoyed researching. After all, one passion deserves another.

Carl Moesche • *Spring 2000*

JANUARY

1

1855 Bill McGunnigle b. Boston, MA.
1857 Tim Keefe b. Cambridge, MA.
1881 John Bell b. Wausau, WI.
1884 Tom Downey b. Lewiston, ME.
1888 Benny Meyer b. Hematite, MO.
1893 Frank Fuller b. Detroit, MI.
1894 Hack Miller b. New York, NY.
1900 Ted Kearns b. Trenton, NJ.
1904 Ethan Allen b. Cincinnati, OH.
1911 Hank Greenberg b. New York, NY.
1931 Foster Castleman b. Nashville, TN.
1948 Randy Bobb b. Los Angeles, CA.
1953 Lynn Jones b. Meadville, PA.
1974 Lee MacPhail takes over as AL President, succeeding the retired Joe Cronin.

2

1854 Sam Crane b. Springfield, MA.
1885 Chick Autry b. Humboldt, TN.
1892 Merlin Kopp b. Toledo, OH.
1893 Jesse Altenburg b. Ashley, MI.
1907 Red Kress b. Columbia, CA.
1926 Stan Hollmig b. Fredericksburg, TX.
1951 Jim Essian b. Detroit, MI.
1963 Edgar Martinez b. New York, NY.
1970 Royce Clayton b. Burbank, CA.

1977 Commissioner Bowie Kuhn suspends Atlanta Braves owner Ted Turner for one year and fines him $10,000 for tampering with soon-to-be free agent, San Francisco OF Gary Matthews.

3

1856 Barney Gilligan b. Cambridge, MA.
1874 Roy Brashear b. Ashtabula, OH.
1899 Buzz Arlett b. Elmhurst, CA.
1904 Bill Cissell b. Perryville, MO.
1910 Frenchy Bordagaray b. Coalinga, CA.
1943 Adrian Garrett b. Brooksville, FL.
1950 Jim Dwyer b. Evergreen Park, IL.
1962 Darren Daulton b. Arkansas City, KS.
1973 George M. Steinbrenner purchases the New York Yankees from CBS for $10 million.

4

1869 Tommy Corcoran b. New Haven, CT.
1884 Al Bridwell b. Friendship, OH.
1903 Alex Metzler b. Fresno, CA.
1914 Herman Franks b. Price, UT.
1944 Tito Fuentes b. Havana, Cuba.
1944 Charlie Manuel b. North Fork, WV.
1963 Daryl Boston b. Cincinnati, OH.

5

1864 Bob Caruthers b. Memphis, TN.
1870 Bill Dahlen b. Nelliston, NY.
1875 Izzy Hoffman b. Bridgeport, NJ.
1880 Dutch Jordan b. Pittsburgh, PA.
1885 Art Fletcher b. Collinsville, IL.
1899 Bob Kinsella b. Springfield, IL.
1899 Bill Hunnefield b. Dedham, MA.
1890 Benny Kauff b. Pomeroy, OH.
1914 Joe Grace b. Gorham, IL.
1920 Boston Red Sox owner Harry Frazee trades OF Babe Ruth to the New York Yankees for $125,000 along with a loan of $350,000 to help finance a broadway show. Fenway Park itself is put up as security for the loan.
1924 Freddie Marsh b. Valley Falls, KS.
1935 Earl Battey b. Los Angeles, CA.
1936 Clyde Bloomfield b. Oklahoma City, OK.
1943 In concession to the war and travel restrictions, major league baseball owners agree to open the season a week late and conduct spring training in Northern cities.
1953 Jim Gantner b. Fond du Lac, WI.
1957 Bob Dernier b. Kansas City, MO.
1958 Ron Kittle b. Gary, IN.
1961 Henry Cotto b. Bronx, NY.
1971 Jason Bates b. Downey, CA.
1975 Houston RHP Don Wilson, age 29, dies of carbon monoxide poisoning in the garage of his Houston home, an apparent suicide victim.
1989 Commissioner Peter Ueberroth signs a $400 million cable television package with ESPN, a month after signing a four-year, $1.06 billion contract with CBS.
1999 Nolan Ryan, George Brett, and Robin Yount are elected to baseball's Hall of Fame, marking the first time that as many first-time candidates are chosen since the Baseball Writers Association's first election in 1936. Ty Cobb, Babe Ruth, Honus Wagner, Walter Johnson, and Christy Mathewson are elected in the inaugural class, but no more than two first-timers had been elected in the same year since.

6

1882 Willis Cole b. Milton Junction, WI.
1897 Buck Crouse b. Anderson, IN.
1900 Clyde Beck b. Bassett, CA.
1903 Fred Eichrodt b. Chicago, IL.
1916 Phil Masi b. Chicago, IL.
1933 Lenny Green b. Detroit, MI.
1936 Ruben Amaro Sr. b. Mexico.
1942 Cleveland RHP Bob Feller becomes the second high profile star to leave major league baseball for the armed services when he enlists in the navy and reports for duty.
1951 Joe Lovitto b. San Pedro, CA.
1955 Doe Boyland b. Chicago, IL.

7

1875 Kitty Bransfield b. Worcester, MA.
1900 Johnny Grabowski b. Ware, MA.
1905 Frank Grube b. Easton, PA.
1910 Johnny McCarthy b. Chicago, IL.
1913 Johnny Mize b. Demorest, GA.
1921 Ted Beard b. Woodsboro, MD.
1922 Alvin Dark b. Comanche, OK.
1933 Commissioner Kenesaw Mountain Landis, sending a Depression-era message to owners, takes a voluntary $25,000 cut in salary.

1942 Jim Lefebvre b. Inglewood, CA.
1945 Tony Conigliaro b. Revere, MA.
1946 Joe Keough b. Pomona, CA.
1967 Rob Maurer b. Evansville, IN.

8

1901 Joe Benes b. Long Island City, NY.
1915 Walker Cooper b. Atherton, MO.
1916 Joe Just b. Milwaukee, WI.
1927 Jim Busby b. Kenedy, TX.
1934 Gene Freese b. Wheeling, WV.
1935 Reno Bertoia b. Italy.
1936 Chuck Cottier b. Delta, CO.
1936 John DeMerit b. West Bend, WI.
1937 Don Dillard b. Greenville, SC.
1949 Wilbur Howard b. Lowell, NC.
1968 Brian Johnson b. Oakland, CA.
1968 Paul Carey b. Boston, MA.
1971 Jason Giambi b. West Covina, CA.
1973 Mike Cameron b. LaGrange, GA.

9

1882 Jack Bliss b. Vancouver, WA.
1895 Ray French b. Alameda, CA.
1903 A peace treaty is signed as the NL agrees to recognize the AL as a major league and both parties agree to honor the reserve clause in player contracts.
1918 Pittsburgh trades RHPs Burleigh Grimes and Al Mamaux, and SS Chuck Ward to Brooklyn for OF Casey Stengel and 2B George Cutshaw.
1918 Ferrell Anderson b. Maple City, KS.
1952 Don Hopkins b. West Point, MS.
1953 Ivan DeJesus b. Puerto Rico.

1953 Phil Mankowski b. Buffalo, NY.
1964 Stan Javier b. Dominican Republic.

10

1859 Tom Dolan b. New York, NY.
1870 John Houseman b. Holland.
1928 Jack Dittmer b. Elkader, IA.
1938 Willie McCovey b. Mobile, AL.
1962 Mario Diaz b. Puerto Rico.
1962 Jim Lindeman b. Evanston, IL.
1991 Baltimore trades RHPs Pete Harnisch and Curt Schilling, and OF Steve Finley to Houston for 1B Glenn Davis.
1992 The New York Yankees trade 2B Steve Sax to the Chicago White Sox for RHPs Domingo Jean, Melido Perez, and Bob Wickman.

11

1868 Silver King b. St. Louis, MO.
1876 Elmer Flick b. Bedford, OH.
1879 Harry McIntire b. Dayton, OH.
1890 Max Carey b. Terre Haute, IN.
1895 Paddy Driscoll b. Evanston, IL.
1911 Roy Hughes b. Cincinnati, OH.
1918 Ernie Andres b. Jeffersonville, IN.
1922 Neil Berry b. Kalamazoo, MI.
1928 Loren Babe b. Pisgah, IA.
1959 Lloyd McClendon b. Gary, IN.

12

1860 Henry Larkin b. Reading, PA.
1876 George Browne b. Richmond, VA.
1899 Joe Hauser b. Milwaukee, WI.
1947 Paul Reuschel b. Quincy, IL.
1951 Bill Madlock b. Memphis, TN.

1956 Juan Bonilla b. Puerto Rico.
1960 Tim Hulett b. Springfield, IL.
1960 Mike Marshall (OF) b. Libertyville, IL.
1961 Chewing gum magnate Phil Wrigley announces that the Chicago Cubs will not have a manager for the upcoming season. Rather, an eight-man coaching committee would run the club. By late fall, the experiment ends.
1961 Casey Candaele b. Lompoc, CA.
1970 Nigel Wilson b. Oshawa, Ontario.
1971 Andy Fox b. Sacramento, CA.

13

1880 Goat Anderson b. Cleveland, OH.
1908 Jimmy Jordan b. Tucapau, SC.
1918 Steve Mesner b. Los Angeles, CA.
1940 Ron Brand b. Los Angeles, CA.
1950 Bob Forsch b. Sacramento, CA.
1962 Kevin Mitchell b. San Diego, CA.
1969 Orlando Miller b. Panama.
1996 Cuban defector and RHP Livan Hernandez receives the largest contract ever for an amateur player $4.5 million from the Florida Marlins.

14

1930 Pete Daley b. Grass Valley, CA.
1937 Sonny Siebert b. St. Mary's, MO.
1942 Dave Campbell b. Manistee, MI.
1943 Ron Clark b. Fort Worth, TX.
1952 Terry Forster b. Sioux City, SD.
1952 Wayne Gross b. Riverside, CA.
1954 New York Yankees CF Joe DiMaggio marries Marilyn Monroe. They divorce only nine months later.

1962 Gary Green b. Pittsburgh, PA.
1963 The Chicago White Sox trade SS Luis Aparicio and OF Al Smith to Baltimore for RHP Hoyt Wilhelm, SS Ron Hansen, 3B Pete Ward and OF Dave Nicholson.
1970 Steve Cooke b. Lihue, HI.
1976 NL owners approve the sale of the Atlanta Braves to Ted Turner, head of Turner Communications, for $12 million.
1998 Houston trades OF James Mouton to San Diego for RHP Sean Bergman.

15

1891 Ray Chapman b. Beaver Dam, KY.
1920 Steve Gromer b. Hamtramck, MI.
1942 Amid the United States' involvement in World War II, President Franklin D. Roosevelt sends baseball commissioner Kenesaw Mountain Landis the infamous "Green Letter" urging baseball to continue to uphold the country's morale. Roosevelt writes, "I honestly think it would be best for the country to keep baseball going."
1943 Mike Marshall (RHP) b. Adrian, MI.
1949 Bobby Grich b. Muskegon, MI.
1956 Rance Mulliniks b. Tulare, CA.
1956 Jerry Narron b. Goldsboro, NC.
1969 Delino DeShields b. Seaford, DE.
1970 The Seattle Pilots trade 1B Don Mincher and INF Ron Clark to Oakland for C Phil Roof, RHPs Lew Krausse and Ken Sanders, and OF Mike Hershberger.
1973 Wayne Gomes b. Langley AFB, VA.

16

1870 Jimmy Collins b. Buffalo, NY.
1904 Jo-Jo Morrissey b. Warren, RI.
1905 The St. Louis Browns trade OF Jesse Burkett to the Boston Puritans for OF George Stone.
1911 Dizzy Dean b. Lucas, AR.
1957 Steve Balboni b. Brockton, MA.
1966 Jack McDowell b. Van Nuys, CA.
1970 St. Louis Cardinals OF Curt Flood files a federal lawsuit challenging baseball's antitrust law and refuses to honor a trade to the Philadelphia Phillies.
1970 Ron Villone b. Englewood, NJ.
1974 New York Yankees CF Mickey Mantle and LHP Whitey Ford become the first pair of teammates elected to baseball's Hall of Fame in the same year.

17

1878 Harry Bay b. Pontiac, IL.
1915 Luman Harris b. New Castle, AL.
1931 Don Zimmer b. Cincinnati, OH.
1944 Denny Doyle b. Glasgow, KY.
1952 Darrell Porter b. Joplin, MO.
1952 Pete LaCock b. Burbank, CA.
1953 Mark Littell b. Gideon, MO.
1960 Chili Davis b. Kingston, Jamaica.

18

1904 Len Koenecke b. Baraboo, WI.
1938 Curt Flood b. Houston, TX.
1944 Carl Morton b. Kansas City, MO.

1964 Brady Anderson b. Silver Spring, MD.
1972 Mike Lieberthal b. Glendale, CA.

19

1887 Chick Gandil b. St. Paul, MN.
1937 In the second year of Hall of Fame balloting, three more players are inducted: Nap Lajoie, Tris Speaker, and Cy Young. It brings the enshrined total to eight after Ty Cobb, Babe Ruth, Honus Wagner, Christy Mathewson, and Walter Johnson were named on the first ballot a year earlier.
1950 Jon Matlack b. West Chester, PA.
1962 Chris Sabo b. Detroit, MI.
1966 Anthony Young b. Houston, TX.
1971 Jeff Juden b. Salem, MA.
1971 Phil Nevin b. Fullerton, CA.

20

1922 Sam Jethroe b. East St. Louis, IL.
1934 Camilo Pascual b. Havana, Cuba.
1947 Negro League C Josh Gibson dies of heart failure, at age 35, less than 12 weeks before baseball allows Jackie Robinson to break the color barrier. Perhaps the greatest receiver of all time, Gibson may have hit nearly 1,000 home runs in the Negro Leagues.
1964 Ozzie Guillen b. Venezuela.
1965 Kevin Maas b. Castro Valley, CA.
1965 Cleveland trades OF Tommie Agee, LHP Tommy John, and C John Romano to the Chicago White Sox for OF Rocky Colavito and C Camilo Carreon. As part of a three-club deal, the Kansas City A's trade Colavito to the

White Sox for OFs Mike Hershberger and Jim Landis, and RHP Fred Talbot.

1970 Marvin Benard b. Nicaragua.

1972 The New York Yankees trade RHP Jack Aker to the Chicago Cubs for OF Johnny Callison.

1977 Baltimore trades OF Paul Blair to the New York Yankees for OF Elliott Maddox and OF Rick Bladt.

1983 Los Angeles trades 3B Ron Cey to the Chicago Cubs for LHP Vance Lovelace.

1997 St. Louis Cardinals OF Curt Flood, who pioneered modern free agency, dies of throat cancer at age 59. Challenging baseball's reserve clause in 1970, Flood took his case all the way to the U.S. Supreme Court before losing, contending he was not a "piece of property" to be sold when the Cardinals traded him to Philadelphia in 1969.

21

1921 Federal judge Kenesaw Mountain Landis begins his seven-year contract as baseball's first commissioner.

1923 Sam Mele b. Astoria, NY.

1946 Johnny Oates b. Sylva, NC.

1966 Chris Hammond b. Atlanta, GA.

1969 Rusty Greer b. Fort Rucker, AL.

1972 Alan Benes b. Evansville, IN.

22

1913 The New York Yankees, no longer tenants of Hilltop Park, receive permission from the New York Giants to use the Polo Grounds as co-tenants.

1918 The New York Yankees trade RHP Urban Shocker, C Les Nunamaker, 2B Joe Gedeon, 3B Fritz Maisel, and OF Nick Cullop to the St. Louis

Browns for LHP Eddie Plank and 2B Del Pratt. After 17 years and 326 wins, the 42-year-old Plank will retire without ever pitching for the Yankees, his spot in the Hall of Fame already secured.

1929 The New York Yankees announce that they will use permanent numbers on the backs of their uniforms corresponding to players' positions in the batting order.

1949 Mike Caldwell b. Tarboro, NC.

1963 Jeff Treadway b. Columbus, GA.

1964 Wayne Kirby b. Williamsburg, VA.

1969 Montreal trades OF Jesus Alou and 1B Donn Clendenon to Houston for OF Rusty Staub. Clendenon refuses to report, forcing the Expos to send RHP Jack Billingham and LHP Skip Guinn to the Astros to complete the trade.

1988 Kirk Gibson and Carlton Fisk are among seven players declared free agents by an arbitrator who rules that owners had acted in collusion against free agents after the 1985 season.

23

1918 Randy Gumpert b. Monocacy, PA.

1930 Frank Sullivan b. Hollywood, CA.

1947 Kurt Bevacqua b. Miami Beach, FL.

1970 Alan Embree b. Vancouver, WA.

1970 Mark Wohlers b. Holyoko, MA.

1981 California trades LHP Frank Tanana, OF Joe Rudi, and RHP Jim Dorsey to Boston for OF Fred Lynn and RHP Steve Renko.

24

1901 Flint Rhem b. Rhems, SC.

1958 Atlee Hammaker b. Carmel, CA.

1964 Rob Dibble b. Bridgeport, CT.
1980 The Payson family, owners of the New York Mets since 1962, sells the franchise for $21.1 million to a group led by Nelson Doubleday and Fred Wilpon.

25

1945 Wally Bunker b. Seattle, WA.
1948 Ed Goodson b. Pulaski, VA.
1951 Vern Ruhle b. Coleman, MI.
1961 The Kansas City A's trade RHPs John Tsitouris and Johnny Briggs to Cincinnati for LHP Joe Nuxhall.
1966 Richie Lewis b. Muncie, IN.
1973 Warren Spahn, the winningest left-handed pitcher of all-time, is elected to the Hall of Fame by the Baseball Writers' Association of America. In 21 NL seasons, mainly with the Boston and Milwaukee Braves, Spahn won 20 games 13 times, finishing with 363 victories.
1973 Terrell Wade b. Rembert, SC.
1974 Dan Serafini b. San Francisco, CA.
1983 The Chicago White Sox trade RHP Warren Brusstar and LHP Steve Trout to the Chicago Cubs for RHPs Dick Tidrow and Randy Martz, SS Scott Fletcher, and 1B Pat Tabler.

26

1945 The New York Yankees are sold to Larry MacPhail, Dan Topping, and Del Webb for $2.8 million.
1963 Baseball's Rules Committee expands the strike zone from the top of the shoulders to the bottom of the knees.
1967 Tim Pugh b. Lake Tahoe, CA.
1967 Jeff Branson b. Waynesboro, MS.

27

1896 Milt Gaston b. Ridgefield Park, NJ.
1927 Ty Cobb, Tris Speaker, and Smokey Joe Wood are found innocent of charges that they conspired to fix a September 25, 1919 game between the Detroit Tigers and the Cleveland Indians.
1947 John Lowenstein b. Wolf Point, MT.
1969 Phil Plantier b. Manchester, NH.
1982 Philadelphia trades then-SS Ryne Sandberg and SS Larry Bowa to the Chicago Cubs for SS Ivan DeJesus.

28

1891 Bill Doak b. Pittsburgh, PA.
1901 The AL makes its major league debut, with Milwaukee, Cleveland, Washington, Baltimore, Detroit, Philadelphia, Boston, and Chicago as charter members, the last three co-existing on National League turf.
1928 Pete Runnels b. Lufkin, TX.
1934 Bill White b. Lakewood, FL.
1950 Larvell Blanks b. Del Rio, TX.
1958 Brooklyn C Roy Campanella has his spinal cord severed in an auto accident in Glen Cove, NY. Paralyzed from the waist down and confined to a wheelchair, Campanella's 10-year career ends prior to the Dodgers' move from Brooklyn to Los Angeles.
1971 California trades OF Bill Voss to Milwaukee for RHP Gene Brabender.
1974 Jermaine Dye b. Oakland, CA.
1982 Baltimore trades 3B Doug DeCinces and LHP Jeff Schneider to California for OF Dan Ford.

29

1919 Bill Rigney b. Alameda, CA.

1919 Bill Voiselle b. Greenwood, SC.

1939 Bobby Bolin b. Hickory Grove, SC.

1958 Stan Musial becomes the NL's first six-figure star when he signs for $100,000 with the St. Louis Cardinals.

1960 Steve Sax b. Sacramento, CA.

1961 Mike Aldrete b. Carmel, CA.

1964 John Habyan b. Bayshore, NY.

1971 Pittsburgh trades OF Matty Alou and LHP George Brunet to St. Louis for OF Vic Davalillo and RHP Nelson Briles.

1973 Jason Schmidt b. Kelso, WA.

30

1926 The Major League Rules Committee grants pitchers permission to use a resin bag during the course of games.

1930 Sandy Amoros b. Havana, Cuba.

1936 After going 38-115 in 1935, the Boston Braves hold a fan contest which changes the team knickname to the Bees. Four years later it changes back to the Braves.

1943 Davey Johnson b. Orlando, FL.

1947 Matt Alexander b. Shreveport, LA.

1958 Commissioner Ford Frick takes the All-Star vote away from the fans, giving it back to the players, coaches, and managers.

1959 Cincinnati trades C Smoky Burgess, LHP Harvey Haddix, and 3B Don Hoak to Pittsburgh for RHP Whammy Douglas, and OFs Jim Pendleton, Frank Thomas, and Johnny Powers.

1962 Cincinnati trades C Jerry Zimmerman to Minnesota for OF Dan Dobbek.

1978 Commissioner Bowie Kuhn overrules the Oakland A's trade of LHP Vida Blue to the Cincinnati Reds for 1B Dave Revering and $1.75 million.

1987 The Chicago Cubs trade 3B Ron Cey to Oakland for SS Luis Quinones.

31

1919 Jackie Robinson b. Cairo, GA.

1931 Ernie Banks b. Dallas, TX.

1947 Nolan Ryan b. Refugio, TX.

1949 Fred Kendall b. Torrence, CA.

1950 The Pittsburgh Pirates make California high school pitcher Paul Petit baseball's first $100,000 bonus baby. Petit will collect only one major league victory and later collect another $100,000 from a movie producer.

FEBRUARY

1

1944 Paul Blair b. Cushing, OK.
1947 Danny Thompson b. Wichita, KS.
1954 The Milwaukee Braves trade LHPs Johnny Antonelli and Don Liddle, C Ebba St. Claire, and SS Billy Klaus to the New York Giants for OF Bobby Thomson and C Sammy Calderone.
1967 Tim Naehring b. Cincinnati, OH.
1968 Kent Mercker b. Dublin, OH.
1972 Rich Becker b. Aurora, IL.
1985 San Francisco trades 1B Jack Clark to St. Louis for OF David Green, SS Jose Uribe, LHP Dave LaPoint, and 1B Gary Rajsich.

2

1876 The NL is formed at Manhattan's Grand Central Hotel with eight charter members: Boston, Chicago, Cincinnati, St. Louis, Hartford, New York, Philadelphia, and Louisville.
1895 George Halas b. Chicago, IL.
1908 Wes Ferrell b. Greensboro, NC.
1923 Red Schoendienst b. Germantown, IL.
1936 Ty Cobb, Babe Ruth, Honus Wagner, Walter Johnson, and Christy Mathewson are named charter members of baseball's new Hall of Fame in Cooperstown, NY, although the new structure is not yet completed.

1937 Don Buford b. Linden, TX.
1957 Baseball owners approve a five-year pension plan offering more liberal benefits to players, coaches, and trainers.
1960 Buddy Biancalana b. Greenbrae, CA.
1968 Scott Erickson b. Long Beach, CA.
1971 Milwaukee trades OF Carl Taylor to Kansas City for C Ellie Rodriguez.
1993 Major League Baseball suspends Cincinnati owner Marge Schott for one year for bringing "disrepute and embarrassment" to the game with her repeated use of racial and ethnic slurs.
1999 San Diego trades OF Greg Vaughn and 1B Mark Sweeney to Cincinnati for OF Reggie Sanders, INF Damian Jackson, and RHP Josh Harris.

3

1876 After pitching the last four years, Albert Spalding resigns as a player and joins his brother J. Walter with $800 to start a sporting goods company.
1885 Slim Sallee b. Higginsport, OH.
1935 Dick Tracewski b. Eynon, PA.
1938 The University of Illinois suspends basketball player Lou Boudreau after learning he's been receiving illegal under-the-table payments from the Cleveland Indians.

11

1947 Joe Coleman b. Boston, MA.

1949 Bake McBride b. Fulton, MO.

1952 Fred Lynn b. Chicago, IL.

1965 Rich Scheid b. Staten Island, NY.

1979 Minnesota trades 1B Rod Carew to California for OF Ken Landreaux, C Dave Engle, RHP Paul Hartzell, and LHP Brad Havens.

1989 Bill White becomes the highest ranking black executive in professional sports when he succeeds A. Bartlett Giamatti as NL president.

4

1949 Steve Brye b. Alameda, CA.

1955 Gary Allenson b. Culver City, CA.

1956 Chris Bando b. Cleveland, OH.

1969 Bowie Kuhn is elected baseball's fifth commissioner. He'll serve until September 30, 1984.

1991 Baseball's Hall of Fame board of directors votes 12–0, with four abstentions, not to allow Pete Rose eligibility for induction because he has been banned from the game by the commissioner.

5

1891 Roger Peckinpaugh b. Wooster, OH.

1928 Don Hoak b. Roulette, PA.

1929 Allan Worthington b. Birmingham, AL.

1934 Hank Aaron b. Mobile, AL.

1936 Lee Thomas b. Peoria, IL.

1946 Vic Correll b. Florence, SC.

1962 Dan Plesac b. Gary, IN.

1968 Roberto Alomar b. Puerto Rico.

1977 Texas trades OF Gene Clines to the Chicago Cubs for LHP Darold Knowles.

1983 Kansas City trades DH Cecil Fielder to Toronto for OF Leon Roberts.

6

1899 Earl Whitehill b. Cedar Rapids, IA.

1901 Glenn Wright b. Archie, MO.

1926 Dale Long b. Springfield, MO.

1927 Smoky Burgess b. Caroleen, MO.

1949 Richie Zisk b. Brooklyn, NY.

1969 Bob Wickman b. Green Bay, WI.

7

1866 Tom Daly b. Philadelphia, PA.

1937 Juan Pizarro b. Puerto Rico.

1949 New York Yankees CF Joe DiMaggio becomes baseball's first $100,000 player.

1950 Burt Hooton b. Greenville, TX.

1951 Benny Ayala b. Puerto Rico.

1954 Dan Quisenberry b. Santa Monica, CA.

1957 Carney Lansford b. San Jose, CA.

1994 The Chicago White Sox announce that they have invited retired Chicago Bulls superstar Michael Jordan to spring training to try out for the team. Jordan flounders in the minor leagues amid flourishing media hype and never reaches the major leagues. He will eventually return to the NBA.

8

1921 Willard Marshall b. Richmond, VA.

1937 Clete Boyer b. Cossville, MO.

1942 Fritz Peterson b. Chicago, IL.

1968 Cincinnati trades C John Edwards to St. Louis for INF Jimy Williams and C Pat Corrales.

1982 The Los Angeles Dodgers break up their more-than-eight-year infield quartet of 3B Ron Cey, SS Bill Russell, 2B Davey Lopes, and 1B Steve Garvey by trading Lopes to the Oakland A's for minor league INF Lance Hudson, who never makes it to the major leagues. Lopes' heir apparent in Los Angeles is Steve Sax, who will win the NL Rookie-of-the-Year Award in 1982 after batting .282 with 49 stolen bases.

9

1920 Baseball's Joint Rules Committee bans the use of all foreign substances and ball-doctoring methods used by pitchers.

1925 Vic Wertz b. York, PA.

1944 Jim Campanis b. New York, NY.

1945 Jim Nash b. Hawthorne, NV.

1961 John Kruk b. Charleston, WV.

1971 Baseball inducts RHP Satchel Paige into its Hall of Fame despite a major league record of 28-31. Paige perhaps won more than 2,000 Negro League games before joining the Cleveland Indians in 1948 at age 42.

1971 Washington trades OF Rick Reichardt to the Chicago White Sox for RHP Gerry Janeski.

10

1894 Herb Pennock b. Kennett Square, PA.

1913 Bill Adair b. Mobile, AL.

1915 Allie Reynolds b. Bethany, OK.

1933 Billy O'Dell b. Whitmere, SC.

1948 Jim Barr b. Lynwood, CA.

1963 Len Dykstra b. Santa Ana, CA.

1965 Len Webster b. New Orleans, LA.

1969 Jayhawk Owens b. Cincinnati, OH.

1970 Bobby J. Jones b. Fresno, CA.

1971 The New York Yankees hire Bill White as baseball's first black announcer.

1971 Los Angeles trades OF Andy Kosco to Milwaukee for LHP Al Downing.

11

1941 Sammy Ellis b. Youngstown, OH.

1949 Ben Oglivie b. Colon, Panama.

1963 Todd Benzinger b. Dayton, KY.

1965 Pittsburgh trades RHP Bob Priddy and OF Bob Burda to San Francisco for C Del Crandall.

1974 Baseball's first arbitration hearing is decided in favor of Minnesota Twins RHP Dick Woodson.

1982 San Diego trades SS Ozzie Smith to St. Louis for SS Garry Templeton.

12

1917 Dom DiMaggio b. San Francisco, CA.

1926 Joe Garagiola b. St. Louis, MO.
1939 Jerry Walker b. Ada, OK.
1942 Pat Dobson b. Depew, NY.
1945 Don Wilson b. Monroe, LA.
1949 Enzo Hernandez b. Venezuela.
1955 Chet Lemon b. Jackson, MS.
1965 Ruben Amaro Jr. b. Philadelphia, PA.
1974 Cleveland trades INF Leo Cardenas to Texas for C Ken Suarez.
1981 Boston C Carlton Fisk is declared a free agent because the Red Sox violated the Basic Agreement by mailing his contract two days beyond the deadline.

13

1883 Hal Chase b. Los Gatos, CA.
1944 Sal Bando b. Cleveland, OH.
1966 Jerry Browne b. Virgin Islands.
1964 Chicago Cubs 2B Ken Hubbs, the NL's 1962 Rookie of the Year, is killed in a plane crash in Provo, UT.
1968 Matt Mieske b. Midland, MI.
1968 San Francisco trades C Tom Haller to Los Angeles for INFs Ron Hunt and Nate Oliver.
1969 Mark Mimbs & Mike Mimbs b. Macon, GA.
1970 Kevin Stocker b. Spokane, WA.

14

1951 Larry Milbourne b. Port Norris, NJ.
1952 Will McEnaney b. Springfield, OH.
1963 John Marzano b. Philadelphia, PA.
1968 Scott Scudder b. Paris, TX.
1970 Kelly Stinnett b. Lawton, OK.

15

1895 Jimmy Ring b. Brooklyn, NY.
1900 George Earnshaw b. New York, NY.
1916 Philadelphia A's 3B Frank "Home Run" Baker, a four-time AL home run champion who sat out the entire 1915 season with a contract dispute, is sold to the New York Yankees for $37,500.
1938 Chuck Estrada b. San Luis Obispo, CA.
1948 Ron Cey b. Tacoma, WA.
1950 Rick Auerbach b. Glendale, CA.
1952 Bill Van Bommel b. Appleton, WI.
1966 Melido Perez b. Dominican Republic.
1969 Brian Williams b. Lancaster, SC.
1980 Texas trades 1B Willie Montanez to San Diego for RHP Gaylord Perry and 1B Tucker Ashford.

16

1866 Billy Hamilton b. Newark, NJ.
1924 Tony Boeckel, a third baseman with both Pittsburgh and the Boston Braves, becomes the first ML player killed in an automobile accident when he crashes in San Diego, CA.
1943 Bobby Darwin b. Los Angeles, CA.
1947 Terry Crowley b. Staten Island, NY.
1952 Barry Foote b. Smithfield, NC.
1952 Jerry Hairston b. Birmingham, AL.

1953 As part of a four-team trade, Cincinnati sends 1B Joe Adcock to the Milwaukee Braves for INF Rocky Bridges.
1960 Eric Bullock b. Los Angeles, CA.
1962 Dwayne Henry b. Elkton, MD.

17

1893 Wally Pipp b. Chicago, IL.
1930 Roger Craig b. Durham, NC.
1934 Willie Kirkland b. Siluria, AL.
1944 Dick Bosman b. Kenosha, WI.
1951 Dave Roberts (INF) b. Lebanon, OR.

18

1889 George Mogridge b. Rochester, NY.
1891 Sherry Smith b. Monticello, GA.
1909 The Boston Red Sox trade RHP Cy Young back to Cleveland, his original club from 1890, for RHPs Charlie Chech and Jack Ryan. Chech and Ryan will pitch only seven years in the major leagues between them, while Young will pitch three more seasons to finish his 22-year career with an ML record 511 wins.
1910 The NL approves a 154-game schedule, a plan already adopted by the AL.
1915 Joe Gordon b. Los Angeles, CA.
1922 Cincinnati trades LHP Rube Marquard to the Boston Braves for SS Larry Kopf and RHP Jack Scott.
1927 Herm Wehmeier b. Cincinnati, OH.
1938 Manny Mota b. Dominican Republic

1939 Dal Maxvill b. Granite City, IL.
1949 Jerry Morales b. Puerto Rico.
1950 Bruce Kison b. Pasco, WA.
1950 John Mayberry b. Detroit, MI.
1952 Marc Hill b. Louisiana, MO.
1954 Washington trades OF Gil Coan to Baltimore for OF Roy Sievers.
1958 Cleveland trades C Jim Hegan and LHP Hank Aguirre to Detroit for LHP Hal Woodeshick and OF J.W. Porter.
1964 Kevin Tapani b. Des Moines, IA.
1967 John Valentin b. Mineola, NY.
1968 Kyle Abbott b. Newburyport, MA.
1970 Tyler Green b. Springfield, OH.
1973 Shawn Estes b. San Bernardino, CA.
1974 Houston trades RHP Pat Darcy to Cincinnati for 3B Denis Menke.
1998 Famed Chicago sportscaster Harry Carey passes away at age 83.
1999 Toronto trades five-time Cy Young Award winner RHP Roger Clemens to the New York Yankees for LHPs David Wells and Graeme Lloyd, and INF Homer Bush.

19

1918 Tom Early b. Roxbury, MA.
1935 Russ Nixon b. Cleveland, OH.
1940 Bill Kelso b. Kansas City, MO.
1944 Bill Zachary b. Knoxville, TN.
1946 New York Giants OF Danny Gardella jumps to the outlaw Mexican League, the first in a group of major leaguers who leave the United States for bigger contracts.
1957 The Kansas City A's trade LHPs Bobby Shantz and Jack McMahon, 3B Clete Boyer, RHP Art Ditmar, 1B Wayne Belardi, and 2B Curt Roberts to

the New York Yankees for LHPs Rip Coleman and Mickey McDermott, SS Billy Hunter, RHP Tom Morgan, 2B Milt Graff, and OF Irv Noren.

1957 Dave Stewart b. Oakland, CA.

1962 Alvaro Espinoza b. Venezuela.

20

1890 Sam Rice b. Morocco, IN.

1913 Tommy Henrich b. Massillon, OH.

1928 Elroy Face b. Stephentown, NY.

1943 Clyde Wright b. Jefferson City, TN.

1963 San Francisco Giants outfielder Willie Mays signs for $100,000—14 years after the Yankees' Joe DiMaggio reaches that plateau.

1966 Baseball hires its first black umpire—the AL's Emmett Ashford.

1966 Derek Lilliquist b. Winter Park, FL.

21

1943 Jack Billingham b. Orlando, FL.

1958 Alan Trammell b. Garden Grove, CA.

22

1862 Connie Mack b. East Brookfield, MA.

1921 Cincinnati trades OF Greasy Neale and RHP Jimmy Ring to the Philadelphia Phillies for LHP Eppa Rixey.

1929 Ryne Duren b. Cazenovia, WI.

1934 Sparky Anderson b. Bridgewater, SD.

1939 Steve Barber b. Tacoma Park, MD.

1948 Bruce Christensen b. Madison, WI.

23

1914 Mike Tresh b. Hazleton, PA.

1921 The Boston Braves trade SS Rabbit Maranville to Pittsburgh for OFs Billy Southworth and Fred Nicholson and INF Walter Barbare.

1929 Elston Howard b. St. Louis, MO.

1941 Ron Hunt b. St. Louis, MO.

1946 Ken Boswell b. Austin, TX.

1960 Demolition begins on Brooklyn's Ebbets Field. Soprano Lucy Monroe, who sang at hundreds of Dodgers games, sings the National Anthem. Four years later, the same baseball-painted wrecking ball will demolish New York's Polo Grounds, former home of the Giants.

1963 Bobby Bonilla b. New York, NY.

1972 Rondell White b. Milledgeville, GA.

24

1874 Honus Wagner b. Carnegie, PA.

1892 Wilbur Cooper b. Bearsville, WV.

1943 With many of their players lost to military service, major league teams advertise for players in *The Sporting News*.

1948 The Chicago White Sox trade LHP Eddie Lopat to the New York Yankees for C Aaron Robinson, RHP Fred Bradley, and LHP Bill Wight.

1956 Eddie Murray b. Los Angeles, CA.

1966 Rod Brewer b. Eustis, FL.

25

1919 Monte Irvin b. Columbia, AL.

1921 Andy Pafko b. Boyceville, WI.

1934 John McGraw, considered by many as the greatest manager of all time, dies of cancer at age 60. In 33 years, including 30 with the New York Giants, McGraw won 2,840 games, 10 NL pennants, and three World Series titles.

1939 Denny Lemaster b. Corona, CA.

1940 Ron Santo b. Seattle, WA.

1951 Cesar Cedeno b. Dominican Republic.

1954 Bob Brenley b. Coshocton, OH.

1963 Paul O'Neill b. Columbus, OH.

1973 Owners and players approve a three-year Basic Agreement that includes binding arbitration and modifications of the controversial reserve clause.

1974 Shannon Stewart b. Cincinnati, OH.

1975 Cleveland trades C Dave Duncan to Baltimore for 1B Boog Powell and LHP Don Hood.

1975 The Chicago Cubs trade OF Brock Davis and LHP Dave LaRoche to Cleveland for RHP Milt Wilcox.

1978 Cincinnati trades 1B Dave Revering to Oakland for RHP Doug Bair.

26

1887 Grover Cleveland Alexander b. Elba, NE.

1915 Preacher Roe b. Ashflat, AR.

1935 Babe Ruth ends his long love affair with New York fans when the Yankees grant him a release to sign with the Boston Braves. Ruth returns to the city where he started his major league career in 1914 with the Red Sox.

1945 Don Secrist b. Seattle, WA.

1950 Jack Brohamer b. Maywood, CA.

1957 The New York Giants trade RHP Hoyt Wilhelm to the St. Louis Cardinals for 1B/OF Whitey Lockman.

1967 David Howard b. Sarasota, FL.

1967 Scott Service b. Cincinnati, OH.

1968 J.T. Snow b. Long Beach, CA.

27

1908 Baseball adopts the sacrifice fly rule, stating that a batter will not be charged with an at-bat if a runner tags up and scores after the catch of his fly ball.

1969 Willie Banks b. Jersey City, NJ.

28

1909 Lefty Bertrand b. Cobden, MN.

1916 Howie Krist b. West Henrietta, NY.

1930 Frank Malzone b. Bronx, NY.

1978 Texas trades LHP David Clyde and DH Willie Horton to Cleveland for OF John Lowenstein and RHP Tom Buskey.

1981 The Chicago Cubs trade OF Dave Kingman to the New York Mets for OF Steve Henderson.

1986 Commissioner Peter Ueberroth hands down one-year suspensions to players Dave Parker, Keith Hernandez, Lonnie Smith, Dale Berra, Jeffrey Leonard, Enos Cabell, and Joaquin Andujar for drug-related activities.

29

1904 Pepper Martin b. Temple, OK.
1924 Al Rosen b. Spartanburg, SC.

1972 Atlanta Braves OF Hank Aaron
signs baseball's first $200,000 contract.

MARCH

1

1944 Vern Fuller b. Menomonie, WI.

1962 Mark Gardner b. Los Angeles, CA.

1969 New York Yankees OF Mickey Mantle retires after 536 home runs, three MVP trophies, and 18 World Series records.

1969 Doug Creek b. Winchester, VA.

1981 Milwaukee trades OF Dick Davis to Philadelphia for LHP Randy Lerch.

2

1909 Mel Ott b. Gretna, LA.

1913 Mort Cooper b. Atherton, MO.

1917 Jim Konstanty b. Strykersville, NY.

1950 Pete Broberg b. West Palm Beach, FL.

1962 Terry Steinbach b. New Ulm, MN.

1965 Ron Gant b. Victoria, TX.

1967 Leo Gomez b. Puerto Rico.

1976 Los Angeles trades OF Willie Crawford to St. Louis for C Ted Simmons.

3

1872 Wee Willie Keeler b. Brooklyn, NY.

1927 The New York Yankees make slugger Babe Ruth the highest paid player in baseball history, signing him for three years at $70,000 per season.

1931 The U.S. Congress and President Herbert Hoover designate "The Star Spangled Banner," written by Francis Scott Key in 1814, the national anthem.

1957 Skeeter Barnes b. Cincinnati, OH.

1968 Bobby Munoz b. Puerto Rico.

1968 Scott Radinsky b. Glendale, CA.

1973 C.J. Nitkowski b. Suffren, NY.

1984 Los Angeles Olympic Committee president Peter Ueberroth is elected baseball's sixth commissioner. He'll take office October 1, 1984.

1999 Orlando Cepeda joins Roberto Clemente as the only Hall of Famers b. in Puerto Rico, when the "Baby Bull" is voted enshrinement by the Veterans Committee. Cepeda was the 1958 NL Rookie of the Year with the San Francisco Giants, and the league's first unanimous MVP in 1967 with the St. Louis Cardinals.

4

1891 Dazzy Vance b. Orient, IN.

1897 Lefty O'Doul b. San Francisco, CA.

1939 Jack Fisher b. Frostburg, MD.

1948 Tom Grieve b. Pittsfield, MA.

1948 Leron Lee b. Bakersfield, CA.

1964 Tom Lampkin b. Cincinnati, OH.

1968 Brian R. Hunter b. El Toro, CA.

1969 Lee Tinsley b. Shelbyville, KY.

1982 San Francisco trades 1B Enos Cabell to Detroit for OF Champ Summers.

5

1922 New York Yankees RF Babe Ruth signs a three-year contract for $52,000 per season.

1930 Del Crandall b. Ontario, CA.

1947 Kent Tekulve b. Cincinnati, OH.

1961 Steve Ontiveros b. Tularosa, NM.

1971 Chad Fonville b. Jacksonville, NC.

1971 Jeff Hammonds b. Plainfield, NJ.

1986 Atlanta trades C Rick Cerone to Milwaukee for C Ted Simmons.

6

1900 Lefty Grove b. Lonaconing, MD.

1917 Pete Gray b. Nanticoke, PA.

1933 Ted Abernathy b. Stanley, NC.

1938 The Philadelphia Phillies trade 1B Dolf Camilli to Brooklyn for OF Eddie Morgan.

1941 Willie Stargell b. Earlsboro, OK.

1945 Former Philadelphia A's C Harry O'Neill is killed in the World War II battle of Iwo Jima. O'Neill caught only one game for the A's in 1939, with no at-bats.

1970 Scott Stahoviak b. Waukegan, IL.

1971 Roger Salkeld b. Burbank, CA.

1987 Andre Dawson gives the Chicago Cubs a blank contract to fill in their own salary amount. He receives $500,000.

7

1884 Ed Willett b. Norfolk, VA.

1924 Cincinnati manager Pat Moran dies of Bright's disease at a hospital in Orlando, FL, the team's spring training site.

1951 Jeff Burroughs b. Long Beach, CA.

1960 Joe Carter b. Oklahoma City, OK.

1965 Jack Armstrong b. Englewood, NJ.

1968 Jeff Kent b. Bellflower, CA.

1981 Atlanta trades OF Jeff Burroughs to Seattle for LHP Carlos Diaz.

8

1900 The NL streamlines its product, reducing the league from 12 teams to eight. The remaining franchises include Brooklyn, Boston, Philadelphia, St. Louis, Cincinnati, Pittsburgh, Chicago, and New York, while exiting franchises include Baltimore, Louisville, Washington, and Cleveland.

1922 Carl Furillo b. Stoney Creek Mills, PA.

1930 New York Yankees RF Babe Ruth signs a record two-year contract at $80,000 per season, proclaiming that he is coming off a better year than President Herbert Hoover, who earns less pay.

1939 Jim Bouton b. Newark, NJ.

1941 Philadelphia Phillies RHP Hugh Mulcahy becomes the first major league player drafted into World War II.

1942 Richie Allen b. Wampum, PA.

1953 Jim Rice b. Anderson, SC.

1999 New York Yankees Hall of Fame CF Joe DiMaggio passes away at age 84. Owner of baseball's record 56-game hitting streak in 1941, DiMaggio led the

Yankees to 10 World Series appearances in his 13 years and finished with a .325 lifetime average with 361 home runs and three MVP awards.

9

1893 Lefty Williams b. Aurora, MO.
1900 The NL expands the strike zone by reshaping home plate from a 12-inch square to a 17-inch wide pentagon.
1912 Arky Vaughan b. Clifty, AR.
1927 Jackie Jensen b. San Francisco, CA.
1932 Ron Kline b. Callery, PA.
1942 Bert Campaneris b. Cuba.
1943 Brooklyn trades 1B Babe Dahlgren to the Philadelphia Phillies for OF Lloyd Waner and INF Al Glossop.
1948 John Curtis b. Newton, MA.
1948 Darrel Chaney b. Hammond, IN.
1950 Doug Ault b. Beaumont, TX.
1963 Terry Mulholland b. Uniontown, PA.
1965 Benito Santiago b. Puerto Rico.

10

1941 The Brooklyn Dodgers announce that their club will become the first to wear protective batting helmets.
1944 Johnny Briggs (OF) b. Patterson, NJ.
1948 Wayne Twitchell b. Portland, OR.
1958 Steve Howe b. Pontiac, MI.
1961 Mike Birkbeck b. Orrville, OH.
1963 John Cangelosi b. Brooklyn, NY.
1973 Cleveland trades OF Alex Johnson to Texas for LHP Rich Hinton.

11

1945 Dock Ellis b. Los Angeles, CA.
1948 Cesar Geronimo b. Dominican Republic.
1959 Phil Bradley b. Bloomington, IN.
1966 Steve Reed b. Los Angeles, CA.
1972 Salomon Torres b. Dominican Republic.
1989 Los Angeles trades OF Mike Devereaux to Baltimore for RHP Mike Morgan.

12

1930 Vernon Law b. Meridian, ID.
1939 Johnny Callison b. Qualls, OK.
1942 Jimmy Wynn b. Cincinnati, OH.
1942 Joe DiMaggio agrees to a $6,250 raise after the New York Yankees first ask him to take a pay cut. DiMaggio is coming off an MVP 1941 season in which he hit in a record 56 straight games, batted .357 with 125 runs scored, and led the Yankees to a World Series championship.
1956 Dale Murphy b. Portland, OR.
1962 Darryl Strawberry b. Los Angeles, CA.
1965 Steve Finley b. Union City, TN.
1971 Greg Hansell b. Bellflower, CA.
1971 Raul Mondesi b. Dominican Republic.
1972 George Arias b. Tucson, AZ.

13

1915 Brooklyn Dodgers manager Wilbert Robinson agrees to catch a baseball dropped from an airplane, but the pilot switches it for a grapefruit which splatters onto his shoulder.

1963 Mariano Duncan b. Dominican Republic.

1964 Will Clark b. New Orleans, LA.

1990 Houston trades SS Dave Silvestri and RHP Daven Bond to the New York Yankees for SS Orlando Miller.

14

1932 Cincinnati trades 2B Tony Cuccinello, 3B Joe Stripp, and C Clyde Sukeforth to Brooklyn for OF Babe Herman, 3B Wally Gilbert, and C Ernie Lombardi.

1950 Dave McKay b. Vancouver, British Columbia.

1961 Kirby Puckett b. Chicago, IL.

1965 Kevin Brown b. McIntyre, GA.

1970 Brent Gates b. Grand Rapids, MI.

15

1869 The Cincinnati Red Stockings announce they are the first team to pay players. Player/manager Harry Wright earns $1200 for the year, exceeded only by his brother, SS George Wright, who will earn $1400.

1898 Rosy Ryan b. Worcester, MA.

1938 Bob Locker b. Hull, IA.

1944 Wayne Granger b. Springfield, MA.

1946 Bobby Bonds b. Riverside, CA.

1959 Harold Baines b. St. Michaels, MD.

1960 Mike Pagliarulo b. Medford, MA.

1968 Kim Batiste b. New Orleans, LA.

1977 Oakland trades 2B Phil Garner, INF Tommy Helms, and RHP Chris Batton to Pittsburgh for RHPs Doc Medich, Dave Giusti, Rick Langford, and Doug Bair, and OFs Mitchell Page, and Tony Armas.

1977 The Chicago Cubs trade RHP Joe Coleman to Oakland for RHP Jim Todd.

1978 Oakland trades LHP Vida Blue to San Francisco for RHPs Dave Heaverlo, Alan Wirth, and Phil Huffman, OF Gary Thomasson, LHP John Henry Johnson, and SS Mario Guerrero.

16

1900 AL President Ban Johnson announces formation of a second franchise in Chicago, where the N.L. Colts (Cubs) also play. The newly formed league now swells to eight franchises: Kansas City, Detroit, Minneapolis, Milwaukee, Indianapolis, Cleveland, Buffalo, and Chicago.

1906 Lloyd Waner b. Harrah, OK.

1943 Rick Reichardt b. Madison, WI.

1972 Oakland A's LHP Vida Blue announces he's retiring from baseball because of contract problems with owner Charlie Finley. Blue finishes 24–8 to win the AL Cy Young Award in 1971. At 22 years of age, Blue reconsiders retirement and plays another 14 years in the major leagues.

17

1871 The National Association of Professional Base Ball Players is born with nine teams: Boston Red Stockings, Chicago White Stockings, Philadelphia A's, New York Mutuals, Washington

Olympics, Troy Haymakers, Fort Wayne Kekiongas, Cleveland Forest Citys, and Rockford Forest Citys.

1899 Charlie Root b. Middletown, OH.

1919 Pete Reiser b. St. Louis, MO.

1919 Hank Sauer b. Pittsburgh, PA.

1922 During a spring training game, Cincinnati's George Harper takes two strikes from Washington RHP Walter Johnson, then heads back to the dugout telling the umpire that he doesn't want the third strike that he has coming.

1938 Jimmie Hall b. Mt. Holly, NC.

1944 Clarence Gaston b. San Antonio, TX.

1959 Danny Ainge b. Eugene, OR.

1965 John Smiley b. Phoenixville, PA.

1969 Atlanta trades 1B Joe Torre to St. Louis for 1B Orlando Cepeda.

1992 Minnesota trades LHP Denny Neagle and OF Midre Cummings to Pittsburgh for LHP John Smiley.

18

1941 Pat Jarvis b. Caryle, IL.

1953 The first ML franchise shift of the 20th century is announced at the league meeting in St. Petersburg, FL. After drawing a paltry 281,000 fans for the entire 1952 season, the Braves will relocate to Milwaukee, leaving Boston without an NL club for the first time since 1876.

1965 Geronimo Berroa b. Dominican Republic.

1990 The baseball owners' 32-day spring training lockout of the players ends with the approval of a new four-year agreement. Spring training is reduced to three weeks, and Opening Day is pushed back to April 9th.

19

1871 Joe McGinnity b. Rock Island, IL.

1894 Bill Wambsganss b. Garfield Heights, OH.

1927 Richie Ashburn b. Tilden, NE.

1962 Ivan Calderon b. Puerto Rico.

1998 Major league baseball owners overwhelmingly approve the sale of the Los Angeles Dodgers to Rupert Murdoch's Fox Group for a reported $311 million, the most ever paid for a professional sports franchise. The ownership transfer ends baseball's oldest family dynasty, with the O'Malley's having had controlling interest in the club since Walter O'Malley bought a majority interest in the then-Brooklyn Dodgers in 1950.

20

1912 Clyde Shoun b. Mountain City, TN.

1941 Pat Corrales b. Los Angeles, CA.

1965 Chris Hoiles b. Bowling Green, OH.

1966 Blas Minor b. Merced, CA.

1971 Manny Alexander b. Dominican Republic.

1973 Baseball waives its five-year rule for Hall of Fame induction by immediately inducting Pittsburgh Pirates OF Roberto Clemente, who was killed 11 weeks earlier in a plane crash during a relief flight to help Nicaraguan earthquake victims. Clemente joins New York Yankees 1B Lou Gehrig as the only Hall of Fame members to have the five-year waiting period waived.

21

1936 Cincinnati trades 1B Jim Bottomley to the St. Louis Browns for SS Johnny Burnett.

1939 Tommy Davis b. Brooklyn, NY.

1944 Manny Sanguillen b. Colon, Panama.

1946 Al Fitzmorris b. Buffalo, NY.

1959 Detroit trades OF Tito Francona to Cleveland for OF Larry Doby.

1963 Shawon Dunston b. Brooklyn, NY.

1988 Philadelphia trades OFs Jeff Stone and Keith Hughes, and 3B Rick Schu to Baltimore for OF Mike Young.

22

1940 Dick Ellsworth b. Lusk, WY.

1963 Rich Monteleone b. Tampa, FL.

1965 Glenallen Hill b. Santa Cruz, CA.

1966 Sean Berry b. Santa Monica, CA.

1968 Ramon Martinez b. Dominican Republic.

1972 The New York Yankees trade 1B Danny Cater to Boston for LHP Sparky Lyle.

1976 About two weeks prior to the California Angels' opening day, groundskeepers discover about 500 marijuana plants coming through the outfield grass. The plants sprouted after a "The Who" concert, which brought in about 55,000 fans, 10,000 of whom were sitting on the outfield grass.

1993 Cleveland RHPs Tim Crews and Steve Olin are killed and LHP Bob Ojeda is seriously injured in a boating accident outside Orlando, FL. Crews and Olin are the first active major league players killed in an accident since New York Yankees catcher Thurman Munson died in a plane crash August 2, 1979.

23

1886 Cy Slapnicka b. Cedar Rapids, IA.

1927 Johnny Logan b. Endicott, NY.

1928 Jim Lemon b. Covington, VA.

1943 Lee May b. Birmingham, AL.

1944 George Scott b. Greenville, MS.

1977 The Chicago White Sox trade RHP Clay Carroll to St. Louis for RHP Lerrin LaGrow.

1989 The Detroit Tigers trade 3B Tom Brookens to the New York Yankees for RHP Charles Hudson.

24

1891 Ernie Shore b. East Bend, NC.

1893 George Sisler b. Manchester, OH.

1917 Dave Bartosch b. St. Louis, MO.

1942 Jesus Alou b. Dominican Republic.

1970 Wilson Alvarez b. Venezuela.

1972 Steve Karsay b. College Point, NY.

1972 Cincinnati trades RHP Tony Cloninger to St. Louis for 2B Julian Javier.

1973 Oakland trades C Dave Duncan and OF George Hendrick to Cleveland for C Ray Fosse and SS Jack Heidemann.

1982 The New York Yankees trade RHP Bill Castro to California for 3B Butch Hobson.

25

1882 Jimmy Sebring b. Liberty, PA.

1937 Newspapers reveal that the

Quaker Oats company paid $25,000 for baseball promotions.

1959 San Francisco trades 1B Bill White and 3B Ray Jablonski to St. Louis for RHPs Don Choate and Sam "Toothpick" Jones.

1966 Tom Glavine b. Concord, MA.

1969 Travis Fryman b. Lexington, KY.

1969 Eric Helfand b. Erie, PA.

1969 Erik Schullstrom b. San Diego, CA.

1969 Dan Wilson b. Arlington Heights, IL.

1971 Brian L. Hunter b. Portland, OR.

1999 Cal Ripken, Sr., who worked for the Baltimore Orioles in 36 of the 45 years the franchise has existed, dies of lung cancer at age 63.

26

1893 Frank Brower b. Gainesville, VA.

1951 New York Yankees' 19-year-old rookie Mickey Mantle smashes an estimated 660 foot home run in an exhibition game against the USC college baseball team in Los Angeles, CA.

1962 Kevin Seitzer b. Springfield, IL.

1966 Mike Remlinger b. Middletown, NY.

1968 Shane Reynolds b. Bastrop, LA.

1968 Jose Vizcaino b. Dominican Republic.

1977 San Francisco trades OF Willie Crawford and INF Rob Sperring to Houston for 2B Rob Andrews.

1984 The Chicago Cubs trade RHP Bill Campbell and C Mike Diaz to Philadelphia for OFs Gary Matthews and Bob Dernier, and RHP Porfi Altamirano.

1997 Florida Marlins OF Gary Sheffield signs the richest contract extention in ML history agreeing to a $61 million, six-year deal.

27

1879 Miller Huggins b. Cincinnati, OH.

1932 Wes Covington b. Laurinburg, NC.

1950 Lynn McGlothen b. Monroe,LA.

1950 J.R. Richard b. Vienna, LA.

1950 Vic Harris b. Los Angeles, CA.

1953 Gary Alexander b. Los Angeles, CA.

1968 Jaime Navarro b. Puerto Rico.

1987 The Chicago White Sox trade OF John Cangelosi to Pittsburgh for RHP Jim Winn.

1987 Kansas City trades RHP David Cone and OF Chris Jelic to the New York Mets for RHPs Rick Anderson and Maurro Gozza, and C Ed Hearn.

1992 Milwaukee trades 3B Gary Sheffield and RHP Geoff Kellogg to San Diego for RHP Ricky Bones, INF Jose Valentin, and OF Matt Mieske.

28

1901 In a move to keep second baseman Nap Lajoie from jumping to the AL Athletics, the Philadelphia Phillies file an injunction to keep him from playing for any other team.

1909 Lon Warneke b. Mt. Ida, AR.

1913 Having finished last or next to last the previous four seasons, the broke St. Louis Browns agree to leave infielder Buzzy Wares to a local minor league team for the season in Alabama, as payment for their spring training facility.

1919 Vic Raschi b. West Springfield, MA.

1931 Former AL President and founder Ban Johnson dies at age 67, just hours after E.S. Barnard, the man who succeeds him, dies of a heart attack at age 56.

1967 Shawn Boskie b. Hawthorne, NV.

1970 Commissioner Bowie Kuhn returns the All-Star Game balloting to the fans with voting done by punch cards and tabulated by computer.

1973 Paul Wilson b. Orlando, FL.

1986 The New York Yankees trade DH Don Baylor to Boston for DH Mike Easler.

1992 Minnesota trades 1B Paul Sorrento to Cleveland for RHPs Oscar Munoz and Curt Leskanic.

1999 The Baltimore Orioles defeat the Cuban National Team, 3–2, in 11 innings, in the first appearance by a major league team in Havana in 40 years.

29

1867 Cy Young b. Gilmore, OH.

1944 Denny McLain b. Chicago, IL.

1960 San Francisco trades RHP Allan Worthington to Boston for 1B Jim Marshall.

1961 Mike Kingery b. St. James, MN.

1962 Billy Beane b. Orlando, FL.

1966 Eric Gunderson b. Portland, OR.

1967 Brian Jordan b. Baltimore, MD.

1968 Juan Bell b. Dominican Republic.

1972 Alex Ochoa b. Miami Lakes, FL.

30

1857 Tom Burns b. Honesdale, PA.

1978 Boston trades RHPs Rick Wise and Mike Paxton, C Bo Diaz, and INF Ted Cox to Cleveland for RHP Dennis Eckersley and C Fred Kendall.

1992 The Chicago White Sox trade OF Sammy Sosa and LHP Ken Patterson to the Chicago Cubs for OF George Bell.

1998 Cleveland trades 1B Sean Casey to Cincinnati for RHP Dave Burba.

31

1920 Dave Koslo b. Menasha, WI.

1959 The Milwaukee Braves trade RHP Gene Conley, SS Joe Koppe, and 2B Harry Hanebrink to Philadelphia for C Stan Lopata, 2B Johnny O'Brien, and INF Ted Kazanski.

1961 The Chicago Cubs trade RHP Moe Drabowsky and LHP Seth Morehead to the Milwaukee Braves for SS Andre Rodgers and INF Daryl Robertson.

1969 The Seattle Pilots trade INF Chico Salmon to Baltimore for RHP Gene Brabender and INF Gordon Lund.

1970 After finishing last in the AL in 1969 with a 64-98 record, the Seattle Pilots relocate from Sicks Stadium to Milwaukee County Stadium where they become the Brewers.

1971 The Chicago White Sox trade C Duane Josephson and RHP Danny Murphy to Boston for 1B Tony Muser and RHP Vicente Romo.

1971 The New York Mets trade OF Ron Swoboda to Montreal for OF Don Hahn.

1994 The New York Mets trade 1B Alan Zinter to Detroit for 1B Rico Brogna.

1996 In the first major league regular season game played in March, Seattle defeats the Chicago White Sox, 3-2, in 12 innings at the Kingdome before 57,467 fans.

1998 Baseball's two expansion teams Arizona and Tampa Bay begin play, marking only the second time in history that the season opens in the month of March. The NL Diamondbacks fall, 9-2, to host Colorado, while the AL Devil Rays also lose, 11-6, to visiting Detroit.

1998 St. Louis 1B Mark McGwire hits a fifth inning grand slam home run against Los Angeles RHP Ramon Martinez to power the Cardinals to a 6-0, Opening Day win before a sellout crowd of 47,972.

1998 Florida C Charles Johnson has his ML record errorless streak end at 172 games in the first inning on Opening Day, an 11-6 win over the Chicago Cubs. Johnson's throw during a steal attempt sails high, allowing a baserunner to take third base on the play.

1998 Houston 2B Craig Biggio, who had the most at-bats in the major leagues last season (619) without grounding into a double play, grounds into a twin-killing on Opening Day against San Francisco.

APRIL

1

1925 Brooklyn Dodgers manager Wilbert Robinson announces a Bonehead Club at $10 per mistake. Soon after, however, Robinson hands the umpire the wrong line-up card, so he owes $10. He dissolves the club.

1930 Chicago Cubs C Gabby Hartnett catches a baseball dropped from a Goodyear blimp at 550 feet. He then asks the blimp to sail higher whereby he proceeds to catch another baseball dropped from 800 feet.

1931 During a scheduled exhibition, 19-year-old Jackie Mitchell becomes the first female baseball pitcher to oppose major league hitters and promptly strikes out Babe Ruth and Lou Gehrig.

1936 Ron Perranoski b. Paterson, NJ.

1939 Phil Niekro b. Blaine, OH.

1944 Rusty Staub b. New Orleans, LA.

1947 Major League Baseball adopts a retirement insurance annuity plan for its players.

1948 Willie Montanez b. Puerto Rico.

1962 Rich Amaral b. Visalia, CA.

1969 Frank Castillo b. El Paso, TX.

1969 The Seattle Pilots trade OF Lou Piniella to Kansas City for OF Steve Whitaker and RHP John Gelnar.

1972 The first player's strike in ML history begins at 12:01 A.M. The strike lasts 12 days and wipes out 86 games.

1974 San Francisco trades RHP Don Carrithers to Montreal for C John Boccabella.

1981 Houston trades RHP Ken Forsch to California for SS Dickie Thon.

1982 Texas trades RHPs Ron Darling and Walt Terrell to the New York Mets for OF Lee Mazzilli.

1985 Author George Plimpton pulls April Fool's Day joke on *Sports Illustrated* readers, profiling New York Mets pitching phenom Sidd Finch, who possesses a 168 mph fastball.

1987 St. Louis trades OF Andy Van Slyke, C Mike LaValliere, and RHP Mike Dunne to Pittsburgh for C Tony Pena.

1989 A. Bartlett Giamatti takes office as baseball's seventh commissioner. He'll serve until his death on September 1, 1989.

1996 NL umpire John McSherry collapses and dies of a heart attack just seven pitches into Cincinnati's home opener against Montreal. McSherry becomes the first umpire fatality on the baseball field.

1996 The New York Mets rally from a 6-0 deficit to defeat St. Louis, 7-6, in the greatest Opening Day comeback of the century.

1997 San Diego's Rickey Henderson scores two runs without playing in the field. As a pinch hitter, Henderson hits a home run. Later that inning he is hit by a pitch and eventually scores.

1998 The AL expansion Tampa Bay Devil Rays win their first game in franchise history, 11-8, over Detroit, as 1B Fred McGriff collects three hits and four RBIs.

1998 Baltimore RHP Scott Erickson pitches a four-hitter for his 100th career win as the Orioles defeat Kansas City, 10-1.

2

1869 Hugh Jennings b. Pittston, PA.
1907 Luke Appling b. High Point, NC.
1927 Billy Pierce b. Detroit, MI.
1937 Dick Radatz b. Detroit, MI.
1938 Al Weis b. Franklin Square, NY.
1945 Reggie Smith b. Shreveport, LA.
1945 Don Sutton b. Clio, AL.
1962 Cleveland trades 1B Vic Power and LHP Dick Stigman to Minnesota for RHP Pedro Ramos, the AL's loss leader each of the past four seasons.
1966 Baseball Commissioner William Eckert voids the contract between the Atlanta Braves and USC RHP Tom Seaver since he signed prior to the collegiate season's ending. For the same $40,000 signing price, only three teams chose to participate in the lottery — the Mets (who got him), the Indians, and Phillies.
1968 Curt Leskanic b. Homestead, PA.
1970 Denny Hocking b. Torrence, CA.
1973 California trades SS Leo Cardenas to Cleveland for 1B Tom McCraw.
1976 Baltimore trades RHPs Mike Torrez and Paul Mitchell, and OF Don Baylor to Oakland for OF Reggie Jackson, LHP Ken Holtzman, and RHP Bill Van Bommel.
1995 Baseball owners end a 234-day work stoppage, inviting striking players back to work. Opening Day for the season is moved back to April 25, and the schedule will allow only 144 games.

1996 Detroit 1B Cecil Fielder, kindly listed at 250 pounds, steals the first base of his 11-year career, which spans 1,097th major league games. Fielder takes off on a full count pitch to Melvin Nieves and swipes second base during a strikeout. The Tigers beat Minnesota, 10-6.
1998 Milwaukee RF Jeromy Burnitz hits two home runs, including an 11th-inning grand slams, as the visiting Brewers beat Atlanta, 8-6, to record their first win since switching to the NL.
1998 Anaheim RHP Ken Hill hurls six shutout innings for his 100th career victory and 3B Dave Hollins hits his 100th career home run as the Angels beat the visiting New York Yankees, 10-2.
1999 Kansas City trades 1B Jeff Conine to Baltimore for RHP Chris Fussell.

3

1923 Expelled "Black Sox" players Hap Felsch and Swede Risberg sue their former club, the Chicago White Sox, for back salary and $400,000 in damages.
1930 Wally Moon b. Bay, AR.
1963 Chris Bosio b. Carmichael, CA.
1968 Mike Lansing b. Rawlins, WY.
1974 Jim Pittsley b. DuBois, PA.
1994 St. Louis beats Cincinnati, 6-4, in the Sunday night opener that sends baseball into a new era with three divisions and a new playoff format.
1998 Baltimore LF B.J. Surhoff hits a three-run homer and RHP Doug Drabek earns his 150th career win as the Orioles defeat Detroit, 10-2.

4

1888 Tris Speaker b. Hubbard, TX.

1916 Mickey Owen b. Nixa, MO.

1924 Gil Hodges b. Princeton, IN.

1942 Jim Fregosi b. San Francisco, CA.

1942 Eddie Watt b. Lamoni, IA.

1947 Ray Fosse b. Marion, IL.

1960 The Chicago White Sox trade 1B Don Mincher and C Earl Battey to Washington for OF Roy Sievers.

1963 Houston trades OF Manny Mota to Pittsburgh for OF Howie Goss.

1969 California trades OF Chuck Hinton to Cleveland for OF Lou Johnson.

1970 Milwaukee trades OF Roy Foster and INF Frank Coggins to Cleveland for 3B Max Alvis and OF Russ Snyder.

1974 In the earliest opener to date in baseball history, Atlanta's Hank Aaron homers off Cincinnati RHP Jack Billingham to tie Babe Ruth for most in career round-trippers with 714.

1975 Scott Rolen b. Evansville, IN.

1978 Pittsburgh trades OF Miguel Dilone, RHP Elias Sosa, and 2B Mike Edwards to Oakland for C Manny Sanguillen.

1988 Toronto DH George Bell becomes the first ML player to hit three home runs on Opening Day as the Blue Jays defeat Kansas City, 5–3. All three of Bell's homers come against Royals starting RHP Bret Saberhagen.

1989 New York LHP Tommy John, age 45, begins his ML record 26th season with an Opening Day assignment against Minnesota. John wins his 287th career game as the Yankees top the Twins, 4-2.

1993 When the Tigers open the year in Boston, Detroit's Sparky Anderson becomes the first skipper since Connie Mack retired in 1950 to manage 24 consecutive seasons.

1994 Chicago OF Karl Rhodes ties an ML record with three home runs on Opening Day, all against New York starting RHP Dwight Gooden. However, the Cubs lose, 12-8, to the Mets at Wrigley Field.

1994 Cleveland debuts Jacobs Field with an 11-inning, 4-3 win over Seattle. Indians 1B Eddie Murray becomes the all-time leader in games played at first base, appearing in his 2,369th at the position.

1994 Toronto OF Carlos Delgado hits his first ML home run, a mammoth 430-foot shot against Chicago White Sox LHP Dennis Cook that hits the window of the Skydome's Hard Rock Cafe.

1998 St. Louis 1B Mark McGwire becomes only the second player in NL history to hit home runs in each of the first four games of the season, leading the Cardinals to an 8-6 win over San Diego. McGwire's sixth-inning, three-run homer ties San Francisco OF Willie Mays' 1971 record.

1999 For the first time, a major league season opener is played in Mexico, as 27,104 fans watch Colorado beat San Diego, 8-2, in Monterrey.

5

1876 Bill Dinneen b. Syracuse, NY.

1900 On a chilly day in New York, Harry Stevens goes shopping for a hot item, stopping at a local butcher to buy sausages then at the bakery to buy rolls. What he creates is later dubbed a "hot dog" by local sports cartoonist Ted Dorgan.

1938 Ron Hansen b. Oxford, NE.

1951 Rennie Stennett b. Colon, Panama.

1971 In their last Opening Day, the Washington Senators blank the Oakland A's, 8-0, before 45,000 fans at RFK Stadium. RHP Dick Bosman is the winning pitcher.

1972 The New York Mets trade SS Tim Foli, 1B Mike Jorgensen, and OF Ken Singleton to Montreal for OF Rusty Staub.

1977 The Chicago White Sox trade SS Bucky Dent to the New York Yankees for OF Oscar Gamble and RHP LaMarr Hoyt.

1982 Baltimore SS Cal Ripken Jr. hits his first ML home run against Kansas City RHP Dennis Leonard.

1993 The NL expansion Florida Marlins win their first game, 6-3, over the Los Angeles Dodgers at Joe Robbie Stadium. The other NL expansion club, the Colorado Rockies, are shutout, 3-0, by the New York Mets.

1998 Los Angeles RHP Ramon Martinez carries a no-hitter into the eighth inning, only to have Cincinnati C Eddie Taubensee spoil it with a one-out single. The Dodgers edge the Reds, 1-0.

1998 After an 0-5 start, the NL expansion Arizona Diamondbacks win for the first time in franchise history, 3-2, over San Francisco. RHP Andy Benes gets the win.

1998 Philadelphia RHP Curt Schilling strikes out 15 Atlanta batters and outduels Braves RHP Greg Maddux, 2-1.

1999 Los Angeles RF Raul Mondesi hits a two-out, three-run home run in the bottom of the ninth inning to tie Arizona, 6-6. He then blasts a game-winning two-out, two-run homer in the 11th inning, lifting the Dodgers over the Diamondbacks, 8-6.

6

1903 Mickey Cochrane b. Bridgewater, MA.

1908 Ernie Lombardi b. Oakland, CA.

1937 Phil Regan b. Otsego, MI.

1943 Marty Pattin b. Charleston, IL.

1951 Bert Blyleven b. Zeist, Holland.

1961 The Chicago Cubs name Vedie Himsl as the first of eight coaches who will rotate as manager during the season. The experiment fails, as the Cubs finish 64-90, 29 games behind NL pennant winner Cincinnati.

1966 Kansas City A's trade LHP John O'Donoghue to Cleveland for RHP Ralph Terry.

1967 Tommy Greene b. Lumberton, NC.

1969 Bret Boone b. El Cajon, CA.

1973 The AL debuts the Designated Hitter (DH). The New York Yankees' Ron Blomberg is the inaugural candidate, and the Yanks lose 15-5, to the Boston Red Sox. Blomberg walks with the bases loaded in the first inning against Boston RHP Luis Tiant.

1973 Minnesota's Tony Oliva hits the first home run by a designated hitter.

1977 The AL expansion Seattle Mariners lose their first game, 7-0, to the California Angels at the Kingdome.

1982 Minnesota debuts the Metrodome, but Seattle spoils the event with an 11-7 win in the opener.

1985 Philadelphia trades RHP Bill Campbell and SS Ivan DeJesus to St. Louis for LHP Dave Rucker.

1989 Los Angeles RHP Orel Hershiser has his record 59-inning scoreless streak end during the first inning of his first start of the season. The Dodgers fall to Cincinnati, 4-3.

1992 Baltimore debuts Camden Yards with a 2-0 win over Cleveland.

1995 Atlanta trades OFs Roberto Kelly and Tony Tarasco and RHP Esteban Yan to Montreal for CF Marquis Grissom.

1999 Atlanta RHP Greg Maddux hits his first home run since 1992 and adds a two-run single in the same fourth inning as the Braves defeat Philadelphia, 11-3.

Maddux becomes the first pitcher with two hits in an inning since St. Louis RHP Todd Stottlemyre did it against Pittsburgh on June 30, 1996.

7

1873 John McGraw b. Truxton, NY.
1918 Bobby Doerr b. Los Angeles, CA.
1942 Tom Phoebus b. Baltimore, MD.
1944 Bill Stoneman b. Oak Park, IL.
1969 The New York Yankees spoil the managerial debut of the Washington Senators' Ted Williams, 8-4, before 45,000 fans, including President Richard M. Nixon.
1969 Cincinnati's Pete Rose hits Los Angeles RHP Don Drysdale's first pitch on Opening Day for a home run, and Bobby Tolan does the same to Drysdale's second pitch. The Dodgers win, however, 3-2.
1969 Philadelphia sends SS Bobby Wine to Montreal as a trade replacement for RHP Larry Jackson, who retires rather than report to the expansion Expos.
1969 Ricky Bones b. Puerto Rico.
1970 The Milwaukee Brewers lose their franchise opener at County Stadium, 12-0, to the California Angels.
1970 The New York Mets win their first home opener after eight years of trying, 5-3, over Pittsburgh in 11 innings.
1970 St. Louis OF Curt Flood is placed on baseball's restricted list for refusing to honor a trade to Philadelphia over the past offseason. Flood will miss the entire 1970 season, lose his case in Federal Court, be traded again, but this time accepts the deal to Washington where he'll play briefly before leaving the game in 1971.

1977 The AL expansion Toronto Blue Jays begin play with a 9-5 victory over the Chicago White Sox at Exhibition Stadium. The Blue Jays' Al Woods becomes baseball's 11th player to pinch-hit a home run in his first ML at-bat.
1979 Houston Astros RHP Ken Forsch no-hits Atlanta to join brother Bob Forsch of the St. Louis Cardinals as the only brother combo to hurl ML no-hitters.
1984 Detroit RHP Jack Morris no-hits the White Sox, 4-0, at Chicago's Comiskey Park.
1991 Philadelphia trades LHP Chuck McElroy and RHP Bob Scanlan to the Chicago Cubs for LHP Mitch Williams.
1993 The expansion Colorado Rockies score their first ever run on their first ever home run, Dante Bichette's long solo blast against New York RHP Bret Saberhagen. It's the only scoring for the Rockies in a 6-1 loss to the Mets.
1994 New York Yankees 1B Don Mattingly collects his 1,000th career RBI during an 18-6 win over Texas.
1997 The Kansas City Royals celebrate their 25th season at Kauffman Stadium by retiring three jersey numbers worn by past heroes George Brett (5), Frank White (20), and the late Dick Howser (10).
1997 The Milwaukee Brewers beat the Texas Rangers, 5-3, in their home opener before 42,893 fans, although the game is nearly forfeited as a giveaway baseball promotion turns ugly forcing three delays. Texas manager Johnny Oates pulls his team off the field twice in the second inning.
1997 New York Mets LHP Joe Crawford makes his ML debut with a few oddities attached. He's a pitcher who debuts as a pinch-hitter; he makes his pitching debut in the same game as his hitting debut, but on different days since he bats before midnight then pitches after midnight.
1999 Baltimore 3B Cal Ripken, Jr.,

misses his first game in 17 years due to injury as the Orioles lose to Tampa Bay, 8-5. Ripken, sitting out with a stiff back, is replaced by rookie Willis Otanez who hits his first ML home run.

1999 Texas Rangers RHP Mike Morgan earns a relief win over Detroit, 10-7, to set an ML record with victories for 10 different clubs. Now in his 19th year, Morgan has won games for the Oakland A's, New York Yankees, Seattle Mariners, Baltimore Orioles, Los Angeles Dodgers, Chicago Cubs, St. Louis Cardinals, Cincinnati Reds, and Minnesota Twins.

8

1943 John Hiller b. Toronto, Ontario, Canada.

1946 Jim "Catfish" Hunter b. Hertford, NC.

1954 Gary Carter b. Culver City, CA.

1960 Los Angeles trades INF Don Zimmer to the Chicago Cubs for LHP Ron Perranoski, INF John Goryl, and OF Lee Handley.

1969 The Montreal Expos play their first regular season game–the first international contest in ML history–and defeat the eventual world champion New York Mets, 10-9, at Shea Stadium. Expos LHP Dan McGinn hits the expansion team's first home run. Baseball's three other expansion teams, the NL's San Diego Padres and the AL's Kansas City Royals and Seattle Pilots, also win their inagural contests.

1973 Alex Gonzalez b. Miami, FL.

1974 Atlanta's Hank Aaron hits his career record 715th home run off Los Angeles LHP Al Downing to break Babe Ruth's all-time record before 54,000 at Atlanta's Fulton County Stadium. The Braves top the Dodgers, 7-4.

1975 Cleveland's Frank Robinson

debuts as the first black manager in ML history and wins, 5-3, over the New York Yankees, thanks to his own home run in the designated hitter role.

1978 Milwaukee 2B Paul Molitor hits his first ML home run against Baltimore RHP Joe Kerrigan.

1981 Boston trades RHP Dick Drago to Seattle for RHP Manny Sarmiento.

1986 San Francisco 1B Will Clark hits a home run on his first swing on his first at-bat in the major leagues.

1986 Seattle 3B Jim Presley hits home runs in both the ninth and tenth innings to help the Mariners to a come-from-behind, 8-4 Opening Day victory over California.

1987 During an interview with ABC's Ted Koppel on "Nightline," Los Angeles vice president Al Campanis says that blacks "lack the necessities" to be major league managers or general managers and is consequently fired for his remarks.

1987 Cleveland RHP Phil Niekro and LHP Steve Carlton team up to beat Toronto, 14-3. Niekro records his 312th victory, while Carlton hurls four shutout innings in relief. Its the first time in ML history that two 300-game winners pitch for the same team in the same game.

1993 Cleveland 2B Carlos Baerga becomes the only player in ML history to homer from both sides of the plate in the same inning. His blasts come against New York Yankees LHP Steve Howe and RHP Steve Farr.

1994 Atlanta LHP Kent Mercker no-hits Los Angeles, 6-0, in his first career complete game. Dodgers RHP Chan Ho Park, who opposes Mercker, becomes the first Korean-born player to appear in the major leagues.

1994 Minnesota OF Kirby Puckett has five hits including his career 2,000th.

1995 Boston trades 3B Scott Cooper and RHP Cory Bailey to St. Louis for

OF Mark Whiten and LHP Rheal Cormier.

1997 The Chicago Cubs match their worst start in their 122-year history with their seventh straight loss, falling, 5-3, to the Florida Marlins.

9

1879 Doc White b. Washington D.C.

1888 Hippo Vaughn b. Weatherford, TX.

1901 Vic Sorrell b. Morrisville, NC.

1909 Claude Passeau b. Waynesboro, MS.

1913 Ebbets Field opens as the new home of the Brooklyn Dodgers, but only 10,000 see their team lose, 1-0, to the Philadelphia Phillies as someone forgets the key to open the front gates.

1946 Nate Colbert b. St. Louis, MO.

1947 Brooklyn Dodgers manager Leo Durocher is suspended for one year by baseball commissioner A.B. "Happy" Chandler for actions detrimental to the game. He is accused of fraternizing with gamblers.

1953 Strapped for funds, St. Louis Browns owner Bill Veeck sells Sportsman's Park to Anheuser-Busch Brewery president August A. Busch, Jr., who renames the park Busch Stadium.

1961 Kirk McCaskill b. Kapuskasing, Ontario.

1963 Jose Guzman b. Puerto Rico.

1964 Milwaukee trades C Bob Uecker to St. Louis for C Jimmie Coker and INF Gary Kolb.

1964 The Los Angeles Dodgers trade RHP Larry Sherry to Detroit for OF Lou Johnson.

1965 Hal Morris b. Fort Rucker, AL.

1965 In the first indoor game played inside Houston's Astrodome, the Colt 45's top the New York Yankees, 2-1, in 12 innings, in an exhibition meeting before 47,000 fans. New York OF Mickey Mantle blasts the first indoor home run.

1967 Graeme Lloyd b. Victoria, Australia.

1969 Chicago LF Billy Williams hits four straight doubles to lead the Cubs past the Philadelphia Phillies, 11-3.

1971 Oakland trades OF Felipe Alou to the New York Yankees for LHP Rob Gardner and RHP Ron Klimkowski.

1981 Los Angeles LHP Fernando Valenzuela hurls a five-hit shutout in his first ML start, blanking Houston, 2-0. The Dodgers rookie southpaw would go on to win his first eight decisions.

1985 Chicago White Sox RHP Tom Seaver makes his record 15th Opening Day start to break Christy Mathewson's record. Seaver hurls 6⅔ innings and gets credit for the 4-2 win over the Milwaukee Brewers.

1987 Baltimore wins the Mason-Dixon battle with Texas, 8-6, as Ken Dixon outpitches Mike Mason on the 122nd anniversary of Robert E. Lee's surrender at Appomattox Courthouse.

1993 Chicago White Sox OF Bo Jackson, who missed the entire 1992 season after hip replacement surgery, hits a home run against New York Yankees LHP Neal Heaton on his first swing of the season. Jackson's surgery was required after injuring the hip while playing football for the NFL's Oakland Raiders.

1993 The Colorado Rockies beat Montreal, 11-4, for their first ever win and set an NL record for attendance in their home debut. The crowd of 80,227 at Mile High Stadium breaks the record of 78,672 set April 18, 1958, by the Los Angeles Dodgers.

1994 Toronto DH Paul Molitor collects his 2,500th career hit, and two pitches later OF Joe Carter hits a two-run home run to tally his 1,000th and 1,001st career RBIs.

1998 Baltimore 3B Cal Ripken Jr. hits a seventh inning leadoff home run to knot the score at 1-1 and move past Lou Gehrig for 45th place on the career hit list with 2,721. Teammate Joe Carter singles home Roberto Alomar for the winning run, 2-1, as the Orioles win their seventh straight game after dropping their season opener.

1999 Yogi Berra ends a self-imposed 14-year exile from Yankee Stadium, returning to throw out the first ball prior to New York's 12-3 home opener win over Detroit. Berra had vowed never to return to New York as long as George Steinbrenner owned the club, having been fired as manager just 14 games into the 1985 season.

1999 Chicago LHP Mike Sirotka ties an AL pitching record with three errors in one inning, as the White Sox lose their home opener to Kansas City, 10-5.

10

1913 President Woodrow Wilson throws out the first ball before Washington edges the newly named New York Yankees, 2-1, in the Senators' home opener. Washington RHP Walter Johnson allows an unearned run in the first inning, but won't yield another run for 56 consecutive innings.

1921 Chuck Connors b. Brooklyn, NY.

1930 Frank Lary b. Northport, AL.

1946 Bob Watson b. Los Angeles, CA.

1949 Lee Lacy b. Longview, TX.

1950 Ken Griffey Sr. b. Donora, PA.

1961 John F. Kennedy becomes the last president to throw out the ceremonial Opening Day first ball at Washington's Griffith Stadium.

1962 The night before their first-ever game, 16 members of the expansion New York Mets are stuck in a hotel elevator for 20 minutes.

1962 The Houston Colt .45s, in the first major league game played in Texas, beat the Chicago Cubs, 11-2, before 25,000 fans. Roman Mejias leads the Houston offense with two home runs.

1962 Los Angeles debuts Dodger Stadium, but Cincinnati spoils the occasion with a 6-3 win.

1963 Mike Devereaux b. Casper, WY.

1963 Marvin Freeman b. Chicago,IL.

1971 The Philadelphia Phillies open Veterans Stadium with a 4-1 win over the Montreal Expos before more than 55,000 fans.

1971 Pittsburgh OF Willie Stargell hits three home runs in a game against Atlanta.

1973 Kansas City debuts Royals Stadium with a 12-1 rout of Texas.

1976 New York Yankees 1B Chris Chambliss calls timeout in the bottom of the ninth, a moment before the Milwaukee Brewers' Don Money connects off LHP Sparky Lyle for an apparent game winning grand slam homer. The umpires rule that time had been called, Money then flies out in his return at-bat, and the Yankees hold on for a 9-7 win.

1976 The Atlanta Braves sign free agent RHP Andy Messersmith to a "lifetime" contract.

1982 Under wintery conditions, Cleveland opens the season at Municipal Stadium with an 8-3 loss to the Texas Rangers. Five hundred tons of snow have to be removed from the field and the game is played in 38-degree temperatures with a wind-chill factor of 17 degrees. Despite the cold, 62,443 fans turn out.

1989 Seattle OF Ken Griffey, Jr., hits his first ML homerun against White Sox RHP Eric King. The blast comes on the same day that Ken Griffey, Sr., celebrates his 39th birthday.

1997 Florida Marlins RHP Alex Fernandez tosses a one-hitter to beat the winless Chicago Cubs, 1-0, in Chicago. The Cubs fall to 0-8, the worst start in their 122-year history.

1999 Making his Arizona debut, LHP Randy Johnson strikes out 15 batters in throwing a six-hitter as the Diamondbacks beat the Braves for the first time in Atlanta, 8-3. Johnson registers his 57th complete game and 103rd double-digit strikeout game of his career.

11

1907 New York Giants C Roger Bresnahan sports shinguards for the first time in major league history.

1912 New York Giants RHP Rube Marquard begins a 19-game winning streak with a 18-3 win over the Brooklyn Dodgers. The Giants hit 13 ground rule doubles since there are no fences, only spectators who line the foul poles and outfield.

1912 Cincinnati celebrates the opening of new Redland Field with a 10-6 win over the Chicago Cubs.

1921 Jim Hearn b. Atlanta, GA.

1954 The New York Yankees trade OF Bill Virdon and RHP Mel Wright to the St. Louis Cardinals for OF Enos Slaughter.

1961 The expansion Los Angeles Angels win their first game, 7-2, at Baltimore, behind RHP Eli Grba's complete game and Ted Kluszewski's two home runs.

1962 In St. Louis, the expansion New York Mets lose their first game, 11-4, as RHP Roger Craig balks home the first Cardinals run in the first inning.

1964 Bret Saberhagen b. Chicago Heights, IL.

1966 Emmett Ashford, age 51, becomes the first black umpire to work an ML game when he takes the field for the Washington Senators' home opener.

1969 The Seattle Pilots win their first game, 7-0, as RHP Gary Bell blanks the Chicago White Sox at Sicks Stadium.

1974 Trot Nixon b. Durham, NC.

1985 Seattle DH Gorman Thomas hits three home runs and drives in six runs to lead the Mariners to a 14-6 win over the A's. Oakland DH Dave Kingman hits an apparent home run, but the ball glances off a speaker in fair territory and is caught for an out inside the Kingdome.

1987 Returning to the Oakland A's after 11 seasons with the Baltimore Orioles, New York Yankees, and California Angels, Reggie Jackson thrills the home crowd with a home run in a 6-4 loss to the Angels. The future Hall of Fame outfielder will hit only 14 more homers to finish a 21-year career with 563 round-trippers.

1990 LHP Mark Langston makes his California Angels debut by combining with RHP Mike Witt on a 1-0 no-hitter over the Seattle Mariners. Langston hurls the first seven innings, Witt the final two.

1992 Cleveland 2B Carlos Baerga collects six hits in a game.

1994 Texas debuts The Ballpark at Arlington with a 4-3 loss to Milwaukee.

1998 Cincinnati and Colorado tie a 115-year-old ML record as eight players collect three or more hits in a game and the Reds beat the home Rockies, 12-5. Six of the eight hitters with three hits are from Cincinnati which totals 21 hits in the contest.

1998 After winning their season opener, the Florida Marlins lose to Pittsburgh, 7-6, dropping their 10th straight game and extending the worst start ever for a defending world champion.

1998 St. Louis 1B Mark McGwire walks with the bases loaded for his 1,000th career RBI to help the Cardinals to a 7-2 win over San Francisco.

1998 Baltimore RHP Mike Mussina allows only two hits over eight innings and notches his 1,000th career strikeout as the Orioles blank Detroit, 2-0.

1999 New York RHP Orlando Hernandez takes a perfect game into the seventh inning, retiring the first 19 Detroit batters, before walking Tigers DH Gregg Jefferies. The Yankees sweep the three-game series, 11-2.

12

1876 Vic Willis b. Wilmington, DE.

1880 Addie Joss b. Juneau, WI.

1909 Philadelphia A's C Mike Powers lunges for a pop foul, crashing into the wall of newly constructed Shibe Park on Opening Day against Boston. Complaining of severe abdominal pains, Powers undergoes surgery to remove part of his intestines, and he suddenly dies on April 26. Shibe Park is the first park made of concrete and steel.

1912 Infielders Joe Tinker (SS), Johnny Evers (2B), and Frank Chance (1B) play their last game after being with the Chicago Cubs since September of 1902.

1916 The Boston Red Sox trade CF Tris Speaker to Cleveland for RHP Sad Sam Jones, 3B Fred Thomas, and $55,000.

1922 Bill Wight b. Rio Vista, CA.

1927 The New York Yankees win on Opening Day and stay in first place all 174 days of the season en route to a 110-44 regular season record and eventual world title by sweeping the Pittsburgh Pirates in the World Series.

1930 Johnny Antonelli b. Rochester, NY.

1933 Charlie Lau b. Romulus, MI.

1940 Woodie Fryman b. Ewing, KY.

1944 Terry Harmon b. Toledo, OH.

1955 Transplanted from Philadelphia, the Kansas City A's win their first game at Municipal Stadium, 6-2 over Detroit.

1960 In front of a crowd of 42,269, the San Francisco Giants defeat the St. Louis Cardinals, 3-1, in the first game at Candlestick Park.

1960 Cleveland trades 1B Norm Cash to Detroit for 3B Steve Demeter.

1961 The Kansas City A's trade RHP Dick Hall and INF Dick Williams to Baltimore for RHP Jerry Walker and OF Chuck Essegian.

1964 Mike McFarlane b. Stockton, CA.

1965 Milwaukee Braves C Joe Torre drills a pair of home runs in the season opener. Exactly one year later, the Braves are in Atlanta, and Torre does it again. Braves 3B Eddie Mathews is the only other ML player with two, two-homer Opening Days.

1965 The expansion Houston Astros lose their Astrodome home opener, 2-0, to Philadelphia, as Richie Allen slugs the first major league indoor home run against RHP Bob Bruce.

1966 An Atlanta crowd of 50,671 welcomes the Braves after they move from Milwaukee but the Pirates' Willie Stargell spoils the occasion with a two-run home run in the 13th inning for a 3-2 Pirates victory.

1980 Cecil Cooper and Don Money each hit a grand slam home run in the second inning of Milwaukee's 18-1 rout of the Boston Red Sox.

1987 Atlanta OF Dion James' line drive to center field strikes and kills a dove before the ball reaches New York Mets CF Kevin McReynolds. James gets credit for a hustling double, while the bird becomes baseball's only fatality caused by a fair ball.

1990 San Francisco OF Brett Butler ties a NL record with five walks in a game.

1992 Boston LHP Matt Young pitches eight no-hit innings at Cleveland but loses, 2-1. In the second game, the Indians manage only two hits off Red Sox RHP Roger Clemens to set an ML record for fewest hits in a doubleheader two.

1994 Boston 3B Scott Cooper hits for the cycle and drives in five runs as the Red Sox hammer Kansas City, 22-11.

1998 Tampa Bay LHP Wilson Alvarez hurls eight strong innings to defeat the Chicago White Sox, 4-1, and improve the Devil Rays' record to 6-4, the best record ever for an expansion team.

1998 The Colorado Rockies complete the worst back-to-back-to-back starting pitching lines in the 1990s as RHP Pedro Astacio gets bombed by Cincinnati for 10 runs and nine hits in five innings. The day before against the Reds, Rockies RHP John Thomson allows nine runs and 11 hits in only two innings. In the series opener April 10th, RHP Darryl Kile gives up eight runs on nine hits in six innings.

1999 Anaheim collects a season-high 20 hits including a club record 10 doubles in beating Texas, 13-5. Angels RF Tim Salmon and 3B Troy Glaus lead the assault with four hits each.

13

1914 The first Federal League game is played in Baltimore as the Terrapins defeat Buffalo, 3-2, behind RHP Jack Quinn. A crowd of 27,000 stands 15 rows deep in the outfield to witness the return of big league baseball to Baltimore.

1921 Former president Woodrow Wilson, current president Warren Harding, and future president Calvin Coolidge are all in attendance to watch the Washington Senators' Opening Day loss to the Boston Red Sox.

1926 Washington RHP Walter Johnson pitches his 14th and last Opening Day game for the Senators, a 1-0, 15-inning win over RHP Ed Rommel and the Philadelphia A's. Both pitchers go the distance.

1953 For the first time in half a century, a new city is represented in baseball as the Boston Braves relocate to Milwaukee. The Braves win their opener in Cincinnati as RHP Max Surkont defeats the Reds, 2-0.

1954 Hank Aaron makes his major league debut in left field for the Milwaukee Braves and goes 0-for-5 during a 9-8 loss to Cincinnati. The Reds' Jim Greengrass hits four doubles in his first game.

1962 On a snowy Friday the 13th, NL baseball returns to New York as new manager Casey Stengel's Mets lose to Pittsburgh, 4-3.

1963 Cincinnati's Pete Rose gets his first major league hit with a triple against Pittsburgh RHP Bob Friend.

1963 Mark Leiter b. Joliet, IL.

1965 Cincinnati Reds 3B Tony Perez hits a home run against Milwaukee Braves LHP Denny Lemaster. It is the first of 379 he will hit in his career.

1966 Wes Chamberlain b. Chicago, IL.

1972 The first player's strike in baseball history ends after 13 days and 86 cancelled games.

1974 Milwaukee SS Robin Yount, still 18 years old, hits his first ML home run, against Baltimore LHP Ross Grimsley. Yount will finish his career with 251 homers.

1984 The Montreal Expos' Pete Rose doubles off Philadelphia LHP Jerry Koosman for his 4,000th career hit. The hit comes exactly 21 years after Rose's first hit.

1987 The San Diego Padres set a major league record when the first three batters in the bottom of the first inning — Marvell Wynne, Tony Gwynn, and John Kruk — all homer off San Francisco starting RHP Roger Mason in the Padres' home opener.

1993 St. Louis RHP Lee Smith breaks the ML record for saves, recording his 358th, against Los Angeles. The next night, Smith, who has pitched in both leagues, breaks the NL record with his 301st.

1995 California trades OF Chad Curtis to Detroit for OF Tony Phillips.

1997 The Chicago Cubs tie a modern NL record for season opening futility, losing their 10th straight game as Atlanta records an 8-6 win in Chicago. Ironically, the Cubs tie the record set by the 1988 Braves.

1997 Chicago White Sox closer and RHP Roberto Hernandez blows a save on both ends of a doubleheader against Detroit, both times on home runs by Tigers 3B Travis Fryman.

1998 Texas DH Lee Stevens hits three home runs to power the Rangers to a 10-1 win over Detroit and give RHP Bobby Witt his 100th career win.

1999 Texas C Ivan Rodriguez sets a franchise record with nine RBIs to lift the Rangers to a 15-6 win over Seattle. Rodriguez has four hits, including a three-run homer and a grand slam homer, and teammate Rusty Greer also goes 4-for-5 as Texas jumps out to a 13-0 lead after three innings.

1999 Oakland defeats Anaheim, 3-2, marking the franchise's 2,500th win since the A's moved to Oakland from Kansas City in 1968. Since 1968, only the New York Yankees, Baltimore Orioles, Cincinnati Reds, Los Angeles Dodgers, Boston Red Sox, and Pittsburgh Pirates have reached the 2,500 plateau.

14

1910 Washington Senators RHP Walter Johnson pitches a one-hit, 3-0 shutout against the Philadelphia A's. Chicago White Sox RHP Frank Smith duplicates the feat against the St. Louis Browns. Prior to the Senators game, William H. Taft becomes the first president to officially throw out the first ball of the season.

1911 Cleveland RHP Addie Joss dies unexpectedly of tubular meningitis at age 31.

1911 New York's Polo Grounds burns down, forcing the NL Giants to play a large portion of the schedule at nearby Hilltop Park, home of the AL New York Highlanders.

1915 On Opening Day in Philadelphia, A's LHP Herb Pennock blanks the Boston Red Sox, 5-0. The only hit allowed is a scratch single by Harry Hooper with two outs in the ninth inning.

1917 Chicago White Sox RHP Ed Cicotte pitches an 11-0 no-hitter over the St. Louis Browns. It's the first of five no-hitters thrown in the AL this year.

1925 Cleveland opens the season with a 21-14 victory over the St. Louis Browns for the most runs scored by one club on opening day. The Indians enjoy a 12-run eighth inning aided by five Browns errors. St. Louis 1B George Sisler commits four errors in the contest.

1927 Don Mueller b. St. Louis, MO.

1935 Marty Keogh b. Oakland, CA.

1936 St. Louis Cardinals OF Eddie Morgan becomes the first player to hit a pinch hit home run in his first ML at bat. It would be Morgan's only homer in a 39-game career.

1941 Pete Rose b. Cincinnati, OH.

1941 President Franklin D. Roosevelt

throws out the first pitch at Washington's Griffith Stadium to open the season. It is Roosevelt's ninth opening ceremony, an all-time presidential record which will go unmatched.

1947 Joe Lahoud b. Danbury, CT.

1953 After moving the franchise from Boston, the Milwaukee Braves win their home opener, 3-2, over St. Louis.

1955 New York Yankees OF Elston Howard breaks the color barrier for the Bronx Bombers with a single in his first major league at-bat at Boston.

1960 The Philadelphia Phillies lose their opener and their manager as Eddie Sawyer is fired after one game and replaced by Gene Mauch.

1966 Greg Maddux b. San Angelo, TX.

1966 Dave Justice b. Cincinnati, OH.

1966 Greg Myers b. Riverside, CA.

1967 Boston rookie LHP Bill Rohr loses a no-hit bid in his first major league start when Elston Howard singles in the ninth inning for the New York Yankees' only hit in a 3-0 loss to the Red Sox. Boston rookie OF Reggie Smith hits his first of a career 314 ML home runs, this one against New York LHP Whitey Ford.

1967 Mike Trombley b. Springfield, MA.

1968 Jesse Levis b. Philadelphia, PA.

1969 Brad Ausmus b. New Haven, CT.

1969 In the first major league game outside the United States, the Montreal Expos top St. Louis, 8-7, before 29,000 fans.

1970 Steve Avery b. Trenton, MI.

1971 Greg Zaun b. Glendale, CA.

1976 New York Mets OF Dave Kingman crushes a tapemeasure home run, more than 550 feet and out of Chicago's Wrigley Field and beyond Waveland Boulevard.

1998 St. Louis 1B Mark McGwire belts three home runs as the Cardinals hammer Arizona, 15-5.

1998 Detroit RHP Scott Sanders gives up 16 hits in only four innings against Texas.

1999 Tampa Bay DH Jose Canseco becomes the 28th ML player to reach 400 home runs, but the Devil Rays lose to Toronto, 7-6, in 11 innings. Born in Cuba, Canseco becomes the first ML player born outside of the United States to accomplish the feat.

1999 New York LHP John Franco becomes the second pitcher to reach 400 saves, as the Mets beat Florida, 4-1. Only retired RHP Lee Smith has more career saves, with 478.

15

1907 The Cleveland Naps buy a $100,000 policy to insure their players against railroad accidents.

1909 New York RHP Leon Ames no-hits Brooklyn for 9 1/3 innings on Opening Day, but the Giants lose to the Dodgers in the 13th inning, 3-0.

1915 New York Giants RHP Rube Marquard no-hits Brooklyn, 2-0.

1940 Willie Davis b. Mineral Springs, AR.

1942 St. Louis Browns SS Vern Stephens hits his first of a career 247 ML home runs, this one against Chicago White Sox RHP Buck Ross.

1944 Washington Senators outfielder Elmer Gedeon is killed in France during World War II. He is one of only two baseball fatalities of the war.

1946 Ted Sizemore b. Gadsden, AL.

1946 New York player/manager Mel Ott hits the last of his 511 career home runs. He has spent his entire 22-year career with the Giants.

1947 Brooklyn 1B Jackie Robinson, age 28, debuts as the first black major league player of the 20th century. Robinson goes 0-for-3 but scores the deciding run as the Dodgers beat the Boston Braves, 5-3, before 26,623 fans at Ebbets Field. An estimated 14,000 of the fans are blacks, eager to see Robinson pioneer major league baseball.

1954 New York Yankees 1B Bill Skowron hits the first of his career 211 ML home runs, against Philadelphia A's LHP Alex Kellner.

1954 Returning to the AL after a 51-year absence, the Baltimore Orioles defeat the Chicago White Sox, 3-1, before 46,354 fans at newly constructed Memorial Stadium.

1957 President Dwight D. Eisenhower officially opens the 1956 season by tossing out the first ball at Griffith Stadium in Washington, D.C. The ball is the 10 millionth Spalding baseball to be used in major league play.

1958 In the first ML game played on the West Coast, San Francisco Giants RHP Ruben Gomez shuts out the Los Angeles Dodgers, 8-0, at Seals Stadium in San Francisco.

1968 The Houston Astros top the New York Mets, 1-0, after 24 innings; six hours and six minutes, as SS Al Weis boots Bob Aspromonte's grounder allowing Norm Miller to score. A total of 20 different Mets strike out, and outfielders Ron Swoboda and Tommy Agee each go 0-for-10. A combined 11 pitchers work without allowing an earned run.

1969 Jeromy Burnitz b. Westminster, CA.

1970 Facing San Francisco RHP Gaylord Perry, Houston 1B John Mayberry hits the first of his ML career 255 home runs. Mayberry would victimize Perry a personal best eight times in his career.

1972 St. Louis trades LHP Jerry Reuss to Houston for RHP Scipio Spinks and LHP Lance Clemons.

1973 Milwaukee OF Gorman Thomas hits his first of a career 268 ML home runs, against Baltimore RHP Jim Palmer.

1976 New York opens a refurbished Yankee Stadium with an 11-4 rout of the Minnesota Twins.

1977 Montreal debuts new Olympic Stadium with a 7-2 loss to Philadelphia.

1987 Milwaukee LHP Juan Nieves no-hits Baltimore, 7-0.

1993 Detroit manager Sparky Anderson picks up the 2,000th win of his managerial career, a 3-2 win over Oakland. He'll finish the year with 2,081 wins, fifth on the all-time list. His Tigers will score 899 runs, the most since the 1953 Brooklyn Dodgers scored 953 runs.

1997 The golden anniversary of Jackie Robinson's breaking baseball's color barrier is celebrated during a Mets- Dodgers game at New York's Shea Stadium. President Clinton delivers a speech near second base, while dignitaries include Robinson's widow Rachel and daughter Sharon, and Branch Rickey III, grandson of the Brooklyn Dodgers owner who signed Robinson in 1947 to set in motion integration in the sport. Acting Commissioner Bud Selig proclaims that no future ML player will wear Robinson's number 42; the Boston Red Sox's Mo Vaughn and the New York Mets' Butch Huskey are the only exceptions.

1997 The Chicago Cubs lose, 10-7, to the Colorado Rockies at Wrigley Field and extend their NL record season-opening losing streak to 11 games, eclipsing the Atlanta Braves' previous record from 1988.

1998 For the first time this century,

four ML teams play regular season games at the same ballpark on the same day. With Yankee Stadium unavailable after a steel joint falls three days earlier, the Yankees move to nearby Shea Stadium and defeat the Anaheim Angels, 6-3, before 40,743 fans. Later that night, 15,955 fans witness a New York sweep as the Mets defeat the Chicago Cubs, 2-1.

1999 Jim Leyland, in his first season as Colorado's manager, earns his 1,000th career win, 6-4 over San Diego, to become the 45th manager to reach that level. Only three other active managers — Tony La Russa, Bobby Cox, and Joe Torre — have reached the 1,000-win plateau. Leyland guided Pittsburgh and Florida before joining the Rockies.

16

1899 Cincinnati Reds RHP John B. Taylor opposes Chicago Cubs RHP John W. Taylor in the last pitching duel of the century between starting pitchers with the same first and last names. The feat is next repeated exactly 100 years later, when Colorado LHP Bobby M. Jones opposes New York Mets RHP Bobby J. Jones.

1903 Paul Waner b. Harrah, OK.

1929 The New York Yankees debut permanent numbers on player's uniforms, assigning them according to spot in the batting order. Babe Ruth bats third, wears number 3; Lou Gehrig hits fourth, wears number 4.

1929 Cleveland OF Earl Averill becomes the first AL player to hit a home run in his first ML at-bat. The Indians defeat Detroit, 5-4, in 11 innings on Carl Lind's double.

1935 After 21 years in the AL, 40-year-old Babe Ruth makes his NL debut with a home run and single off New York Giants LHP Carl Hubbell in a 4-2 Boston Braves win.

1938 The St. Louis Cardinals trade Dizzy Dean to the Chicago Cubs for RHP Curt Davis, LHP Clyde Shoun, OF Tuck Stainback, and $185,000.

1940 Cleveland RHP Bob Feller tosses an Opening Day no-hitter, a 1-0 win over the Chicago White Sox at Comiskey Park.

1940 President Franklin D. Roosevelt's errant first pitch goes into the camera lens of a Washington Post photographer at Washington's Griffith Stadium.

1940 WGN-TV televises an ML baseball game for the first time during an exhibition game at Chicago's Wrigley Field. Jack Brickhouse does the first play-by-play announcing.

1943 Jim Lonborg b. Santa Maria, CA.

1944 Bob Montgomery b. Nashville, TN.

1945 Wendell Smith, sports editor of the *Pittsburgh Courier*, arranges a tryout with the Boston Red Sox for Jackie Robinson and two other black players. Red Sox manager Joe Cronin is impressed, but Boston declines and becomes the last team to integrate in 1959.

1955 Bruce Bochy b. France.

1959 Philadelphia Phillies PH Dave Philley connects for his ninth consecutive pinch hit, after ending ending the 1958 season with eight straight.

1969 Fernando Vina b. Sacramento, CA.

1972 Chicago Cubs RHP Burt Hooton no-hits the Philadelphia Phillies, 4-0 at Wrigley Field.

1975 Facing Pittsburgh RHP Dock Ellis, Montreal Expos 3B Larry Parrish hits his first of a career 256 ML home runs.

1978 St. Louis RHP Bob Forsch no-hits Philadelphia, 5-0. Less than a year later, brother Ken Forsch of the Houston Astros hurls a no-hitter against Atlanta to become the only brother combination to throw no-hitters in the major leagues.

1983 San Diego 1B Steve Garvey plays in his 1,118th consecutive game at Los Angeles to break the NL record formerly held by Chicago's Billy Williams.

1984 Oakland A's DH Dave Kingman hits three home runs, including a grand slam in his first three at-bats. He collects eight RBIs during Oakland's 9-6 win over Seattle.

1999 Atlanta trades RHP Mark Wohlers to Cincinnati for RHP John Hudek.

17

1851 Cap Anson b. Marshalltown, IA.

1892 In the first Sunday night game in NL history, Cincinnati beats St. Louis, 5-1.

1925 New York Yankees RF Babe Ruth undergoes surgery for an intestinal abcess, an injury that will sideline him until June 1.

1945 Pete Gray, an outfielder with only one arm, makes his ML debut going 1-for-4 in helping the St. Louis Browns beat Detroit, 7-1. Gray would play only during the 1945 season and retire with a .218 batting average in 77 games.

1950 Pedro Garcia b. Puerto Rico.

1951 In his first ML game, New York Yankees OF Mickey Mantle goes 1-for-4 in a 5-0 win over the Boston Red Sox.

1953 New York Yankees OF Mickey Mantle blasts the longest recorded home run — an estimated 565 feet — off of LHP Chuck Stobbs and out of Washington's Griffith Stadium.

1955 Detroit OF Al Kaline belts two home runs in one inning against the Kansas City A's.

1956 At Griffith Stadium in Washington, D.C., President Dwight D. Eisenhower throws out the ceremonial first ball to open the season then watches New York CF Mickey Mantle blast a 500-foot home run against Washington RHP Camilo Pascual as the Yankees win, 10-4.

1960 Cleveland trades OF Rocky Colavito to Detroit for OF Harvey Kuenn.

1964 Philadelphia 1B Richie Allen hits the first of his career 351 ML home runs. Chicago Cubs LHP Dick Ellsworth is the pitcher.

1964 The New York Mets open Shea Stadium with a 4-3 loss to Pittsburgh as the Pirates' Willie Stargell hits the first home run at the new ballpark.

1967 Marquis Grissom b. Atlanta, GA.

1969 Montreal RHP Bill Stoneman no-hits Philadelphia, 7-0, in only the 10th game in Expos franchise history.

1969 Facing New York RHP Cal Koonce, Pittsburgh 1B Al Oliver hits his first of a career 219 ML home runs.

1976 The Philadelphia Phillies overcome a 12-1 deficit and beat the Chicago Cubs, 18-16, in 10 innings. The Phillies tie the NL record for best rally as 3B Mike Schmidt hits four home runs and a single for eight RBIs. Two of Schmidt's homers are against RHP Rick Reuschel, and the last one comes against his brother, RHP Paul Reuschel.

1987 Toronto 1B Fred McGriff hits his first ML home run, a blast off of Boston RHP Bob Stanley.

1994 Los Angeles OF Cory Snyder hits a blast off of three home runs for seven RBIs as the Dodgers pound Pittsburgh, 19-2.

18

1880 Sam Crawford b. Wahoo, NE.

1892 Jack Scott b. Ridgeway, NC.

1899 Baltimore Orioles John McGraw plays third and makes his major league managerial debut in a 5-3 win over the New York Giants.

1923 Yankee Stadium, the largest facility in the country, opens before 74,214 fans as Babe Ruth's three-run homer lifts New York to a 4-1 win over the Boston Red Sox. John Philip Sousa leads the teams on the field at the head of the Seventh Regiment Band. Governor Alfred E. Smith throws out the first ball.

1925 Brooklyn owner Charles Ebbets dies on the morning of his Dodgers' home opener against the New York Giants at Ebbets Field.

1942 Steve Blass b. Cannan, CT.

1946 Pittsburgh OF Ralph Kiner hits his first of a career 369 ML home runs, this one against St. Louis LHP Howie Pollet. Kiner would go on to lead the league in homers in the first seven of his 10 ML seasons.

1946 Cincinnati trades RHP Jim Konstanty to the Boston Braves for OF Max West.

1947 Brooklyn 1B Jackie Robinson hits his first of a career 137 ML home runs. New York Giants LHP Dave Koslo yields the homer.

1950 Cleveland 3B Al Rosen hits his first of a career 192 ML home runs, this one against Detroit RHP Fred Hutchinson.

1951 Doug Flynn b. Lexington, KY.

1956 During a game between the New York Yankees and Washington Senators, Ed Rommel becomes the first major league umpire to wear glasses.

1957 Cleveland OF Roger Maris hits his first of a career 275 ML home runs, this one against Detroit RHP Jack Crimian.

1958 The Los Angeles Dodgers set an NL home debut attendance record as 78,672 fans see a 6-5 win over San Francisco.

1958 Facing Pittsburgh RHP Ron Kline, Cincinnati OF Vada Pinson hits his first of a career 256 ML home runs.

1959 Jim Eisenreich b. St. Cloud, MN.

1959 Dennis Rasmussen b. Los Angeles, CA.

1964 Minnesota OF Tony Oliva hits the first of a career 220 ML home runs, facing Washington RHP Steve Ridzik.

1970 Rico Brogna b. Turner Falls, MA.

1977 Cleveland RHP Pat Dobson gives up Baltimore 1B Eddie Murray's first ML home run.

1980 Minnesota Twins RHP Terry Felton gets the first of his ML record 16 consecutive losses to start a career which runs through September 12, 1982. Although he earns three saves in 1982, Felton is still winless, ending a four-year career at 0-16.

1987 Philadelphia 3B Mike Schmidt hits his 500th career homer with two outs in the ninth inning against Pittsburgh RHP Don Robinson to rally the Phillies to a 8-6 win over the Pirates at Three Rivers Stadium.

1990 Chicago White Sox 3B Robin Ventura hits his first ML home run as he faces Boston RHP Roger Clemens.

1991 The Chicago White Sox debut new Comiskey Park in forgettable fashion, getting hammered by Detroit, 16-0. The Tigers' Cecil Fielder hits the first home run at the new park against Chicago ace RHP Jack McDowell.

1999 Atlanta CF Andruw Jones goes

5-for-6 with a home run, triple, and career high six RBIs, as the Braves set a team scoring record in routing Colorado, 20-5, in Denver.

19

1909 Bucky Walters b. Philadelphia, PA.

1919 New York Governor Alfred E. Smith signs a bill permitting Sunday baseball throughout the state.

1938 In the first inning on Opening Day at Philadelphia's Baker Bowl, Brooklyn OF Ernie Koy homers in his first ML at-bat. In the bottom half of the first inning, Phillies 2B Emmett Mueller also homers in his first ML at-bat.

1948 Rick Miller b. Grand Rapids, MI.

1949 In pregame ceremonies at Yankee Stadium, granite monuments honoring Babe Ruth, Lou Gehrig, and Miller Huggins are unveiled beyond the center field wall.

1952 Boston Braves 3B Eddie Mathews hits the first of his 512 ML home runs, this one against Philadelphia LHP Ken Heintzelman.

1960 Frank Viola b. East Meadow, NY.

1961 Spike Owen b. Cleburne, TX.

1966 Boston 3B George Scott hits his first of a career 271 ML home runs, this one against Detroit RHP Joe Sparma.

1966 New York Yankees OF Roy White hits his first of a career 160 ML home runs, as he faces Cleveland LHP Sam McDowell.

1968 Brent Mayne b. Loma Linda, CA.

1969 Cleveland trades RHPs Sonny

Siebert and Vicente Romo and C Joe Azcue to Boston for LHPs Dick Ellsworth and Juan Pizzaro and OF Ken Harrelson.

1987 Facing Atlanta LHP Jeff Dedmon, San Francisco 3B Matt Williams hits his first ML home run.

1997 The Chicago Cubs match the longest losing streak in their 122-year history with their 13th straight defeat, 6-3, to the New York Mets at Shea Stadium. Relief pitcher Turk Wendell, who wears number 13, takes the loss.

1998 The New York Mets equal their biggest shutout in club history with a 14-0 pasting of Cincinnati. Mets LF Bernard Gilkey becomes only the fourth player in club history to score five runs.

1999 Baltimore 3B Cal Ripken, Jr.'s, bad back forces him onto the disabled list for the first time in his 19-year career.

20

1910 Cleveland RHP Addie Joss no-hits the Chicago White Sox for the second time in his career, and the second time by the same 1-0 score. The first time was a perfect game.

1912 Fenway Park opens in Boston with the Red Sox winning a 7-6, 11-inning contest over the New York Yankees on a two-out single by OF Tris Speaker. The newspaper headlines are still filled with the recent sinking of the Titanic disaster.

1912 Tiger Stadium opens in Detroit with the Tigers winning a 6-5, 11-inning contest.

1920 Philadelphia Phillies manager Gavvy Cravath calls his own number to pinch-hit, and he connects on a three-run home run for a 3-0 win over the New York Giants. The round-tripper would be Cravath's last of his career total of 119.

1937 Detroit OF Gee Walker becomes the first ML player to hit for the cycle on Opening Day. He accomplishes the feat in reverse order (home run, triple, double, and single) as the Tigers beat Cleveland, 4-3.

1939 Opening Day at Fenway Park in Boston, Red Sox rookie Ted Williams doubles off New York Yankees RHP Red Ruffing for his first major league hit. Yankees 1B Lou Gehrig goes 0-for-4 in his 2,123 straight game, the only occasion he and Williams are on the field together.

1943 Boston Braves manager Casey Stengel suffers a broken leg when he is hit by a Boston taxi cab. The injury will sideline him for most of the season.

1950 Milt Wilcox b. Honolulu, HI.

1961 Don Mattingly b. Evansville, IN.

1967 New York RHP Tom Seaver records his first ML win, a 6-1 triumph over the Chicago Cubs.

1973 Todd Hollandsworth b. Dayton, OH.

1981 San Francisco trades 1B Mike Ivie to Houston for 1B Dave Bergman and OF Jeffrey Leonard.

1985 Philadelphia 2B Juan Samuel ties a major league record recording 12 assists from his position.

1988 The Baltimore Orioles set a major league record, losing their 14th straight game to open a season, this time 8-6 to the Milwaukee Brewers.

1988 Oakland moves into first place in the AL West and wins 18 of its next 19 games to stay atop its division for the remaining 165 days of the season. The A's will finish with the best record in baseball at 104-58, but will lose the World Series to Los Angeles in five games.

1990 Pete Rose, baseball's all time hit leader with 4,256, is convicted of tax evasion and receives a sentence of five months and a $50,000 fine. He begins serving his sentence August 8th at the Marion, Illinois, Federal Prison Camp. One of the camp guards is the brother of Ray Fosse, the Cleveland Indians catcher that Rose bowled over to win the 1970 All-Star Game.

1990 Seattle RHP Brian Holman loses his bid for a perfect game with two outs in the bottom of the ninth inning against Oakland when A's pinch-hitter Ken Phelps connects for a home run. Holman then completes the Mariners' 6-1 win.

1997 Oakland 1B Mark McGwire becomes only the fourth ML player to homer over the left field roof at Detroit's Tiger Stadium in the A's 9-2 loss. The four previous players were Harmon Killebrew in 1962, Frank Howard in 1968, and Cecil Fielder in 1990.

1997 The Chicago Cubs end a season-opening losing streak at 14 games with a 4-3 win in the second game of the doubleheader at New York. The 0-14 start set an NL record for season opening futility and is the second worst ever behind the 1988 Baltimore Orioles, who began 0-21.

1999 Before 37,717 fans, Los Angeles edges Atlanta, 5-4, to go over the 100 million mark in attendance at Dodger Stadium since the facility opened in 1962.

21

1887 Joe McCarthy b. Philadelphia, PA.

1898 Philadelphia Phillies RHP Bill Duggleby hits a grand slam home run in his first major league at-bat. He's the only player ever to do it.

1910 Detroit spoils the opening of Cleveland's League Park with a 5-0 win over the Indians.

1912 Cincinnati SS Jimmy Esmond hits the first home run at Redland Park, an inside-the-park dash. During the deadball era, no one will hit a ball out of the stadium for a home run. Reds OF Pat Duncan finally does it in 1921.

1918 Chicago Cubs RHP Grover Cleveland Alexander, age 31, is drafted into World War I. After a 2-1 start, Alexander misses the rest of the season and has his string of three straight 30-win seasons end. In his 12 seasons following the end of the war, Alexander won't reach that plateau again, but his 373 career wins will be third best all-time.

1937 Gary Peters b. Grove City, PA.

1947 Al Bumbry b. Fredericksburg, VA.

1955 The Brooklyn Dodgers beat the Philadelphia Phillies, 14-4, at Ebbets Field for their 10th straight victory to start the season, an ML record that lasts until 1981.

1957 Jesse Orosco b. Santa Barbara, CA.

1961 The Minnesota Twins, transplanted from Washington, begin ML baseball in Minneapolis, MN, by losing to the "new," expansion Washington Senators, 5-3.

1963 Ken Caminiti b. Hanford, CA.

1966 Philadelphia trades RHP Ferguson Jenkins, OF Adolfo Phillips, and 1B John Hernstein to the Chicago Cubs for RHP Larry Jackson and RHP Bob Buhl.

1967 After 737 consecutive games, the Dodgers are rained out against St. Louis, their first rainout since moving to Los Angeles from Brooklyn to start the 1958 season.

1971 Pittsburgh OF Willie Stargell hits three home runs to pace the Pirates to a 10-2 win over Atlanta. It is the second time in 11 days that Stargell hits three homers in a game against the Braves.

1972 The Texas Rangers make their Texas debut with a 7-6 win over California at Arlington Stadium.

1978 The Houston Astros pull their second triple play in 15 days and fourth in club history. Shortstop Roger Metzger has a hand in all of them.

1982 Atlanta beats Cincinnati, 4-3, for its ML record 13th straight win to open the season.

1984 Montreal Expos RHP David Palmer hurls five perfect innings against St. Louis when rain washes the game out. It would be the fourth major league perfect game of less than nine innings.

1987 The Milwaukee Brewers' 13-game winning streak from the start of the season ends with a 7-1 loss to the Chicago White Sox. The 13-game win streak to start a season equals the Atlanta Braves' 1982 start.

1989 Braves OF Dale Murphy hits his 336th career home run, establishing the Atlanta club record. Hank Aaron hit 335 of his 755 lifetime homers while with Atlanta.

1994 Cleveland Indians 1B Eddie Murray homers from both sides of the plate, a career record 11th time, in a 10-6 win over Minnesota. With his first homer, his 443rd career, he passes Dave Kingman for 20th place all-time.

1996 Baltimore Orioles RF Brady Anderson leads off his fourth straight game with a home run, an ML record.

1999 New York RHP Roger Clemens ties the AL record by winning his 17th consecutive decision, a 4-2 win over Texas. Clemens equals the mark set by Cleveland RHP Johnny Allen in 1936-37 and tied by Baltimore LHP Dave McNally in 1968-69.

1999 Houston 1B Jeff Bagwell hits three home runs to set a franchise record for career homers as the Astros beat Chicago, 10-3. Bagwell runs his Houston total to 225, two more than Jimmy Wynn, who played for the club from 1963 to 1973.

22

1876 Boston Red Caps OF Jim O'Rourke singles off Philadelphia A's RHP Alonzo Knight for the first hit in the first game in NL history. The Red Caps win, 6-5.

1903 The New York Highlanders lose their first game in franchise history, 3-1, at Washington before 11,950 fans.

1915 The New York Yankees fashion pinstripes on their uniforms for the first time.

1918 Mickey Vernon b. Marcus Hook, PA.

1922 St. Louis Browns OF Ken Williams becomes the first player of the 20th century to hit three home runs in a game. He'll lead the AL with a season high 39 round-trippers.

1955 After moving from Philadelphia, the Athletics win their ML debut in Kansas City, 6-2, over the Detroit Tigers before a standing room crowd of 32,147, the largest paid crowd for any event in Kansas City.

1957 Philadelphia becomes the final NL team to break the color barrier when John Kennedy pinch runs for the Phillies in their 4-1 loss to Brooklyn.

1959 The Chicago White Sox score 11 runs with only one hit in the seventh inning of a 20-6 rout of the Kansas City A's. Chicago OF Johnny Callison collects the only hit in the inning, a single. The White Sox are aided by 10 walks — five with the bases loaded — three Kansas City errors and one hit batsman.

1961 Jimmy Key b. Huntsville, AL.

1962 New York Yankees SS Tom Tresh hits his first of a career 153 ML home runs. Cleveland RHP Dick Donovan is the pitcher.

1966 Mickey Morandini b. Kittanning, PA.

1966 The Braves win their first game since moving from Milwaukee to Atlanta, beating the New York Mets, 8-4.

1968 Mike Bell b. Lewiston, NJ.

1970 New York Mets RHP Tom Seaver strikes out 19 San Diego Padres in a 2-1 win. Seaver allows just two hits and sets an ML record striking out 10 batters consecutively for the last outs of the game.

1971 Philadelphia trades OF Johnny Briggs to Milwaukee for 1B Pete Koegel and RHP Ray Peters.

1982 After opening the season with an ML record 13 straight wins, Atlanta falls to Cincinnati, 2-1.

1985 Minnesota OF Kirby Puckett hits his first ML home run as he faces Seattle LHP Matt Young.

1986 Texas RHP Bobby Witt becomes the first pitcher since David Clyde in 1973 to register his first pro victory at the major league level when he beats Toronto. Witt was 0-6 at Class AA Tulsa in 1985.

1988 St. Louis trades 2B Tommy Herr to Minnesota for OF Tom Brunansky.

1993 Seattle RHP Chris Bosio no-hits Boston, 7-0. After walking the first two batters, Bosio retires the next 27 in a row.

1996 Seattle sets an ML record for home runs in the month of April with 39, breaking the Chicago White Sox' 1984 mark of 38. The Mariners will finish the month with a new high of 44 round-trippers.

1997 The New York Yankees acquire the rights to 28-year-old Japanese RHP Hideki Irabu from San Diego for OF

Ruben Rivera, RHP Rafael Medina, and $3 million. The Padres had earlier purchased Irabu's rights through a working agreement with the Chiba Lotte Marines.

1999 Tampa Bay LHP Tony Saunders carries a no-hitter into the eighth inning when Baltimore SS Mike Bordick ends his bid with a single to center field. Saunders and two Devil Rays relievers settle for the one-hit, 1-0 shutout against the Orioles.

1999 Colorado plays its first game since a shooting incident at suburban Denver Columbine High School two days earlier, and defeats San Francisco, 8-5 at 3Com Park. The Rockies postponed games at Coors Field against Montreal because of the shootings, which killed 15 people.

23

1886 Harry Coveleski b. Shamokin, PA.

1888 James Scott b. Deadwood, SD.

1896 Elam Vangilder b. Cape Girardeau, MO.

1900 Jim Bottomley b. Oglesby, IL.

1903 The New York Highlanders win their first game, 7-2, over the Washington Senators.

1905 Baseball traditionally had not been played on Sundays, but this Sunday the Brooklyn Dodgers don't charge admission. However, they do sell four different priced scorecards with discriminating seating.

1914 In a Federal League contest, the Chicago Whales christen new Weeghman Park — the future Wrigley Field — with a 9-1 victory over the Kansas City Packers.

1919 A slimmed down 140-game ML schedule opens in Washington, D.C.,

where Senators RHP Walter Johnson shuts out the Philadelphia A's, 1-0.

1921 Warren Spahn b. Buffalo, NY.

1939 Boston rookie OF Ted Williams goes 4-for-5 and hits the first of a career 521 ML home runs as he faces Philadelphia RHP Bud Thomas. The Red Sox lose to the A's, 12-8.

1946 Brooklyn RHP Ed Head no-hits the Boston Braves, 5-0.

1952 New York Giants RHP Hoyt Wilhelm homers in his first major league at bat and never hits another in 21 years and 1,070 games. The victim is Boston Braves LHP Dick Hoover, who will make only one other appearance in the season (a no-decision) and leave the major leagues.

1952 Cleveland Indians RHP Bob Feller and St. Louis Browns LHP Bob Cain match one-hitters as the Browns eke out a 1-0 win.

1954 Milwaukee OF Hank Aaron hits his first ML homer against St. Louis RHP Vic Raschi in a 7-5 Braves win. Aaron will retire in 1976 as baseball's all time home run champion with 755 round-trippers.

1955 Chicago hits seven home runs and ties a modern scoring record during the White Sox' 29-6 victory at Kansas City. Chicago C Sherm Lollar collects two hits in each of the second and sixth innings to become only the third player in history with this double-double.

1962 After an 0-9 start, the New York Mets beat Pittsburgh to win their first game, 9-1, behind RHP Jay Hook.

1964 Houston Colt 45's RHP Ken Johnson becomes the only ML pitcher to lose a complete game no-hitter, as a couple of errors lead to his 1-0 defeat by Cincinnati.

1967 Rheal Cormier b. New Brunswick, Canada.

1968 Los Angeles trades RHP Phil Regan and OF Jim Hickman to the

Chicago Cubs for OF Ted Savage and
LHP Jim Ellis.

1982 Facing Pittsburgh RHP Eddie
Solomon, Chicago Cubs 2B Ryne Sandberg hits the first of 282 ML home runs.

1989 Texas RHP Nolan Ryan comes
within two outs of a career sixth no-hitter, losing it when Toronto's Nelson
Liriano triples in the ninth inning. The
Rangers still win, 4-1, as Ryan settles for
his career 10th one-hitter.

1991 Cincinnati RHP Rob Dibble ties
an NL single game record by striking out
six batters consecutively in a relief role.

1994 Baltimore RHP Lee Smith
becomes the fastest reliever in history to
reach nine saves, earning it in the Orioles' 16th game.

1999 St. Louis 3B Fernando Tatis sets
an ML record with two grand slam
home runs in one inning as the Cardinals rout Los Angeles, 12-5. Tatis hits
both slams against Dodgers RHP Chan
Ho Park and sets another ML record
with eight RBIs in the third inning.

24

1894 Howard Ehmke b. Silver Creek,
NY.

1901 The AL debuts its first game at
the Chicago Cricket Club as the host
White Sox defeat Cleveland, 8-2, before
14,000 fans. The other three scheduled
AL openers are rained out.

1917 New York Yankees LHP George
Mogridge no-hits the Red Sox in
Boston, 2-1.

1927 Frank Lucchesi b. San Francisco,
CA.

1944 Bill Singer b. Los Angeles, CA.

1945 A.B. "Happy" Chandler is elected
baseball's second Commissioner, suceed-
ing Judge Kenesaw Mountain Landis,
who passed away the previous November.

Chandler will serve until July 15, 1951.

1958 Lee Walls hits three homers and
collects eight RBIs as the Chicago Cubs
shell Los Angeles, 15-2.

1958 Bill Krueger b. Waukegan, IL.

1962 Los Angeles LHP Sandy Koufax
becomes the first pitcher in ML history
to twice strike out 18 batters in nine
inning games, beating Chicago, 10-2.
Koufax also fanned 18 San Francisco
Giants on August 31, 1959.

1965 New York Mets manager Casey
Stengel records his 3,000th career win
with a 7-6 decision over San Francisco.

1965 Mike Blowers b. Wurzburg,
West Germany.

1967 Omar Vizquel b. Venezuela.

1968 Todd Jones b. Marietta, GA.

1970 Kansas City OF Amos Otis hits
his first of a career 193 ML home runs,
this one against Baltimore LHP Mike
Cuellar.

1972 Chipper Jones b. DeLand, FL.

1986 Sixteen Seattle Mariners batters
strike out against Oakland, five days
after the Mariners had 16 whiffs against
the same A's pitchers.

1996 Greg Myers and Paul Molitor each
collect five RBIs as Minnesota sets a team
record for runs in routing Detroit, 24–11.

1998 Los Angeles C Mike Piazza ties
an ML record with his third grand slam
home run in a month as the Dodgers
rout the Chicago Cubs, 12-4. Cincinnati
OF Eric Davis is the only other NL
player to do it (May 1987), while it has
been done four times in the AL.

1999 Houston 3B Ken Caminiti drives
in two runs with his 1,500th career hit
to lead the Astros to a 4-3 win over
Cincinnati.

25

1876 The NL Chicago White Stockings franchise debuts with a 4-0 win

over Louisville as RHP Al Spalding hurls the shutout in defeating RHP Jim Devlin. Devlin would pitch in all 68 Louisville games that year. Chicago would become the only professional baseball team to field a club the first year and remain active every year thru the present, changing its name from the White Stockings to Colts to Orphans and finally to the Cubs.

1884 Pop Lloyd b. Gainesville, FL.

1901 Cleveland 2B Erve Beck hits the first home run in AL history.

1901 In an AL opener at Detroit's Bennett Park, the Tigers beat Milwaukee after trailing, 13-4, going into the bottom of the ninth inning. Detroit erupts for 10 runs and a 14-13 win.

1904 New York Yankees RHP Jack Chesbro records the first of what will be an ML record 41 wins on the season.

1924 Philadelphia A's OF Al Simmons hits his first of a career 307 ML home runs, this one against Washington RHP Walter Johnson.

1933 New York Yankees LHP Russ Van Atta shuts out Washington, 16-0, collecting a record four hits himself in his ML debut.

1943 Lew Krausse b. Media, PA.

1948 Cincinnati 1B Ted Kluszewski hits the first of his 279 ML home runs, this one against Pittsburgh RHP Hal Gregg.

1952 New York Giants RHP Hoyt Wilhelm triples in his second major league at-bat. He had hit his first home run in his first career at-bat. Wilhelm would never again homer or triple in his 21-year career covering 1,070 games.

1959 Tony Phillips b. Atlanta, GA.

1976 Chicago CF Rick Monday rescues the American Flag from two protesters who try to set it on fire at Dodger Stadium. It happens during the fourth inning of the Cubs' 5-4, 10-inning loss to the Dodgers.

1977 Cincinnati bombs Atlanta, 23-9, in Atlanta as the Reds tie an NL scoring record with 12 runs in the fifth inning. George Foster hits two homers for seven RBIs and scores five runs.

1985 Denny McLain, baseball's last 30-game winner, is sentenced to 23 years in prison after his conviction on racketeering, cocaine possession, and extortion.

1995 The season finally begins with both the AL and the NL being forced to play a 144-game schedule instead of the customary 162 games, because of the length of the owners'/players' strike. The longest strike in sports history, which began August 12, 1994, cancelled that year's playoffs and World Series for the first time since 1904.

1997 Seattle OF Ken Griffey Jr. hits three home runs in a 13-8 win over Toronto to set an ML record for home runs in April with 13.

1997 Matt Williams hits three home runs, David Justice hits two more, and Cleveland hits a club record eight in all during an 11-4 win at Milwaukee. The Brewers hit three homers of their own to match the ML record with 11 round-trippers in a nine inning night game.

26

1888 Ray Caldwell b. Corydon, PA.

1900 Hack Wilson b. Elwood City, PA.

1902 Cleveland RHP Addie Joss makes his ML debut, firing a one-hitter in blanking the St. Louis Browns, 3-0.

1905 Chicago Cubs OF Jack McCarthy turns three double plays in a game.

1917 Sal Maglie b. Niagra Falls, NY.

1919 Virgil Trucks b. Birmingham, AL.

1927 Granny Hamner b. Richmond, VA.

1945 Roger Bresnahan becomes the first catcher elected to baseball's Hall of Fame. A 17-year veteran, Bresnahan is credited with sporting shin guards for the first time.

1947 Amos Otis b. Mobile, AL.

1959 Cincinnati Reds RHP Willard Schmidt becomes first player to be hit by a pitch twice in one inning as the Reds top Milwaukee, 11-10.

1961 New York Yankees RF Roger Maris hits his first homer of the season against Detroit RHP Paul Foytack in the 11th game of the season. The 10-day draught will be Maris' longest of the year as he finishes the season with a then-record 61 homers.

1970 San Francisco 1B Willie McCovey and C Dick Dietz hit grand slam home runs against Montreal, marking the first time in Giants history that two players do it in the same game.

1980 Philadelphia Phillies LHP Steve Carlton hurls the sixth one-hitter of his career in a 2-0 win over St. Louis. A second inning single by the Cardinals' Ted Simmons is the only hit.

1990 Texas Rangers RHP Nolan Ryan ties Bob Feller's major league record of twelve one-hitters in blanking Chicago, 1-0. Ryan strikes out 16 White Sox batters and allows only Ron Kittle's second inning single.

1996 AL RHP Milt Gaston passes away at age 100. Playing for the New York Yankees, St. Louis Browns, Washington Senators, Boston Red Sox, and Chicago White Sox from 1924-34, Gaston had more Hall-of-Fame teammates and managers than any player in baseball history. He played with Babe Ruth, Lou Gehrig, George Sisler, Sam Rice, Luke Appling, Al Simmons, and 11 other Cooperstown honorees. In January, he became just the eighth former major leaguer to reach age 100.

1997 Chicago Cubs' Ryne Sandberg connected for his 267th career home run in a 7-6 win against Pittsburgh, eclipsing the previous mark for second basemen, held by Joe Morgan.

27

1896 Rogers Hornsby b. Winters, TX.

1916 Enos Slaughter b. Roxboro, NC.

1918 After an ML record 0-9 start, the Brooklyn Dodgers get into the win column with a 5-3 win over the New York Giants in the first game of a doubleheader.

1943 The Boston Braves trade C Ernie Lombardi to the New York Giants for 2B Connie Ryan and C Hugh Poland.

1944 Boston Braves RHP Jim Tobin hits a home run during his no- hitter over Brooklyn, 2-0.

1947 New York celebrates Babe Ruth Day at Yankee Stadium before more than 58,000 fans. New York plays "emotionally wrecked," losing to Washington, 1-0. Ruth will die from cancer a year later at age 53.

1961 Ty Cobb throws out the first pitch at Los Angeles' Wrigley Field for the home opener of the expansion Angels. It is Cobb's last visit to a ballpark; at age 74 he'll die of cancer in three months.

1965 Bob MacDonald b. East Orange, NJ.

1968 Baltimore RHP Tom Phoebus no-hits Boston, 6-0.

1970 Washington trades 3B Ken McMullen to California for 3B Aurelio Rodriguez and OF Rick Reichardt.

1971 Atlanta OF Hank Aaron hits his 600th career home run against San Francisco RHP Gaylord Perry during the Braves' 10-inning, 6-5 loss to the Giants.

1973 Facing Detroit, Kansas City Royals RHP Steve Busby hurls the first of his two no-hitters, 3-0.

1974 Cleveland trades 1B Chris Chambliss, RHP Dick Tidrow, and RHP Cecil Upshaw to the New York Yankees for LHP Fritz Peterson, RHP Fred Beene, RHP Tom Buskey, and RHP Steve Kline.

1981 Los Angeles rookie LHP Fernando Valenzuela hurls his fourth shutout in five starts, blanking San Francisco, 5-0.

1983 Houston RHP Nolan Ryan whiffs Montreal's Brad Mills for his 3,509th career strikeout, eclipsing the all-time record held by Walter Johnson which stood for 56 years. Ryan will eventually conclude his 27-year career with an unapproachable 5,714 strikeouts.

1994 Facing Milwaukee, Minnesota Twins RHP Scott Erickson hurls the first franchise no-hitter in 27 years, 6-0. This, a year after Erickson led the AL in hits, runs allowed, and losses.

1994 Toronto Blue Jays OF Joe Carter collects a record 31st RBI in April.

1999 Baltimore LF B.J. Surhoff goes 5-for-5 (including two doubles and a home run) to lift the Orioles to an 8-4 win over Kansas City.

28

1901 Cleveland pitcher Bock Baker gives up a record 23 singles as the Chicago White Sox win, 13-1.

1902 Red Lucas b. Columbia, TN.

1909 For the fourth straight day, the Detroit Tigers win in their final at-bat.

1921 Cleveland RHP George Uhle collects six RBIs in this game.

1930 Tom Sturdivant b. Gordon, KS.

1934 Detroit OF Goose Goslin hits

into four consecutive double plays, but the Tigers still win, 4-1.

1935 Pedro Ramos b. Cuba.

1956 Cincinnati OF Frank Robinson hits his first of a career 586 ML home runs, this one against Chicago Cubs LHP Paul Minner.

1960 Tom Browning b. Casper, WY.

1961 Five days after his 40th birthday, Milwaukee Braves LHP Warren Spahn collects his second career no-hitter, a 1-0 win over San Francisco.

1962 The New York Mets hit a club record five home runs during an 8-6 win over Philadelphia at the Polo Grounds. Frank Thomas, Charlie Neal, and Gil Hodges hit consecutive homers in the sixth inning.

1964 Barry Larkin b. Cincinnati, OH.

1965 At the Houston Astrodome, New York Mets announcer Lindsey Nelson broadcasts the game from inside a gondola suspended above second base from the apex of the dome.

1988 The winless Baltimore Orioles set an AL record losing their 21st straight game, 4-2, this one to Minnesota.

1989 New York Yankees OF Rickey Henderson sets an ML record when he leads off a game with a home run for the 36th time of his career, breaking a tie with OF Bobby Bonds.

1998 During the Rangers 7-2 win over Minnesota, Texas RF Juan Gonzalez drives in two runs to set an ML record with 35 RBIs in April.

1999 Colorado RF Larry Walker hits three home runs, driving in eight runs to tie a team record. The Rockies win, 9-7, over St. Louis.

29

1913 Having forgotten to load their uniforms on the train, Cincinnati loses to the Chicago Cubs, 7-2, wearing borrowed Chicago White Sox uniforms.

1918 Cleveland CF Tris Speaker executes the fourth unassisted double play of his career, but the Indians still lose to Chicago, 8-4.

1929 Brooklyn RHP Clise Dudley, who bats left-handed, becomes the first modern pitcher to hit a home run in his first at bat.

1931 Cleveland Indians RHP Wes Ferrell, whose catcher is brother Rick, no-hits the St. Louis Browns, 9-0. Wes also drives in four runs with a homer and a double.

1933 In a strange play at home plate, Washington Senators C Luke Sewell tags out two New York runners on the same play. The Yankees Lou Gehrig holds up, thinking a fly ball would be caught, and Dixie Walker, who is a baserunner behind, catches up to Gehrig on the play.

1934 Luis Aparicio b. Venezuela.

1937 Detroit C Rudy York hits his first of a career 277 ML home runs, this one against Cleveland LHP Earl Whitehill.

1947 Tom House b. Seattle, WA.

1951 Rick Burleson b. Lynwood, CA.

1953 Milwaukee Braves 1B Joe Adcock becomes the first ML player to hit a home run to center field — 475 feet away — at New York's Polo Grounds.

1960 After 1,513 games in the outfield for the St. Louis Cardinals, Stan Musial plays in his 1,000th game at first base, making him the first player to reach the plateau at two positions.

1962 New York Mets OF Frank Thomas ties an ML record by being hit by pitches twice in the same inning.

1967 Kansas City A's OF Rick Monday hits the first of his 241 career ML home runs. Boston Red Sox RHP Don McMahon is the pitcher.

1971 Sterling Hitchcock b. Fayetteville, NC.

1974 Houston 1B Lee May goes 5-for-5 including two home runs in the sixth inning, as the Astros clobber the Chicago Cubs, 18-2.

1981 Philadelphia Phillies LHP Steve Carlton records his 3,000th career strikeout, whiffing Montreal 3B Tim Wallach.

1986 Boston RHP Roger Clemens strikes out an ML record 20 batters in the Red Sox' 3-1 win over Seattle in the Kingdome. Clemens whiffs every-one in the Mariners' starting lineup at least once, allows three hits and no walks.

1988 Baltimore shuts out the Chicago White Sox, 9-0, ending the Orioles' ML record season-opening losing streak at 21 games.

1990 Chicago Cubs RHP Greg Maddux ties the ML record of seven putouts by a pitcher in a game.

1995 Kansas City OF Jon Nunnally becomes the 70th ML player to homer in his first at-bat when he connects against New York RHP Melido Perez to lead off the game. The Yankees win, however, 10-3.

1998 Chicago hits six home runs in routing Baltimore, 16-7. Will Cordero and Albert Belle connect twice, while White Sox teammates Frank Thomas and Robin Ventura add one each.

1999 Seattle CF Ken Griffey, Jr., hits a pair of home runs, including a grand slam during an 11-run fifth inning, as the Mariners set a team scoring record with a 22-6 rout of Detroit. The Tigers had not given up 11 runs in one inning in 40 years.

30

1903 The New York Highlanders, ancestors of the New York Yankees, win their first home game in New York AL history, 6-2. More than 16,000 fans watch RHP Jack Chesbro gain the victory over Washington at Hilltop Park.

1912 Chet Laabs b. Milwaukee, WI.

1913 Chicago Cubs SS Al Bridwell hits his first home run after more than 3,600 at bats and early into his ninth major league season. Bridwell will hit only one more homer, closing out an 11-year career in 1915.

1922 Chicago White Sox rookie RHP Charlie Robertson becomes only the third modern pitcher to hurl a perfect game, a 2-0 gem against the Detroit Tigers. Catcher Ray Schalk handles his record fourth no-hitter.

1936 St. Louis 1B Johnny Mize hits the first of his career 359 ML home runs. New York Giants RHP Harry Gumbert is the pitcher.

1937 Philadelphia A's INF Ace Parker becomes the first AL player to hit a home run as a pinch-hitter in his first ML at-bat. Parker will hit only one more homer in his two-year career, then opt for professional football, which carries him to the NFL Hall of Fame.

1939 Cleveland Indians RHP Bob Feller pays for his mother to see him pitch on Mother's Day. However, during the contest a foul ball hit off of Feller strikes his mother, knocking her unconscious.

1940 Brooklyn Dodgers RHP James "Tex" Carlton no-hits Cincinnati, 3-0.

1944 In the first game of a doubleheader, the New York Giants clobber Brooklyn, 26-8. New York OF Mel Ott scores six times (record second time in career), and 1B Phil Weintraub collects 11 RBIs. The Dodgers pitchers aid in their own demise, surrendering 17 walks in the contest. Brooklyn earns a split, however, with a 5-4 win in the nightcap.

1946 Cleveland Indians RHP Bob Feller strikes out 11 New York Yankees en route to the second of his three career no-hitters, 1-0, at Yankee Stadium.

1949 Phil Garner b. Jefferson City, TN.

1955 The Philadelphia Phillies trade C Smoky Burgess, OF Stan Palys, and RHP Steve Ridzik to Cincinnati for C Andy Seminick, OF Glen Gorbous, and OF Jim Greengrass.

1961 San Francisco OF Willie Mays belts four homers, two against Milwaukee starting RHP Lew Burdette, as the Giants pound the Braves, 14-4.

1962 The Milwaukee Braves trade RHP Bob Buhl to the Chicago Cubs for LHP Jack Curtis.

1964 Jeff Reboulet b. Dayton, OH.

1967 Baltimore LHP Steve Barber carries a no-hitter into the ninth inning against Detroit, but RH reliever Stu Miller has it slip away as SS Mark Belanger's error leads to a 2-1 Tigers win.

1969 Facing Houston, Cincinnati RHP Jim Maloney hurls his third and last no-hitter, 10-0.

1988 Cincinnati manager Pete Rose shoves an umpire during an argument, prompting Commissioner A. Bartlett Giamatti to suspend him for 30 days.

1989 The New York Yankees trade LHP Al Leiter to Toronto for OF Jesse Barfield.

1996 The New York Yankees defeat Baltimore, 13-10, in the longest nine inning game in history: 4:21. The record was eclipsed during the 2000 season.

1997 Atlanta 1B Fred McGriff hits two home runs, and LF Michael Tucker collects five hits as the Braves hammer Cincinnati, 12-3, to set an ML record for their 19th win in April.

1997 Colorado RF Larry Walker ties an NL record with his 11th home run in April as the Rockies defeat the Chicago Cubs, 11-5. Walker joins Willie Stargell (1971), Mike Schmidt (1976), Gary Sheffield (1996), and Barry Bonds (1996).

MAY

1

1891 Behind RHP Cy Young, Cleveland inaugurates League Park, beating Cincinnati, 12–3, in front of 9,000 fans.

1901 The Detroit Tigers commit 12 errors against the Chicago White Sox. Two Chicago players, Dummy Hoy and Herm McFarland, hit grand slams in the game to become the first AL hitters to hit slams. They are also the only White Sox players since to ever hit grand slams in the same contest.

1906 Philadelphia Phillies LHP Johnny Lush no-hits the Dodgers in Brooklyn, 6-0.

1920 Babe Ruth hits his first home run as a member of the New York Yankees.

1920 The Boston Braves and Brooklyn Dodgers battle for 26 innings and a 1-1 tie before the game is called due to darkness. Braves RHP Joe Oeschger and Dodgers RHP Leon Cadore each goes the distance without a decision.

1941 Dodgers President Larry MacPhail submits a patent application on the "Brooklyn Safety Cap," a hat lined with plastic to protect players from bean balls.

1948 Von Joshua b. Oakland, CA.

1951 New York Yankees CF Mickey Mantle hits the first of his 536 ML home runs, this one against Chicago White Sox RHP Randy Gumpert.

1957 The Chicago Cubs trade INF Gene Baker and 1B Dee Fondy to Pittsburgh for 1B Dale Long and OF Lee Walls.

1959 The Chicago White Sox' 39-year-old RHP Early Wynn is the whole show against the Boston Red Sox. Besides pitching a one-hitter with 14 strikeouts, he clubs a double and a home run to account for his 1-0 victory.

1961 Charlie O'Brien b. Tulsa, OK.

1964 Jose Lind b. Puerto Rico.

1969 Houston Astros RHP Don Wilson no-hits Cincinnati, 4-0, just one day after Reds RHP Jim Maloney no-hit the Astros, 10-0, and nine days after Wilson absorbed a 14-0 pounding by Cincinnati.

1973 The San Francisco Giants score seven runs with two outs in the ninth inning to beat Pittsburgh, 8-7.

1975 Milwaukee DH Hank Aaron drives in two runs during the Brewers' 17-3 romp over Detroit, to become baseball's all-time RBI leader with 2,212. Aaron passes Babe Ruth on the career list and will finish with a new mark of 2,297 RBIs.

1980 New York Mets LHP Pete Falcone ties an ML record by striking out the first six batters of the game against Philadelphia. He finishes up with only eight strikeouts, however, in a seven-inning, 2-1 loss.

1985 Toronto LHP Jimmy Key defeats Kansas City, 6-3, ending a more-than-four-year drought since a Blue Jays left-handed starter registered a victory, the last coming on October 4, 1980 by Paul Mirabella.

1991 In a 7-4 win over New York Yankees, Oakland A's OF Rickey Henderson surpasses Lou Brock as baseball's career stolen base leader with his 939th theft.

1991 Texas Rangers RHP Nolan Ryan hurls his seventh career no-hitter, striking out 16 Blue Jays in 3-0 win over Toronto. At age 44, Ryan becomes the oldest pitcher to throw a no-hitter.

1992 The Dodgers postponed a three-game series against Montreal because of rioting in Los Angeles as a result of the Rodney King trial.

1992 Oakland A's OF Rickey Henderson steals his 1,000th career base in first inning at Tiger Stadium in Detroit.

1999 During the Tigers' 4-3 loss at Tampa Bay, Detroit RHP Brian Moehler is ejected from the game for having sandpaper on his thumb.

2

1876 Chicago Cubs 2B Ross Barnes hits the first home run in NL history.

1887 Eddie Collins b. Millerton, NY.

1908 Jack Norworth copyrights "Take Me Out to the Ballgame," although he had not seen a baseball game when he wrote the lyrics and wouldn't until 1940.

1909 Pittsburgh SS Honus Wagner steals second, third, and home in succession for the third time in his career.

1917 Cincinnati RHP Fred Toney and Chicago LHP James "Hippo" Vaughn no-hit each other's teams through nine innings. In the tenth inning, football star Jim Thorpe's infield dribbler, the second hit of the inning, proves to be the game winner for the Reds, 1-0.

1923 Washington RHP Walter Johnson records his first shutout of the season and the 100th of his major league record 113 career shutouts as the Senators defeat the New York Yankees, 3-0.

1923 New York Yankees SS Everett Scott plays in his 1,000th consecutive game.

1939 New York 1B Lou Gehrig's consecutive games played streak ends at 2,130 as Babe Dahlgren takes his spot. Dahlgren homers as the Yankees destroy Detroit, 22-2.

1941 Clay Carroll b. Clanton, AL.

1948 Brooklyn OF Duke Snider hits his first of a career 407 ML home runs, this one against Philadelphia LHP Curt Simmons.

1954 St. Louis Cardinals OF Stan Musial hits an ML record five home runs in a doubleheader against the New York Giants. Musial hits three in the first game and two more in the nightcap. In attendance is eight-year-old Nate Colbert, who will duplicate the feat as a member of the San Diego Padres in 1972.

1962 Baltimore 1B Boog Powell hits his first of a career 339 ML home runs. Minnesota LHP Jim Kaat is the pitcher.

1963 Cleveland trades RHP Jim Perry to Minnesota for LHP Jack Kralick.

1964 Minnesota's Tony Oliva, Bob Allison, Jimmie Hall, and Harmon Killebrew hit consecutive home runs in the top of the 11th inning to propel the Twins to a 7-4 win at Kansas City.

1995 Boston SS John Valentin and 1B Mo Vaughn hit grand slams in consecutive innings to account for all the scoring in the Red Sox' 8-0 win over the New York Yankees.

1995 San Francisco beats Los Angeles, 4-3, in 13 innings after neither team scores through the first 12 frames. Dodgers Japanese League import RHP

Hideo Nomo makes his ML debut, collecting seven strikeouts and yielding only one hit in five innings of work.

1996 Seattle's game with Cleveland is suspended in the seventh inning when a 5.4 magnitude earthquake shakes the Kingdome.

1999 Texas DH Rafael Palmeiro has three hits, including the 2,000th of his career, and RF Juan Gonzalez hits his third home run in as many games, to lead the Rangers to an 8-6 win over Cleveland.

3

1891 Eppa Rixey b. Culpeper, VA.

1904 Red Ruffing b. Granville, IL.

1920 Brooklyn falls to the Boston Braves, 2-1, in 19 innings. The Dodgers played 58 innings over a three day period, scored just five runs, lost two games and tied once, and played in a different city each time.

1927 Brooklyn RHP Jesse Barnes and New York RHP Virgil Barnes become the first pair of brothers to oppose each other as starting pitchers. Jesse defeats Virgil, 7-6.

1934 Chuck Hinton b. Rocky Mount, NC.

1936 New York CF Joe DiMaggio has three hits in his ML debut against the St. Louis Browns as the Yankees cruise, 14-5.

1938 Boston Red Sox LHP Robert "Lefty" Grove begins his 20-game consecutive win streak at Fenway Park.

1942 Cincinnati 1B Hank Sauer hits his first of a career 288 ML home runs, this one against New York Giants RHP Bob Carpenter.

1942 Boston Braves RHP Jim Tobin becomes the only pitcher of the 20th century to hit three home runs in a

game. He'll finish the season with six round-trippers.

1946 Davey Lopes b. Providence, RI.

1950 New York Yankees RHP Vic Raschi commits an ML record four balks in a game.

1951 New York Yankee rookie Gil McDougald drives in six runs in one inning to tie a major league record as the Yankees hammer the St. Louis Browns, 17-3, at Sportsman's Park. McDougald hits a two-run triple and a grand slam home run in an 11-run ninth inning.

1952 Washington trades OF Sam Mele to the Chicago White Sox for OF Jim Busby and INF Mel Hoderlein.

1959 Detroit OF Charlie Maxwell hits four consecutive home runs in a double-header sweep of the New York Yankees, 4-2 and 8-2, at Briggs Stadium.

1963 Cincinnati 2B Pete Rose hits his first of a career 160 ML home runs, this one against St. Louis RHP Ernie Broglio.

1986 In the top of the seventh inning at Pittsburgh's Three Rivers Stadium, a skunk wanders out onto the playing field delaying the game between the Pirates and Philadelphia Phillies for seven minutes.

1994 The Chicago Cubs break a 92-year-old club record losing their 12th straight home game.

1994 Florida OF Chuckie Carr has the expansion club's first five-hit game as the Marlins top Atlanta, 6-3.

1995 Cleveland 3B David Bell makes his ML debut in a 14-7 win over Detroit, making the Bell family the second three-generation family in baseball history. The Boones were the first.

1999 In the first ever game between the Cuban National Team and a major league team played in the United States, Cuba defeats the Baltimore Orioles, 12-6, at Camden Yards.

4

1910 The Browns and Cardinals both play home games in St. Louis before President William H. Taft. In an effort not to offend either club, he attends parts of both games at Robinson Field and Sportsman's Park.

1929 New York Yankees 1B Lou Gehrig hits three home runs in a game for the third time in his career.

1944 The two St. Louis clubs — the Cardinals and the Browns — announce that blacks no longer have to sit in only the bleachers or pavillion seats.

1961 The Los Angeles Dodgers trade OF Don Demeter and 3B Charley Smith to Philadelphia for RHP Dick Farrell and SS Joe Koppe.

1968 The Chicago Cubs trade OF Byron Browne to Houston for OF Aaron Pointer.

1969 The Houston Astros turn seven double plays against the San Francisco Giants. Astros 1B Curt Blefary is the recipient of all seven second putouts.

1969 Kansas City Royals 1B Bob Oliver collects six hits four singles, a double, a homer against the California Angels.

1975 Houston OF Bob Watson races around the bases on Milt May's home run and crosses the plate at San Francisco's Candlestick Park to score major league baseball's one millionth run, seconds ahead of Cincinnati's Dave Concepcion.

1975 San Francisco trades OF Garry Maddox to Philadelphia for 1B Willie Montanez.

1979 Texas trades SS Bert Campaneris to California for SS Dave Chalk.

1980 Normally a first baseman, the Chicago White Sox' Mike Squires becomes just the second left-handed

catcher in the major leagues in three quarters of a century with an inning of work against Milwaukee. Dale Long of the 1958 Chicago Cubs was the first left-handed receiver to catch in a big league game.

1981 New York Yankees RHP Ron Davis strikes out eight consecutive Angels in relief, preserving a 4-2 win over California.

1989 Toronto's Junior Felix becomes the 53rd player in ML history to hit a home run in his first at-bat with a third-inning shot off California RHP Kirk McCaskill. The Angels win, however, 3-2, in 10 innings.

1990 Boston trades RHP Lee Smith to St. Louis for OF Tom Brunansky.

1991 Cleveland OF Chris James drives in a club record nine runs with two homers and two singles during a 20-6 rout of the Oakland A's.

1994 Detroit 1B Cecil Fielder hits his 200th career home run, a 475-foot blast that lands on the left field roof at Tiger Stadium.

1995 Oakland RHP Dennis Eckersley runs his AL record for consecutive errorless games by a pitcher to 470. The streak began May 1, 1987.

1996 Baltimore RF Brady Anderson becomes the fastest player ever to reach 15 home runs in a season with a blast against Milwaukee RHP Steve Sparks.

1997 Milwaukee RHP Calvin Eldred becomes the eighth ML pitcher to give up back-to-back home runs in back-to-back innings.

5

1883 Chief Bender b. Brainerd, MN.

1904 Boston Red Sox RHP Cy Young hurls the AL's first perfect game, a 3-0 gem over the Philadelphia A's. It's the second of his three career no-hitters, and it runs his hitless innings streak to 18. Young also becomes the first pitcher with a no-hitter thrown in each league.

1917 St. Louis Browns LHP Ernest Koob no-hits the Chicago White Sox, 1–0.

1925 Detroit player/manager Ty Cobb goes 6-for-6, accounting for a modern ML record 16 total bases with three home runs, a double, and two singles in a 14-8 win against the St. Louis Browns.

1933 St. Louis Cardinal 3B Pepper Martin hits two doubles, a triple, and a home run in a 5-3 win over Philadelphia.

1941 Tommy Helms b. Charlotte, NC.

1947 Larry Hisle b. Portsmouth, OH.

1955 In his first ML start, Brooklyn LHP Tommy Lasorda ties a record throwing three wild pitches in one inning.

1962 Facing Baltimore, California Angels LHP Bo Belinsky hurls the first no-hitter for an expansion team, 2-0.

1963 Detroit C Bill Freehan hits his first of a career 200 ML home runs, this one against Baltimore RHP Dick Hall.

1967 Charles Nagy b. Fairfield, CT.

1972 Kansas City trades 1B Bob Oliver to California for RHP Tom Murphy.

1978 Cincinnati 3B Pete Rose becomes the 14th ML player to reach the 3,000 hit plateau with a single off Montreal RHP Steve Rogers during the Reds' 4-3 loss to the Expos.

1980 NL President Chub Feeney suspends Pittsburgh 3B Bill Madlock for 15 days and fines him $5,000 for shoving his glove in the face of umpire Gerry Crawford.

1996 Cincinnati OF Eric Davis becomes the 18th player in ML history to hit a grand slam home run in consecutive games.

1998 Milwaukee RHP Paul Wagner becomes the second Brewers starter in as many days against San Diego to give up 11 runs in a game. Milwaukee RHP Jose Mercedes starts the fireworks May 4th, as the pair of Brewers become the only duo in the 1990s to turn the trick.

1999 Colorado becomes the first team in 35 years and the third in this century to score in every inning in beating the Chicago Cubs, 13-6, at Wrigley Field.

6

1903 The Chicago White Sox commit 12 errors against Detroit, almost exactly two years to the day that the Tigers had bungled a dozen against Chicago.

1915 Babe Ruth, a 20-year-old rookie LHP with the Boston Red Sox, hits his first ML home run against New York Yankees RHP Jack Warhop. Ruth also has two singles in a 13-inning, 5-3 loss to New York.

1917 St. Louis Browns RHP Bob Groom no-hits the Chicago White Sox, 3-0. It's the second no-hitter in as many days for the Browns against the White Sox as LHP Ernie Koob turned the trick just 24 hours earlier.

1919 George Halas makes his major league debut in RF for the New York Yankees, going 1-for-4. He'll get one more big league hit, vacate the spot for the acquired Babe Ruth, and go on to coach the NFL Chicago Bears.

1925 New York Yankees manager Miller Huggins benches SS Everett Scott, ending his consecutive games played streak at 1,307, a streak he started in 1916 with the Boston Red Sox It's the longest streak prior to Lou Gehrig's.

1930 The Boston Red Sox trade two-time AL loss leader RHP Red Ruffing to the New York Yankees for OF Cedric

Durst. Ruffing, 39-99 in six-plus years with Boston, resurrects his career with New York going 231-124 in 15 seasons, including a stretch of four straight 20-win seasons en route to his eventual Hall of Fame selection.

1931 Willie Mays b. Westfield, AL.

1933 Cincinnati signs RHP Jack Quinn, two months short of his 50th birthday, and the NL save leader in each of the past two seasons. In 14 games, he goes 0-1 to close out a 23-year career with a 247-217 record.

1940 Bill Hands b. Rutherford, NJ.

1950 Boston beats Cincinnati, 15-11, belting five home runs in the process and giving the Braves a record 13 homers over a three-game span.

1951 Pittsburgh LHP Cliff Chambers no-hits the Boston Braves, 3-0.

1953 St. Louis Browns RHP Alva "Bobo" Holloman no-hits the Philadelphia A's, 6-0, in his first ML start. The no-hitter would be Holloman's only shutout and complete game of his one-year career, in which he wins only three games.

1982 With a 7-3 win over the New York Yankees, Seattle RHP Gaylord Perry becomes the 15th pitcher in ML history to reach 300 victories.

1994 Kansas City RHP David Cone notches his 100th career victory and 3B Gary Gaetti hits his 250th career home run as the Royals defeat the Chicago White Sox, 6-5.

1994 Chicago RHP Anthony Young wins as a starter for the first time in more than two years as the Cubs rout Pittsburgh, 10-1.

1998 Chicago Cubs RHP Kerry Wood sets an NL record, a rookie record, and ties the ML record by striking out 20 batters in a nine inning game. During his one-hitter, a 2-0 win over Houston, Wood strikes out every Astros player at least once, walks none, and has only two balls hit out of the infield.

7

1896 Tom Zachary b. Graham, NC.

1906 In the fifth inning of a New York-Washington game, umpire Tim Hurst punches Senators manager Clark Griffith in the mouth and is suspended for five days.

1917 Boston Red Sox LHP Babe Ruth outduels Washington RHP Walter Johnson, 1-0, winning the game himself with a sacrifice fly.

1918 The Boston Braves set a franchise record for largest shutout win, hammering Brooklyn, 16-0.

1922 New York Giants RHP Jesse Barnes no-hits the Philadelphia Phillies, 6-0, missing a perfect game by only a fifth inning walk.

1925 Pittsburgh SS Glenn Wright turns an unassisted triple play against the St. Louis Cardinals.

1928 Dick Williams b. St. Louis, MO.

1940 The Brooklyn Dodgers become the first NL team to travel by air, taking two planes from St. Louis to Chicago.

1941 Detroit slugger Hank Greenberg reports for duty in the U.S. Army, one of several major leaguers who would leave baseball to fight in World War II.

1956 New York Giants 1B Bill White hits the first of his career 202 ML home runs in his first at-bat against St. Louis RHP Ben Flowers.

1957 Cleveland LHP Herb Score is struck in the eye by a line drive by the New York Yankees' Gil McDougald, essentially ending a promising ML career. Score, who led the AL in strikeouts in his first two seasons in 1955-56 and posted a combined 36-19 record, never really recovers, winning only 19 more games while losing 27 over the next six seasons.

1959 The largest crowd ever to see a major league game, 93,103, show up for an exhibition contest at Los Angeles Coliseum to pay tribute to catcher Roy Campanella, who was crippled in an automobile accident two years earlier.

1960 Los Angeles Dodgers C Norm Sherry, a last minute replacement, hits an 11th inning home run to give his brother, relief pitcher Larry Sherry, a 3-2 win over Philadelphia.

1975 Atlanta trades 1B Richie Allen and C Johnny Oates to Philadelphia for C Jim Essian and OF Barry Bonnell.

1978 Detroit SS Alan Trammell, facing Oakland RHP Matt Keough, hits his first ML home run.

1980 Kansas City collects nine consecutive hits, one short of the AL record, en route to beating Texas, 12-5.

1995 Minnesota and Cleveland play the longest game in either team's history, a 17-inning contest won by the Indians, 10-9, in 6:36. The teams also combine to leave on base a season-high 39 runners.

1999 Cleveland overcomes a 9-1 deficit by scoring 18 runs in its final three innings to beat Tampa Bay, 20-11. Indians LF David Justice hits two home runs, 3B Travis Fryman adds a three-run shot, and 2B Roberto Alomar adds a grand slam. Devil Rays 1B Fred McGriff sets an ML record by hitting a home run in his 34th ballpark.

1999 Chicago LF Carlos Lee becomes the first White Sox player and 75th ML player to hit a home run in his first ML at-bat in a 7-1 win over Oakland.

8

1858 Dan Brouthers b. Sylvan Lake, NY.

1893 Edd Roush b. Oakland City, IN.

1906 On Mother's Day, Connie Mack's Philadelphia A's are out of outfielders, so pitcher Chief Bender fills in and contributes two inside-the-park homers. He later comes in to pitch and earns the win in relief.

1907 Boston Braves RHP Big Jeff Pfeffer no-hits Cincinnati, 6-0.

1911 The Boston Braves begin their NL record of 14 consecutive home losses streak which runs through May 24, 1911.

1929 New York Giants LHP Carl Hubbell no-hits Pittsburgh, 11-0.

1935 Cincinnati C Ernie Lombardi hits four doubles in consecutive innings (sixth, seventh, eighth, and ninth) against four different Philadelphia pitchers. Lombardi also singles as the Reds beat the Phillies, 15-4.

1937 Mike Cuellar b. Cuba.

1943 Baseball's two-week "dead ball" era comes to an end when Albert G. Spalding's "war ball" is replaced with a more lively ball.

1945 The St. Louis Cardinals trade LHP John Antonelli and OF Glenn Crawford to the Philadelphia Phillies for OF Buster Adams.

1949 Steve Braun b. Trenton, NJ.

1951 Dennis Leonard b. Brooklyn, NY.

1961 The New York Yankees trade RHP Ryne Duren, OF/1B Lee Thomas and RHP Johnny James to the Los Angeles Angels for RHP Tex Clevenger and OF Bob Cerv.

1963 Milwaukee Braves RHP Bob Buhl sets a record for hitting futility, going hitless in his 88th straight at bat.

1963 Pittsburgh OF Willie Stargell hits his first of a career 475 ML home runs, this one against Chicago Cubs RHP Lindy McDaniel.

1963 St. Louis OF Stan Musial hits a

home run during an 11-5 loss to Los Angeles, giving him 1,357 extra base hits for his career and breaking Babe Ruth's record. Musial's eventual mark of 1,377 extra base hits will stand until Hank Aaron tops it 10 years later.

1965 Felix Jose b. Dominican Republic.

1965 Facing Chicago Cubs RHP Lindy McDaniel, Houston Astros 2B Joe Morgan hits his first of a career 268 ML home runs.

1966 San Francisco trades 1B Orlando Cepeda to St. Louis for LHP Ray Sadecki.

1966 Baltimore RF Frank Robinson becomes the only player to hit a home run out of the Orioles' Memorial Stadium with a 451 foot blast against Cleveland RHP Luis Tiant during the second game of a doubleheader.

1968 Oakland RHP Jim "Catfish" Hunter hurls the 10th perfect game in ML history, a 4-0 win over Minnesota. Hunter contributes three hits and all four RBIs in the first night no-hitter and first AL perfect game in 46 years. At age 22, Hunter is the youngest ever to throw an ML no-hitter.

1971 Washington trades 1B Mike Epstein and LHP Darold Knowles to Oakland for LHP Paul Lindblad, 1B Don Mincher, and C Frank Fernandez.

1971 Cleveland trades OF Buddy Bradford to Cincinnati for INF Kurt Bevacqua.

1974 Kansas City 3B George Brett hits the first of his ML total 317 home runs, this one against Texas RHP Ferguson Jenkins.

1975 Milwaukee trades OF Bobby Coluccio to the Chicago White Sox for OF Bill Sharp.

1984 Minnesota rookie OF Kirby Puckett ties a record with four hits in his first ML game as the Twins win at California, 5-0.

1998 St. Louis 1B Mark McGwire becomes the 26th and fastest player to reach 400 career home runs, but the Cardinals still lose, 9-2, to the New York Mets. McGwire's home run (his 20th of the season) comes in his 4,726th at-bat, besting Babe Ruth's previous record of 4,854 at-bats to reach the milestone.

1999 In the first Shane vs. Shane matchup in ML history, Houston RHP Shane Reynolds pitches against Montreal with Shane Andrews playing third base. The Expos win, 6-5.

9

1901 Cleveland RHP Earl Moore no-hits the Chicago White Sox for nine innings the first 20th Century no-hitter but then loses, 4-2, in the 10th inning.

1915 Philadelphia A's LHP Bruno Haas walks 16 Detroit batters in his major league debut. The other A's and Tigers pitchers combine for 14 more walks for a major league record of 30 in the contest.

1929 New York Giants LHP Carl Hubbell no-hits Pittsburgh, 11-0, for the first no-hitter by a left-hander since 1916.

1960 Tony Gwynn b. Los Angeles, CA.

1961 Baltimore Orioles 1B Jim Gentile hits two consecutive grand slams in consecutive innings against Minnesota in 13-5 rout.

1961 Boston Red Sox OF Carl Yastrzemski hits the first of a career 452 ML home runs, this one against Los Angeles Angels RHP Jerry Casale.

1975 San Francisco trades LHP Ron Bryant to St. Louis for OF Larry Herndon.

1984 Chicago and Milwaukee put to bed the oldest game in ML history: 8:06. The game starts on May 8 at

Chicago's Comiskey Park, but is suspended after 17 innings due to the AL curfew rule. A home run by White Sox RF Harold Baines in the bottom of the 25th inning lifts Chicago to a 7-6 win. Baines shares the ML record for most plate appearances in a game (12), and shares the AL record for most innings by an outfielder (25) in a game.

1987 Baltimore 1B Eddie Murray becomes the first ML player to homer from both sides of the plate in consecutive games as the Orioles defeat the White Sox, 15-6, at Chicago's Comiskey Park.

1990 Baltimore SS Cal Ripken Jr. becomes only the third shortstop in ML history to reach 200 home runs, joining Ernie Banks and Vern Stephens.

1995 Kenny Lofton, Carlos Baerga, and Paul Sorrento all hit home runs as Cleveland ties an ML record scoring eight runs in the first inning before making an out. The Indians rout Kansas City, 10-0.

1999 Pittsburgh SS Pat Meares has five hits and 1B Brant Brown hits a three-run inside-the-park home run to lead the Pirates to a 12-9 win over St. Louis.

10

1918 Pittsburgh LHP Earl Hamilton gets off to a 6-0 start with a 0.83 ERA, then enlists in the Navy for World War I.

1929 Boston Braves CF Earl Clark handles an ML record 13 chances in a nine-inning game.

1934 In a game against the Chicago White Sox, New York Yankees 1B Lou Gehrig asks manager Joe McCarthy to come out in the fifth inning because he feels sick. To that point, Gehrig has contributed two homers, two doubles, and seven RBIs.

1937 Jim Hickman b. Henning, TN.

1939 Philadelphia Phillies rookie C Dave Coble catches a ball dropped from the 521 foot Philadelphia City Hall.

1950 Cincinnati trades C Walker Cooper to the Boston Braves for 2B Connie Ryan.

1953 New York Yankees SS Frank Verdi walks to the plate for the first time ever, but when the opposing manager changes pitchers, Yankees manager Casey Stengel calls for a pinch hitter. Verdi will never again get to bat in the major leagues.

1967 Atlanta OF Hank Aaron hits the only inside-the-park home run of his 755 career homers. Philadelphia RHP Jim Bunning is the pitcher.

1969 Baltimore begins its ML record of 23 straight wins over the Kansas City Royals, a skein that stretches until August 12, 1970.

1969 Pete Schourek b. Austin, TX.

1970 During a 6-5 loss to St. Louis, Atlanta RHP Hoyt Wilhelm becomes the first hurler to appear in his 1,000th ML game.

1973 Cleveland trades RHP Steve Dunning to Texas for RHP Dick Bosman and OF Ted Ford.

1981 Montreal RHP Charlie Lea becomes the first French-born pitcher to throw a no-hitter as the Expos beat the San Francisco Giants, 4-0, in the second game of a doubleheader.

1998 Javy Lopez, Andres Galarraga, Andruw Jones, and Ryan Klesko all hit home runs as Atlanta ties a franchise record connecting for a home run in its 22nd straight game. The Braves beat San Diego, 8-5.

1999 During the Red Sox' 12-4 win over Seattle, Boston SS Nomar Garciaparra hits two grand slam home runs and adds a two-run homer to become the first AL player with 10 RBIs in a game since 1975. Garciaparra becomes the 11th major leaguer to hit two slams in a game and the third Boston player to do it, following Rudy York (1946) and Jim Tabor (1939).

11

1897 Washington Senators C Duke Farrell throws out an ML record eight would-be basestealers.

1903 Charlie Gehringer b. Fowlerville, MI.

1904 Boston Red Sox RHP Cy Young has his 23-inning, no-hit string end.

1907 Rip Sewell b. Decatur, AL.

1919 Washington RHP Walter Johnson pitches 12 scoreless innings only to tie the New York Yankees at the Polo Grounds. Johnson allows only two hits and retires 28 batters in a row. Going 0-for-5 in the Yankees leadoff spot is future NFL pioneer George Halas.

1919 Cincinnati RHP Horace Eller no-hits the St. Louis Cardinals, 6-0.

1923 The Philadelphia Phillies outslug the St. Louis Cardinals, 20-14, in a game featuring 10 home runs. Phillies CF Cy Williams accounts for three homers himself.

1925 Chicago White Sox C Ray Schalk catches a ball dropped 460 feet from the Tribune Tower in Chicago.

1927 At Sportsmans Park in St. Louis, New York Yankees RF Babe Ruth hits his eighth of an eventual then-record 60 home runs in a season. Browns RHP and future NFL Hall of Fame running back Ernie Nevers is the pitcher.

1929 Cleveland defeats the New York Yankees, 4-3, in the first game ever in which both teams wear numbered uniforms.

1939 Milt Pappas b. Detroit, MI.

1949 Jerry Martin b. Columbia, SC.

1955 Chicago SS Ernie Banks hits a grand slam home run — the first of five on the season — to lead the Cubs to a 10-8 victory over Brooklyn, snapping the Dodgers' 11-game winning streak.

1955 The New York Yankees trade RHP Johnny Sain and OF Enos Slaughter to the Kansas City A's for RHP Sonny Dixon.

1956 St. Louis trades RHPs Stu Miller and Ben Flowers and LHP Harvey Haddix to Philadelphia for RHPs Murry Dickson and Herm Wehmeier.

1959 New York Yankees C Yogi Berra has his string of 950 errorless chances end when he muffs a play against Cleveland.

1960 The Kansas City A's trade LHP George Brunet to the Milwaukee Braves for RHP Bob Giggie.

1963 Los Angeles LHP Sandy Koufax pitches the second of his career four no-hitters in beating San Francisco, 8-0.

1964 Bobby Witt b. Arlington, VA.

1971 Cleveland Indians RHP Steve Dunning hits a grand slam homer off Oakland RHP Diego Segui to become the last AL pitcher with a grand slam. Phil Hennigan earns the win in relief for the Indians, 7-5.

1972 The San Francisco Giants trade Hall of Famer Willie Mays back to New York — where he started his career — this time to the Mets, in exchange for RHP Charlie Williams.

1974 Chicago Cubs 1B Andre Thornton hits the first of a career 253 ML home runs, this one against New York Mets LHP Ray Sadecki.

1977 After an 8-21 start under manager Dave Bristol, Atlanta Braves owner Ted Turner manages the team for a day and loses, 2-1, to Pittsburgh in extra innings.

1990 The New York Yankees trade OF

Dave Winfield to California for RHP Mike Witt.

1996 Facing the Rockies, Florida LHP Al Leiter throws the first no-hitter in the Marlins' four-year history, 11-0.

1998 Chicago RHP Kerry Wood sets an ML record for strikeouts in consecutive games with 33, whiffing 13 Arizona batters in a 4-2 Cubs win. Wood had set the NL record and tied the ML record a week earlier with 20 strikeouts against Houston in his previous start.

1998 Andruw Jones homers twice and Andres Galarraga adds a three-run shot to power Atlanta to an 8-1 win over Cincinnati and give the Braves a franchise record with 23 consecutive games hitting a home run.

1999 Houston sets a team record with 10 doubles, equals the team record with 19 runs, and collects 18 hits in pounding Pittsburgh, 19-8. Astros CF Carl Everett leads the attack with three hits and five RBIs.

1999 In the first matchup in 100 years of starting pitchers with the same first and last names, Colorado LHP Bobby M. Jones beats New York Mets RHP Bobby J. Jones, 8-5.

12

1910 Philadelphia A's RHP Chief Bender no-hits Cleveland, 4-0.

1915 Philadelphia C Wally Schang throws out six potential basestealers, but the A's still lose to the St. Louis Browns, 3-0.

1919 The Washington Senators and New York Yankees play 15 innings when the game is declared a tie, 4-4 by darkness. The day before, Washington RHP Walter Johnson and New York RHP Jack Quinn had shut out each other's team for 12 innings in another darkness-ended

tie. After two days and 27 innings played, there was still no victor.

1925 Yogi Berra b. St. Louis, MO.

1926 Washington RHP Walter Johnson wins his 400th career game, a 7-4 victory over the St. Louis Browns. Johnson is only the second pitcher to reach the plateau following Cy Young.

1935 Felipe Alou b. Dominican Republic.

1936 St. Louis Cardinals SS Leo Durocher and Brooklyn Dodgers manager Casey Stengel meet under the Ebbets Field stands and fight after a ballgame.

1941 Boston Red Sox LHP Robert "Lefty" Grove wins the last of 20 straight games at Fenway Park, a home streak that began May 3, 1938.

1947 Bob Heise b. San Antonio, TX.

1955 Chicago Cubs RHP Sam "Toothpick" Jones no-hits Pittsburgh, 4-0. After walking the bases loaded in the ninth, Jones finishes strong by striking out Dick Groat, Roberto Clemente, and Frank Thomas to close out the first no-hitter at Wrigley Field in 38 years.

1956 Brooklyn RHP Carl Erskine hurls his second career no-hitter, a 3-0 win over the New York Giants.

1957 Lou Whitaker b. Brooklyn, NY.

1968 Mark Clark b. Bath, IL.

1970 Chicago 1B Ernie Banks hits his 500th career home run and drives in his 1,600th run. RHP Pat Jarvis is the victim, and the Cubs beat Atlanta, 4-3.

1970 The Chicago Cubs trade OF Boots Day to Montreal for C Jack Hiatt.

1982 Minnesota trades RHP Doug Corbett and 2B Rob Wilfong to California for OF Tom Brunansky and RHP Mike Walters.

1996 Houston C Jerry Goff ties an ML record for passed balls when he has six during the Astros 7-6 loss to Montreal. Goff is sent to the minor leagues the next day.

1998 Atlanta ties the NL record by hitting a home run in its 24th consecutive game when 1B Andres Galarraga connects for his league-leading 15th round-tripper as the Braves beat Cincinnati, 5-1.

1998 St. Louis 1B Mark McGwire hits the longest home run in the 32-year history of Busch Stadium. The 527-feet shot helps the Cardinals to a 6-5, 10-inning win over Milwaukee.

13

1888 DeWolf Hopper gives the first public reading of Ernest Thayer's immortal baseball poem, "Casey at the Bat." The poem is possibly inspired by Philadelphia Phillies LHP Dan Casey, who one summer day in 1887 struck out (as RHH) with two outs and the bases loaded against New York.

1911 The New York Giants score 10 runs against St. Louis before making their first out of the game.

1927 Dusty Rhodes b. Mathews, AL.

1929 For the first time in ML history, both teams put numbers on their backs and make them a permanent uniform addition as the Cleveland Indians beat the New York Yankees, 4-3, at League Park.

1933 John Roseboro b. Ashland, OH.

1934 Leon Wagner b. Chattanooga, TN.

1945 Philadelphia Phillies 1B Jimmie Foxx becomes the first ML player to hit a pinch-hit grand slam home run in both leagues, after earlier in his career connecting for the AL Philadelphia A's.

1950 Juan Beniquez b. Puerto Rico.

1955 New York Yankees OF Mickey Mantle hits three homers — one left-handed and two right-handed — in a 5-2 win over Detroit.

1958 Teammates Willie Mays and Darryl Spencer have four long hits apiece as San Francisco beats the Dodgers in Los Angeles, 16-9. Mays has two homers, two triples, and a single for four RBIs; Spencer has two homers, a triple, and a double for six RBIs for a combined 28 total bases.

1958 St. Louis OF Stan Musial collects his 3,000th career hit, a pinch-hit double off Chicago RHP Moe Drabowski, and the Cardinals rally past the Cubs, 5-3.

1960 The Chicago Cubs trade 2B Tony Taylor and C Cal Neeman to Philadelphia for RHP Don Cardwell and 1B Ed Bouchee.

1965 Jose Rijo b. Dominican Republic.

1967 New York OF Mickey Mantle hits his 500th career home run, this one off Baltimore RHP Stu Miller. The Yankees win, 6-5, over the Orioles.

1969 Lyle Mouton b. Lafayette, LA.

1976 Kansas City 3B George Brett sets an ML record by collecting at least three hits for the sixth straight game as the Royals club the Chicago White Sox, 13-2.

1982 The Chicago Cubs record their 8,000th franchise victory, 5-0 over Houston in the Astrodome.

1989 Minnesota CF Kirby Puckett becomes the 35th player in ML history to hit four doubles in a game.

1993 Kansas City 3B George Brett hits his 300th career home run to help the Royals to a 7-3 win over Cleveland. Brett joins only Hank Aaron, Willie Mays, Carl Yastrzemski, Stan Musial, and Al Kaline as the only ML players with at least 3,000 hits and 300 home runs.

1994 California RF Tim Salmon ties an AL record for most hits in a three-game series stretch by collecting his 13th hit in 15 at-bats.

1998 Atlanta sets an NL record and ties the ML record by hitting a home run in its 25th straight game when LF Ryan Klesko connects during the Braves' 10-2 win over St. Louis.

1999 Baltimore 3B Cal Ripken, Jr., returns from his first-ever stay on the disabled list, but the Orioles lose to Texas, 15-7. Ripken had been out since April 18 because of a nerve problem in his lower back.

14

1881 Ed Walsh b. Plains, PA.

1892 Brooklyn utility player Tom Daly connects for the first ML pinch-hit home run against the Boston Beaneaters.

1899 Earle Combs b. Pebworth, KY.

1904 After Chicago Cubs OF Jack McCarthy sprains an ankle tripping over the umpire's broom at home plate, the NL orders use of pocket-size whisk brooms. The AL follows suit in 1905.

1913 Washington RHP Walter Johnson gives up a run in the fourth inning against the St. Louis Browns to end his scoreless-innings streak at 56. The Senators win, however, 10-5.

1914 Chicago White Sox RHP James Scott no-hits Washington for nine innings, but gives up two hits in the tenth to lose, 1-0.

1918 Washington, D.C., officials repeal the ban against night baseball in the nation's capital, citing the need for more wartime recreational outlets.

1920 Washington RHP Walter Johnson wins his 300th game, a 9-8 decision over the Detroit Tigers.

1928 New York Giants manager John McGraw is hit by a car while crossing a street outside Chicago's Wrigley Field. The injury will sideline him for six weeks.

1937 Dick Howser b. Miami, FL.

1941 Chicago White Sox LHP Eddie Smith gives up the first hit in New York Yankees Joe DiMaggio's 56-game hitting streak.

1942 Tony Perez b. Cuba.

1947 Dick Tidrow b. San Francisco, CA.

1948 Dave LaRoche b. Colorado Springs, CO.

1949 St. Louis Browns OF Roy Sievers hits his first of a career 318 ML home runs, this one against Detroit RHP Fred Hutchinson.

1950 Pittsburgh 1B Johnny Hopp hits two home runs and four singles in six at bats to lead the Pirates to a 16-9 victory over the Cubs in the second game of a doubleheader at Wrigley Field.

1955 Dennis Martinez b. Nicaragua.

1963 Pat Borders b. Columbus, OH.

1965 Joey Cora b. Puerto Rico.

1969 The Chicago White Sox trade 2B Sandy Alomar, Sr., and RHP Bob Priddy to California for 2B Bobby Knoop.

1972 In his first game with the New York Mets, Willie Mays hits a fifth-inning home run against RHP Don Carrithers to provide the winning run in 5-4 contest over his former club, the San Francisco Giants.

1972 Boston OF Ben Oglivie hits his first of a career 235 ML home runs. Oakland RHP Jim "Catfish" Hunter is the pitcher.

1973 Brad Rigby b. Altamonte Springs, FL.

1977 Kansas City RHP Jim Colborn no-hits Texas, 6-0.

1977 Roy Halladay b. Arvada, CO.

1981 Los Angeles Dodgers rookie LHP Fernando Valenzuela runs his record to 8-0 by defeating Montreal before 53,906, the largest Dodger Stadium crowd in seven years.

1986 California DH Reggie Jackson blasts his 537th career home run to move past Mickey Mantle into sixth place on the all-time list. Jackson will finish sixth all-time with 563 round-trippers.

1988 After using up seven pitchers, the St. Louis Cardinals bring in utility infielder Jose Oquendo to pitch the 16th inning against Atlanta. Oquendo shuts out the Braves for three innings, then gives up two runs in the 19th inning to lose, receiving the first decision by a non-pitcher in 20 years.

1989 Pittsburgh's Benny Distefano becomes the first left-handed catcher in a major league game in nine years, and only the third in ML history, when he handles the ninth inning of the Pirates' 5-2 loss to Atlanta. Mike Squires caught two games for the Chicago White Sox in 1980, while Dale Long of the Chicago Cubs was the first in 1958.

1991 Milwaukee trades DH Dave Parker to California for OF Dante Bichette.

1994 Minnesota DH Dave Winfield passes Frank Robinson with his 1,817th RBI, moving into 12th place all-time.

1994 The Kansas City Royals retire 3B George Brett's number 5, the first retired number in team history, then lose to Oakland, 5-4, despite 3B Gary Gaetti's seventh career triple play.

1994 St. Louis SS Ozzie Smith homers in back-to-back games for the first time in his 16-year career.

1995 Cleveland DH Eddie Murray hits his 463rd career home run in a 3-1 victory over Baltimore to tie teammate Dave Winfield for 18th place on the all-time list.

1996 New York Yankees RHP Dwight Gooden no-hits Seattle, 2-0. It's the eighth no-hitter in Yankees history and the first in Gooden's career.

1999 New York 1B John Olerud becomes the 14th player to reach the right field upper deck at Veterans Stadium in the Mets' 7-3 win at Philadelphia. New York also gets homers from 3B Robin Ventura and 2B Edgardo Alfonso.

1999 Anaheim DH Mo Vaughn hits his eighth career grand slam home run and ties a career high with six RBIs as the Angels beat Tampa Bay, 8-3.

15

1906 New York Giants LHP Hooks Wiltse becomes the first pitcher since 1893 to strike out seven straight batters.

1912 Detroit Tigers OF Ty Cobb goes into the stands against a heckler in New York and attacks pressman Claude Leuker, an act that draws an indefinite suspension. Cobb's Tiger teammates go on a one day strike to get him reinstated after a replacement Detroit team gets clobbered by the Philadelphia A's, 24-2. Cobb would be fined $50 for the incident, and his teammates would each get a $100 fine for walking out.

1918 Washington RHP Walter Johnson hurls a 1-0, 18-inning shutout over LHP Lefty Williams of the Chicago White Sox, who also goes the distance.

1919 In the 13th inning as the Reds blank the Dodgers 10-0 after 12 scoreless innings, Cincinnati scores 10 runs against Brooklyn RHP Al Mamaux.

1944 Cincinnati LHP Clyde Shoun no-hits the Boston Braves, 1-0.

1948 Bill North b. Seattle, WA.

1952 In a 1-0 win over Washington, Detroit RHP Virgil Trucks hurls the first of his two no-hitters of the summer.

1953 George Brett b. Moundsville, WV.

1960 Chicago RHP Don Cardwell becomes the first ML pitcher to throw a no-hitter in his first start after being traded, as the Cubs defeat St. Louis, 4-0, at Wrigley Field.

1967 John Smoltz b. Warren, MI.

1973 California Angels RHP Nolan Ryan no-hits Kansas City, 3-0. It's the first no-hitter in Angels franchise history, the first of Ryan's record-tying two in the same year, and the first of his ML career record seven no-hitters. Angels C Jeff Torborg is on the receiving end of his third no-hitter after catching by two Los Angeles Dodgers LHP Sandy Koufax and RHP Bill Singer.

1974 A.J. Hinch b. Midwest City, OK.

1976 Detroit Tigers RHP Mark "The Bird" Fidrych makes his first major league start.

1981 Cleveland Indians RHP Len Barker throws the first perfect game in 13 years, a 3-0 gem against Toronto.

1998 Los Angeles trades C Mike Piazza and 3B Todd Zeile to Florida for C Charles Johnson, 3B Bobby Bonilla, and OFs Gary Sheffield and Jim Eisenreich.

1998 With four of its regular players absent awaiting finalization of a trade to Los Angeles, Florida sets a team record with nine consecutive hits during the first inning of its 8-7 win over St. Louis.

16

1902 In the only time two deaf baseball players oppose each other, New York Giants RHP Luther "Dummy" Taylor hurls eight strong innings to defeat Cincinnati, 5-3, with Reds OF William "Dummy" Hoy, collecting two hits.

1909 The Chicago White Sox trade OF Gavvy Cravath, LHP Nick Altrock, and OF Jiggs Donahue to Washington for LHP Bill Burns.

1928 Billy Martin b. Berkeley, CA.

1933 Washington 3B Cecil Travis makes his ML debut with five hits in a 12-inning game against Chicago.

1939 In the first night game in AL history, Cleveland beats the Philadelphia A's, 8-3, in 10 innings at Shibe Park.

1949 Rick Reuschel b. Quincy, IL.

1953 The Chicago White Sox load the bases against the New York Yankees in the ninth inning, but Vern Stephens, who had 10 grand slams in his career, is lifted for a pinch hitter. Pitcher Tommy Byrne, the substitute batter, connects with a grand slam against RHP Ewell Blackwell.

1956 Jack Morris b. St. Paul, MN.

1959 The Philadelphia Phillies trade INF Granny Hamner to Cleveland for RHP Humberto Robinson.

1959 Mitch Webster b. Larned, KS.

1965 Baltimore RHP Jim Palmer, age 19, wins his first ML game and also hits his first ML home run off RHP Jim Bouton, as the Orioles beat the New York Yankees, 7-5.

1967 Doug Brocail b. Clearfield, PA.

1972 At Veterans Stadium in Philadelphia, Phillies LF Greg Luzinski hits a monster home run striking a suspended Liberty Bell which hangs beyond the center-field wall.

1975 Oakland trades INF Ted Kubiak to San Diego for RHP Sonny Siebert.

1981 Houston SS Craig Reynolds hits three triples to lead the Astros to a 6-1 win over the Chicago Cubs.

1983 New York Mets OF Darryl Strawberry hits his first ML home run against Pittsburgh RHP Lee Tunnell.

1994 Los Angeles 3B Tim Wallach collects four RBIs, giving him 1,000 for his career.

1998 St. Louis 1B Mark McGwire hits "the best ball I've ever hit," a Busch Stadium record 545-foot home run, to lead the Cardinals past Florida, 5-4.

1998 Houston 2B Craig Biggio thrills the largest regular season crowd in Astrodome history — 51,526 — with a bottom of the ninth inning home run to lift the Astros to a 3-2 win over Atlanta.

17

1903 Having to move a regulation game from Cleveland to Columbus, Ohio due to Sunday restrictions, the Cleveland Indians beat the New York Highlanders, 9-2.

1903 James Thomas "Cool Papa" Bell b. Starkville, MS.

1925 Cleveland Indians OF Tris Speaker collects his 3,000th career hit, against Washington LHP Tom Zachary in a 2-1 loss to the Senators.

1927 Boston Braves RHP Bob Smith hurls a 22-inning complete game, but loses, 4-3, to the Chicago Cubs.

1948 Carlos May b. Birmingham, AL.

1956 The St. Louis Cardinals trade OF Bill Virdon to Pittsburgh for LHP Dick Littlefield and OF Bobby Del Greco.

1961 New York Yankees RF Roger Maris hits his first home run of the season at Yankee Stadium (fourth overall) on his way to a record 61.

1963 Houston Colt 45s RHP Don Nottebart hurls the second no-hitter by an expansion club, a 4-1 win over Philadelphia. Los Angeles Angels LHP Bo Belinsky was the first just a year earlier.

1970 Atlanta OF Hank Aaron singles off Cincinnati RHP Wayne Simpson for his 3,000th career hit. The occasion makes Aaron the only major league player with 3,000 hits and 500 career home runs. Stan Musial, the only other living member of the 3,000 hit club, is in attendance.

1971 Washington Senators 1B Tom McCraw hits what is likely the shortest home run ever. On a pop fly to shallow left center, Cleveland SS Jack Heidemann, CF Vada Pinson, and LF John Lowenstein all collide and fall dazed to the ground. McCraw circles the bases on his 160 foot tater.

1978 Los Angeles trades OF Glenn Burke to Oakland for OF Billy North.

1979 The Chicago Cubs erupt for a 13-run rally against the Philadelphia Phillies and still lose. The Cubs fall behind 21-9, tie the game, then lose 23-22 in 10 innings at Wrigley Field. Chicago OF Dave Kingman hits three home runs, while Philadelphia 3B Mike Schmidt hits two. The slugfest combines 11 home runs and 50 hits.

1984 Cincinnati RHP Mario Soto ties an ML record striking out four batters in one inning.

1992 Boston 3B Wade Boggs collects his 2,000th career hit, against California LHP Mark Langston.

1992 Toronto surpasses the one million mark in attendance faster than any team in ML history, needing just 21 dates to draw 1,006,294 fans.

1996 Milwaukee DH Dave Nilsson becomes the first Brewers player in history and the 12th in AL history to hit two home runs in the same inning. His two blasts come during an 11-run sixth in a 12-1 win at Minnesota.

1996 Atlanta OF Jermaine Dye becomes the 71st player in history to hit a home run in his first ML at bat.

1998 New York LHP David Wells becomes the 15th pitcher in modern ML history to throw a perfect game, and the Yankees blank Minnesota, 4-0. Wells joins RHP Don Larsen as the only

Yankees pitchers to hurl perfect games, and extends his consecutive batters-retired streak to an AL record 37 over two games.

1998 Chicago rookie RHP Kerry Wood strikes out eight Cincinnati batters before leaving the contest with a cut on his pitching finger, as the Cubs bury the Reds, 10-1. Wood's strikeout total of 41 over his last three starts is two shy of the ML mark set by New York Mets RHP Dwight Gooden.

18

1882 Louisville pitcher Tony Mullane pitches ambidextrously to left-handed and right-handed Baltimore hitters, but he still loses, 9-8. Mullane's off-field antics lead to Louisville's instituting the first Ladies Day promotion.

1912 As Detroit Tiger players walk off the field contesting Ty Cobb's suspension, college pitcher Aloysius Travers makes his first, last, and only ML appearance. In eight innings against the Philadelphia A's, he yields 26 hits, seven walks, and allows an AL record 24 runs. He gets paid $50 to be a scab. Teammate Ed Irvin, filling in at third base, goes 2-for-3 with two triples in his only major league at-bats.

1929 Jack Sanford b. Wellesley Hills, MA.

1937 Brooks Robinson b. Little Rock, AR.

1946 Reggie Jackson b. Wyncote, PA.

1950 St. Louis Cardinals 3B Tommy Glaviano makes three consecutive errors on three straight batted balls as the Cardinals blow an 8-5 lead to Brooklyn and lose.

1951 Jim Sundberg b. Galesburg, IL.

1957 Baltimore OF Dick Williams hits a ninth inning, game-tying solo home run against Chicago LHP Paul LaPalme seconds before 10:20 P.M., a time set as a curfew so that the White Sox can catch a train out of Baltimore. If Williams does anything else, Chicago wins the game. Instead, the game is replayed from the beginning and the Orioles go on to win.

1965 Erik Hanson b. Kinnelon, NJ.

1966 Washington Senators 1B Frank Howard hits a record 10th homer over six games as Senators top Detroit, 8-4. The previous mark was seven homers in six games.

1967 Eric Young b. New Brunswick, NJ.

1969 Minnesota's Rod Carew and Cesar Tovar each steal home in the third inning, providing the Twins' only runs in an 8-2 loss to Detroit.

1972 Darren Dreifort b. Wichita, KS.

1972 San Diego trades OF Ollie Brown to Oakland for OF Curt Blefary and LHP Mike Kilkenny.

1976 The Chicago White Sox trade OF Carlos May to the New York Yankees for LHP Ken Brett and OF Rich Coggins.

1979 Atlanta OF Dale Murphy hits three home runs in a game against San Francisco.

1984 Philadelphia Phillies 3B Mike Schmidt hits his 400th career home run at Los Angeles against Dodgers RHP Bob Welch.

1997 Chicago White Sox 1B Frank Thomas goes 4-for-4 with a walk in a 10-4 win over Oakland to extend his consecutive plate appearance streak to 12 straight times reaching base safely. Thomas is four shy of the ML record set by Ted Williams in 1957.

1998 Oakland 3B Mike Blowers becomes the 99th AL and the 218th ML player to hit for the cycle as the A's bury the Chicago White Sox, 14-0.

19

1910 Cleveland RHP Cy Young wins his 500th game, a 5-4 squeaker over Washington in 11 innings. The following season, Young will conclude his 22-year career with an all-time record of 511 victories.

1928 Gil McDougald b. San Francisco, CA.

1929 Curt Simmons b. Egypt, PA.

1933 The Ferrell brothers — RHP Wes of Cleveland and C Rick of Boston — both hit home runs in the same game for the first time in ML history that a brother act accomplishes the feat. Rick hits his homer against Wes, while Wes hits his on a pitch called for by brother Rick.

1952 Dan Ford b. Los Angeles, CA.

1960 In his first game with the San Francisco Giants, RHP Juan Marichal hurls a one-hitter in beating Philadelphia, 2-0.

1967 Turk Wendell b. Pittsfield, MA.

1970 St. Louis trades RHP Jerry Johnson to San Francisco for RHP Frank Linzy.

1971 San Diego trades C Chris Cannizzaro to the Chicago Cubs for INF Garry Jestadt.

1972 Cincinnati trades OF Bernie Carbo to St. Louis for OF Joe Hague.

1979 Major League umpires end their six-week strike and return to work. Amateur and minor league umpires are called in during their absense to work major league contests.

1987 Facing the White Sox, Milwaukee drops its 12th straight decision, 5-1. When the streak began, the Brewers were 20-3 and leading the AL East.

1998 St. Louis 1B Mark McGwire hits three two-run home runs — the 45th multiple home run game in his career — as the Cardinals edge Philadelphia, 10-8.

1999 Cincinnati LF Jeffrey Hammonds hits three home runs, and 1B Sean Casey adds two homers and a career high six RBIs as the Reds pound Colorado, 24-12, to complete a three game sweep of the Rockies. Cincinnati pounds out 28 hits against seven Colorado pitchers.

1999 Cleveland 1B Richie Sexson drives in a career-high five runs with his second career grand slam home run and an RBI single, and the Indians pound out 18 hits to beat the Chicago White Sox, 13-7, to complete a three-game sweep.

20

1907 The St. Louis Cardinals end New York's 17-game winning streak, beating the Giants, 6-4, at the Polo Grounds.

1920 Police disguised as soldiers and farmers raid the Wrigley Field bleachers and arrest 24 Cubs fans for gambling while RHP Grover Cleveland Alexander shuts out Philadelphia, 6-0.

1921 Hal Newhouser b. Detroit, MI.

1925 Cleveland scores six runs in the last of the ninth inning to beat the New York Yankees, 10-9. Indians OF Tris Speaker scores the winning run from first base on a single.

1931 Ken Boyer b. Liberty, MO.

1940 Detroit 3B Pinky Higgins hits three consecutive home runs as the Tigers outslug Boston, 10-7.

1941 Chicago White Sox OF Taffy Wright sets an AL record by driving in a run for his 13th straight game. Surprisingly, in six of the games during the streak, Wright did not get a hit.

1945 One-armed OF Pete Gray leads a St. Louis Browns doubleheader sweep of the New York Yankees, with three hits and two RBIs in the opener, then scores the winning run in the nightcap, while making seven putouts in the field.

1946 Bobby Murcer b. Oklahoma City, OK.

1947 The Pittsburgh Pirates defeat the Boston Braves, 4-3, in a game with a combined 22 hits — all singles.

1953 In only their 13th game of the season, the Milwaukee Braves surpass their 1952 attendance of 281,278, when the franchise was in Boston.

1956 Washington Senators LHP Chuck Stobbs loses a pitch and has the ball flip into the stands equidistant from home plate and first base about 30 rows up.

1959 Detroit beats New York, dropping the Yankees into last place for the first time since May 1940.

1960 Fog arrives in the middle of a Milwaukee Braves-Chicago Cubs contest and leads to its suspension.

1963 David Wells b. Torrence, CA.

1965 Todd Stottlemyre b. Yakima, WA.

1969 The Seattle Pilots trade RHP Jack Aker to the New York Yankees for RHP Fred Talbot.

1975 Cleveland trades RHP Jim Perry and RHP Dick Bosman to Oakland for RHP Blue Moon Odom.

1976 Boston Red Sox 1B Carl Yastrzemski homers twice against the New York Yankees, a day after he hit three homers in Detroit to tie the major league mark of five homers in two games.

1978 Pittsburgh OF Willie Stargell hits a 535-foot home run against Montreal RHP Wayne Twitchell — the longest home run in Montreal's Olympic Stadium — to highlight the Pirates' 6-0 win. The homer is Stargell's 407th, tying him with Duke Snider on the all-time list.

1995 Minnesota OF Marty Cordova ties an ML rookie record by homering in

his fifth straight game, a 10-6 loss to Seattle.

1998 American League President Gene Budig fines and suspends five players who participated in a bench-clearing brawl between the Baltimore Orioles and New York Yankees the previous day. After giving up a three-run home run which put New York ahead, 7-5, Baltimore reliever Armando Benitez throws at Yankees 1B Tino Martinez on the next pitch, inciting the riot. Benitez himself is suspended for eight games and fined. The Yankees win the game, 9-5.

1999 New York 3B Robin Ventura becomes the first ML player to hit a grand slam home run in both games of a doubleheader in leading the Mets to a sweep over the Milwaukee Brewers, 11-10 and 10-1.

21

1902 Earl Averill b. Snohomish, WA.

1919 New York Giants OF Jim Thorpe is dealt to the Boston Braves for the $1,500 waiver price. He'll play 60 more games, then leave baseball with a .252 batting average over six seasons, and make his mark as an NLF Hall of Famer.

1926 Chicago White Sox 1B Earl Sheely hits a home run and three doubles against the Boston Red Sox, giving him a record seven consecutive extra base hits.

1941 Bobby Cox b. Tulsa, OK.

1952 Cincinnati RHP Ewell Blackwell retires Brooklyn leadoff hitter Billy Cox, but never retires another hitter during an eventual 19-1 Dodgers blowout. Three Reds relievers fail to stem the first inning tide as an ML record 19 consecutive Brooklyn batters reach base. Eventually, a record 15 runs score, 12 coming after two outs for another record. All told, a final record 21 hitters come to bat in the inning.

1957 Boston baseball writers, reaffirming a decision to bar women from the Fenway Park pressbox, deny a seat to Cleveland feature writer Doris O'Donnell, who is following the Indians.

1960 Kent Hrbek b. Minneapolis, MN.

1961 Milwaukee Braves C Joe Torre hits his first of a career 252 ML home runs, this one against Cincinnati RHP Joey Jay, an ex-Braves hurler traded to the Reds before the season started.

1970 New York Yankees RHP Mel Stottlemyre ties the ML record by walking 11 batters in a game, but still combines for a shutout win.

1992 The California Angels team bus crashes on the New Jersey Turnpike, injuring manager Buck Rodgers and 11 others.

1996 Seattle CF Ken Griffey, Jr., becomes the seventh youngest ML player to hit 200 home runs, and RF Jay Buhner homers for the fifth straight game as the Mariners bury Boston, 13-7, at Fenway Park. Griffey is 26 years, 181 days old at the time.

1997 Cleveland 1B Jim Thome steals his only base all season, home plate, to account for the only scoring of the Indians' 1-0 win over Kansas City.

22

1884 Chicago-Pittsburgh RHP Hugh "One Arm" Daily strikes out 13 Baltimore batters in a Union Association game. Daily would lead the league in strikeouts with 483, more than 100 more than his nearest rival.

1902 Al Simmons b. Milwaukee, WI.

1943 Tommy John b. Terre Haute, IN.

1956 Mark Brouhard b. Burbank, CA.

1962 New York RF Roger Maris walks five times — four intentionally — as the Yankees prevail, 2-1, in 12 innings over the California Angels.

1963 Batting left-handed, New York CF Mickey Mantle claims he never hit one harder than this home run against the Kansas City A's RHP Bill Fischer. The ball hits the facade at the top of the upper deck at Yankee Stadium, just six feet short of going over the roof. Experts claim it would've gone well over 600 feet.

1965 San Francisco trades SS Jose Pagan to Pittsburgh for SS Dick Schofield, Sr.

1966 Jose Mesa b. Dominican Republic.

1968 Pittsburgh OF Willie Stargell hits three home runs, a double, and a single in a 13-6 win over the Chicago Cubs at Wrigley Field. Stargell's double just misses being his fourth homer of the afternoon as the ball hits the railing on the left field bleachers.

1976 St. Louis Cardinals OF Reggie Smith hits three home runs — two right-handed and one left-handed — to drive in five runs in a 7-6 win over Philadelphia. His third homer comes with two outs in the ninth inning and breaks a 6-6 tie.

1977 Boston and Milwaukee combine for an ML record-tying 11 home runs as the Red Sox win, 14-10, in the first game of a doubleheader at Fenway Park. Boston hits six homers, while Milwaukee collects five.

1983 Toronto's Cliff Johnson ties the ML record with his 18th career pinch-hit home run against Baltimore LHP Tippy Martinez.

1998 Florida trades C Mike Piazza to the New York Mets for OF Preston

Wilson and LHPs Eddie Yarnell and Geoff Goetz.

1999 New York Yankees RHP Roger Clemens sets an AL record winning his 18th straight decision, a 10-2 victory over the Chicago White Sox in the first game of a doubleheader.

1999 Anaheim knuckleballer RHP Steve Sparks ties an ML record hitting three consecutive batters in the third inning, two of them with the bases loaded, during the Angels' 8-6 win at Tampa Bay. Sparks, who receives no decision, also hits a fourth batter to tie the ML record for most batters hit in a nine-inning game.

1999 Cincinnati RHP Pete Harnisch hits his first career home run in 341 at-bats and hurls his second shutout of the season, a 3-0 gem over San Diego.

23

1888 Zack Wheat b. Hamilton, MO.

1901 Philadelphia A's 2B Nap Lajoie becomes the first ML player to draw an intentional walk with the bases loaded to force home a run against Boston. Lajoie is well on his way to winning the triple crown with 14 home runs, 125 RBIs, and a .426 batting average, and also leads the league with 48 doubles, 145 runs scored, and a .639 slugging average.

1901 Cleveland scores nine runs with two outs in the ninth inning to beat Washington, 14-13.

1906 Willis Hudlin b. Wagoner, OK.

1945 The St. Louis Cardinals trade RHP Mort Cooper to the Boston Braves for RHP Red Barrett.

1946 Prior to the Chicago Cubs-Brooklyn Dodgers contest, a full-fledged brawl breaks out between the two teams during batting practice. Hard feelings from a fight between the two teams the night before ignite a second altercation.

1954 Cincinnati C Ed Bailey doesn't catch a single pitch in an inning as the first two batters single on the first pitch, and the next three batters all fly out on their first pitches as well.

1957 New York Yankees CF Mickey Mantle becomes the first AL switch hitter to hit for the cycle. The first NL batter to accomplish the feat was Pittsburgh OF Max Carey in 1925.

1962 New York OF Joe Pepitone hits two home runs in the eighth inning as the Yankees beat Kansas City, 13-7.

1970 The San Diego Padres and San Francisco Giants play a 15-inning seesaw battle won by the Padres, 17-16. Nate Colbert leads San Diego with five hits and four RBIs.

1970 Ricky Gutierrez b. Miami, FL.

1979 The Chicago Cubs trade RHP Ray Burris to the New York Yankees for RHP Dick Tidrow.

1984 The Detroit Tigers win their 16th straight road game, this one 4-2 at California, tying an AL record.

1991 Philadelphia RHP Tommy Greene, making only his 15th ML start, no-hits the Montreal Expos, 2-0.

1994 Seattle CF Ken Griffey, Jr., hits his 21st home run, breaking Mickey Mantle's record for the most homers in two months, but the Mariners lose at Oakland, 7-5.

1995 Los Angeles trades INF Jeff Treadway and OF Henry Rodriguez to Montreal for OF Roberto Kelly and LHP Joey Eischen.

1995 Chicago Cubs RHP Kevin Foster and Colorado RHP Marvin Freeman hit home runs off each other during the Cubs' 7-6 win at Coors Field. They become just the 10th duo to accomplish the feat this century.

1999 Baltimore CF Brady Anderson sets an AL record by getting hit by a pitch twice in the same inning, and scoring each time in a 10-run first inning, as the Orioles rout Texas 15-6.

24

1878 Jack Pfiester b. Cincinnati, OH.

1918 Cleveland RHP Stan Coveleski pitches all 19 innings as the Indians outlast the New York Yankees, 3-2.

1929 Chicago White Sox RHP Ted Lyons throws a 21-inning, complete game victory over Detroit.

1935 In the first night game in ML history, Cincinnati tops Philadelphia, 2-1, in 10 innings before 20,422 fans at Crosley Field. President Franklin D. Roosevelt pushes a button from the White House to turn on 363 1,000-kilowatt bulbs on eight towers.

1936 New York 2B Tony Lazzeri hits two grand slams, adds a solo homer and a two-run triple for an AL record 11 RBIs as the Yankees drub the Philadelphia A's, 25-2. Teammate Ben Chapman reaches base safely all seven times during the nine inning contest to set another record.

1940 The first night games are played at the Polo Grounds in New York and Sportsman's Park in St. Louis.

1946 Chicago RHP Ted Lyons, 45, the oldest major leaguer in World War II, gives up pitching to replace Jimmy Dykes as manager of the White Sox. Lyons is 1-4 at the time with a 2.32 ERA. He had missed the 1943-45 seasons because of the war, and had spent his entire 21-year pitching career with Chicago.

1964 Minnesota 3B Harmon Killebrew hits the longest home run in Baltimore's Memorial Stadium, a 471 foot shot against Orioles RHP Milt Pappas.

1968 Jerry DiPoto b. Jersey City, NJ.

1990 Cincinnati intentionally walks Chicago OF Andre Dawson five times to break the ML record shared by Roger Maris and Garry Templeton.

1991 Hal McRae is named manager of the Kansas City Royals, becoming the fourth father in ML history to manage his son. The other three are Connie Mack, Yogi Berra, and Cal Ripken, Sr.

1994 The St. Louis Cardinals set an ML record, stranding 16 runners without scoring, in a 4-0 loss to Philadelphia.

1994 Baltimore SS Cal Ripken, Jr., hits his 300th career home run, this shot against Milwaukee LHP Teddy Higuera in a 13-5 win at Milwaukee. The Brewers extend their team record 13th straight loss.

1995 Oakland RHP Dennis Eckersley becomes the sixth pitcher in ML history to reach 300 saves in a 5-2 win over Baltimore.

1995 The Texas Rangers and Chicago White Sox play the longest doubleheader in major league history, 7 hours and 39 minutes at Comiskey Park.

1995 Seattle 3B Mike Blowers ties a team record with eight RBIs during a 15-6 win over Boston. He also sets a Mariners record for extra base hits in one game with two doubles, a triple, and a home run.

1996 Seattle CF Ken Griffey, Jr., blasts three home runs against the New York Yankees to complete the only father-son duo with three round-trippers in one game. Father Ken Griffey, Sr., hit three homers playing for Atlanta in 1986 against Philadelphia.

25

1906 Boston LHP Jesse Tannehill snaps his team's 20-game losing streak hurling the Red Sox past the Chicago White Sox, 3-0.

1906 Martin Dihigo b. Cuba.

1923 Detroit Tigers OF Ty Cobb scores his 1,741st run, passing Honus Wagner for the all-time lead. Cobb will retire after the 1928 season with 2,245 runs scored, a record which still stands.

1935 Playing for the Boston Braves, Babe Ruth hits his final three career home runs at Pittsburgh's Forbes Field. He adds a single for a total of six RBIs, but the Pirates win, 11-7. His third homer becomes the first ever to clear the roof in right field. Five days later, hitting just .181, Ruth retires from the game with 714 career homers.

1937 Detroit C Mickey Cochrane homers in his third inning at-bat, forcing New York RHP Bump Hadley to brush him back on his next at-bat. Hadley beans Cochrane, whereupon the catcher is rushed to the hospital with a skull fracture. He will never play again, retiring with a 13-year, .320 lifetime average and 119 homers.

1941 Boston LHP Lefty Grove allows a single to New York's Joe DiMaggio in the 11th game of DiMaggio's eventual 56-game hitting streak. In September 1927, Grove had yielded a grand slam homer to Babe Ruth. Grove and Chicago White Sox RHP Ted Lyons would be the only two pitchers involved in both Ruth's 60-homer season and in DiMaggio's record consecutive game hitting streak.

1950 John Montefusco b. Long Branch, NJ.

1951 New York Giants rookie CF Willie Mays goes 0-for-5 in his ML debut against Philadelphia.

1953 In only his eighth ML season, Pittsburgh OF Ralph Kiner reaches the 300 home run plateau. Kiner, who led the NL in home runs in each of his first seven seasons, will lose this year's title to Milwaukee 3B Eddie Mathews.

1953 Milwaukee RHP Max Surkont strikes out an ML record eight straight batters during a 10-3 win over Cincinnati.

1963 The Kansas City A's trade C Joe Azcue and SS Dick Howser to Cleveland for C Howard Edwards.

1966 Dave Hollins b. Buffalo, NY.

1989 Montreal trades LHP Randy Johnson, RHP Brian Holman, and RHP Gene Harris to Seattle for LHP Mark Langston and RHP Mike Campbell.

1998 St. Louis 1B Mark McGwire breaks the ML record with his 25th home run before June 1st, during the Cardinals 6-1 loss to Colorado. Seattle CF Ken Griffey, Jr., hit 24 homers prior to June 1, 1997 and finished the year with 56.

1999 Arizona ties a 68-year ML record with three double plays started by a catcher, and LHP Randy Johnson strikes out 12 batters on a six-hitter as the Diamondbacks blank San Diego, 4-0. Johnson has two pitches clocked at 100 mph.

26

1894 The Pittsburgh Pirates lead the Cleveland Spiders, 12-3, in the eighth inning at Cleveland, when the home fans start a seat cushion fight that carries over onto the playing field. The Pirates are awarded a 9-0 forfeit win.

1916 New York Giants OF Benny Kauff, who led the NL in stolen bases the last two years, gets on base three times and gets picked off all three times as well.

1929 Pinch-hitters Pat Crawford of the New York Giants and Les Bell of the Boston Braves both hit grand slam home runs during New York's 15-9 victory.

1930 Cleveland 3B Joe Sewell strikes out twice against Chicago LHP Pat Caraway. Sewell would not whiff again all year, finishing with three K's in 353 at-bats.

1930 Washington Senators Goose Goslin and Joe Judge become the first AL players to hit back-to-back home runs twice in the same game.

1937 Commissioner Kenesaw Mountain Landis takes away the All-Star votes from the fans and instead decrees that the two managers will select future teams.

1947 Darrell Evans b. Pasadena, CA.

1949 Ed Crosby b. Long Beach, CA.

1955 In a game against Pittsburgh, Brooklyn RHP Don Newcombe becomes the last pitcher to steal home.

1956 Cincinnati RHPs John Klippstein, Hershell Freeman, and Joe Black combine for 9⅓ hitless innings, but the Reds later lose to the Philadelphia Phillies, 2-1, in 11 innings.

1959 Pittsburgh LHP Harvey Haddix pitches 12 perfect innings against Milwaukee, but loses 1-0 in the 13th inning on a double by Joe Adcock. Adcock's blow is actually a home run, but he passes baserunner Hank Aaron, who heads for the dugout after the ball clears the fence. Braves starter Lew Burdette allows 12 singles in 13 innings.

1960 Rob Murphy b. Miami, FL.

1962 Los Angeles LHP Sandy Koufax strikes out 16 Philadelphia Phillies in the Dodgers' 6-3 win.

1963 Philadelphia Phillies 1B Roy Sievers becomes the second ML player to hit a pinch-hit grand slam in both leagues when he connects against Cincinnati LHP Bill Henry.

1964 Willie Fraser b. New York, NY.

1965 Ricky Jordan b. Richmond, CA.

1971 Jason Bere b. Cambridge, MA.

1971 The New York Yankees trade INF Curt Blefary to Oakland for LHP Rob Gardner.

1975 Travis Lee b. Olympia, WA.

1996 Chicago becomes the 16th team in AL history to hit four home runs in one inning during the White Sox' 12-1 win over Milwaukee. Frank Thomas, Harold Baines, and Robin Ventura hit consecutive homers, and Chad Kreuter adds another during Chicago's seven-run eighth inning.

1997 Chicago's Sammy Sosa and Pittsburgh's Tony Womack hit inside-the-park home runs in the sixth inning of the Cubs' 2-1 win. Its the first time two inside-the-park homers have been hit in the same inning in 20 years.

1999 Tampa Bay LHP Tony Saunders breaks his left humerus while throwing a pitch against the Texas Rangers. Since 1989, three ML pitchers have experienced such an injury, with none returning to professional baseball.

27

1902 To keep Philadelphia A's 2B Nap Lajoie from returning to the NL, AL president Ban Johnson shifts his contract from the A's to the Cleveland Indians.

1904 New York Giants 1B Dan McGann becomes the first ML player to steal five bases in a game.

1937 In a rare relief role, New York Giants LHP Carl Hubbell hurls two scoreless innings and wins a record 24th straight decision over a two-year period, this one a 3-2 squeaker over Cincinnati. Giants OF Mel Ott contributes a home run.

1944 Jim Holt b. Graham, NC.

1948 Gary Nolan b. Herlong, CA.

1955 Boston Red Sox 1B Norm

Zauchin collects 10 RBIs with three home runs and a double in the first five innings of a 16-0 blowout of the Washington Senators.

1959 Ron Tingley b. Presque Isle, ME.

1960 Baltimore C Clint Courtney uses a "big mitt" for the first time in catching knuckleballer Hoyt Wilhelm as the Orioles edge the New York Yankees, 3-2. Designed by Orioles manager Paul Richards, the "big mitt" is 50 percent larger than a normal-size catchers mitt.

1960 Pittsburgh trades 2B Julian Javier and RHP Eduardo Bauta to St. Louis for INF Dick Gray and LHP Wilmer Mizell.

1965 Jacob Brumfield b. Bogalusa, LA.

1966 John Jaha b. Portland, OR.

1968 Montreal and San Diego are awarded new NL franchises as the league expands for the first time in seven years.

1968 Jeff Bagwell b. Boston,MA.

1968 Frank Thomas (1B) b. Columbus, GA.

1969 Todd Hundley b. Martinsville, VA.

1977 Mike Caruso b. Coral Springs, FL.

1980 California trades OF Al Cowens to Detroit for 1B Jason Thompson.

1998 Texas RF Juan Gonzalez singles home a run during the Rangers' 6-5 loss to Minnesota to rank him seventh all-time on the RBI list in his 1,000th ML game with 852. The six players ahead of him, Hank Greenberg, Joe DiMaggio, Al Simmons, Lou Gehrig, Jimmie Foxx, and Ted Williams, are all in the Hall of Fame.

1999 Detroit DH Luis Polonia goes 5-for-5 to lead the Tigers to a 10-5 win over the Chicago White Sox.

28

1888 Jim Thorpe b. Prague, OK.

1946 The Washington Senators beat the New York Yankees, 2-1, in the first night game at Yankee Stadium. The first ball is thrown out by General Electric president Charles E. Wilson.

1951 New York Giants CF Willie Mays hits the first of his 660 career ML home runs, this one against Boston Braves LHP Warren Spahn. Mays will victimize Spahn a personal best 18 times during his 22-year career.

1956 Pittsburgh 1B Dale Long hits a home run in a record eighth straight game, a 3-2 win over Brooklyn and RHP Carl Erskine.

1956 Chicago White Sox SS Luis Aparicio hits his first ML home run against the Kansas City A's LHP Tommy Lasorda.

1957 The NL approves the West Coast relocation of the New York Giants and Brooklyn Dodgers, provided both clubs go at the same time.

1957 Kirk Gibson b. Pontiac, MI.

1966 Atlanta trades 1B Lee Thomas and LHP Arnie Early to the Chicago Cubs for RHP Ted Abernathy.

1968 The AL announces that the league will split into two divisions for the 1969 season. The East division will consist of Baltimore, Boston, Cleveland, Detroit, New York, and Washington, while California, Chicago, Kansas City, Minnesota, Oakland, and Seattle will make up the West.

1973 Chicago White Sox LHP Wilbur Wood gets two wins in one day, completing a suspended game against Cleveland, then winning the regularly scheduled game.

1979 Kansas City 3B George Brett hits for the cycle and adds another home run to lift the Royals to a 6-5, 16-inning win over Baltimore.

1986 Chicago White Sox RHP Joe Cowley becomes the first pitcher in the 20th century to strike out the first seven batters in a game when he turns the trick against Texas. Cowley lasts only 4⅔ innings, however, as the Rangers beat him, 6-3. His record will stand only until September 23rd when Houston LHP Jim Deshaies strikes out the first eight batters to start a game.

1993 For the first time since 1925, two 3,000-hit players oppose each other as Kansas City 3B George Brett and Milwaukee CF Robin Yount face off in a 5-1 Brewers win.

1994 Minnesota DH Dave Winfield passes Rod Carew, moving into 15th place all-time with his 3,054th career base hit.

1995 The Detroit Tigers and Chicago White Sox combine for an ML record 12 home runs in Chicago's 14-12 win at Tiger Stadium. Four players had at least two homers to set an AL record and tie the ML mark, and the 10 solo homers set another ML record. The participants include Chad Curtis (2), Cecil Fielder (2), Kirk Gibson (2), and Lou Whitaker for Detroit, and Ron Karkovice (2), Ray Durham, Craig Grebeck, and Frank Thomas for Chicago.

1995 San Diego ties an NL record scoring nine runs in the 10th inning to beat Philadelphia, 13-5. The Phillies score once in the bottom of the 10th inning.

1996 Baltimore SS Cal Ripken, Jr., playing in his 2,174th straight game, enjoys the first three-home run–game of his career as the Orioles win at Seattle, 12–8.

1998 Arizona intentionally walks San Francisco LF Barry Bonds with two outs and the bases loaded in the bottom of the ninth inning to force home a run, then hangs on to an 8-7 win over the Giants.

1998 The Chicago White Sox beat Detroit, 11-7, in 10 innings, scoring four runs in the top of the 10th inning without a base hit.

29

1916 New York RHP Christy Mathewson defeats Boston, 3-0, for the Giants 17th straight win, all on the road.

1922 The U.S. Supreme Court rules that organized baseball is primarily a sport and not a business, therefore, not subject to anti-trust laws and interstate commerce regulations.

1945 John "Blue Moon" Odom b. Macon, GA.

1952 New York Giants OF Willie Mays enlists in the U.S. Army, which will not return him to ML baseball until Opening Day 1954.

1962 Taken off the field by stretcher four days earlier after getting beaned, Chicago Cubs 1B Ernie Banks hits three home runs in his first game back.

1965 Philadelphia 1B Richie Allen hits a 529-foot home run over the roof at Connie Mack Stadium off Chicago RHP Larry Jackson as the Phillies win, 4-2.

1965 Charlie Hayes b. Hattiesburg, MS.

1965 The Chicago Cubs trade OF Len Gabrielson and C Dick Bertell to San Francisco for C Ed Bailey, RHP Bob Hendley, and OF Harvey Kuenn.

1967 Bill Risley b. Chicago, IL.

1967 Baltimore trades 1B Mike Epstein and LHP Frank Bertaina to Washington for LHP Pete Richert.

1970 St. Louis trades INF Phil Gagliano to the Chicago Cubs for RHP Ted Abernathy.

1971 Atlanta 3B Darrell Evans hits the first of his 414 ML home runs, this one against St. Louis RHP Bob Gibson.

1971 Cincinnati trades SS Frank Duffy and RHP Vern Geishert to San Francisco for OF George Foster.

1976 Houston Astros RHP Joe Niekro defeats brother RHP Phil Niekro of the Atlanta Braves, 6-3, adding a career-only home run in the win.

1989 Hitting just .203 with only six home runs after 42 games into the season, Philadelphia 3B Mike Schmidt announces his retirement, ending an 18-year career with the Phillies. Schmidt, a 10-time Gold Glove Award winner and a three-time NL MVP (1980-81, 1986), paced the senior circuit in home runs eight times and finished with 548 round-trippers, seventh best all-time. He'll be inducted into the Hall of Fame in 1995.

1990 Oakland LF Rickey Henderson steals his 893rd career base, breaking Ty Cobb's AL record during the A's 2-1 loss to Toronto.

1994 Cincinnati trades OF Roberto Kelly and LHP Roger Etheridge to Atlanta for OF Deion Sanders.

1998 The New York Yankees beat the Boston Red Sox, 6-2, for the 1,000th time in the storied rivalry of the two franchises. The Yankees improve to 1,000-813 against the Red Sox since they began playing in 1903. Boston becomes the fifth franchise that New York has beaten at least 1,000 times.

1999 Arizona RHP Byung-Hyun Kim, 20, from South Korea, makes his ML debut in the ninth inning and earns the save striking out New York C Mike Piazza to end the game and preserving the Diamondbacks' 8-7 win.

30

1871 Amos Rusie b. Mooresville, IN.

1883 The Cincinnati Red Stockings lose a 1-0 morning game against the New York Giants, then take the train to Philadelphia to edge the Phillies, 10-9, to complete a unique Memorial Day doubleheader split.

1887 New York Giants LHP Bill George gives up an ML record 16 walks against the Chicago White Stockings.

1894 Boston 2B Bobby Lowe becomes the first ML player to hit four home runs in a game, connecting each time against Cincinnati RHP Elton "Icebox" Chamberlain, during the Beaneaters' 20-11 win. Lowe also has a single for a record 17 total bases.

1904 Chicago Cubs 1B Frank Chance gets hit by pitches five times in a doubleheader against Pittsburgh.

1922 Between games of a morning-afternoon Memorial Day doubleheader, the Chicago Cubs and St. Louis Cardinals swap outfielders Max Flack for Cliff Heathcote who each play in the second game against his former team. They are the only players to play for both teams in a single day.

1934 New York RHP Burleigh Grimes earns his 270th and final victory of a 19-year career with a 5-4 relief win over Washington. Grimes' win is the last in ML history by a pitcher permitted to throw a spitball.

1946 At Brooklyn's Ebbets Field, Boston Braves OF Bama Rowell breaks the center-field scoreboard clock with a tremendous home run against the Dodgers.

1961 New York CF Mickey Mantle, RF Roger Maris, and 1B Bill Skowron each hit two home runs, and C Yogi Berra adds one as the Yankees pound Boston, 12-3.

1962 Cleveland RHP Pedro Ramos tosses a three-hitter and helps his own cause with two home runs, including a grand slam, for a 7-0 win over Baltimore.

1968 Mike Oquist b. LaJunta, CO.

1969 California trades OF Vic Davalillo to St. Louis for OF Jim Hicks.

1972 Manny Ramirez b. Dominican Republic.

1977 Cleveland RHP Dennis Eckersley no-hits California, 1-0.

1982 Baltimore 3B Cal Ripken, Jr., begins his consecutive games played streak in which he will overtake Lou Gehrig's mark of 2,130 straight on September 6, 1995, and continue on.

1987 Cincinnati OF Eric Davis becomes the first NL player to hit three grand slams in a month when he connects against Pittsburgh in a 6-2 Reds win. The slam is also Davis' NL record 19th homer for the months of April and May.

1992 New York RHP Scott Sanderson becomes the ninth pitcher in ML history to beat all 26 teams as the Yankees rout Milwaukee, 9-1. Sanderson joins RHPs Nolan Ryan, Don Sutton, Mike Torrez, Rick Wise, Gaylord Perry, Doyle Alexander, and Rich Gossage, and LHP Tommy John.

1995 Former Los Angeles Dodger and Oakland A's OF Glenn Burke passes away at age 42, reportedly the first ML player to die from complications from the HIV virus causing AIDS.

1997 Baltimore RHP Mike Mussina's bid for the club's first-ever perfect game ends after 25 batters are retired consecutively as Cleveland C Sandy Alomar Jr. singles in the ninth inning. Mussina settles for a one-hitter.

31

1914 Chicago White Sox RHP Joe Benz no-hits Cleveland, 6-1.

1920 In his first season in New York following his trade from Boston, Yankees RF Babe Ruth ties teammate Wally Pipp's single-season home run record with 12, which led the AL in 1916. Ruth would finish the season with a new ML record of 54 homers.

1921 Boston Red Sox 1B Stuffy McInnis begins his 1,700 consecutive errorless-chances streak which runs thru June 2, 1922.

1927 Philadelphia A's 1B Jimmie Foxx hits the first of his career 534 home runs, this one against New York Yankees RHP Urban Shocker.

1927 Detroit 1B Johnny Nuen turns a rare unassisted triple play, the day after Chicago Cubs SS Jimmy Cooney does it.

1935 Philadelphia Phillies RHP Jim Bivin retires Babe Ruth on an infield grounder in the Babe's final major league at-bat. Only 28 games into the season with the NL Boston Braves, Ruth calls it quits with his .181 batting average.

1937 New York LHP Carl Hubbell has his 24-game winning streak end as Brooklyn routs the Giants, 10-3.

1938 New York Yankees 1B Lou Gehrig plays in his 2,000th straight game during a win over Boston.

1938 Ray Washburn b. Pasco, WA.

1962 Joe Orsulak b. Glen Ridge, NJ.

1964 The second game of a doubleheader between the New York Mets and San Francisco Giants lasts for seven hours and 23 minutes before the Giants win, 8-6 in 23 innings. For the day, the two clubs play 32 innings covering 10 hours and 16 minutes.

1967 Kenny Lofton b. East Chicago, IL.

1979 Detroit LHP Pat Underwood makes his ML debut against his brother, Toronto LHP Tom Underwood.

1981 The Los Angeles Dodgers reach the one million attendance mark on their 22nd home date, a new major league record eclipsing the 25th date they had earlier set in 1978.

1996 Montreal OF Henry Rodriguez hits his 20th home run, setting a NL record for most home runs thru May, in a 7-4 win over San Francisco.

JUNE

1

1913 The New York Yankees trade 1B Hal Chase to the Chicago White Sox for 1B Babe Borton and INF Rollie Zeider.

1923 The NL's best team, the New York Giants (95–58) torture baseball's worst team, the Philadelphia Phillies (50–104), scoring in every inning of a 22–8 rout. It will be 76 years before the Colorado Rockies duplicate the feat, beating the Cubs, 13–6, on May 5, 1999.

1925 New York 1B Lou Gehrig begins his 2,130 consecutive games played streak by pinch hitting for SS Pee Wee Wanninger in a 5–3 loss to Washington.

1937 Chicago White Sox RHP Bill Dietrich no-hits the St. Louis Browns, 8–0.

1941 Dean Chance b. Wooster, OH.

1941 The New York Yankees begin a streak of hitting at least one home run in 25 straight games. In that stretch, the Yankees hit a total of 40 homers.

1942 Randy Hundley b. Martinsville, VA.

1942 Ken McMullen b. Oxnard, CA.

1965 Houston trades OF Al Spangler to the Los Angeles Angels for RHP Don Lee.

1974 St. Louis trades INFs Ed Crosy and Luis Alvarado to Cleveland for 2B Jack Heidemann.

1975 California RHP Nolan Ryan

notches his 100th career win and ties Sandy Koufax with his fourth no-hitter in blanking Baltimore, 1–0. Ryan collects nine strikeouts in the win.

1977 Seattle's Ruppert Jones homers off Cleveland RHP Dennis Eckersley in the fifth inning to snap Eckersley's no-hit string of 22⅓ innings, just two short of Cy Young's ML record. The Indians still win, 7–1.

1978 Seattle trades OF Steve Braun to Kansas City for RHP Jim Colborn.

1979 Philadelphia Phillies LHP Steve Carlton bats eighth in the order, ahead of SS Bud Harrelson, who hits ninth.

1986 Texas OF Ruben Sierra hits his first ML home run against Kansas City LHP Charlie Leibrandt.

1987 Cleveland RHP Phil Niekro pitches a 9–6 win over Detroit, giving himself and his brother, Joe, an ML record 530 combined victories, surpassing brothers Gaylord and Jim Perry.

1995 Texas LHP Kenny Rogers runs his season-high scoreless innings streak to 39 before giving up a run against Minnesota in a 6–3 Rangers win.

1999 New York RHP Roger Clemens extends his AL-record of 20 straight decisions in beating Cleveland, 11–5. Clemens passes Rube Marquard for third best all-time, trailing only Elroy Face and Carl Hubbell, who set the ML record with 24 straight decisions in 1936–37. Clemens has not lost in 30 starts dating back to May 29, 1998.

2

1863 Wilbert Robinson b. Bolton, MA.

1892 Benjamin Harrison becomes the first president to attend a game while in office, witnessing Cincinnati's 7–4, 11-inning win over Washington.

1899 Sloppy Thurston b. Fremont, NE.

1917 Boston Braves C Hank Gowdy becomes the first major league player to leave the game and volunteer to enlist in the armed services during World War I.

1925 New York 1B Wally Pipp leaves the lineup with a headache in favor of Lou Gehrig. Pipp never returns to the Yankees lineup.

1928 Boston 3B Les Bell hits three home runs and a triple driving in six runs, but Cincinnati defeats the Braves nonetheless, 20–12.

1931 Larry Jackson b. Nampa, ID.

1935 Boston Braves president Emil Fuchs gives 41-year-old Babe Ruth his unconditional release. It's just eight days after his three-homer game at Pittsburgh gave him 714 career round-trippers.

1940 Jim Maloney b. Fresno, CA.

1941 Former Yankees great Lou Gehrig dies at age 37 in New York of Amyotrophic Lateral Sclerosis, "Lou Gehrig's Disease," which forced his retirement two years earlier.

1949 The Philadelphia Phillies tie an ML record hitting five home runs in one inning. The eighth inning barrage against Cincinnati includes two homers by Andy Seminick, and one each for Del Ennis, Schoolboy Rowe, and Willie "Puddin' Head" Jones.

1959 At Chicago's Comiskey Park, the visiting Baltimore Orioles and White Sox are locked in a tight game when millions of gnats arrive at the stadium,

halting play. After smoke bombs and fireworks, the gnats leave, and Baltimore rallies to win, 3–2.

1962 Darnell Coles b. San Bernardino, CA.

1963 Bryan Harvey b. Chattanooga, TN.

1964 St. Louis trades RHP Lew Burdette to the Chicago Cubs for RHP Glen Hobbie.

1966 Cleveland trades RHP Don McMahon and RHP Lee Stange to Boston for RHP Dick Radatz.

1967 Boston trades RHP Don McMahon and P Rob Snow to the Chicago White Sox for 2B Jerry Adair.

1967 Mike Stanton b. Houston, TX.

1969 Kurt Abbott b. Zanesville, OH.

1970 Reid Cornelius b. Thomasville, AL.

1970 Mike Kelly b. Los Angeles, CA.

1989 Philadelphia trades OF Chris James to San Diego for INF Randy Ready and OF John Kruk.

1990 Seattle LHP Randy Johnson hurls the first no-hitter in franchise history, 2–0 over Detroit. It's also the first no-hitter thrown in the Kingdome since it opened in 1977.

1995 Boston Red Sox SS John Valentin goes 5-for-5 with a double and three HRs for 15 total bases in a 6–5 win over Seattle. Valentin finishes just one total base shy of the AL record last reached by former Red Sox OF Fred Lynn in 1975.

1998 The San Diego Padres select Long Beach (CA) high school 3B Sean Burroughs with the ninth pick in the first round of baseball's Free Agent Draft. The selection is baseball's second only father-son first round combination, as Jeff Burroughs was a top pick by the Washington Senators in 1969. Tom Grieve (Washington 1969) and son Ben Grieve (Oakland 1994) were baseball's first duo.

1998 Five beanballs and two bench-clearing brawls lead to 12 ejections during Anaheim's 7–5 win over Kansas City. Both Angels manager Terry Collins and Royals manager Tony Muser are ejected along with seven players and three coaches.

1998 Atlanta RHP Dennis Martinez ties Juan Marichal as the winningest Latin American pitcher in baseball history with 243 victories, scattering 12 hits in a 9–0 shutout over Milwaukee. The 43-year-old Martinez improves his 22-year career record to 243–189 with his first complete game since May 26, 1996. Martinez notches his 30th career shutout and 122nd complete game. Marichal compiled a 243–142 record in 16 seasons from 1960–1975; 238 of the wins in 14 years with San Francisco.

1999 The Arizona Diamondbacks tie a team record for runs in a game and set a franchise record with 20 hits in drubbing Montreal, 15–2.

3

1851 The New York Knickerbockers are the first team to wear uniforms, taking the field in blue trousers, white shirts, and straw hats.

1888 Ernest L. Thayer's "Casey at the Bat" is first published.

1897 New York Giants LHP Cy Seymour becomes the first hurler to win two complete games in one day, after the mound is moved back to its present distance of 60 feet six inches from the plate. Seymour beats Louisville, 6–1 and 10–6.

1902 St. Louis Cardinals RHP Mike O'Neill becomes the first ML player to belt a pinch-hit grand slam home run when he connects against the Boston Braves.

1912 New York Giants RHP Rube Marquard notches his 19th consecutive win over two seasons, a new record.

1918 Boston Red Sox LHP Dutch Leonard throws his second career no-hitter, 5–0 over Detroit. Babe Ruth supplies all the support needed with a home run.

1925 Chicago White Sox player/manager Eddie Collins joins baseball's 3,000 hit club in a game against Detroit.

1932 New York 1B Lou Gehrig becomes the first modern ML player to hit four home runs (consecutive) in one game as the Yankees pound the Philadelphia A's, 20–13. Gehrig connects three times against starting RHP George Earnshaw and finishes with six RBIs.

1932 John McGraw retires after managing for 33 years — 31 of them with the New York Giants — with 4,879 games and 2,840 wins, both totals second only to Philadelphia A's manager Connie Mack.

1933 New York Yankees RHP Walter "Jumbo" Brown, 6–4 and 295 pounds, strikes out 12 batters in 6⅓ innings in relief to get a victory over the Philadelphia A's.

1952 The Boston Red Sox trade 1B Walt Dropo, LHP Bill Wight, INF Fred Hatfield, INF Johnny Pesky, and OF Don Lenhardt to Detroit for RHP Dizzy Trout, 3B George Kell, SS Johnny Lipon, and OF Hoot Evers.

1953 The St. Louis Browns begin their ML record of 20 consecutive home losses, which lasts through July 7, 1953.

1955 The St. Louis Cardinals trade C Del Rice to Milwaukee for OF Pete Whisenant.

1960 Barry Lyons b. Biloxi, MS.

1963 Houston OF Rusty Staub hits his first of a career 292 ML home runs, this one against Los Angeles RHP Don Drysdale.

1971 Carl Everett b. Tampa, FL.

1971 Chicago Cubs LHP Ken Holtzman hurls his second no-hitter, 1–0 over Cincinnati.

1976 Milwaukee trades OF Bobby Darwin and RHP Tom Murphy to Boston for OF Bernie Carbo.

1978 Philadelphia pinch hitter Davey Johnson hits a grand slam for the second time during the year, making him the only player in baseball history with two pinch slams in the same season. The Phillies beat Los Angeles, 5–1.

1989 Los Angeles and Houston play 22 innings at the Astrodome in the longest night game in NL history: 7 hours and 14 minutes. The Astros win on Rafael Ramirez's RBI single off Jeff Hamilton, normally the Dodgers' third baseman. At the game's conclusion, Los Angeles has LHP Fernando Valenzuela at first base and regular first baseman Eddie Murray at third base.

1989 Texas RHP Nolan Ryan hurls his 11th career one-hitter and strikes out 11 as the Rangers beat Seattle, 6–1. It is Ryan's career 16th low-hit (none or one) game, breaking Cleveland RHP Bob Feller's record of 15.

1995 Montreal RHP Pedro Martinez takes a perfect game into extra innings, but a leadoff double by San Diego's Bip Roberts ends his bid. Expos RHP Mel Rojas comes in to relieve and preserves a 1–0 victory. Martinez and Harvey Haddix (1959 with Pittsburgh) are the only pitchers to pitch nine perfect innings without gaining a victory.

1998 Cuban defector RHP Orlando Hernandez wins his ML debut, hurling seven innings and striking out seven batters for the New York Yankees in his 7–1 win over Tampa Bay.

1998 Texas defeats Oakland, 16–10, marking the first time in the 1990s that both starters — Rangers RHP Aaron Sele and A's RHP Blake Stein — allow nine runs or more. Sele allows 10 runs and 12 hits in four innings, while Stein gives up nine runs and nine hits in 4⅓ innings.

4

1911 Cincinnati hammers the Boston Braves, 26–3, marking the worst run differential in NL history at 23.

1913 Cleveland OF Shoeless Joe Jackson hits the first ever home run over the roof at the Polo Grounds in New York.

1936 Detroit player/manager Mickey Cochrane collapses in a Shibe Park dugout and is hospitalized on the threshold of a career-threatening nervous breakdown.

1938 Art Mahaffey b. Cincinnati, OH.

1943 St. Louis Cardinals RHP Mort Cooper blanks Philadelphia, 5–0, for his second consecutive one-hit shutout.

1947 Doug Griffin b. South Gate, CA.

1951 Pittsburgh's Gus Bell hits for the cycle to lead the Pirates to a 12–4 win over the Phillies in Philadelphia.

1964 Los Angeles LHP Sandy Koufax hurls his third career no-hitter, striking out 12 Philadelphia Phillies in a 3–0 win.

1957 Tony Pena b. Dominican Republic.

1967 Scott Servais b. LaCrosse, WI.

1967 Rick Wilkins b. Jacksonville, FL.

1967 Boston trades OF Don Demeter and 1B Tony Horton to Cleveland for RHP Gary Bell.

1968 Los Angeles RHP Don Drysdale blanks Pittsburgh, 5–0, for his NL record sixth consecutive shutout. The shutout innings streak ends in his next start at 58⅔.

1972 An ML record five teams are shutout on the same day.

1974 On 10¢ beer night in Cleveland, fans become unruly in the bottom of the ninth inning as the Indians tie Texas,

5–5. The umpires are forced to forfeit the game to the Rangers as over 30 people are arrested.

1974 Darin Erstad b. Jamestown, ND.

1990 Los Angeles RHP Ramon Martinez strikes out 18 Braves, hurling a three-hit, 6–0 triumph over Atlanta. Martinez enters the ninth inning needing just one strikeout to tie the NL record held by both Steve Carlton and Tom Seaver, but comes up empty.

1997 Milwaukee RHP Cal Eldred gives up nine hits, eight runs, three home runs, and a wild pitch, but still sees a 7–0 deficit to Boston erased, as he somehow emerges as the winning pitcher.

1998 The Los Angeles Dodgers trade RHPs Hideo Nomo and Brad Clontz to the New York Mets for RHPs Greg McMichael and Dave Mlicki.

1998 The New York Yankees trade RHP Willie Banks to Arizona for RHPs Scott Brow and Joe Lisio.

5

1874 Jack Chesbro b. North Adams, MA.

1905 Boston Red Sox OF Buck Freeman sets an ML record, playing his 5,341st consecutive inning in the field. The record stands until Cal Ripken, Jr., erases it in 1985.

1911 Boston Red Sox RHP Smokey Joe Wood strikes out three straight Chicago White Sox pinch hitters in the ninth inning to preserve a 5–4 win.

1924 Lou Brissie b. Anderson, SC.

1938 Cincinnati RHP Johnny Vander Meer hurls a three hitter. He will then hurl back-to-back no-hitters in his next two starts for a total of only three hits allowed over three starts. No one had ever allowed fewer than five.

1949 Commissioner Happy Chandler lifts the five-year suspensions for 18 players who jumped to the Mexican League in 1946.

1955 New York Yankees CF Mickey Mantle homers against White Sox LHP Billy Pierce as the ball clears Chicago's Comiskey Park left field roof for an estimated 550 feet.

1959 Pittsburgh 1B Dick Stuart hits the longest home run ever at Forbes Field, a blast over the center-field wall against Chicago Cubs RHP Glen Hobbie.

1961 Detroit trades 2B Chuck Cottier to Washington for LHP Hal Woodeshick.

1966 Cincinnati SS Leo Cardenas hits four home runs in a doubleheader split against the Chicago Cubs. Cardenas hits two in each game as the Reds win the opener, 8–3, but lose the nightcap, 9–5.

1966 Pittsburgh OF Willie Stargell goes 5-for-5 to help the Pirates past Houston, 10–5. Stargell's performance gives him nine straight hits over two games.

1966 Bill Spiers b. Orangeburg, SC.

1967 Ray Lankford b. Modesto, CA.

1973 The San Diego Padres select Minnesota All-American Dave Winfield as the first pick in the June amateur draft. Winfield is also drafted by the NFL Minnesota Vikings as a tight end, and by the NBA Atlanta Hawks and ABA Utah Stars as a forward.

1979 During the first day of the June draft, the Kansas City Royals select two future NFL Hall of Fame quarterbacks who both decline baseball for football. In the fourth round, the Royals select RHP Dan Marino of Pittsburgh's Central Catholic High School; and in the 19th round they select Granada Hills High School, Northridge, CA OF John Elway. Elway will become the first pick of the 1983 NFL draft with the Indianapolis Colts, who will trade his rights to the Denver Broncos, while Marino will also be tabbed in the first round in 1983 with the Miami Dolphins.

1979 Seattle DH Willie Horton hits a towering fly ball against Detroit LHP John Hiller and is credited with a single when his drive hits a left field speaker in the Kingdome. Without interference, it would've been Horton's 300th career homer. He'll get it the next day, however, against Tigers RHP Jack Morris.

1986 San Diego 1B Steve Garvey is ejected for the first time in his career arguing a close play at home plate. As the on-deck hitter, Garvey protests a called triple play by umpire Charlie Williams. Replay shows that Garvey's teammate, Bip Roberts, was indeed safe, and the Padres still lose, 4–2.

1989 The Toronto Blue Jays lose their Skydome debut as Milwaukee OF Glenn Braggs hits a two-run home run in the Brewers' 5–3 win. The complex costs $375 million to build.

1997 During a 14–6 rout of Detroit, Seattle's 21-year-old SS Alex Rodriguez becomes the first player in the history of the franchise to hit for the cycle in a nine inning game.

1998 St. Louis 1B Mark McGwire eclipses the Busch Stadium single-season record for home runs with his 18th, passing Richie Allen (1970), Ted Simmons (1979), Jack Clark (1987), and Ron Gant (1996).

1999 Boston RHP Tom Gordon blows his first save opportunity in more than a year as Atlanta scores twice in the ninth inning to beat the Red Sox, 6–5. Since April 14, 1998, Gordon had converted an ML record 54 consecutive chances.

6

1903 The Pittsburgh Pirates run their ML record consecutive wins streak to six games. Their consecutive shutout innings streak of 56 straight will run through June 9th.

1907 Bill Dickey b. Bastrop, LA.

1913 The New York Yankees lose to the Cleveland Indians, 2–1, extending their worst losing streak in franchise history to 13 games.

1925 New York Yankees 1B Lou Gehrig begins his record of 885 consecutive games at first base. The streak runs through September 27, 1930.

1939 Cincinnati gets two outs in the New York half of the fourth inning when the roof caves in at the Polo Grounds. Before the inning is over, Harry Danning, Frank Demaree, Burgess Whitehead, Manny Salvo, and Joe Moore will homer as the Giants score eight times en route to a 17–3 laugher.

1943 Merv Rettenmund b. Flint, MI.

1944 Baseball cancels its schedule as Americans brace for D-Day — the invasion of Europe on the beaches of Normandy, France.

1944 Bud Harrelson b. Niles, CA.

1953 Dave Bergman b. Evanston, IL.

1972 By a 5–3 vote, the U.S. Supreme Court rules against OF Curt Flood, who is in trying to gain his freedom after being traded by St. Louis to Philadelphia. The Court rules that baseball is still exempt from anti-trust laws and the reserve clause remains intact.

1973 St. Louis trades RHP Jim Bibby to Texas for C John Wockenfuss and RHP Mike Nagy.

1990 New York Yankees manager Bucky Dent, fired unceremoniously by owner George Steinbrenner, becomes the only skipper let go during the entire season.

1996 Boston SS John Valentin hits for the cycle during the Red Sox' 7–4 win over Chicago to become the first player in history to both hit for the cycle and turn an unassisted triple play in a career.

1998 Atlanta's Bobby Cox becomes the 19th manager in ML history to collect 1,000 wins as the Braves defeat the Baltimore Orioles, 10–5, in an interleague contest.

1999 Chicago DH Frank Thomas drives in three runs, including the 1,000th of his career, to lead the White Sox to a 4–3 interleague win over Pittsburgh.

7

1884 Providence Grays RHP Charlie Sweeney strikes out 19 Boston Beaneaters batters to set an NL record.

1892 Cleveland Spiders utility player Jack Doyle collects the first pinch hit in ML history.

1906 The Chicago Cubs shell two New York Giants Hall of Fame RHPs — Joe McGinnity and Christy Mathewson — for 11 runs in the first inning en route to a 19–0 shellacking.

1907 The Boston Red Sox trade 3B Jimmy Collins to the Philadelphia A's for 3B John Knight.

1933 Herb Score b. Rosedale, NY.

1938 Cleveland RHP Johnny Allen walks off the mound in the second inning and doesn't return because home plate umpire Bill McGowan wants Allen's dangling sweatshirt sleeve to be cut off since it is distracting Boston Red Sox hitters. Allen is fined $250 by manager Ossie Vitt, and the shirt ends up in the Hall of Fame.

1945 George Mitterwald b. Berkeley, CA.

1947 Don Money b. Washington D.C.

1947 Thurman Munson b. Akron, OH.

1966 Heathcliff Slocumb b. Jamaica, NY.

1966 Trevor Wilson b. Torrence, CA.

1970 St. Louis C Ted Simmons hits his first of a career 248 ML home runs.

1981 Seattle 2B Julio Cruz handles a ML record 19 chances for his position in an 11-inning game.

1981 Houston trades RHP Joaquin Andujar to St. Louis for OF Tony Scott.

1982 Los Angeles 1B Steve Garvey plays in his 1,000th straight game, ranking him fifth all-time behind Lou Gehrig, Everett Scott, Billy Williams, and Joe Sewell.

1983 Philadelphia LHP Steve Carlton strikes out St. Louis OF Lonnie Smith in the third inning for his 3,522nd career strikeout to overtake RHP Nolan Ryan for the all-time record. The Phillies lose, however, 2–1.

1989 Toronto C Ernie Whitt has three hits and drives in three runs as the Blue Jays beat the Milwaukee Brewers, 4–2, in the first game in ML history played both indoors and outdoors on the same day. With dark clouds and thunder in the distance threatening rain, the Sky-Dome's $100 million retractable roof begins closing in the fifth inning. The closing operation begins at 8:48 P.M. and ends at 9:22 P.M., too late to prevent a brief stoppage in play.

1994 Oakland OF Rickey Henderson steals his 1,100th base.

1998 Atlanta RHP Greg Maddux ends Baltimore's 128-game scoring streak by blanking the Orioles in interleague play, 9–0. Prior to the contest, Baltimore retires former 1B Eddie Murray's uniform number 33, making it just the fifth jersey enshrined after those of Earl Weaver (4), Brooks Robinson (5), Frank Robinson (20), and Jim Palmer (22).

1998 Cleveland RHP Dave Burba hits a two-run home run — the first by an Indians pitcher in 26 years — in an 8–1 interleague win over Cincinnati.

1998 Chicago RF Sammy Sosa and LF Jose Hernandez each hit three-run homers and have five RBIs apiece in leading the Cubs to their ninth straight win, a 13–7 victory over the cross town White Sox. The Cubs complete their third consecutive three-game series sweep for the first time since September 1938.

8

1911 Van Mungo b. Pageland, SC.

1923 In the third inning against the Philadelphia A's, St. Louis Browns 3B Homer Ezzell reaches base but then calls time to use the bathroom. Manager Connie Mack permits the Browns to use courtesy runner Pat Collins while Ezzell temporarily leaves the field. Later in the game, Collins pinch-hits, making him the only ML player to both pinch-run and pinch-hit in the same game.

1925 Del Ennis b. Philadelphia, PA.

1926 New York Yankees RF Babe Ruth homers over the right field roof of Detroit's Tiger Stadium. The ball rolls down Plum street and comes to rest about 850 feet from home plate.

1940 Cincinnati OF Harry Craft connects for a home run, triple, double, and two singles in seven at-bats to lead a 27-hit attack as the Reds pound the Dodgers, 23–2 at Brooklyn.

1944 Mark Belanger b. Pittsfield, MA.

1950 The Boston Red Sox collect 28 hits to hammer the St. Louis Browns, 29–4, at Fenway Park and set ML records: most runs scored by one team; most long hits in a game, 17 (nine doubles, one triple, and seven homers); most total bases, 60; most extra bases on long hits, 32; most runs for two games, 49; most hits in two games, 51.

1961 In the seventh inning against Cincinnati, the Milwaukee Braves' Eddie Mathews, Hank Aaron, Joe Adcock, and Frank Thomas hit a major league record four consecutive home runs.

1961 Kevin Gross b. Downey, CA.

1965 Major League Baseball institutes a free agent summer draft with Arizona State OF Rick Monday becoming the inaugural selection to the Kansas City A's, who'll sign him for $104,000.

1968 Los Angeles RHP Don Drysdale has his scoreless inning streak end at 58⅔ as Philadelphia OF Howie Bedell's sacrifice fly scores Tony Taylor. It would be Bedell's only RBI of the season. The Dodgers beat the Phillies, however, 5–3.

1969 The Chicago White Sox trade RHP Bob Locker to the Seattle Pilots for RHP Gary Bell.

1969 The New York Yankees retire number 7 on Mickey Mantle Day. Nearly 60,000 fans come to Yankee Stadium to see Mantle and watch New York sweep a doubleheader from the Chicago White Sox, 3–1 and 11–2.

1977 California RHP Nolan Ryan strikes out 19 Toronto batters, reaching that single game mark for an ML record fourth time in his career.

1992 New York Yankees LHP Steve Howe is placed on baseball's disqualified list by Commissioner Fay Vincent after a seventh incident involving illegal drugs.

1995 Montreal trades RHP Reid Cornelius to the New York Mets for 1B David Segui.

1995 Cincinnati trades LHP John Courtright to Minnesota for 1B David McCarty.

1997 Seattle LHP Randy Johnson carries a no-hitter into the eighth inning and records 15 strikeouts as the Mariners blank Detroit, 2–0. The Seattle ace strikes out at least 10 batters for the 74th time in his career, tying him with LHP Sam McDowell for fourth place on the career list.

1998 Chicago RF Sammy Sosa ties a team record by homering in his fifth straight game and the Cubs extend their winning streak to 10 games by beating Minnesota, 8–1.

1998 Florida 3B Todd Zeile singles home the winning run in the bottom of the 17th inning as the Marlins beat Toronto, 4–3. The game is the longest in the Marlins' six-year history and the longest in interleague play. It also matches the longest in Toronto's 22-year history.

1999 St. Louis 1B Mark McGwire hits his 18th home run of the season and 475th of his career, tying him with Stan Musial and Willie Stargell for 17th place all-time, during the Cardinals' 11–10 loss to Kansas City.

9

1901 The New York Giants set an ML record with 31 hits against Cincinnati during a 25–13 win. Giants OF Kip Selbach goes 6-for-7 with two doubles and four singles, and scores four runs.

1906 The Boston Beaneaters beat St. Louis, 6–3, snapping a 19-game losing streak. By season's end, Boston will have four 20-game losers and finish 49–102, 66½ games behind NL champion Chicago, which finishes 116–36.

1908 In the fifth inning against the Boston Red Sox, the Cleveland Naps set an ML record with all nine batters in the order getting a hit and scoring a run.

1914 Pittsburgh SS Honus Wagner becomes the first 20th century player to collect 3,000 hits. Chicago Cubs 1B Cap Anson first reached the milestone in 1897.

1931 Bill Virdon b. Hazel Park, MI.

1932 The St. Louis Browns trade RHP Dick Coffman to Washington for LHP Carl Fischer.

1946 New York Giants manager Mel Ott is the first skipper to be ejected twice in the same day as the Pittsburgh Pirates sweep a doubleheader, 2–1 and 5–1.

1951 Dave Parker b. Cincinnati, OH.

1961 Tom Edens b. Ontario, OR.

1963 Playing the first Sunday night game in ML history, the Houston Colt 45s hand the San Francisco Giants their seventh straight loss, 3–0 in Houston. Permission is granted to play at night due to extreme heat.

1966 The Minnesota Twins explode in the seventh inning against the Kansas City A's as Rich Rollins and Zoilo Versalles start the assault with home runs. After two outs, Tony Oliva, Don Mincher, and Harmon Killebrew also connect. The five home runs in the inning ties the ML mark, as the Twins win, 9–4.

1981 A day after being selected in the third round by the San Diego Padres, OF Tony Gwynn is drafted by the NBA San Diego Clippers in the 10th round. The San Diego State product chooses baseball.

1984 Five days after being selected by the Atlanta Braves in the second round, LHP Tom Glavine is drafted by the NHL Los Angeles Kings in the fourth round, 69th pick overall.

1986 Chicago White Sox RHP Tom Seaver (306 wins) and California Angels RHP Don Sutton (298 wins) become the highest composite win total (604) to face each other since Washington Senators RHP Walter Johnson (406) faced Chicago White RHP Red Faber (197) in 1926 (603). Sutton beats the White Sox, 3–0.

1990 Los Angeles 1B Eddie Murray hits home runs from both sides of the plate in a game for the 10th time, tying Mickey Mantle's major league record.

Murray will finish his career with a record 11 times accomplishing the feat.

1990 Milwaukee trades OF Glenn Braggs and 2B Billy Bates to Cincinnati for RHP Ron Robinson and RHP Bob Sebra.

1992 The New York Mets trade RHP Tim Burke to the New York Yankees for LHP Lee Guetterman.

1999 Pittsburgh CF Brant Brown goes 5-for-5 with five RBIs and hits a home run over the right field roof at Tiger Stadium to lead the Pirates to a 15–3 interleague win over Detroit.

1999 Kansas City 3B Joe Randa goes 5-for-5 and scores four runs to lead the Royals to a 17–13 interleague win over St. Louis.

10

1890 Pittsburgh RHP Billy Gumbert becomes the first NL player to hit a home run in his first at-bat.

1892 Baltimore Orioles C Wilbert Robinson becomes the first ML player to collect seven hits in a nine inning game.

1907 The Philadelphia Phillies trade LHP Johnny Lush to the St. Louis Cardinals for RHP Charlie Brown.

1921 New York Yankees RF Babe Ruth becomes baseball's all-time home run leader by hitting his 120th against Cleveland RHP Jim Bagby Sr. The Indians win, however, 8–6.

1938 Boston Red Sox LHP Bill Lefebvre becomes the first AL pitcher to hit a home run in his first at-bat. It's the only home run of Lefebvre's four-year career.

1944 At 15 years, 10 months, and 11 days, Cincinnati LHP Joe Nuxhall becomes the youngest ever to appear in an ML game. In ⅔ of an inning, St. Louis lights him up for five runs on two hits and five walks en route to an 18–0

wipeout. Nuxhall won't appear in the major leagues again for eight years, but will finish with a 16-year career.

1959 Cleveland OF Rocky Colavito becomes only the third player in ML history to hit four consecutive home runs, during an 11–8 Indians win at Baltimore.

1961 The Chicago White Sox trade OF Wes Covington, RHP Bob Shaw, RHP Gerry Staley, and OF Stan Johnson to the Kansas City A's for RHP Don Larsen, RHP Ray Herbert, 3B Andy Carey, and OF Al Pilarcik.

1966 Cleveland RHP Sonny Siebert no-hits Washington, 2–0.

1972 Atlanta LF Hank Aaron hits his 14th career grand slam home run, tying Gil Hodges' NL record, and helping the Braves to a 15–3 romp over Philadelphia. Aaron's blast also puts him ahead of Willie Mays into second place on the career list with 649 round-trippers.

1973 Pokey Reese b. Columbia, SC.

1974 Philadelphia 3B Mike Schmidt hits a roof speaker in the Houston Astrodome against LHP Claude Osteen and is credited with a double in what would've been an easy 400 foot home run otherwise. The speaker is 117 feet off the floor and 329 feet from home plate when struck by the ball, which was still rising.

1978 The Chicago Cubs trade RHP Ron Davis to the New York Yankees for LHP Ken Holtzman.

1981 Philadelphia 1B Pete Rose singles in the first inning against Houston RHP Nolan Ryan for his 3,630th career hit, tying Stan Musial's NL record. The Phillies beat the Astros, 5–4, before more than 57,000 at Veteran's Stadium.

1986 Former Yale University President A. Bartlett Giamatti is named NL president.

1995 Baltimore 3B Jeff Manto becomes the 24th ML player to homer in four consecutive at-bats when he connects in the second inning of a 6–2 win over California. Manto had two homers June 9th, and homered in his last at-bat in the previous game. All told, Manto socked five home runs in six at-bats in the three games.

1997 Florida RHP Kevin Brown carries a perfect game into the eighth inning, then settles for a 9–0 no-hitter against the Giants in San Francisco.

1998 St. Louis 1B Mark McGwire becomes the second fastest player in ML history to 30 home runs, reaching the mark in his 64th game, an 11-inning, 10–8 loss to the Chicago White Sox. In 1928, Babe Ruth hit his 30th homer in the New York Yankees' 63rd game. White Sox 3B Robin Ventura hits a pair of homers including the one out, two-run game winner in the 11th inning.

1999 San Diego RHP Trevor Hoffman earns his 12th save of the season and 200th in his career as the Padres edge Oakland, 2–1.

1999 Colorado and Seattle combine for 10 home runs in a 16–11 rain-delayed Rockies win at Coors Field in Denver.

11

1879 Roger Bresnahan b. Toledo, OH.

1903 Ernie Nevers b. Willow River, MN.

1904 Chicago Cubs RHP Bob Wicker no-hits the New York Giants for nine innings, yields a hit in the 10th, but still wins, 1–0.

1915 New York Yankees RHP Ray Caldwell, a left-handed hitter, becomes the first ML player with pinch-hit home runs in consecutive games after connecting today and yesterday.

1926 Philadelphia 1B Russ Wright-

stone hits a home run, a triple, and two doubles in six at-bats as the Phillies edge Pittsburgh, 13–11.

1929 Frank Thomas (OF) b. Pittsburgh, PA.

1934 The Chicago Cubs trade 1B Dolf Camilli to the Philadelphia Phillies for 1B Don Hurst.

1937 The Boston Red Sox trade brothers Rick Ferrell (C) and Wes Ferrell (RHP) to Washington for OF Ben Chapman and RHP Bobo Newsom.

1938 Cincinnati LHP Johnny Vander Meer no-hits the Boston Braves, 3–0, for the first of back-to-back no-hitters in successive starts.

1948 Dave Cash b. Utica, NY.

1964 In a three-team deal, the Los Angeles Angels trade INF Frank Kostro to Minnesota and INF Billy Moran to Cleveland. Cleveland sends INF Jerry Kindall to Minnesota, and the Twins send 1B Vic Power and OF Lenny Green to Los Angeles.

1966 Chicago 1B Ernie Banks ties a modern day record hitting three triples, as the Cubs beat Houston, 8–2, at the Astrodome. Teammate Adolfo Phillips strikes out four straight times to tie an all-time mark of eight whiffs in two consecutive games.

1967 The Chicago Cubs hit seven homers and the New York Mets hit four during the second game of a doubleheader, tying the ML mark of 11 set by the New York Yankees (6) and the Detroit Tigers (5) in 1950.

1968 Atlanta trades RHPs Clay Carroll and Tony Cloninger, and SS Woody Woodward to Cincinnati for RHP Milt Pappas, LHP Ted Davidson, and INF Bob Johnson.

1969 Los Angeles trades OF Ron Fairly and INF Paul Popovich to Montreal for SS Maury Wills and OF Manny Mota. The Expos then trade Popovich to the Chicago Cubs for OF Adolfo Phillips and RHP Jack Lamabe.

1970 Milwaukee trades OF Steve Hovley to Oakland for LHP Al Downing and 1B Tito Francona.

1971 St. Louis trades OF Leron Lee and LHP Fred Norman to San Diego for RHP Al Santorini.

1985 Philadelphia OF Von Hayes becomes the 21st player in ML history to hit two home runs in one inning. Hayes sparks a nine-run first inning as the Phillies pound the New York Mets, 26–7.

1990 Texas RHP Nolan Ryan, age 43, hurls a record sixth no-hitter, 5–0 at Oakland. Ryan becomes the oldest pitcher to throw a no-hitter and the only pitcher to do it in three different decades and with three different teams (Angels, Astros, Rangers).

1992 Going against their long-standing policy of opposing investors from outside of the United States and Canada, Major League Baseball owners approve the sale of the Seattle Mariners to a group headed by Nintendo Company Limited of Japan.

1995 Montreal OF Rondell White collects six hits in hitting for the cycle and scores five runs in a 13–inning, 10–8 win over San Francisco.

1995 Oakland 1B Mark McGwire hits three solo home runs against Boston LHP Zane Smith in an 8–1 A's win to tie the ML record with five homers in consecutive games.

1995 California RHP Lee Smith sets an ML record with a save in his 16th consecutive appearance, pitching a scoreless ninth to preserve the Angels' 5–4 win over Baltimore.

1997 Toronto RHP Roger Clemens has his 11-game season opening win streak end as Seattle defeats him, 5–1 in Toronto.

1999 Oakland SS Miguel Tejeda hits three home runs and drives in five runs in leading the A's to a 12–6 win over Los Angeles.

1999 Kansas City 3B Joe Randa goes 3-for-3 with two home runs, drives in four runs, and sets a Royals record by getting hits in nine consecutive at bats, in a 10–3 win over Pittsburgh.

1999 Cleveland RHP Dwight Gooden hits his eighth career home run, most by any active pitcher, and 1B Richie Sexson hits a solo homer in the ninth to help the Indians to an 8–6 interleague win over Cincinnati.

12

1880 Worcester LHP Lee Richmond hurls the first perfect game in NL history, 1–0 over Cleveland.

1922 St. Louis LHP Hub Pruett strikes out Babe Ruth three consecutive times as the Browns top the New York Yankees, 7–1.

1922 The St. Louis Cardinals collect a record-tying 10 hits in a row in the sixth inning and outslug the Philadelphia Phillies, 14–8.

1928 New York 1B Lou Gehrig collects two triples and two home runs in a 15–5 win over the Chicago White Sox.

1932 The Boston Red Sox trade OF Earl Webb to Detroit for 1B Dale Alexander and OF Roy Johnson. Webb, who set an ML record with 67 doubles in 1931 while batting .333, would be out of baseball by the end of the 1933 season with his production dropping off sharply.

1939 Baseball's Hall of Fame opens in Cooperstown, NY, with 10 of the first 12 inductees present: Honus Wagner, Grover Cleveland Alexander, Tris Speaker, Napoleon Lajoie, George Sisler, Walter Johnson, Eddie Collins, Babe Ruth, Connie Mack, Cy Young, and Ty

Cobb. Two inductees — Christy Mathewson and Wee Willie Keeler — had
passed away prior to enshrinement.

1954 Milwaukee Braves RHP Jim
Wilson no-hits the Philadelphia Phillies,
2–0.

1959 San Francisco LHP Mike
McCormick throws a five-inning no-hitter against Philadelphia which is called
by rain.

1970 Damon Buford b. Baltimore,
MD.

1970 Pittsburgh RHP Dock Ellis no-
hits San Diego, 2–0, in the first game of
a doubleheader. Ellis, who walks eight
batters, later admits that he took LSD
prior to the game.

1971 Ryan Klesko b. Westminster,
CA.

1971 Philadelphia trades 2B Tony
Taylor to Detroit for pitchers Carl
Cavanaugh and Mike Fremuth.

1972 San Diego trades C Bob Barton
to Cincinnati for C Pat Corrales.

1972 San Diego trades LHP Mike
Kilkenny to Cleveland for INF Fred
Stanley.

1981 Major League baseball begins its
first major strike, 50 days worth, wiping
out 714 games before resuming in
August. The players are protesting an
attempt by owners to undercut free
agency by demanding compensation in
either cash or a comparable player for
every experienced player who becomes a
free agent.

1981 The Chicago Cubs trade RHP
Rick Reuschel to the New York Yankees
for RHPs Doug Bird and Mike Griffin.

1990 Baltimore SS Cal Ripken Jr.
moves into second place on the all-time
ironman list with his 1,308th straight
game, a 4–3 win over Milwaukee.

1996 Major League Baseball suspends
Cincinnati Reds owner Marge Schott
thru the 1998 season after her racist

comments regarding Adolf Hitler. It's
her second suspension in four years for
similiar conduct.

1997 Major league baseball begins
interleague play for the first time in history with four games: San Francisco 4,
Texas 3; Seattle 12, Colorado 11; Oakland 5, Los Angeles 4; and Anaheim 8,
San Diego 4. San Francisco leadoff hitter
Darryl Hamilton singles in the first
inning against Darren Oliver for the first
interleague hit. San Francisco OF Stan
Javier later hits the first interleague home
run.

1998 San Diego RF Ruben Rivera hits
a three-run home run to cap a seven-run
eighth inning as the Padres beat San
Francisco, 10–3, in front of the largest
crowd ever in San Diego 60,789.

1999 Toronto trades LHP Dan Plesac
to Arizona for SS Tony Batista and RHP
John Frascatore.

13

1905 New York RHP Christy Mathewson hurls his second career no-hitter,
but the Giants need a ninth inning run
against Chicago RHP Mordecai Brown
to edge the Cubs, 1–0.

1910 Boston Braves RHP Cliff Curtis
takes the first of what would be a record
23 straight losses. The Braves would
finish last in the NL, 50½ games behind
the Chicago Cubs with a 53–100 record
and would have three 20-game losers on
their staff. Curtis won't win again until
May 22, 1911.

1912 New York Giants RHP Christy
Mathewson earns his 300th career victory and 20th win of the season by
defeating the Chicago Cubs, 3–2.

1922 Mel Parnell b. New Orleans, LA.

1924 The New York Yankees are
awarded a 9–0 forfeit win against the

Tigers when a ninth inning players' fight escalates into a full-scale fan riot at Detroit's Navin Field.

1925 Cleveland has a commanding 15–3 lead over Philadelphia after seven innings, but the A's tally 14 times over the final two frames for a 17–15 win. The Indians record the biggest blown lead ever.

1930 The St. Louis Browns trade OF Heinie Manush and RHP General Crowder to Washington for OF Goose Goslin.

1937 In the third game of a three-game series between the New York Yankees and the St. Louis Browns, Joe DiMaggio has three at-bats, gets three hits, scores three runs, and has three RBIs. Defensively, DiMaggio has three putouts.

1948 On the 25th anniversary date of Yankee Stadium, Babe Ruth's uniform number 3 is retired in a ceremony that marks the Bambino's final appearance at Yankee Stadium. He'll pass away 64 days later.

1957 Cleveland trades OF Jim Busby to Baltimore for OF Dick Williams.

1960 Cleveland trades C Russ Nixon and OF Carroll Hardy to Boston for LHP Ted Bowsfield and OF Marty Keough.

1966 The Kansas City A's trade OF Jose Tartabull, RHP Roland Shelton, and RHP John Wyatt to Boston for RHP Ken Sanders, OF Jim Gosger, and LHP Giudo Grilli.

1966 The Chicago White Sox trade RHP Eddie Fisher and OF Ken Faulkner to Baltimore for 2B Jerry Adair and OF John Riddle.

1969 San Diego trades OF Tony Gonzalez to Atlanta for C Walt Hriniak, INF Van Kelly, and OF Andy Finley.

1970 Houston trades OF Jim Beauchamp and INF Leon McFadden to St. Louis for RHP George Culver.

1973 Cincinnati trades OF Gene Locklear to San Diego for LHP Fred Norman.

1975 St. Louis trades SS Eddie Brinkman to Texas for OF Willie Davis.

1975 Cleveland trades RHP Gaylord Perry to Texas for RHP Jim Bibby, LHP Rick Waits, and RHP Jackie Brown.

1984 The Chicago Cubs trade OFs Joe Carter and Mel Hall, and RHP Don Schulze to Cleveland for RHPs Rick Sutcliffe and George Frazier, and C Ron Hassey.

1994 Texas DH Jose Canseco blasts three home runs and has a career high eight RBIs in a 17–9 win over Seattle. Canseco also has two singles to set a Rangers team record with 14 total bases.

1994 New York 1B Don Mattingly plays in his 1,469th game at first base, moving past Wally Pipp into second place in Yankees history, behind Hall of Famer Lou Gehrig.

1999 Baltimore 3B Cal Ripken, Jr., has a career high six hits, including two home runs as the Orioles explode for the most runs scored in franchise history, 22–1 over Atlanta.

1999 Houston manager Larry Dierker collapses in the dugout with a grand mal seizure in the eighth inning of the Astros game with San Diego. The game is suspended with Houston leading, 4–1, to be resumed at a later date. Dierker is scheduled for brain surgery two days later.

14

1889 Indianapolis Hoosiers Paul Hines and Jerry Denny become the first NL pair to hit back-to-back home runs twice in the same game.

1926 Don Newcombe b. Madison, NJ.

1952 Boston Braves LHP Warren

Spahn strikes out 18 Cubs in a 3–1, 15-inning loss to Chicago.

1956 The St. Louis Cardinals trade OF Jackie Brandt, 2B Red Schoendienst, SS Bobby Stephenson, LHP Dick Littlefield and C Bill Sarni to the New York Giants for SS Alvin Dark, C Ray Katt, LHP Don Liddle, and OF Whitey Lockman.

1957 Greg Brock b. McMinnville, OR.

1963 New York OF Duke Snider hits his 400th career home run to highlight a 10–3 Mets win over Cincinnati.

1965 Cincinnati RHP Jim Maloney no-hits the New York Mets for 10 innings, striking out 18 batters, but yields two hits in the 11th to lose, 1–0. Mets OF Johnny Lewis homers for the game's only run. The no-hitter is the first of three in Maloney's career.

1966 Boston trades RHP Earl Wilson and OF Joe Christopher to Detroit for OF Don Demeter and RHP Julio Navarro.

1969 Oakland RF Reggie Jackson collects 10 RBIs against Boston with two home runs, a double, and two singles. The A's bury the Red Sox in Fenway Park, 21–7.

1969 Detroit trades OF Ron Woods to the New York Yankees for OF Tom Tresh.

1972 Montreal trades C John Bateman to Philadelphia for C Tim McCarver.

1974 California RHP Nolan Ryan strikes out 19 Boston Red Sox batters, a new high for an extra inning game as the Angels win, 4–3, in 15 innings. Ryan hurls 12 innings and strikes out Cecil Cooper six times. Boston RHP Luis Tiant goes all 15 innings in taking the loss.

1975 Milwaukee trades OF Johnny Briggs to Minnesota for OF Bobby Darwin.

1978 Cincinnati 3B Pete Rose has two hits in a 3–1 win over Chicago to begin his 44-game hitting streak.

1979 Cleveland trades OF Paul Dade to San Diego for 1B Mike Hargrove.

1990 The NL announces that it will expand from 12 to 14 teams for the 1993 season. The two new franchises become the Colorado Rockies and Florida Marlins.

1991 Cleveland trades INF/OF Tim Costo to Cincinnati for 1B Reggie Jefferson.

1995 San Francisco 3B Mike Benjamin goes 6-for-7, including the game winning hit in the 15th inning as Giants top Chicago, 4–3. The performance gives Benjamin a record 14 hits in three consecutive games. His six hits also ties a Giants team record last accomplished by Jesus Alou in 1964.

1995 Los Angeles RHP Hideo Nomo strikes out 16 Pittsburgh batters during the Dodgers 8–5 win.

1998 New York ties the ML record by winning or splitting its 24th straight series with a 4–2 win over Cleveland. The Yankees tie the 1912 Boston Red Sox and 1970 Cincinnati Reds for most consecutive non-losing series.

15

1925 Trailing Cleveland, 15–4, after 7½ innings, the Philadelphia A's erupt for 13 runs in the bottom of the eighth inning to win, 17–15.

1925 Gene Baker b. Davenport, IA.

1937 Boston Red Sox OF Ben Chapman records seven straight outs on consecutive fly balls hit to him.

1938 Billy Williams b. Whistler, AL.

1938 Cincinnati LHP Johnny Vander Meer pitches his second consecutive no-hitter, 6–0 over the Dodgers, spoiling the first night game at Brooklyn's Ebbets Field. Vander Meer's feat comes only four days after he no-hits the Boston Braves, 3–0. His hitless innings streak reaches a record 21⅔.

1942 Bruce Dal Canton b. California, PA.

1946 Ken Henderson b. Carroll, IA.

1948 Detroit becomes the final AL team to host a night game, defeating the Philadelphia A's, 4–1 at Briggs Stadium.

1949 Dusty Baker b. Riverside, CA.

1949 Philadelphia Phillies 1B Eddie Waitkus is shot in the chest by Ruth Ann Steinhagen in her room at the Edgewater Beach Hotel in Chicago, ending his season after 54 games. He'll return to the World Series-bound Phillies in 1950 and play six more years.

1949 The Chicago Cubs trade OFs Peanuts Lowrey and Harry Walker to Cincinnati for OFs Hank Sauer and Frankie Baumholtz.

1952 St. Louis rallies from a 11–0 deficit to beat the New York Giants, 14–12, for the best rally in NL history.

1956 Lance Parrish b. McKeesport, PA.

1957 St. Louis RHP Von McDaniel, age 18, throws a two-hit, 2–0 shutout against the Brooklyn Dodgers.

1957 The Milwaukee Braves trade RHP Ray Crone, OF Bobby Thomson, and 2B Danny O'Connell to the New York Giants for 2B Red Schoendienst.

1957 The New York Yankees trade 2B Billy Martin, OF Woody Held, RHP Ralph Terry, and OF Bob Martyn to Kansas City for 1B Harry Simpson, OF Jim Pisoni, and RHP Ryne Duren.

1957 Brett Butler b. Los Angeles, CA.

1958 The Chicago White Sox trade OF Tito Francona and RHP Bill Fischer to Detroit for RHP Bob Shaw and INF Ray Boone.

1958 Kansas City trades OF Woody Held and 1B Vic Power to Cleveland for OF Roger Maris, 1B Preston Ward, and RHP Dick Tomanek.

1958 Wade Boggs b. Omaha, NE.

1960 Cincinnati trades OFs Tony Gonzalez and Lee Walls to Philadelphia for OFs Wally Post and Harry Anderson, and 1B Fred Hopke.

1961 Pittsburgh trades OF Gino Cimoli to Milwaukee for SS Johnny Logan.

1963 Milwaukee trades RHP Lew Burdette to St. Louis for C Gene Oliver and RHP Bob Sadowski.

1963 San Francisco RHP Juan Marichal becomes the first Latin American to throw a no-hitter, 1–0 over Houston, at Candlestick Park.

1964 The Chicago Cubs trade OF Lou Brock, LHP Jack Spring, and RHP Paul Toth to St. Louis for LHP Bobby Shantz, RHP Ernie Broglio and OF Doug Clemens.

1964 Cleveland trades RHP Jim "Mudcat" Grant to Minnesota for RHP Lee Stange and INF George Banks.

1965 St. Louis trades LHP Mike Cuellar and RHP Ron Taylor to Houston for LHP Hal Woodeshick and RHP Chuck Taylor.

1967 Baltimore trades INF-OF Woody Held to California for LHP Marcelino Lopez; it is the third time in his career that Held is traded on June 15th.

1967 Houston trades RHP Claude Raymond to Atlanta for LHP Wade Blasingame.

1967 The Chicago White Sox trade OF Ed Stroud to Washington for OF Jim King.

1968 Cleveland trades OF Vic Davalillo to California for OF Jimmie Hall.

1969 Montreal trades 1B Donn Clendenon to the New York Mets for RHP

Steve Renko, P Jay Carden, P Dave Colon, and INF Kevin Collins.

1970 The Chicago White Sox trade OF Buddy Bradford and RHP Tommie Sisk to Cleveland for RHP Bob Miller and LHP Barry Moore.

1970 Baltimore trades SS Bobby Floyd to the Kansas City Royals for RHP Moe Drabowsky.

1970 Baltimore trades OF Dave May to Milwaukee for RHP Dick Baney and RHP Buzz Stephen.

1972 Philadelphia trades LHP Joe Hoerner to Atlanta for RHP Jim Nash and RHP Gary Neibauer.

1972 Tony Clark b. Newton, KS.

1972 Andy Petitte b. Baton Rouge, LA.

1976 Oakland A's owner Charlie Finley sells LF Joe Rudi and RHP Rollie Fingers to the Boston Red Sox, and LHP Vida Blue to the New York Yankees in seperate deals which are subsequently voided by Commissioner Bowie Kuhn.

1976 In a 10-player trade, the New York Yankees send C Rick Dempsey, LHP Rudy May, LHP Tippy Martinez, RHP Dave Pagan, and LHP Scott McGregor to the Baltimore Orioles for LHP Ken Holtzman, RHP Doyle Alexander, LHP Grant Jackson, C Ellrod Hendricks, and LHP Jimmy Freeman.

1976 A deluge of rain of up to 10 inches in some spots washes out an indoor game between Pittsburgh and Houston in the Astrodome. Players are inside taking batting practice, but no others can get thru the storm.

1977 St. Louis trades LHP Doug Capilla to Cincinnati for RHP Rawley Eastwick.

1977 Houston trades OF Willie Crawford to Oakland for 1B Denny Walling.

1978 The Chicago Cubs trade OF Hector Cruz to San Francisco for RHP Lynn McGlothen.

1984 Atlanta trades LHP Ken Dayley and 1B Mike Jorgensen to St. Louis for 3B Ken Oberkfell.

1995 Chicago Cubs RHP Frank Castillo retires the firt 19 batters faced, but loses a perfect game against San Francisco on a Mike Benjamin base hit. Castillo is lifted in the ninth inning of the 3–1 win.

16

1916 Boston Braves RHP Tom Hughes throws his second career no-hitter, 2–0 over Pittsburgh.

1938 Boston 1B Jimmy Foxx walks an ML record six consecutive times against the St. Louis Browns, during the Red Sox' 12–8 win.

1952 Ron LeFlore b. Detroit, MI.

1953 The St. Louis Browns beat New York, 3–1, to end the Yankees' 18-game winning streak, and also snap a 14-game losing streak of their own.

1957 Chicago RHP Dixie Howell hits two home runs during the 3⅔ innings he hurls in relief to lead the White Sox to a 8–6 win over the Washington Senators in the second game of a doubleheader.

1962 Wally Joyner b. Atlanta, GA.

1963 The New York Mets begin their modern ML record of 22 consecutive losses on the road. The streak runs through July 28, 1963.

1969 Kevin Young b. Alpena, MI.

1971 Chris Gomez b. Los Angeles, CA.

1977 Kerry Wood b. Irving, TX.

1978 After three ninth inning near misses in his 12-year career, Cincinnati RHP Tom Seaver hurls a no-hitter against the St. Louis Cardinals, winning 4–0.

1986 Baltimore trades RHP Dennis Martinez to Montreal for INF Rene Gonzales.

1991 Philadelphia rookie RHP Andy Ashby strikes out the side in the fourth inning against Cincinnati on just nine pitches. Ashby becomes only the 12th NL pitcher and the first Phillies pitcher to accomplish the feat.

1991 Atlanta CF Otis Nixon ties an ML record with six stolen bases against Montreal. Philadelphia A's 2B Eddie Collins set the mark in 1912.

1994 Boston trades C Dave Valle to Milwaukee for OF Tom Brunansky.

1994 St. Louis ties a NL record turning seven double plays in a 10-inning loss to Pittsburgh.

1995 Florida OF Andre Dawson hits his 400th career NL home run, and his 429th overall, against Philadelphia LHP David West during a 2–1 Marlins win.

1996 Longtime radio announcer Mel Allen, voted into the Hall of Fame in 1978, passes away at age 83. The voice of the New York Yankees and a broadcaster for 58 years, Allen was the only announcer to call baseball games in seven decades.

1998 Atlanta LHP Denny Neagle throws a four-hit shutout as the Braves blank Florida, 7–0, to make manager Bobby Cox the winningest manager in franchise history with his 1,005th win. Cox passes Frank Selee, who managed the Braves from 1890–1901.

1998 Baltimore rookie RHP Sidney Ponson and LHP Arthur Rhodes combine on a two-hitter as the Orioles beat New York, 2–0, ending the Yankees' ML record streak of non-losing series at 24. By winning the first two games of the three-game series, Baltimore assures the Yankees of not splitting or winning a series for the first time since opening the season with two straight losses in Anaheim.

1999 Playing in his 2,000th career game, Toronto 3B Tony Fernandez has two hits to raise his batting average to a major league–leading .404 during the Blue Jays' 3–2 win over Anaheim.

17

1880 Providence RHP Monte Ward hurls the second perfect game in NL history, 5–0 over Buffalo.

1885 Brooklyn Dodgers LHP John Francis "Phenomenal" Smith, arrogant and disliked by his teammates, loses, 18–5, in his debut against the St. Louis Cardinals. Smith's teammates commit 20 errors to ensure his downfall. The players are each fined $500 for the incident, and Smith is shortly released.

1910 Joe Bowman b. Argentine, KS.

1915 Chicago Cubs RHP George "Zip" Zabel enters the game against Brooklyn with two outs in the first inning. The game is later tied, and Zabel blanks the Dodgers into the 19th inning when the Cubs win, 4–3. Zabel finishes with the longest relief job in history, 18⅓ innings of shutout ball.

1941 New York Yankee CF Joe DiMaggio hits a routine infield grounder, but it takes a bad hop and bounces off the shoulder of Chicago White Sox SS Luke Appling. The ball is ruled a hit and extends DiMaggio's hitting streak to 30 games, en route to his record 56-game streak.

1943 The Philadelphia A's lead Boston, 4–2, when Red Sox manager Joe Cronin inserts himself into the lineup as a pinch-hitter with two runners on base. He connects for a three-run homer as Boston wins, 5–4. In the nightcap, Philadelphia again leads when Cronin again inserts himself into the lineup with two men on base. Again he hits a three-run homer, but this time the A's hang on to win, 8–7.

1948 Dave Concepcion b. Venezuela.

1960 Boston LF Ted Williams hits his 500th career home run, against Cleveland RHP Wynn Hawkins.

1961 Mickey Brantley b. Catskill, NY.

1962 Epitomizing the futility of the expansion New York Mets, 1B Marv Throneberry forgets to touch second base (and also misses first base) on an apparent triple.

1965 Manny Lee b. Dominican Republic.

1966 Shawn Abner b. Hamilton, OH.

1969 Detroit utility player Ike Brown becomes the last Negro League player to integrate to the major leagues. Brown was a member of the 1960 Kansas City Monarchs.

1971 Chicago SS Don Kessinger goes 6-for-6 with five singles and a double in a 7–6, 10-inning win over St. Louis.

1974 Boston Red Sox 1B Cecil Cooper strikes out an ML record–tying six times in a 15-inning game.

1978 New York Yankees LHP Ron Guidry strikes out 18 California Angels batters to set an AL record for left-handers. Guidry fans 15 in the first six innings as the Yankees win, 4–0.

1985 New York Yankees CF Rickey Henderson has his first career five-hit game.

1987 Kansas City Royals manager Dick Howser, age 51, dies of a brain tumor. Howser led the Royals to a World Series championship in 1985.

1993 Baseball owners vote 26–2 in favor of expanding the playoffs for the first time in 25 years, doubling the teams that qualify to eight starting in 1994.

1998 With 28,673 fans in attendance at Wrigley Field to see Chicago lose to Milwaukee, 6–5, the Cubs surpass the one million mark in home attendance.

The Cubs have reached the milestone every year since 1968 with the exception of the 1981 strike-shortened season.

1999 Atlanta RHP Kevin Millwood loses a perfect game in the seventh inning on a Craig Biggio single, but the Braves' relievers hold on to beat Houston, 8–5.

18

1911 Detroit rallies from a 13–1 deficit to beat Chicago, 16–15, for a record 12-run comeback.

1939 Lou Brock b. El Dorado, AR.

1947 Cincinnati RHP Ewell Blackwell no-hits Boston, 6–0.

1950 Cleveland scores 14 runs in the first inning for an AL record en route to trouncing the Philadelphia A's, 21–2.

1953 The Boston Red Sox send 23 men to bat in the seventh inning against Detroit and score 17 runs on 14 hits all records. Boston SS Gene Stephens collects three hits in the inning, C Sammy White scores three runs in the inning — more records — as the Red Sox trounces Detroit, 23–3.

1960 The New York Giants fire Bill Rigney and name Tom Sheehan as manager. At 66 years, two months, and 18 days, Sheehan becomes the oldest man to debut as manager of an ML team.

1961 Andres Galarraga b. Venezuela.

1966 Sandy Alomar, Jr. b. Puerto Rico.

1967 Houston RHP Don Wilson pitches the first of his two no-hitters, 2–0 over Atlanta. Wilson faces 30 batters and strikes out 15.

1975 Boston Red Sox rookie CF Fred Lynn belts three home runs, a triple and a single for 10 RBIs in a 15–1 massacre of Detroit.

1976 Commissioner Bowie Kuhn, acting "in the best interests of the game," vetoes three Charlie Finley player sales. Finley, the Oakland A's owner, tried to sell off LHP Vida Blue to the New York Yankees for $1.5 million, and LF Joe Rudi and RHP Rollie Fingers to the Boston Red Sox for $1 million each.

1986 California RHP Don Sutton becomes the 19th ML pitcher to win 300 games, allowing Texas only three hits in a 5–1 win. Sutton becomes the first 300-game winner needing more than 20 seasons to reach the milestone having been a 20-game winner only once (1976).

1989 The New York Mets trade CF Lenny Dykstra, RHP Roger McDowell, and RHP Tom Edens to Philadelphia for OF Juan Samuel.

1989 San Francisco trades LHP Terry Mulholland, LHP Dennis Cook, and 3B Charlie Hayes to Philadelphia for RHP Steve Bedrosian and INF Rick Parker.

1995 Detroit manager Sparky Anderson moves into third place on the all-time win list with his 2158th, a 10–8 win over Baltimore. Anderson trails only Connie Mack (3,731) and John McGraw (2,763).

1997 The New York Yankees win the first subway series in 40 years, beating the New York Mets, 3–2, at Yankees Stadium, in the third game of the interleague series.

1998 St. Louis 1B Mark McGwire sets an ML record with his 33rd home run thru June as the Cardinals beat Houston, 7–6. Seattle CF Ken Griffey, Jr., hit 32 homers thru June in 1994.

1998 Chicago CF Brant Brown hits three home runs as the Cubs bury Philadelphia, 12–5.

19

1846 In the earliest game of record under Cartwright rules, the New York

Knickerbockers defeat the New York Nine, 24–1, in four innings at Elysian Fields in Hoboken, NJ.

1884 Eddie Cicotte b. Detroit, MI.

1889 Washington OF William "Dummy" Hoy throws three Indiana Hoosier runners out at the plate, but the Senators still lose, 8–3. Hoy gets his nickname being both deaf and mute, forcing umpires to use hand signals to convey balls and strikes.

1903 Lou Gehrig b. New York, NY.

1927 Philadelphia Phillies RHP Jack Scott, age 35, becomes the oldest hurler to throw two complete games in one day.

1942 Boston Braves OF Paul Waner becomes baseball's seventh member of the 3,000-hit club with a single against Pittsburgh RHP Rip Sewell.

1949 Jerry Reuss b. St. Louis, MO.

1950 Jim Slaton b. Long Beach, CA.

1950 Duane Kuiper b. Racine, WI.

1952 Brooklyn RHP Carl Erskine hurls the first of his two career no-hitters, a 5–0 victory over the Chicago Cubs.

1954 Johnnie LeMaster b. Portsmouth, OH.

1961 New York Yankees RF Roger Maris connects for his 25th home run of the season against Kansas City LHP Jim Archer. Maris is seven games ahead of Babe Ruth's 60-home run pace of 1927.

1963 Detroit OF Gates Brown becomes the first AL black player to hit a home run in his first at-bat.

1967 St. Louis CF Curt Flood turns an unassisted double play.

1977 Boston hits five home runs in an 11–1 rout of the New York Yankees, giving the Red Sox a major league record 16 round-trippers in three games. The Red Sox hit six homers on the 17th, and five more on the 18th, all against the

Yankees. New York had no home runs in the series.

1994 Detroit ties an ML record, set by the 1941 Yankees, by hitting a home run in its 25th straight game, a 3–1 win over Toronto.

1994 Atlanta RHP John Smoltz becomes the 14th ML pitcher to allow four home runs in one inning. Cincinnati touches him for seven runs in the first inning of a 12–4 loss.

1999 Colorado 1B Todd Helton hits for the cycle in only four at-bats as the Rockies defeat Florida, 10–2.

1999 Toronto 3B Tony Fernandez has two RBI singles raising his major-league-leading average to .409 as the Blue Jays blank Kansas City, 7–0. Fernandez' second hit ties Julio Franco for most hits by a Dominican player with 2,177.

1999 Tampa 3B Wade Boggs collects his 1,000th career RBI as the Devil Rays edge Minnesota, 4–3.

20

1901 Chicago Cubs RHP John W. Taylor begins an incredible run of 188 straight complete games. He won't need relief until August 9, 1906; by that time he will have amassed 1,727 straight innings pitched.

1912 The New York Giants outslug the Boston Braves, 21–12, with both teams scoring a total of 17 runs in the ninth inning. The Giants score seven runs to take a 21–2 lead and the Braves finish the inning scoring 10 runs of their own.

1925 Pittsburgh OF Max Carey becomes the first switch-hitter to hit for the cycle.

1943 Andy Etchebarren b. Whittier, CA.

1951 Cleveland 2B Bobby Avila hits three home runs, a double and a single in a 14–8 pasting of the Red Sox in Boston.

1961 Gary Varsho b. Marshfield, WI.

1980 California SS Freddie Patek, one of baseball's smallest players at 5-foot-5, hits three home runs and a double to lead the Angels to a 20–2 romp over the Red Sox at Boston.

1982 Philadelphia 1B Pete Rose becomes the fifth ML player to appear in 3,000 games, and extends a personal consecutive games streak to 523 in a 3–1 loss to the Pirates in Pittsburgh.

1986 Multi-sport star Bo Jackson, the 1985 Heisman Trophy winner, shuns the NFL Tampa Bay Buccaneers by instead signing with the Kansas City Royals.

1992 Kelly Saunders becomes only the second woman to serve as public address announcer during an ML game when she fills in for Rex Barney at Baltimore.

1998 Chicago RF Sammy Sosa hits two home runs for the second straight day to set an ML with 16 homers in June, as the Cubs beat Philadelphia, 9–4. Babe Ruth (1930), Bob Johnson (1934), Roger Maris (1961), and Pedro Guerrero (1985) all hit 15 home runs in June. Sosa will hit four more homers before the month ends to set a new one month record of 20.

1999 Anaheim RHP Troy Percival sets a club record with his 127th career save during the Angels 4–2 win against the New York Yankees.

21

1866 Matt Kilroy b. Philadelphia, PA.

1901 Cincinnati RHP Harley Parker gives up 21 runs on 26 hits over eight innings during his only game of the season and final game of his four-year ML career.

1916 Boston Red Sox RHP Rube Foster no-hits the New York Yankees, 2–0.

1918 Ed Lopat b. New York, NY.

1938 Boston Red Sox 3B Pinky Higgins collects his 12th consecutive hit over a two-day, four-game stretch against Chicago and Detroit.

1941 Boston Red Sox LHP Lefty Grove finally loses at home, 13–9 to the St. Louis Browns, snapping a streak of 20 straight wins at Fenway Park.

1953 Charlie Moore b. Portsmouth, VA.

1956 In a rare double one-hitter, Chicago LHP Jack Harshman outduels Baltimore's RHPs Connie Johnson and George Zuverink, as the White Sox beat the Orioles, 1–0.

1956 Rick Sutcliffe b. Independence, MO.

1964 Philadelphia Phillies RHP Jim Bunning hurls only the second NL perfect game in 84 years by blanking the New York Mets, 6–0, on Father's Day. The feat also gives Bunning a no-hitter in each league as he earlier pitched one for Detroit in 1958. Phillies C Gus Triandos becomes the first receiver to handle no-hitters in both leagues as he handled RHP Hoyt Wilhelm's 1958 gem for Baltimore.

1969 Donovan Osborne b. Roseville, CA.

1970 Detroit SS Cesar Gutierrez, wearing uniform number 7, collects seven hits — six singles and double — in seven at-bats during a 12-inning, 9–8 win over Cleveland.

1973 Just sixteen days after being selected first in the amateur draft, San Diego OF Dave Winfield hits his first ML home run against Houston RHP Ken Forsch.

1989 Texas OF Sammy Sosa hits his first ML home run against Boston RHP Roger Clemens.

1989 Chicago C Carlton Fisk hits his 307th career home run as a catcher, eclipsing Yogi Berra's AL record in a 7–3 White Sox win over the New York Yankees.

1989 The New York Yankees trade OF Rickey Henderson to Oakland for OF Luis Polonia, RHP Eric Plunk, and LHP Greg Cadaret.

22

1889 The Louisville Colonels of the American Association drop their 26th straight game in a season where they will go thru four managers and finish with a 27–111 mark, 66½ games behind champion Brooklyn.

1903 Carl Hubbell b. Carthage, MO.

1925 Pittsburgh beats up the St. Louis Cardinals, 24–6, as Kiki Cuyler and Pie Traynor hit grand slam home runs and Max Carey collects two hits in each of the first and eighth innings.

1932 NL officials, after a long holdout, approve the use of numbers to identify their players for both home and road games.

1934 Russ Snyder b. Oak, NE.

1947 Cincinnati RHP Ewell Blackwell carries a no-hitter into the ninth inning against Brooklyn when Eddie Stanky singles thru Blackwell's legs and Jackie Robinson also singles. Blackwell settles for a two-hitter, just four days after he no-hit the Boston Braves.

1982 Philadelphia OF Pete Rose doubles off St. Louis RHP John Stuper for his 3,772nd career hit, passing Hank Aaron for second place all-time behind Ty Cobb. The Cardinals win, however, 3–2.

1994 Seattle OF Ken Griffey, Jr., hits

his 31st home run in a 12–3 win over California, breaking Babe Ruth's record for most home runs hit by the end of June.

1994 New York Mets LHP John Franco breaks Dave Righetti's record for saves by a left-hander with his 253rd.

1997 Baltimore 3B Cal Ripken, Jr., hits his 500th and 501st career doubles, passing Goose Goslin for 31st place on the all-time list, as the Orioles beat the Blue Jays, 5–2 in Toronto.

1997 The first four hitters in the Atlanta batting order all hit home runs against Philadelphia in the same inning, but not in order. The Braves have to bat around for number two hitter Michael Tucker to join the other three.

1998 Oakland LF Rickey Henderson hits a home run against San Francisco for his 1,706th career hit and into sole possession of third place on the all-time A's list, passing former INF Jimmy Dykes.

1999 The Chicago Cubs overcome an eight-run deficit to win at Colorado, 13–12.

23

1917 Boston Red Sox RHP Ernie Shore relieves Babe Ruth in the first inning and proceeds to throw a perfect game against the Washington Senators, winning 4–0. Ruth is ejected along with catcher Pinch Thomas for arguing balls and strikes after walking Washington leadoff hitter Ray Morgan. Morgan is thrown out attempting to steal as Shore retires 27 men in order. New Red Sox C Sam Agnew chips in with three hits.

1933 Dave Bristol b. Macon, GA.

1946 Chicago Cubs 1B Eddie Waitkus and OF Marv Rickert hit back-to-back inside-the-park home runs at the Polo Grounds in New York. The Giants, however, win the contest, 15–10.

1950 Outfielder Hoot Evers' two-run inside-the-park home run in the bottom of the ninth inning lifts Detroit to a 10–9 win over New York. The Tigers and Yankees combine for a then-record 11 homers, with all 11 accounting for the game's 19 runs. New York blasts six, and Detroit five.

1958 Marty Barrett b. Arcadia, CA.

1959 Cincinnati trades 1B Walt Dropo to Baltimore for 1B Whitey Lockman.

1960 Jim Deshaies b. Massena, NY.

1963 New York Mets OF Jimmy Piersall celebrates his 100th career home run by running around the bases backwards, much to the displeasure of Philadelphia RHP Dallas Green and Commissioner Ford Frick, who is in attendance.

1966 The Kansas City A's trade OF/1B Ken Harrelson to Washington for RHP Jim Duckworth.

1971 Twenty days after being no-hit, 1–0, by Chicago Cubs LHP Ken Holtzman, Cincinnati is again no-hit, 4–0, this time by Philadelphia RHP Rick Wise. Wise also becomes the first ML pitcher to hit two home runs in the same game he throws a no-hitter.

1973 Philadelphia Phillies LHP Ken Brett hits a home run in an ML record fourth consecutive game. They are Brett's only homers of the entire season in 80 at-bats.

1977 Eddie Stanky manages Texas for one day, a 10–8 win over Minnesota, then steps down.

1984 Chicago wins a thriller, 12–11 over St. Louis in 11 innings. Cubs 2B Ryne Sandberg goes 5-for-6 with 7 RBIs and keeps the locals alive with game-tying home runs off Cardinals relief ace

Bruce Sutter in both the bottom of the ninth and 10th innings. St. Louis OF Willie McGee hits for the cycle and drives in six runs.

1988 New York Yankees owner George Steinbrenner fires manager Billy Martin for a fifth time, replacing him with Lou Piniella, the manager he had earlier replaced.

1992 Cincinnati Reds RHP Rob Dibble reaches the 500 career strikeout plateau in the fewest innings pitched in ML history, 368.

1994 Oakland RHP Bobby Witt comes within one controversial call of a perfect game against Kansas City. In the sixth inning, Royals SS Greg Gagne is ruled safe during a foot-race to first base with Witt, but replays show that he is out.

1996 Florida Marlins C Charles Johnson begins his ML record 171 consecutive errorless games streak which runs until Opening Day 1998.

1996 St.Louis 3B Gary Gaetti hits his 300th career home run during a 3–2 loss to Montreal.

1998 Arizona trades RHP Russ Springer to Atlanta for LHP Alan Embree.

1999 New York Mets C Mike Piazza goes 0-for-4, ending a club-tying 24-game hitting streak during the Mets' 6–3 win over Florida. Piazza also suffers a slight concussion when he is hit under the helmet by a batter's swing in the seventh inning and has to leave the game.

24

1882 Richard Higham becomes the only umpire ever banned from baseball when evidence proves that he bet on games he worked in Detroit.

1936 New York Yankees CF Joe DiMaggio homers twice in the same inning and adds two doubles during an 18–4 win over the St. Louis Browns.

1938 Don Mincher b. Huntsville, AL.

1951 Ken Reitz b. San Francisco, CA.

1955 Five days shy of his 19th birthday, Washington 3B Harmon Killebrew hits the first of his 573 ML home runs against Detroit LHP Billy Hoeft. The Tigers crush the Senators, 18–7.

1957 Doug Jones b. Covina, CA.

1962 New York and Detroit are tied, 7–7, in the 22nd inning when seldom used outfielder Jack Reed belts a two-run homer to win it for the Yankees, 9–7. It would be the 29-year-old Reed's only ML homer. Detroit OF Rocky Colavito collects seven hits in 10 at-bats.

1968 Detroit OF Jim Northrup hits two grand slams in a 14–3 trouncing of Cleveland. Five days later against Chicago, Northrup will set the major league mark with his third grand slam in a week.

1977 Milwaukee 2B Don Money sets an AL record with 12 assists in a nine inning game.

1983 Milwaukee RHP Don Sutton becomes the eighth pitcher in ML history to record 3,000 strikeouts when he fans Cleveland's Alan Bannister.

1983 New York Yankees 1B Don Mattingly hits the first of his career 222 ML home runs against Boston LHP John Tudor.

1994 Houston 1B Jeff Bagwell becomes the 28th ML player to hit two home runs in one inning. Later in the same game against Los Angeles, Bagwell will hit his third homer of the day during a 16–4 Astros win.

1997 Seattle's Randy Johnson sets an AL strikeout record for left-handers with 19 whiffs against Oakland, but loses,

4–1, thanks in part to A's 1B Mark McGwire, who blasts a 538 foot home run. Johnson falls one strikeout short of the record 20 in a nine inning game set twice by Boston RHP Roger Clemens.

1998 Chicago RF Sammy Sosa ties the ML record for home runs in a month with his 18th, but Detroit rallies to beat the Cubs, 7–6, in 11 innings. Sosa's homer, his 32nd of the season, ties Detroit 1B Rudy York's August 1937 record.

1998 Houston 1B Jeff Bagwell socks his 200th and 201st career home runs, but the Astros fall to Colorado, 8–6.

1999 Chicago 1B Frank Thomas has three hits including two doubles to reach the 1,500 plateau as the White Sox beat Minnesota, 5–3.

25

1903 Boston Braves LHP Wiley Piatt loses two complete games in the same day to Pittsburgh, 1–0 and 5–3.

1924 New York Giants OF Hack Wilson hits his first of a career 244 ML home runs, this one against Brooklyn RHP Burleigh Grimes.

1924 Pittsburgh LH reliever Emil Yde doubles in the ninth inning to tie the score against the Chicago Cubs, then triples in the 14th to win the game.

1934 New York RHP John Broaca ties an ML record by striking out five consecutive times, but pitches the Yankees to an 11–2 win over the Chicago White Sox. New York 1B Lou Gehrig fares better, hitting for the cycle.

1937 Chicago OF Augie Galan becomes the first NL switch-hitter to hit home runs left-handed and right-handed in the same game as the Cubs beat the Brooklyn Dodgers, 11–2.

1945 Dick Drago b. Toledo, OH.

1948 Clay Kirby b. Washington, D.C.

1950 Pittsburgh OF Ralph Kiner hits for the cycle including two home runs for eight RBIs, as the Pirates beat Brooklyn, 16–11.

1950 Chicago OF Hank Sauer hits two home runs and two doubles to lead the Cubs to an 11–8 win over the Philadelphia Phillies.

1959 Alejandro Peña b. Dominican Republic.

1961 Baltimore and California use an ML record 16 pitchers, eight by each side, as the Orioles win, 9–8 in 14 innings on a Ron Hansen home run.

1963 Mike Stanley b. Fort Lauderdale, FL.

1968 San Francisco rookie OF Bobby Bonds hits a grand slam in his first ML game, against Los Angeles RHP John Purdin, becoming the only player in the 20th century to do so.

1970 Aaron Sele b. Golden Valley, MN.

1971 Billy Wagner b. Trannersville, VA.

1971 Montreal trades OF Ron Swoboda to the New York Yankees for OF Ron Woods.

1972 Carlos Delgado b. Puerto Rico.

1988 Baltimore SS Cal Ripken Jr. plays in his 1,000th consecutive game during the Orioles' 10–3 loss to Boston.

1995 Colorado 1B Andres Galarraga becomes only the fourth player in ML history to homer in three straight innings during an 11–3 win at San Diego.

1996 Oakland 1B Mark McGwire hits two home runs to reach the 300th of his career.

1998 Chicago RF Sammy Sosa sets an ML record for home runs in a month with his 19th home run, but the Cubs lose, 6–4, to Detroit.

1999 St. Louis RHP Jose Jimenez no-hits Arizona, 1–0, becoming the first Cardinals rookie to accomplish the feat since Paul Dean beat Brooklyn in 1934. Losing pitcher, LHP Randy Johnson, strikes out 14 St. Louis batters to reach the 2,500 plateau.

26

1916 Cleveland tinkers with the idea of uniform numbers and printed numbers for a scorecard in a game with the Chicago White Sox. Thirteen years later, the New York Yankees make the idea stick.

1938 Cincinnati 2B Lonnie Frey collects eight hits in a doubleheader split with Philadelphia. Frey has three hits in a 10–3 opening game loss, then finishes with five hits in a 8–5 nightcap win.

1943 Bill Robinson b. McKeesport, PA.

1944 In an effort to raise funds for war bonds, more than 50,000 fans jam New York's Polo Grounds for a unique exhibition the Yankees, Dodgers, and Giants would take turns against each other with one team sitting out each inning. Final score: Dodgers 5, Yankees 1, Giants 0.

1962 Boston RHP Earl Wilson hits a home run during his 2–0 no-hitter over the Los Angeles Angels at Fenway Park.

1970 Baltimore RF Frank Robinson ties an ML record hitting two grand slams in the same game, lifting the Orioles to a 12–2 rout of Washington.

1970 New York Mets OF Ken Singleton hits his first of a career 246 ML home runs, this one against Montreal RHP Bill Stoneman.

1974 Derek Jeter b. Pequannock, NJ.

1974 Jason Kendall b. San Diego, CA.

1976 Texas SS Toby Harrah plays both ends of a doubleheader, 18 innings against the Chicago White Sox, without taking part in any fielding plays — no assists and no putouts. The Rangers win the first game in the bottom of the ninth on Harrah's grand slam.

1983 New York OF Rusty Staub collects his ML record-tying eighth consecutive pinch hit during the Mets' 8–4 loss to Philadelphia.

1994 Minnesota OF Kirby Puckett becomes the Twins' all-time hits leader when he picks up three safeties, giving him 2,088 for a career. Rod Carew finished his career with 2,085 hits.

1999 Chicago RF Sammy Sosa hits his 300th career home run, but the Cubs lose to Philadelphia, 6–2.

1999 Boston scores 11 runs in the first inning and cruises to a 17–1 pasting of the Chicago White Sox. The Red Sox celebrate their biggest first inning since August 13, 1933 when they score 11 runs against the Philadelphia A's.

1999 Baltimore LHP Jesse Orosco makes his major league record 1,051st relief appearance during the Orioles' 9–8 loss to the New York Yankees. In 20 major league seasons, Orosco has pitched in 1,055 games, 16 short of the record held by RHP Dennis Eckersley.

27

1876 Philadelphia Phillies SS Davy Force becomes the first NL player to go 6-for-6 in a nine inning game. In his 10-year ML career, Force will finish with only a .211 lifetime average.

1887 Chicago Cubs LHP George Van Haltren walks 16 Boston Braves batters. He'll later switch to the OF where over 17 seasons he'll accumulate a lifetime .316 batting average.

1932 Eddie Kasko b. Linden, NJ.

1939 Brooklyn and Boston battle for 23 innings and more than five hours before settling for a 2–2 tie at Braves Field.

1943 Rico Petrocelli b. Brooklyn, NY.

1966 Jeff Conine b. Tacoma, WA.

1970 Jim Edmonds b. Fullerton, CA.

1972 Atlanta purchases the contract of RHP Denny McLain in exchange for Oakland purchasing the contract of 1B Orlando Cepeda.

1973 Texas debuts 18-year-old LHP David Clyde, who has recently signed out of high school as the first pick in the June amateur draft and goes right to the major leagues. Before a sellout crowd of 35,698, Clyde walks the bases loaded then strikes out the side in his first inning. In five innings, he allows one hit and earns a 4–3 win over Minnesota. Clyde's spectacular prep career at Houston's Westchester High School included a national record 843 strikeouts in 475 innings.

1977 San Francisco 1B Willie McCovey hits two grand slams against Cincinnati. He performed the same feat four years earlier to become the only player in ML history with a pair of two-grand slam games.

1978 San Diego rookie LHP Dennis Kinney gives up a pinch-hit grand slam home run to San Francisco's Jack Clark to become the only pitcher to give up a pair of pinch grand slams in the same season. Earlier in the year while with Cleveland, Kinney allowed a pinch grand slam to California's Merv Rettenmund.

1991 Toronto trades OFs Mark Whiten and Glenallen Hill and LHP Denis Boucher to Cleveland for RHP Tom Candiotti and OF Turner Ward.

1994 Chicago Cubs LHP Randy Myers records his 200th career save in a 2–1 win over Pittsburgh.

1998 San Diego LHP Sterling Hitchcock no-hits Anaheim through seven innings when Angels C Phil Nevin hits a home run leading off the eighth to spoil it. Hitchcock finishes with a two-hitter with nine strikeouts in a 5–1 win.

1999 In their final home game at the Kingdome after 22½ years, the Seattle Mariners say goodbye in grand fashion, 5–2 over Texas, as CF Ken Griffey, Jr., steals the show with a three-run homer and later adds a wall-scaling catch on a potential three-run homer by Juan Gonzalez. The Mariners will debut Safeco Field July 15, 1999.

28

1907 Washington steals a record 13 bases against the New York Yankees and C Branch Rickey en route to a 16–5 win.

1910 Chicago Cubs SS Joe Tinker becomes the first ML player to steal home twice in the same game.

1911 In the first game played at New York's Polo Grounds, the Giants defeat the Boston Braves, 3–0.

1922 Washington RHP Walter Johnson outduels New York Yankees RHP Waite Hoyt, 1–0, recording his 95th career shutout.

1939 The New York Yankees smash a doubleheader record 13 home runs out of Shibe Park in a 23–2 and 10–0 sweep over the Philadelphia A's.

1941 Al Downing b. Trenton, NJ.

1949 Don Baylor b. Austin, TX.

1964 Mark Grace b. Winston-Salem, NC.

1979 San Francisco trades OF Hector Cruz to Cincinnati for RHP Pedro Borbon.

1986 California RHP Don Sutton and Cleveland RHP Phil Niekro hook up in the first battle of 300-game winners in nearly 100 years. Neither Sutton nor

Niekro figures in the decision in the Angels 9–3 win.

1987 On his 38th birthday, Boston Red Sox DH Don Baylor is hit by New York RHP Rick Rhoden. It is the 244th time Baylor has been plunked, breaking Ron Hunt's record. Baylor will finish with a career mark of 255 times being hit by a pitch.

1987 Oakland 1B Mark McGwire ties two ML records as the A's bury Cleveland, 10–0. McGwire homers twice to tie the record with five homers over two games, and also ties a record with his ninth run scored in two consecutive games.

1995 Houston trades C Scott Servais and OF Luis Gonzales to the Chicago Cubs for C Rick Wilkins. Both catchers celebrated their 28th birthdays on the same date just three weeks earlier.

1997 Florida RHP Livan Hernandez, a Cuban defector, earns his first ML victory, 4–2 against Montreal.

1998 Pittsburgh trades OF Jermaine Allensworth to Kansas City for RHP Manuel Bernal.

1999 Boston 2B Jose Offerman collects his first grand slam and first multi-homer game, driving in six runs, as the Red Sox rout the Chicago White Sox, 14–1. Offerman enters the game with only 23 homers in 3,845 career at-bats in his 10 ML seasons.

29

1888 Bobby Veach b. Island, KY.

1897 The Chicago Cubs set a scoring record in thrashing the Louisville Colonels, 36–7. Infielder Barry McCormick goes 6-for-8 and scores five times.

1915 Dizzy Trout b. Sandcut, IN.

1916 The Chicago Cubs and Cincin-

nati Reds play a nine inning game with just one baseball.

1923 Brooklyn 1B Jacques Fournier goes 6-for-6 with a home run, two doubles, and three singles as the Dodgers beat the Philadelphia Phillies, 14–5.

1936 Harmon Killebrew b. Payette, ID.

1937 Chicago Cubs 1B Rip Collins plays an entire game without a putout or an assist.

1941 In a doubleheader against the Washington Senators, New York Yankees CF Joe DiMaggio ties and breaks the AL record of hitting safely in 41 consecutive games. DiMaggio doubles in the opener, then singles in the nightcap to break the record held by the St. Louis Brown's George Sisler in 1922.

1954 Rick Honeycutt b. Chattanooga, TN.

1967 Detroit trades RHP Larry Sherry to Houston for OF Jim Landis.

1968 Detroit OF Jim Northrup belts his third grand slam home run in a week as the Tigers beat the Chicago White Sox, 5–2.

1975 Willie Mays hits a three-run homer off Early Wynn in an Old-Timers Game at Milwaukee's County Stadium.

1984 Montreal Expos 1B Pete Rose snaps Hank Aaron's record for career games played when he appears for the 3,309th time.

1986 The Detroit Tigers beat the Milwaukee Brewers, 9–5, to give manager Sparky Anderson his 600th AL win. Having won 863 games as manager of the NL Cincinnati Reds from 1970–78, Anderson becomes the only manager to win 600 games in both leagues.

1990 Oakland RHP Dave Stewart pitches the first of two no-hitters on the day, beating Toronto, 5–0. Los Angeles LHP Fernando Valenzuela later no-hits St. Louis, 6–0. It's the first time in ML history that two no-hitters are thrown in both leagues on the same day and the first time this century that two pitchers have complete game no-hitters on the same day.

1994 San Francisco CF Darren Lewis extends his ML record for most consecutive errorless games by an outfielder to 392 games. During the streak which began August 21, 1990, Lewis also handles a record 938 chances without a miscue. The streak will end the next day.

1995 Chicago 3B Robin Ventura has five hits in the White Sox' 17–13 win over Milwaukee. The teams combine for a season-high 36 hits in the contest.

1995 Los Angeles RHP Hideo Nomo strikes out 13 Colorado Rockies in a 3–0 win, giving him a Dodgers record 50 strikeouts in four games. The previous mark of 49 whiffs over four games was set three times by Hall of Fame LHP Sandy Koufax.

1998 Major League baseball takes a rare day off, marking the first time since April 30, 1973 — aside from All Star breaks and labor stoppages — that there has been a day and night during the season without any games being played.

30

1894 Louisville OF Fred Clarke collects five hits in his first NL game.

1908 Boston Red Sox RHP Cy Young, at 41 years and three months, becomes the oldest pitcher to toss a no-hitter in beating the New York Yankees, 8–0. It is Young's third career no-hitter.

1909 The Chicago Cubs spoil Pittsburgh's opening of new Forbes Field, posting a 3–2 win over the Pirates.

1933 St. Louis RHP Dizzy Dean strikes out 17 Chicago Cubs batters in an 8–2 Cardinals win.

1934 New York Yankees 1B Lou

Gehrig hits three triples in 4½ innings at Washington, but the game is washed out, erasing his feat.

1934 Detroit OF Gee Walker gets picked off first base twice in a game against the St. Louis Browns, and is subsequently suspended for 10 games for his inattentiveness. During the World Series the same year, Walker will be picked off first base again as he is distracted while arguing with someone on the St. Louis Cardinals bench.

1944 Ron Swoboda b. Baltimore, MD.

1948 Cleveland RHP Bob Lemon no-hits Detroit, 2–0.

1949 New York Yankees CF Joe DiMaggio plays in his first series of the year after recovering from a bone spur operation. DiMaggio will hit .455 with four home runs and nine RBIs as the Yankees will sweep a series from the Red Sox in Boston.

1957 Bud Black b. San Mateo, CA.

1962 Los Angeles Dodgers LHP Sandy Koufax hurls the first of his four no-hitters, a 5–0 victory over the New York Mets.

1962 Tony Fernandez b. Dominican Republic.

1970 Mark Grudzielanek b. Milwaukee, WI.

1972 Garret Anderson b. Los Angeles, CA.

1973 Chan Ho Park b. Kong Ju City, Korea.

1978 Larry Doby becomes the second black manager in baseball, following Cleveland's Frank Robinson in 1975, by taking over the helm of the Chicago White Sox for Bob Lemon. Doby, who was also the AL's first black player in 1947, will finish the White Sox season at 37–50, and be replaced by Don Kessinger as manager in 1979.

1978 San Francisco 1B Willie McCovey hits his 500th career home run, this one against Atlanta LHP Jamie Easterly, during the Giants' 10–9 loss to the Braves.

1991 Boston 1B Mo Vaughn hits his first ML home run against California RHP Jeff Robinson.

1995 Cleveland DH Eddie Murray becomes the 19th ML player to collect his 3,000th career hit with a single against Minnesota RHP Mike Trombley during the Indians' 4–1 win.

1996 Colorado 2B Eric Young ties a modern ML record stealing six bases in a game, during the Rockies 16–15 win over Los Angeles.

1997 Baltimore 3B Cal Ripken, Jr., hits his second grand slam of the season, and RHP Mike Mussina wins his 100th career game as the Orioles win an 8–1 interleague contest over the Philadelphia Phillies.

1998 St. Louis 1B Mark McGwire ties Reggie Jackson's 1969 record for home runs before the All-Star break with his 37th, a 472-foot, upper deck shot against Kansas City LHP Glendon Rusch. The Cardinals don't score again and lose to the Royals, 6–1.

1998 Chicago RF Sammy Sosa hits his 20th home run in June, to conclude the most prolific month in ML history, but the Cubs lose to Arizona, 5–4. Sosa's homer is his 34th of the season.

1999 With President Bill Clinton in attendance, Chicago LF Sammy Sosa calls his home run and delivers a solo blast and NL-leading 30th of the season to help the Cubs past Milwaukee, 5–4.

1999 Arizona LHP Randy Johnson strikes out 17 Cincinnati batters, but still loses 2–0, as his Diamondbacks teammates are allowed only one hit by Reds LHP Ron Villone and RHP Scott Williamson.

JULY

1

1910 The St. Louis Browns spoil Chicago's opening of Comiskey Park with a 2–0 win. Dimensions are huge: 362 feet at the foul lines and 420 feet to straight away center field. White Sox RHP Ed Walsh helped design this pitcher's paradise, ironically the same year he would lead the AL in losses with a career-worst of 20.

1917 Cincinnati RHP Fred Toney pitches complete game victories in a doubleheader against Pittsburgh. Toney throws a three-hitter in each, winning 4–1 and 5–1, to set a record for fewest hits allowed by a pitcher in a doubleheader.

1920 Washington RHP Walter Johnson no-hits the Boston Red Sox, 1–0.

1941 New York Yankees CF Joe DiMaggio singles against Boston RHP Jack Wilson to tie Wee Willie Keeler's 1897 hitting streak at 44 games.

1951 Cleveland RHP Bob Feller hurls the third and final no-hitter of his career, a 2–1 win over Detroit.

1978 Los Angeles trades OF Jeffrey Leonard and SS Rafael Landestoy to Houston for C Joe Ferguson.

1990 New York Yankees RHP Andy Hawkins hurls a no-hitter against the Chicago White Sox, but still loses, 4–0, a victim of walks and errors by his teammates.

1994 Baltimore and California combine for an ML record-tying 11 home runs as the Orioles win, 14–7, at Camden Yards.

1999 Milwaukee SS Jose Valentin hits two-run homers from both sides of the plate and the Brewers match their season high with 21 hits in a 19–12 slugfest over the Chicago Cubs at Wrigley Field.

1999 Atlanta LHP Tom Glavine wins his 13th consecutive decision against Montreal, dating back to 1992, as the Braves top the Expos, 4–1.

2

1903 Washington Nationals 1B Ed Delahanty apparently dies of an alcohol related drowning in Niagra Falls, NY, near the International bridge. During a night train ride from Detroit to Washington, the conductor has him removed from the train at this spot for being drunk and obnoxious. His body is found the next morning. He was 35.

1929 Chuck Stobbs b. Wheeling, WV.

1933 The St. Louis Cardinals are blanked for 27 innings in a doubleheader loss to the New York Giants. In game one, Giants ace LHP Carl Hubbell goes the distance and beats RHP Tex Carleton, 1–0, in 18 innings, allowing six hits and no walks. In game two, Giants RHP Roy Parmelee strikes out 13, walks none, and beats RHP Dizzy Dean by the same 1–0 margin.

1941 New York Yankees CF Joe DiMaggio hits a home run to extend his consecutive game hitting streak to 45 games, surpassing Wee Willie Keeler's 1897 record of 44 straight games.

1943 The New York Yankees allow a team record 12 runs in one inning at Cleveland.

1947 Detroit 1B Roy Cullenbine begins his ML record streak of receiving at least one base on balls in 22 straight games.

1961 The Kansas City A's trade OF Wes Covington to Philadelphia for OF Bobby Del Greco.

1963 San Francisco CF Willie Mays hits a home run in the bottom of the 16th inning to lift the Giants to a 1–0 win over Milwaukee. Giants RHP Juan Marichal, 25, and Braves LHP Warren Spahn, 42, both go the distance.

1964 Jose Canseco b. Havana, Cuba.

1965 Steve Sparks b. Tulsa, OK.

1966 Tim Spehr b. Excelsior Springs, MO.

1970 Detroit Tigers RHP Joe Niekro loses a no-hitter to the New York Yankees in the ninth inning on a base hit by Horace Clarke. It's the third time in less than a month that a pitcher almost no-hit the Yankees, and all three times Clarke breaks it up with a single. The other pitchers were Kansas City LHP Jim Rooker and Boston RHP Sonny Siebert.

1982 Boston Red Sox DH Tony Perez collects his 2,500th career hit this one against Milwaukee LHP Bob McClure.

1989 Milwaukee CF Robin Yount singles for his 2,500th career hit in his 16-year career. At age 33, he's the fifth youngest player to reach that plateau.

1993 After starting their double-header at 4:35 P.M., Philadelphia and San Diego agree to complete the second game — pushed back three times by rain delays — even though it doesn't start until 1:23 A.M. on July 3rd. Phillies reliever Mitch Williams wins the 10-inning marathon with a single at 4:40 A.M., the latest finish in ML history. San Diego wins the opener, 5–2.

1995 Los Angeles RHP Hideo Nomo becomes the first Japanese player to be picked for baseball's annual All-Star Game. Nomo leads the NL in strikeouts and is second in ERA at the time of selection.

1999 Texas RHP Jeff Zimmerman defeats Seattle LHP Jordan Zimmerman, 7–6, marking the first time brothers have pitched against each other since 1998 when Greg and Mike Maddux squared off.

1999 Tampa Bay DH Jose Canseco celebrates his 35th birthday hitting his 29th home run of the season as the Devil Rays edge Toronto, 8–7. Canseco's homer is his 426th, tying him with Billy Williams for 24th place on the career list.

1999 During a 9–5 home loss to Arizona, St. Louis 1B Mark McGwire hits his 24th and 25th home runs of the season for his 56th career multihomer game to move ahead of Jimmie Foxx for fourth on the career list.

1999 The New York Mets suffer their worst shutout loss ever, 16–0, as Atlanta 3B Chipper Jones hits a pair of two-run homers and RHP Greg Maddux scatters two hits over six innings.

3

1893 Dickie Kerr b. St. Louis, MO.

1909 The St. Louis Cardinals commit a record 17 errors in a doubleheader.

1912 New York Giants LHP Rube Marquard defeats Brooklyn, 2–1, for his record 19th straight win of the season and 21st in a row over two years. He'll finish the year at 26–11.

1925 Brooklyn 2B Milt Stock collects four hits in a record fourth day in a row.

1931 Ed Roebuck b. East Millsboro, PA.

1939 St. Louis Cardinals 1B Johnny Mize hits two home runs, a triple, and a double to help his club to a 5–3 win over the Chicago Cubs.

1940 Cesar Tovar b. Venezuela.

1953 Frank Tanana b. Detroit, MI.

1960 Chicago Cubs 3B Ron Santo hits his first of a career 342 ML home runs, this one against Cincinnati LHP Jim O'Toole.

1964 Warren Newson b. Newnan, GA.

1965 Greg Vaughn b. Sacramento, CA.

1966 Moises Alou b. Atlanta, GA.

1966 Atlanta Braves RHP Tony Cloninger hits two grand slams collecting a record nine RBIs for a pitcher, during a 17–3 win over the San Francisco Giants at Candlestick Park.

1968 Cleveland Indians RHP Luis Tiant strikes out 19, walks none, and scatters six hits in a 1–0, 10-inning win over Minnesota.

1970 California Angels LHP Clyde Wright needs only 98 pitches in 1:51 to no-hit the Oakland A's, 4–0.

1973 In the only meeting for these brothers to face each other, Detroit RHP Jim Perry squares off against Cleveland RHP Gaylord Perry. Neither finishes the game, but Gaylord takes the loss, 5–4.

1983 Texas OF Bobby Jones, a Vietnam veteran, collects five hits, including two doubles in the Rangers' 12-run, 15th inning in Oakland, the largest extra inning outburst in history.

1994 Atlanta 1B Fred McGriff hits his 250th career home run and drives in five runs during a 12–6 win over Florida.

1995 Toronto 2B Roberto Alomar has his AL record consecutive errorless game streak end after 104 games.

1995 Colorado 1B Andres Galarraga collects six hits including two home runs in a 15–10 win over Houston.

1998 The New York Mets trade RHP John Hudek to Cincinnati for INF/OF Lenny Harris.

1998 The New York Yankees edge Baltimore, 3–2, to set a record for most wins in the first half of the season since the inception of the 162-game schedule in 1962. The Yankees, 59–20, eclipse the previous best mark of the 1970 Cincinnati Reds, who went 58–23 after 81 games.

4

1880 George Mullin b. Toledo, OH.

1905 The Philadelphia A's score two runs in the 20th inning to give LHP Rube Waddell a 4–2 win over RHP Cy Young and the Boston Red Sox. Both pitchers go the entire game with Young not allowing a walk.

1908 New York Giants LHP George "Hooks" Wiltse no-hits the Philadelphia Phillies, winning 1–0 in 10 innings. Wiltse loses his perfect game in the ninth inning when he hits opposing pitcher George McQuillan with a pitch after getting two strikes on him.

1911 Chicago RHP Ed Walsh stops Detroit, 7–3, ending Ty Cobb's 40-game hitting streak.

1912 Detroit RHP George Mullin celebrates his 32nd birthday with a 7–0 no-hitter against the St. Louis Browns.

1929 Chuck Tanner b. New Castle, PA.

1932 In a Fourth of July battle

between New York and Washington, Yankees C Bill Dickey punches Senators OF Carl Reynolds, breaking his jaw. The incident costs Dickey a 30-day suspension and a $1,000 fine.

1939 New York Yankees 1B Lou Gehrig makes his famous "I'm the luckiest man on the face of the earth" speech at Yankee Stadium as he and Babe Ruth hug and speak to each other for the first time in years.

1939 During an Independence Day doubleheader, the Boston Red Sox and Philadelphia A's celebrate with a record 54 runs and 65 hits. Boston wins both games, 17–7 and 18–12. Red Sox 3B Jim Tabor drives in 11 runs during the doubleheader with a single, double, and four home runs, two of which are same-game grand slams, which ties an ML record.

1945 The Cleveland Indians tie an ML league record by not recording any assists in a 4–2 win over the New York Yankees.

1963 Jose Oquendo b. Puerto Rico.

1967 Vinny Castilla b. Mexico.

1976 Philadelphia C Tim McCarver loses a grand slam home run when he passes teammate Garry Maddox on the basepaths. The Phillies still beat the Pirates, 10–5.

1980 Houston Astros RHP Nolan Ryan reaches his 3,000th career strikeout by fanning Cesar Geronimo, who in 1974 was also St. Louis Cardinals RHP Bob Gibson's 3,000th victim.

1983 Oakland A's LF Rickey Henderson steals three bases to tie a AL record of seven steals in two consecutive games. Henderson stole four bases on July 3rd.

1983 New York Yankees LHP Dave Righetti no-hits Boston, 4–0.

1985 The New York Mets defeat Atlanta, 16–13, in 19 innings in one of the wackiest games ever played, finishing at 3:55 A.M. the next morning. Before the nearly seven hours concludes, Mets 1B Keith Hernandez hits for the cycle; Braves relief pitcher Rick Camp, an .060 lifetime hitter, hits his only ML home run, against New York LHP Tom Gorman, who gets his last ML victory; Mets RF Darryl Strawberry and manager Davey Johnson get thrown out at 2:30 A.M. for arguing a called third strike; Mets C Gary Carter catches every offering from seven different pitchers. New York sets a team record with 28 hits. All told, there are 155 official at-bats, 23 strikeouts, 22 walks, and 43 players used. The July 4th fireworks celebration begins at 4:01 A.M. on July 5th.

1999 Kansas City DH Mike Sweeney ties the AL record with an RBI in his 13th consecutive game, and RF Jermaine Dye homers twice driving in a career high six runs as the Royals defeat Cleveland, 10–9.

1999 Toronto RF Shawn Green hits two home runs, the second the 100th of his career, and RHP Pat Hentgen gets his 100th career victory as the Blue Jays defeat Tampa Bay, 6–3.

5

1884 Jack Quinn b. Jeanesville, PA.

1904 The Philadelphia Phillies defeat New York, 6–5 in 10 innings, ending the Giants' 18-game winning streak.

1914 The last place Boston Braves begin to dig themselves out and win the pennant going away by 10 games. They are the only team to go from last to first from July 4th to October.

1929 The New York Giants become the first ML team to use a public address system in a game against the Pittsburgh Pirates.

1935 Brooklyn's Tony Cuccinello and brother Al, of New York, both hit home runs marking the first time that brothers on opposing teams collect round-trippers in the same contest. The Dodgers defeat the Giants, 14–4.

1937 Chicago's Frank Demaree goes 6-for-7 in the first game of a double-header three doubles and three singles as the Cubs beat the Cardinals, 13–12, in 14 innings. Demaree added two more singles in the nightcap as the Cubs win again, 9–7.

1946 Brooklyn manager Leo Durocher tells a reporter that New York Giants manager Mel Ott is a "nice guy" and that "nice guys finish last." The Giants indeed finish last and by 1948 replace Ott with Durocher.

1947 Cleveland Indians OF Larry Doby becomes the first black to play in the AL. He strikes out as a pinch hitter in a 6–5 loss to the Chicago White Sox.

1950 Gary Matthews b. San Fernando, CA.

1951 Rich Gossage b. Colorado Springs, CO.

1955 Cincinnati manager Birdie Tebbetts and St. Louis manager Harry Walker argue at home plate, trade punches, and are both ejected and fined $100 each for their conduct.

1967 In a matchup featuring the second pair of brothers to oppose each other as starting pitchers, Atlanta Braves RHP Phil Niekro defeats his brother, RHP Joe Niekro, and the Chicago Cubs, 8–3.

1987 San Francisco trades LHPs Mark Davis and Keith Comstock, 3B Chris Brown and RHP Mark Grant to San Diego for LHPs Craig Lefferts and Dave Dravecky, and OF Kevin Mitchell.

1997 San Diego LF Rickey Henderson collects his 2,500th career hit to become the 74th ML player to reach that plateau, but the Padres fall to Los Angeles, 7–3.

1998 Cincinnati trades RHP Jeff Shaw to Los Angeles for 1B Paul Konerko and LHP Dennis Reyes.

1998 Toronto RHP Roger Clemens becomes the 11th pitcher in ML history to reach 3,000 strikeouts when he fans Tampa Bay's Randy Winn in the third inning of the Blue Jays' 2–1 victory. Clemens finishes with seven whiffs in seven innings to stand at 3,002 career strikeouts.

1999 Arizona LHP Randy Johnson strikes out 12 St. Louis batters to equal Dwight Gooden's 1984 NL record of 43 whiffs over three starts, but loses another heartbreaker, 1–0 to the Cardinals. The Diamondbacks have been shut out in each of Johnson's last three starts and have just three hits for him in that span.

1999 Baltimore 3B Cal Ripken, Jr., collects his 1,000th career extra base hit with a double, and also homers in leading the Orioles to a 9–1 win over the New York Yankees.

6

1929 The St. Louis Cardinals set a modern ML record for runs, and an NL record for hits (28) in pounding the Philadelphia Phillies, 28–6, in the second game of a doubleheader. The Cardinals score 10 runs in the first and fifth innings, receive nine walks, and are led by 1B Jim Bottomley and OF Chick Hafey, who belt grand slam home runs.

1933 In the first All-Star Game held at Chicago's Comiskey Park, New York Yankees RF Babe Ruth fittingly hits the first ever home run of the annual classic which proves to score the winning runs in the AL's 4–2 win.

1936 Cleveland's 17-year-old rookie RHP Bob Feller pitches three innings of an exhibition game against St. Louis and strikes out eight Cardinals batters.

1938 Coming off back-to-back no-hitters only a month before, Cincinnati LHP Johnny Vander Meer thrills the home crowd at Crosley Field hurling three scoreless innings to pace the NL to a 4–1 win in the All Star Game.

1942 In the first war-time All-Star Game played at the Polo Grounds in New York, Cleveland SS Lou Boudreau leads off with with a home run and moments later Detroit 1B Rudy York adds a two-run shot to provide all the scoring in the AL's 3–0 win. The game begins at 7:22 P.M. after a blackout test.

1949 New York Giants C Walker Cooper drives in 10 runs in a regular season game.

1954 Willie Randolph b. Holly Hill, SC.

1958 San Francisco OF Leon Wagner hits his first of a career 211 ML home runs against St. Louis RHP Jim Brosnan.

1963 Lance Johnson b. Lincoln Heights, OH.

1983 California OF Fred Lynn drills the All-Star Game's first grand slam home run leading the AL to a convincing 13–3 victory at Comiskey Park in Chicago. On the 50th Anniversary of the first All-Star Game held at the same site, the AL breaks an 11-year losing streak. San Francisco LHP Atlee Hammaker sets the All-Star Game record for earned runs allowed with seven.

1985 Former Cy Young Award winner Denny McLain is scheduled to pitch for his team, the Detroit Denny's, in the Atlanta Federal Penitentiary, but is rained out. McLain last pitched in the major leagues in 1972.

1986 Atlanta trades RHP Duane Ward to Toronto for RHP Doyle Alexander.

1986 Atlanta 3B Bob Horner becomes the first modern player to hit four

home runs in a losing cause, as the Braves are beaten, 11–8, at Montreal. Horner's first three homers are against Expos starting RHP Andy McGaffigan.

1987 Oakland 1B Mark McGwire becomes the first rookie to hit 30 home runs before the All-Star break, and teammate Jose Canseco also homers twice in leading the A's to a 6–3 win over Boston.

1989 Despite retiring on May 29, 1989, Philadelphia 3B Mike Schmidt is elected by the fans to start in the annual All-Star Game.

1992 The AL sets All-Star Game records with 19 hits, including seven straight singles in the first inning, against Atlanta LHP Tom Glavine, en route to a convincing 13–6 victory at Jack Murphy Stadium in San Diego. Seattle OF Ken Griffey, Jr., leads the assault going 3-for-3 with a home run, two runs scored and two RBIs.

1996 New York Yankees closer John Wetteland sets an ML record by picking up his 20th save in 20 straight appearances, breaking the mark of 19 held by Chicago Cubs RHP Lee Smith in 1983.

1999 Chicago CF Chris Singleton becomes the first AL rookie to hit for the cycle since Texas' Oddibe McDowell did it in 1985, but the White Sox still lose to Kansas City, 8–7.

7

1883 George Suggs b. Kinston, NC.

1900 Boston Beaneaters RHP Kid Nichols wins his 300th career game, 11–4 over the Chicago Cubs. Nichols will finish his 15-year career six years later with 360 wins — seventh best all-time.

1906 Satchel Paige b. Mobile, AL.

1909 Billy Herman b. New Albany, NY.

1914 Philadelphia A's owner Connie

Mack rejects the chance to purchase the minor league contracts of Babe Ruth and two other players for $10,000.

1918 Boston SS Rabbit Maranville starts his 10-day leave from the Navy, but chooses not to relax at home. Maranville will hit .316 in 11 games, his only games of the year for the Braves, before getting shipped back out.

1919 New York Giants C Mike Gonzalez allows eight stolen bases in one inning.

1922 Pittsburgh OF Max Carey reaches base all nine times with six hits and three walks in a regular season game.

1923 Boston LHP Lefty O'Doul allows a record 13 runs in the sixth inning during Cleveland's 27–3 rout of the Red Sox. The Indians set a record for runs scored, and the 24-run differential is the second worst all time. O'Doul will later switch to the outfield and hit over .300 in six of the next seven years to finish with a lifetime .349 mark and win two batting titles.

1931 The St. Louis Browns and the Chicago White Sox play their game without a single batter striking out.

1936 The NL wins the All-Star Game for the first time with a 4–3 triumph at Braves Field in Boston. A pair of Chicago Cubs aid the win as C Gabby Hartnett hits a run-scoring triple and OF Augie Galan blasts a home run.

1937 New York Yankees 1B Lou Gehrig paces the AL to an 8–3 win in the All-Star Game, with four RBIs including a two-run home run against St. Louis RHP Dizzy Dean. Dean will never be the same pitcher again after having his toe broken by an Earl Averill line drive. New York Yankees LHP Lefty Gomez claims his third All-Star victory for the AL, which wins for the fourth time in five games.

1945 Bill Melton b. Gulfport, MS.

1948 Cleveland Indians owner Bill Veeck gives 42-year-old RHP Satchel Paige a birthday present by signing him to a contract for the rest of the season. *The Sporting News* calls the event "a travesty on baseball"; however, baseball's oldest rookie will hurl a pair of shutouts winning six of seven decisions as the Indians squeeze past the Boston Red Sox to win the AL pennant.

1959 In the first of two All-Star Games scheduled for the year, the NL scores the tying and winning runs in the bottom of the eighth inning at Pittsburgh's Forbes Field. Milwaukee OF Hank Aaron singles home a run, then scores on a triple by San Francisco OF Willie Mays for the 5–4 victory.

1964 Philadelphia OF Johnny Callison blasts a three-run home run in the bottom of the ninth inning against Boston RHP Dick Radatz to give the NL a 7–4 win in the All Star Game at New York's Shea Stadium.

1966 Dave Burba b. Dayton, OH.

1968 Chuck Knoblauch b. Houston, TX.

1979 Philadelphia Phillies 3B Mike Schmidt hits three home runs in a game against San Francisco.

1982 Chicago RF Harold Baines hits three consecutive home runs, including a grand slam in leading the White Sox to a 7–0 win over the Detroit Tigers.

1995 Oakland RHP Ariel Prieto makes his ML debut, becoming the first 1995 draftee to reach the majors barely a month after the Cuban defector is drafted. Pieto hurls six innings, allows seven hits and four earned runs in a 4–2 loss to Toronto.

1998 The first All-Star Game in Coors Field in Denver lives up to its high scoring forecast, as the AL collects 19 hits in a 13–8 victory. The teams combine for a record 21 runs scored, and tie a mark with 31 total hits. Baltimore 2B Roberto Alomar has three hits including a home run to earn MVP honors, and along with his brother, Cleveland C Sandy Alomar, Jr., continues a record for brothers playing in their fifth All-Star Game together.

1999 The Arizona Diamondbacks tie a club record with five home runs, including two by CF Steve Finley, to beat Houston, 13–7.

8

1902 The AL Baltimore Orioles lose manager John McGraw, who jumps to the NL New York Giants taking five players with him.

1918 Boston Red Sox OF Babe Ruth loses a home run against Cleveland when his game-winning blow under current rules credits him with only a triple as it is all that is needed to drive home the winning run. In all, 37 players lost homers under similiar rules circumstances until 1920.

1927 New York Yankee RF Babe Ruth hits an inside-the-park home run against Detroit RHP Don Hankins, the only homer of Ruth's eventual season total of 60 that won't clear a fence.

1935 The AL wins its third straight All-Star Game, 4–1, as Philadelphia A's 1B Jimmie Foxx provides all the runs needed with a first inning two-run home run.

1941 Ken Sanders b. St. Louis, MO.

1941 Pittsburgh SS Arky Vaughan becomes the first All-Star Game player to homer twice in the annual classic, but the AL pulls it out with two outs in the bottom of the ninth inning, 7–5, as Boston Red Sox LF Ted Williams hits a game-ending three-run homer. Ameri-

can League outfielders Joe (Yankees) and Dom DiMaggio (Red Sox) become the first brother combination to appear in the same All Star Game.

1943 George Culver b. Salinas, CA.

1947 At Chicago's Wrigley Field, the AL scratches out a 2–1 All-Star Game comeback win on singles by Boston Red Sox 2B Bobby Doerr and Washington OF Stan Spence.

1948 Lerrin LaGrow b. Phoenix, AZ.

1949 Brooklyn RHP Don Newcombe faces New York 2B Hank Thompson in the first encounter between a black pitcher and a black hitter.

1951 Alan Ashby b. Long Beach, CA.

1952 In the only rain-shortened All-Star Game in history, the NL wins, 3–2, in five innings at Shibe Park in Philadelphia on home runs by Brooklyn 2B Jackie Robinson and Chicago Cubs OF Hank Sauer.

1958 In the first All-Star Game played without an extra base hit, the AL wins, 4–3, at Baltimore's Memorial Stadium. San Francisco OF Willie Mays singles on the first pitch of the game, and 12 more singles will follow.

1962 St. Louis RF Stan Musial hits three home runs in a 15–1 drubbing of the New York Mets.

1965 Jerome Walton b. Newnan, GA.

1969 Bobby Ayala b. Ventura, CA.

1971 Minnesota trades C Paul Ratliff to Milwaukee for C Phil Roof.

1980 Cincinnati OF Ken Griffey, Sr., hits a single and a home run to rally the NL to a 4–2 All-Star Game victory at Dodger Stadium in Los Angeles.

1988 Cleveland LHP Bud Black ties an ML record hitting three batters in one inning.

1994 Boston Red Sox SS John Valentin becomes only the 10th ML player to record an unassisted triple play.

1997 Cleveland C Sandy Alomar, Jr., breaks a 1–1 tie with a two-run home run against San Francisco LHP Shawn Estes to power the AL to a 3–1 All-Star Game win before the home crowd at Jacobs Field.

9

1874 Jack Powell b. Bloomington, IL.

1921 A ruling by the city of Pittsburgh's director of public safety allows fans for the first time to keep balls hit into the stands.

1929 Wally Post b. St. Wendelin, OH.

1940 The NL records the first All-Star Game shutout, 4–0, as five pitchers limit the AL to only three hits. Boston Braves OF Max West provides all the offense needed with a first inning three-run home run against New York Yankees RHP Red Ruffing.

1946 After restrictions canceled festivities in 1945, the All-Star Game returns. The AL wins in resounding fashion as Boston Red Sox LF Ted Williams delights the home crowd belting two home runs along with two singles in a 12–0 wipeout at Fenway Park.

1948 Cleveland Indians 42-year-old rookie RHP Satchel Paige makes his ML debut against the St. Louis Browns. Paige had been a Negro League star, winning perhaps 2,000 games, before signing with Indians owner Bill Veeck.

1955 Willie Wilson b. Montgomery, AL.

1957 Chicago White Sox OF Minnie Minoso makes a bottom of the ninth inning running catch of Gil Hodges' line drive with the tying run on base to preserve the AL's 6–5 win in the All-Star Game at Busch Stadium in St. Louis.

1963 San Francisco OF Willie Mays collects a single, steals two bases, scores twice, and drives in two runs to lead the NL to a 5–3 win in the All-Star Game at Cleveland's Municipal Stadium. St. Louis OF Stan Musial sets an ML record with his 24th All-Star Game appearance.

1968 In the first All-Star Game played indoors, San Francisco OF Willie Mays scores the only run on a first inning double play ball to give the NL a 1–0 win inside the Houston Astrodome. Six NL hurlers combine for the first All-Star Game shutout in eight years.

1971 Oakland beats California, 1–0 in 20 innings, striking out a record 26 batters in the longest shutout in ML history. A's starter, LHP Vida Blue, strikes out 17 Angels batters in the first 11 innings. Oakland's Angel Mangual singles home the only run at 1:08 A.M. right before a curfew would have suspended the contest.

1974 Tom Evans b. Kirkland, WA.

1991 Oakland skipper Tony LaRussa becomes the first manager to win three consecutive All-Star Games, with his ace reliever Dennis Eckersley becoming the first hurler to save three games in a row, as the AL wins its fourth straight for the first time since 1946–49, 4–2 at Toronto's Skydome. Baltimore SS Cal Ripken, Jr., is named MVP after hitting a three-run homer in the third inning for the margin of victory.

1994 Boston SS John Valentin turns the 10th unassisted triple play in ML history.

1996 Los Angeles C Mike Piazza hits a home run and a double to help the NL to a 6–0 All-Star Game victory at Philadelphia's Veterans Stadium. For the first time in All-Star Game history, neither team issues a walk.

1998 Baseball owners instill acting commissioner Bud Selig as their first true commissioner in six years, giving the former Milwaukee Brewers owner a

five-year contract. Selig had served as
acting commissioner since September 9,
1992. He becomes baseball's ninth commissioner.

1998 St. Louis RHP Todd Stottlemyre
becomes the first pitcher since 1979 not
to hit ninth in the batting order when
manager Tony LaRussa bats him eighth
against Houston. Cardinals rookie 2B
Placido Polanco bats ninth as the
Astros win, 5–4. Philadelphia Phillies
LHP Steve Carlton batted eighth in the
order on June 1, 1979, ahead of SS Bud
Harrelson.

1998 Milwaukee CF Marquis Grissom
drives in five runs with a home run and
a double as the Brewers defeat Chicago,
12–9, in the Cubs' first visit to County
Stadium since August 29, 1965.

10

1917 Hugh Alexander b. Buffalo, MO.

1928 Washington RHP Milt Gaston
shuts out Cleveland, 9–0, allowing an
AL record 14 hits during the blanking.
Its the second time in Gaston's career
he has hurled a shutout despite allowing double digit hits.

1929 The Philadelphia Phillies and
Pittsburgh Pirates both hit a home run
in every inning, no more and no less.

1932 Cleveland SS John Burnett collects an ML record nine hits seven singles and two doubles in 11 at-bats
during an 18-inning, 18–17 loss to the
Philadelphia A's. The Indians set an ML
record with 33 hits in a losing cause.
Philadelphia 1B Jimmie Foxx hits three
home runs, a double, and two singles.
A's RHP Ed Rommel allows 29 hits and
14 runs in an ML record 17 relief
innings, in what would be his final victory of a 171-win, 13-year career.

1934 New York Giants LHP Carl

Hubbell strikes out Babe Ruth, Lou
Gehrig, Jimmy Foxx, Al Simmons, and
Joe Cronin consecutively in the All-Star
Game at New York, but the AL rallies to
pull out the contest, 9–7.

1935 Chicago Cubs 2B Babe Herman
hits the first night game home run at
Cincinnati's Crosley Field.

1936 Philadelphia OF Chuck Klein
hits four home runs, driving in six
runs, as the Phillies outscore Pittsburgh
in 10 innings, 9–6.

1940 Gene Alley b. Richmond, VA.

1945 The All-Star Game is cancelled
due to wartime travel restrictions.

1946 Hal McRae b. Avon Park, FL.

1947 Cleveland RHP Don Black no-
hits the Philadelphia A's, 3–0.

1951 Bob Bailor b. Connellsville, PA.

1951 For the first time in All-Star
Game history, the NL wins two straight
contests as Stan Musial, Bob Elliott,
Ralph Kiner, and Gil Hodges all hit
home runs in an 8–3 win at Briggs Stadium in Detroit.

1954 Andre Dawson b. Miami, FL.

1956 The NL rides home runs by San
Francisco OF Willie Mays and St. Louis
OF Stan Musial to a 7–3 All-Star Game
victory at Griffith Stadium in Washington.

1958 Pittsburgh 1B Dick Stuart hits
his first of a career 228 ML home runs,
against Chicago Cubs RHP Don Elston.

1962 In the final year of two All-Star
Games, the NL wins the first contest at
D.C. Stadium in Washington, 3–1,
behind Pittsburgh OF Roberto
Clemente's three hits.

1964 San Francisco OF Jesus Alou
becomes the first Giants player in
nearly 40 years to collect six hits in a
game. All come against different pitchers as San Francisco defeats the Chicago
Cubs, 10–3.

1968 Both AL and NL officials agree

on the 1969 expansion format: two divisions in each league, a 162 game schedule, and a best-of-five league championship series.

1969 Marty Cordova b. Las Vegas, NV.

1979 Philadelphia Phillies OF Del Unser sets an ML record with his third consecutive pinch-hit home run.

1984 New York Mets RHP Dwight Gooden, age 19, becomes the youngest player to compete in an All-Star Game, as pitching carries the NL to a 3–1 win at San Francisco's Candlestick Park. Gooden and Los Angeles Dodgers LHP Fernando Valenzuela combine to strike out a record six batters in a row, eclipsing New York Giants LHP Carl Hubbell's 1934 record of five straight established exactly 50 years earlier. A record 21 batters strike out as Oakland RHP Bill Caudill also strikes out the side in his inning of work.

1990 Six AL pitchers limit the NL to an All-Star Game low two hits in a 2–0 win at Chicago's Wrigley Field under the lights.

1992 Pittsburgh trades 3B Steve Buechele to the Chicago Cubs for LHP Danny Jackson.

1997 New York Yankees RHP Hideki Irabu, making his first ML start since coming over from Japan, strikes out nine Detroit batters in 6⅔ innings to win his debut, 10–3, before 51,901 fans at Yankee Stadium.

11

1914 Nineteen-year-old Boston rookie LHP Babe Ruth makes his first ML start and gets credit for a 4–3 win over Cleveland. Ruth is lifted in the seventh inning for pinch-hitter Duffy Lewis who singles to give Ruth and the Red Sox the victory.

1934 Bob Allison b. Raytown, MO.

1939 Cleveland RHP Bob Feller comes in to relieve, getting an inning-ending double play ball in the sixth, then throws three shutout innings to help the AL win the All-Star Game, 3–1 at Yankee Stadium. Yankees CF Joe DiMaggio delights the hometown fans with a fifth inning home run to seal the victory.

1944 Chicago Cubs 1B Phil Cavarretta reaches base an All-Star Game record five times with a triple, single, and three walks to lead the NL to a 7–1 win at Forbes Field in Pittsburgh.

1949 Jack Heidemann b. Brenham, TX.

1950 In the first extra-inning affair in All-Star Game history, St. Louis 2B Red Schoendienst hits a 14th inning home run to lift the NL to a 4–3 win at Comiskey Park in Chicago. Pittsburgh OF Ralph Kiner hits a ninth inning home run to tie the game, sending it into extra innings.

1954 Philadelphia rookie 3B Jim "Igor" Command hits a grand slam in his first major league at-bat off Brooklyn ace RHP Carl Erskine. Command will get only three more major league hits and retire.

1957 Milwaukee recalls OF Bob "Hurricane" Hazle from the minor leagues. He goes on to hit .403 with seven home runs to help the pennant winning Braves during their mid-summer stretch run. The following year, Hazle is traded to Detroit and is soon thereafter out of baseball.

1960 The NL wins the first of two All-Star Games played within three days, 5–3 at Kansas City's Municipal Stadium as San Francisco OF Willie Mays has a single, double, and triple.

1961 In the first of two All-Star Games, Pittsburgh OF Roberto Clemente singles home San Francisco

OF Willie Mays in the bottom of the 10th inning to lift the NL to a 5–4 victory at Candlestick Park in San Francisco.

1962 The New York Yankees trade OF Don Lock to Washington for 1B Dale Long.

1967 Andy Ashby b. Kansas City, MO.

1967 Cincinnati 3B Tony Perez hits a home run off Kansas City A's RHP Jim "Catfish" Hunter in the top of the 15th inning to give the NL a 2–1 win in the longest All-Star Game in history, held at California's Anaheim Stadium. Solo homers by third basemen account for all the scoring as Philadelphia's Richie Allen connects for the NL in the second inning, and Baltimore's Brooks Robinson answers for the AL with a sixth inning blast.

1967 The New York Mets trade INF Chuck Hiller to Philadelphia for 2B Phil Linz.

1978 Los Angeles 1B Steve Garvey becomes the first two-time MVP in All-Star Game history with a two-run single and a triple to lift the NL to a 7–3 win at San Diego's Jack Murphy Stadium.

1985 Houston RHP Nolan Ryan becomes the first pitcher in ML history to reach the 4,000 strikeout plateau when he fans New York OF Danny Heep on three pitches leading off the sixth inning. The Astros beat the Mets, 4–3, in 12 innings as 2B Bill Doran collects five hits.

1989 Kansas City OF Bo Jackson steals the show at the annual All-Star Game, a 5–3 AL win, at California's Anaheim Stadium. Jackson leads off the bottom of the first inning with a mammoth 448 foot home run against San Francisco RHP Rick Reuschel. In the second inning, he knocks in the go-ahead run with a groundout, and later

singles and steals a base to be named the game's MVP. Texas RHP Nolan Ryan, age 42, earns his first All-Star Game victory by striking out three batters in two innings of work as the AL wins back-to-back All-Star Games for the first time since 1957–58.

1995 Florida Marlins 1B Jeff Conine becomes baseball's 10th player to hit a home run in his first at-bat in an All-Star Game, lifting the NL to a 3–2 win at The Ballpark in Arlington, Texas. Solo homers account for all of the NL scoring as Houston 2B Craig Biggio and Los Angeles C Mike Piazza also connect prior to Conine's eighth-inning game-winner.

12

1900 Cincinnati LHP Frank "Noodles" Hahn throws the first no-hitter of the 20th Century, 4–0 over Philadelphia.

1901 Boston RHP Cy Young wins his 300th game as the Red Sox beat the Philadelphia A's, 5–3.

1931 New York Giants OF Mel Ott becomes the youngest player in ML history to reach 100 home runs at 22 years and four months.

1938 Ron Fairly b. Macon, GA.

1945 Boston OF Tommy Holmes goes hitless in the Braves' 6–1 loss to the Chicago Cubs to end his consecutive-game hitting streak at 37 games, a NL mark that will stand until Pete Rose breaks it in 1978.

1949 Major League owners pass a rule requiring each stadium to install a cinder "warning track" by the start of the 1950 season.

1949 In the first All-Star Game featuring black players, the AL wins 11–7 at Brooklyn's Ebbets Field. Brooklyn's

Jackie Robinson starts at second base for the NL, and teammates Don Newcombe, and Roy Campanella, and Cleveland's Larry Doby all participate for the first time.

1951 New York Yankees RHP Allie Reynolds hurls the first of his two no-hitters of the season, a 1–0 victory over Cleveland.

1954 Major league players formally organize themselves into a group entitled the Major League Baseball Players Association. J. Norman Lewis is hired to represent the players in negotiations with owners.

1954 Cleveland scores an AL record eight runs in the first inning against Baltimore before the first out is made.

1955 St. Louis OF Stan Musial hits a solo home run in the bottom of the 12th inning to lift the NL to a 6–5 win at the All-Star Game at Milwukee County Stadium. Milwaukee RHP Gene Conley strikes out the side in the top of the 12th setting up Musial's heroics as the NL erases an early 5–0 deficit.

1965 Mike Munoz b. Baldwin Park, CA.

1966 Los Angeles SS Maury Wills singles home St. Louis C Tim McCarver in the 10th inning to give the NL a 2–1 All-Star Game win in 105 degree heat at Busch Stadium in St. Louis.

1979 At Chicago's Comiskey Park, fans are admitted for $.98 during disco demolition night. During the trashing of records between games of a doubleheader, 5,000 fans refuse to leave the field, forcing the second game to be forfeited. The White Sox lose the first game to Detroit, and the second game to disco.

1985 The Chicago White Sox trade OF Tom Paciorek to the New York Mets for INF-OF Dave Cochrane.

1988 Oakland A's C Terry Steinbach drives in both runs with a home run and a sacrifice fly as the AL wins the All-Star Game, 2–1 at Cincinnati's Riverfront Stadium.

1990 Chicago RHP Melido Perez hurls a record-tying seventh no-hitter of the season as the White Sox blank the New York Yankees, 8–0.

1990 Atlanta trades LHP Derek Lilliquist to San Diego for RHP Mark Grant.

1994 San Diego OF Tony Gwynn slides past Texas C Ivan Rodriguez to score the winning run in the bottom of the 10th inning to give the NL an 8–7 All-Star Game victory at Three Rivers Stadium in Pittsburgh. The win snaps a record six-game losing streak for the NL which has won all nine extra inning All-Star Game contests played.

1997 Pittsburgh RHPs Francisco Cordova and Ricardo Rincon combine for a 10-inning no-hitter as the Pirates win on a pinch-hit three-run home run by Mark Smith, 3–0 over the Houston Astros. Cordova pitches the first nine innings and joins Rincon for the eighth combined no-hitter in ML history, and the first in extra innings. The game is seen by 44,119 fans on Jackie Robinson Night, the first non-Opening Day sellout in Pittsburgh since June 5, 1977.

1998 Baltimore RF Eric Davis hits his 10th career grand slam and drives in five runs as the Orioles beat Boston, 11–7.

1998 St. Louis 1B Mark McGwire becomes the fastest player to reach 40 home runs in a season, breaking his own record, during a 6–4 win over Houston. McGwire belts his 39th and 40th homers of the season in only 281 at-bats, breaking his 1996 mark of 296 at-bats during a season in which he'll finish with 70 homers.

1999 St. Louis 1B Mark McGwire belts a record 13 first round home runs during the All-Star Home Run Derby held at Boston's Fenway Park.

13

1889 Stan Coveleski b. Shamokin, PA.

1896 Philadelphia Phillies OF Ed Delahanty becomes the second ML player to hit four home runs in a game. He also adds a single, with all five hits coming against Chicago Cubs RHP Adonis Terry.

1927 Ruben Gomez b. Puerto Rico.

1934 New York RF Babe Ruth hits his 700th career home run, against Detroit RHP Tommy Bridges, during the Yankees' 4–2 win.

1935 Philadelphia A's OF Doc Cramer goes 6-for-6 in a nine inning game, tying the AL record. He becomes the only AL player to accomplish the feat twice, having first done it in 1932.

1940 Jack Aker b. Tulare, CA.

1943 Boston Red Sox 2B Bobby Doerr blasts a second inning, three-run home run to pace the AL to a 5–3 win in the first night-time All-Star Game played at Shibe Park in Philadelphia.

1948 Despite injuries to four of its top players Joe DiMaggio, Ted Williams, George Kell, and Hal Newhouser the AL overcomes an early 2–0 deficit to win the All-Star Game, 5–2 at Sportsman's Park in St. Louis.

1954 In the highest scoring contest in All-Star Game history, the AL belts a record 17 hits in an 11–9 win at Cleveland's Municipal Stadium. Washington LHP Dean Stone is credited with the victory, yet never throws a pitch as with two outs in the eighth inning, St. Louis 2B Red Schoendienst is thrown out trying to steal home. The AL rallies with three runs in the eighth inning and Chicago White Sox RHP Virgil Trucks

comes in to save the game in the ninth for Stone.

1960 The NL completes its two-game All-Star Game sweep, winning 6–0 at Yankee Stadium in New York. As he does in the first game, San Francisco OF Willie Mays has three hits, this time including a home run to pace the senior circuit.

1963 In his eighth attempt, 43-year-old RHP Early Wynn finally wins his 300th (and last) game, as Cleveland defeats Kansas City, 7–4.

1965 The NL jumps out to an early 5–0 lead and holds on for a 6–5 win in the All-Star Game at Metropolitan Stadium in Minnesota. San Francisco OF Willie Mays scores the game-winner on a seventh inning infield hit, then preserves the victory with a leaping, backhanded catch with two runners on base in the bottom of the eighth inning.

1971 The AL snaps an eight-game All-Star Game losing streak as Oakland OF Reggie Jackson, Baltimore OF Frank Robinson, and Minnesota 1B Harmon Killebrew all smack two-run home runs for a 6–4 win at Tiger Stadium in Detroit. All told, six home runs are hit by six different players, tying an All-Star Game record. Robinson's home run marks the first time a player does it for both leagues as he connected for Cincinnati in the second of two All-Star Games in 1959.

1973 Montreal's Hal Breeden becomes the first NL player to pinch hit home runs in both games of a doubleheader. Joe Cronin of the 1943 Boston Red Sox was the first AL player to do it.

1976 Cincinnati OF George Foster and Houston OF Cesar Cedeno each hit two-run home runs to power the NL to a 7–1 All-Star Game victory at Veterans Stadium in Philadelphia.

1982 In the first All-Star Game played outside of the United States, Cincinnati

SS Dave Concepcion hits a two-run home run to carry the NL to its 11th straight victory, 4–1, at Montreal's Olympic Stadium. The win is also the NL's 19th in the last 20 Summer Classics.

1991 Four Baltimore Orioles pitchers combine to no-hit Oakland, 2–0. RHP Bob Milacki (6 IP), LHP Mike Flanagan (1 IP), RHP Mark Williamson (1 IP), and RHP Gregg Olson (1 IP) become baseball's first foursome to accomplish the feat.

1993 The AL extends its All-Star Game winning streak to six straight with a 9–3 win at Baltimore's Camden Yards. Minnesota OF Kirby Puckett hits a home run and a two-run double in earning MVP honors as the AL extends its All-Star Game winning streak, which had never been more than four consecutive victories in the contest's 60-year history.

1998 Toronto INF Tony Fernandez collects his 2,000th career hit.

1999 Boston RHP Pedro Martinez electrifies the home crowd at Fenway Park by striking out an All-Star Game record first four batters faced, and five of the first six, to earn MVP honors in a 4–1 AL victory. In an appropriate and emotional ending to the last All-Star Game at Fenway Park, legendary Boston Hall of Famer Ted Williams throws out the first pitch.

14

1908 Johnny Murphy b. New York, NY.

1929 Bob Purkey b. Pittsburgh, PA.

1934 New York Yankee Lou Gehrig preserves his games-played streak despite a lumbago seizure the previous day. Listed as a shortstop, Gehrig leads

off the game with a single and is promptly removed from the lineup after the hit.

1946 Cleveland Indians SS/manager Lou Boudreau becomes the first AL player to collect five extra base hits in a game with four doubles and a home run. The Tribe loses, 11–10, to Boston, however, as Ted Williams hits three home runs and collects eight RBIs. Between games of the doubleheader, the "Boudreau Shift" is invented for Williams with both the Cleveland third baseman and shortstop moving to the right side of second base, and the center fielder moving deep into right-center.

1948 Earl Williams b. Newark, NJ.

1953 The NL wins its fourth straight All-Star Game, rapping out 10 hits in a 5–1 win at Crosley Field in Cincinnati. St. Louis Cardinals OF Enos Slaughter leads the attack with two singles, a walk, two runs scored and an RBI.

1956 Boston Red Sox LHP Mel Parnell no-hits the Chicago White Sox, 4–0.

1963 Houston OF Jimmy Wynn hits the first of a career 291 ML home runs against New York Mets LHP Don Rowe.

1967 Robin Ventura b. Santa Maria, CA.

1967 Houston 3B Eddie Mathews, in his only year with the Astros, connects for his 500th career home run against another future Hall of Famer — RHP Juan Marichal — in the Astros' 8–6 win over San Francisco at Candlestick Park.

Mathews becomes the seventh player to reach the historic plateau, following Mickey Mantle, who became the sixth member exactly two months earlier.

1968 Derrick May b. Rochester, NY.

1968 Houston RHP Don Wilson strikes out 18 Cincinnati batters.

1968 Atlanta Braves OF Hank Aaron

hits his 500th career home run, just the eighth ML player to reach the plateau. At age 34, Aaron joins only Babe Ruth and Willie Mays to reach 500 homers before their 35th birthdays.

1970 Playing in front of the home crowd, Cincinnati RF Pete Rose crashes into Cleveland C Ray Fosse to score the winning run in the bottom of the 12th inning and give the NL a 5–4 All-Star Game victory at Cincinnati's new Riverfront Stadium. For the first time since 1957, the fans vote for the starting lineups. The NL wins its 12th straight Summer Classic, while Fosse's career will never be the same after the shoulder injury.

1972 Brothers Tom and Bill Haller spend several hours just inches apart. Tom is the Detroit catcher this day and Bill is the home plate umpire, an ML first for brothers.

1974 Texas Rangers manager Billy Martin becomes the first AL skipper to get ejected by umpires during both games of a doubleheader.

1987 After 12 scoreless innings, Montreal OF Tim Raines hits a two-out triple in the top of the 13th inning to score Ozzie Virgil and Hubie Brooks with the only runs as the NL wins the All-Star Game, 2–0, at the Oakland Coliseum.

1994 St. Louis SS Ozzie Smith breaks Luis Aparicio's career assist record with his 8,017th in an 8–1 loss to Colorado.

1995 Los Angeles Dodgers RHP Ramon Martinez no-hits the Florida Marlins, 7–0. A lone seventh inning walk spoils the perfect game.

15

1876 In the first no-hitter in NL history, St. Louis Reds RHP George

Bradley defeats the Hartford Blues, 2–0. For the season, Bradley would account for every decision in all 64 games for the Reds with 45 wins to rank second in the league, and only 19 losses. He would lead the NL in ERA at 1.23 and in shutouts with 16.

1895 Baltimore Orioles SS Hugh Jennings handles 20 chances without a miscue during a 15-inning, 11–10 win over the Boston Beaneaters.

1901 New York Giants RHP Christy Mathewson hurls the first of his two career no-hitters, 5–0 over the St. Louis Cardinals.

1939 Mike Shannon b. St. Louis, MO.

1952 Detroit 1B Walt Dropo collects seven straight hits in seven at-bats during a doubleheader at Washington to give him a record-tying 12 straight hits over a two-day period. Boston Red Sox 3B Pinky Higgins set the record in 1938.

1965 Scott Livingstone b. Dallas, TX.

1965 Kirt Manwaring b. Elmira, NY.

1969 Cincinnati 1B Lee May hits four home runs in a doubleheader split with Atlanta. May collects two homers and five RBIs in each game, a 9–8 loss in the opener, and a 10–4 win in the nightcap.

1969 Minnesota's Rod Carew steals home against Chicago LHP Jerry Nyman in a 6–2 Twins win. It's Carew's seventh steal home of the season tying Pete Reiser's 1946 major league mark.

1973 California Angels RHP Nolan Ryan strikes out 17 Detroit Tigers en route to a 6–0 no-hitter, his second no-hitter of the year. Realizing he's the final out with no chance of success against Ryan, Detroit 1B Norm Cash carries a table leg instead of a bat to the batter's box. He promptly whiffs to end the game.

1975 The NL scores three runs in the top of the ninth inning for a 6–3 All-Star Game victory at Milwaukee's

County Stadium. Chicago Cubs 3B Bill Madlock, who has a key single in the inning and New York Mets LHP Jon Matlack become the first players to share the game's MVP Award. Boston PH Carl Yastrzemski accounts for all the AL scoring with a three-run home run. Milwaukee PH Hank Aaron delights the hometown crowd making his 24th All-Star Game appearance, tying Stan Musial and Willie Mays for the most all-time.

1986 Los Angeles LHP Fernando Valenzuela ties an All-Star Game record striking out five consecutive batters, but the AL wins the contest, 3–2, inside the Houston Astrodome. Valenzuela's victims are Don Mattingly, Cal Ripken, Jr., Jesse Barfield, Lou Whitaker, and Teddy Higuera. The five straight whiffs tie New York Giants LHP Carl Hubbell's 1934 record when he fanned future Hall of Famers Babe Ruth, Lou Gehrig, Jimmie Foxx, Al Simmons, and Joe Cronin in order.

1991 Montreal trades RHP Tim Burke to the New York Mets for RHP Ron Darling and LHP Mike Thomas.

1995 Seattle LHP Randy Johnson strikes out an AL season high 16 batters during his 3-hit, 3–0 win over Toronto.

1996 Cal Ripken, Jr., ends his streak of consecutive games played while at shortstop at 2,216, moving to third base in favor of Manny Alexander.

1997 After a nine-year period in which no one hit a ball into the right field upper deck in Cincinnati, St. Louis OF Ray Lankford hits two in two at-bats.

1999 San Diego scores twice in the top of the ninth inning to rally past Seattle, 3–2, spoiling the Safeco Field grand opener before 44,607 fans.

1999 Milwaukee's contest with Kansas City is postponed due to a fatal crane accident the previous day at nearby Miller Park. Three construction workers died in the accident.

16

1887 Shoeless Joe Jackson b. Brandon Mills, SC.

1909 Detroit RHP Ed Summers allows only seven hits and hurls all 18 innings in a 0–0 tie with Washington, marking the longest scoreless game in AL history.

1920 Larry Jansen b. Verboort, OR.

1920 Pittsburgh LHP Earl Hamilton shuts out the New York Giants for 16 innings, then gives up seven runs in the 17th to lose, 7–0.

1920 New York OF Babe Ruth breaks his own season record of 29 home runs with his 30th as the Yankees beat the St. Louis Browns, 5–2. Ruth finishes the year with 54.

1924 New York 1B George Kelly sets an ML record when he hits a home run in his sixth straight game, an 8–7 win over Pittsburgh.

1941 New York Yankees CF Joe DiMaggio extends his hitting streak to 56 games with a 3-for-4 day in a 10–3 win over Cleveland.

1944 Brooklyn snaps a 16-game losing streak, scoring eight unearned runs in beating the Boston Braves, 8–5. The Dodgers will then begin a five-game losing streak.

1948 After 8½ years as the Brooklyn Dodgers manager, Leo Durocher stuns the baseball world by taking over the helm of the arch rival New York Giants.

1960 Terry Pendleton b. Los Angeles, CA.

1970 Bill VanLandingham b. Columbia, TN.

1970 Pittsburgh debuts Three Rivers Stadium with a 3–2 loss to Cincinnati.

1985 Five NL pitchers allow the AL hitters only five singles and an unearned run during a 6–1 All-Star Game win at the Minnesota Metrodome. The victory is the NL's 21st in the last 23 summer classic meetings.

1998 Seattle LHP Randy Johnson loses his no-hitter bid on an eighth inning single by Brent Gates, as the Mariners blank Minnesota, 3–0.

17

1914 New York Giants LHP Rube Marquard beats Pittsburgh RHP Babe Adams, 3–1 in 21 innings, with both pitchers going the distance.

1917 Lou Boudreau b. Harvey, IL.

1924 St. Louis RHP Jesse Haines no-hits the Boston Braves, 5–0.

1930 Roy McMillan b. Bonham, TX.

1931 The Chicago White Sox beat the St. Louis Browns, 10–8 in 12 innings, without a single batter striking out.

1936 New York LHP Carl Hubbell begins a 24-game winning streak that spans two years pitching a five-hitter as the Giants blank Pittsburgh, 6–0.

1938 Deron Johnson b. San Diego, CA.

1941 Cleveland LHP Al Smith and RHP Jim Bagby, Jr., combine to halt New York OF Joe DiMaggio's 56-game hitting streak. Indians 3B Ken Keltner makes two great plays against DiMaggio before a night game record crowd of 67,468. During the streak, which started on May 15th, DiMaggio batted .408 with 15 home runs and 55 RBIs. Had he reached 57 games, DiMaggio would have collected $10,000 from the Heinz 57 company.

1942 Don Kessinger b. Forrest City, AR.

1956 Boston LF Ted Williams hits his 400th career home run.

1961 New York Yankees RF Roger Maris loses what would have been his 36th home run of the season to rain in Baltimore. The game becomes washed out before it becomes official.

1961 Commissioner Ford Frick rules that Babe Ruth's 60 home run record must be surpassed in 154 games, otherwise the new mark would go into the record books with an asterisk. Roger Maris' eventual record of 61 homers in the same year will become the only record in the history of the game with an asterisk.

1961 Ty Cobb dies in Atlanta, GA., at age 74. His lifetime batting average of .367 is baseball's all-time best.

1969 Minnesota LHP Jim Kaat, winner of seven straight Gold Gloves, is charged with three errors, but the Twins still top Chicago, 8–5.

1974 St. Louis RHP Bob Gibson strikes out Cincinnati OF Cesar Geronimo to become the second pitcher in ML history and the first NL hurler to reach 3,000 strikeouts. The Reds win the contest, however, 6–4.

1978 Texas RHP George "Doc" Medich saves the life of a 61-year-old fan who suffers a heart attack just prior to the Rangers game in Baltimore. Medich, a medical student, administers heart massage until help arrives.

1979 New York Mets OF Lee Mazzilli walks with the bases loaded in the top of the ninth inning to score the winning run, giving the NL a 7–6 All-Star Game win inside Seattle's Kingdome. In the eighth inning, Mazzilli momentarily ties the game with an oposite field home run in his first All-Star Game at-bat.

1984 The Chicago White Sox trade RHP Doug Drabek and LHP Kevin Hickey to the New York Yankees for SS Roy Smalley, III.

1987 New York 1B Don Mattingly sets

an ML record with nine home runs over seven consecutive games as the Yankees beat Texas, 8–4.

1990 Boston survives hitting into an ML record two triple plays and edges Minnesota, 1–0. Both triple plays are pulled off by the same fielders: 3B Gary Gaetti, who receives the ground ball and steps on third for the first out; 2B Al Newman, who receives Gaetti's throw for the second out; and 1B Kent Hrbek, who finishes the play catching Newman's throw to retire the batter. The first triple play is also Gaetti's fifth lifetime, establishing a record for third basemen.

1991 Baltimore DH Sam Horn ties an ML record with six strikeouts in a game, this one of 15 innings.

1993 Florida trades RHP Cris Carpenter to Texas for RHP Robb Nen and RHP Kurt Miller.

1998 Pittsburgh trades RHP Esteban Loaiza to Texas for RHP Todd Van Poppel and 2B Warren Morris.

1998 St. Louis 1B Mark McGwire hits a pair of home runs his 41st and 42nd to set an ML record for most homers by the end of July, as the Cardinals beat Los Angeles, 4–1. McGwire passes the previous mark held by both Babe Ruth and Jimmie Foxx.

1998 Baltimore 1B Rafael Palmeiro hits his 300th career home run as the Orioles defeat Anaheim, 4–1.

1998 Chicago LF Albert Belle hits his 300th career home run — his 10th in 10 games since the All-Star break — as the White Sox defeat Cleveland, 4–3.

1999 Seattle 3B Russ Davis hits the first home run at new Safeco Field, and teammates Alex Rodriguez and Raul Ibanez also connect for round-trippers as the Mariners win, 9–1, over San Diego, in their third try in their new $517 million home.

1999 Philadelphia LHP Randy Wolf becomes the first Phillies pitcher in 19 years to win his first five decisions. Phillies LF Ron Gant drives in five runs in a 11–3 win at Boston.

1999-Baltimore DH Harold Baines hits a sixth inning home run which proves to be the game winner in a 2–1 Orioles victory over Montreal. Baines' home run is his 220th as a designated hitter, breaking a tie atop the career list with Don Baylor.

18

1897 Cap Anson, who plays his entire 22-year career with the Chicago Cubs, collects his 3,000th major league hit at age 45. Anson is the first player to reach this milestone.

1906 Washington RHP Cy Falkenberg becomes the first AL pitcher to hit a grand slam home run. It would be the only home run during his 12-year career.

1927 Philadelphia A's OF Ty Cobb becomes the first ML player to reach the 4,000 hit plateau, with a double against his former team, the Detroit Tigers.

1927 New York Giants OF Mel Ott hits his first of a career 511 ML home runs, this one against Chicago Cubs RHP Hal Carlson.

1940 Joe Torre b. Brooklyn, NY.

1944 Rudy May b. Coffeyville, KS.

1948 Chicago White Sox OF Pat Seerey hits four home runs, driving in seven runs against the Philadelphia A's. His final homer wins the contest, 12–11, in the 11th inning.

1954 The St. Louis Cardinals forfeit a regular season game for stalling tactics while the sun goes down.

1962 Minnesota becomes the first team to hit two grand slam home runs

in the same inning as Harmon Killebrew and Bob Allison both connect in
an 11-run first inning. They go on to
eventually rout Cleveland 14–3.

1963 Mike Greenwell b. Louisville,
KY.

1970 San Francisco OF Willie Mays
becomes the 10th player in ML history
to reach 3,000 hits when he bounces a
base hit through the left side of the
infield against Montreal RHP Mike
Wegener. The Giants romp over the
Expos, 10–1.

1983 Philadelphia manager Pat Corrales is fired with the Phillies in first
place. General Manager Paul Owens
names himself as new manager and the
club wins 47 of its last 77 games to capture the NL pennant.

1987 New York Yankees 1B Don Mattingly homers for the eighth straight
game, tying the ML record set by Pittsburgh's Dale Long in 1956. The 10
homers Mattingly hits in that span is a
new eight-game record.

1989 Cincinnati trades OF Kal
Daniels and INF Lenny Harris to Los
Angeles for SS Mariano Duncan and
RHP Tim Leary.

1993 San Diego trades 1B Fred
McGriff to Atlanta for OF Melvin
Nieves, OF Vincent Moore, and RHP
Donnie Elliott.

1994 Houston overcomes an 11–0
deficit after three innings to beat St.
Louis, 15–12, tying the NL record for
best comeback.

1994 Toronto LF Joe Carter hits his
20th home run of the season, marking
the ninth straight year he has hit at
least that many.

1994 San Francisco LF Barry Bonds
hits his 250th career home run in a 7–5
win over Philadelphia.

1995 Florida 1B Greg Colbrunn hits
two home runs and has seven RBIs dur-

ing the Marlins' 14-inning, 12–10 win
over San Francisco.

1999 New York RHP David Cone
becomes the third Yankees hurler in
history to throw a perfect game with a
6–0 win over the Montreal Expos.
Moments before the first pitch, Don
Larsen greets Cone and tosses out the
first pitch to Yogi Berra in a recreation
of Larsen's perfect 1956 World Series
game. Several other Yankees legends are
on hand for this special "Yogi Berra
Day." Yankees RF Paul O'Neill becomes
the first ML player to play on the winning side in three perfect games with
Cone and Yankees LHP David Wells in
1998, and also as a member of the 1988
Cincinnati Reds during LHP Tom
Browning's gem.

19

1896 Bob Meusel b. San Jose, CA.

1909 Cleveland SS Neal Ball turns the
first major league unassisted triple play
against Boston. The year before, Ball
led the majors in errors with 80 and in
worst fielding percentage at .898.

1910 Cleveland RHP Cy Young
notches his 500th career win, an 11-
inning, 5–2 win over Washington. He'll
finish with 11 more wins over the
course of one more season, his 22nd, to
become baseball's all-time leader in victories.

1915 Washington beats Cleveland,
11–4, stealing an ML record eight bases
in the first inning against Indians C
Steve O'Neill.

1916 Phil Cavaretta b. Chicago, IL.

1918 U.S. Secretary of War Newton
Baker issues a "Work or Fight" order,
forcing all able-bodied Americans into
jobs considered essential to the war.

1924 St. Louis rookie RHP Herman

"Hi" Bell becomes the last pitcher to win both ends of a doubleheader with a 6–1 and 2–1 complete-game sweep of the Boston Braves.

1927 The Chicago Cubs spoil John McGraw Day at the Polo Grounds by beating the Giants. McGraw is honored for 25 years as the Giants' manager.

1949 Gene Locklear b. Lumberton, NC.

1955 Detroit rookie RHP Babe Birrer comes on in relief in the sixth inning, throws four shutout innings and drills a pair of three-run homers for six RBIs, as the Tigers clobber Baltimore, 12–4. The six runs Birrer drives home are his only RBIs in his three ML seasons.

1966 David Segui b. Kansas City, KS.

1977 Cincinnati 2B Joe Morgan and Philadelphia OF Greg Luzinski each hit first inning home runs against Baltimore RHP Jim Palmer, as the NL jumps out to a 4–0 lead and holds on to a 7–5 All-Star Game win at New York's Yankee Stadium.

1982 At Washington's R.F.K. Stadium, 75-year-old Hall of Fame SS Luke Appling leads off the first inning of the Old-Timers Game with a home run over the left field wall against fellow inductee LHP Warren Spahn. It is Appling's first home run since 1949, the year before he retired from baseball following 20 years of service with a career mark of only 45 round-trippers.

1985 Texas trades 3B Buddy Bell to Cincinnati for OF Duane Walker and RHP Jeff Russell.

1989 Cleveland LF Joe Carter hits three home runs to tie an ML record with five homers in two consecutive games, having hit two the previous day.

1990 Pete Rose pleads guilty to income tax evasion in a Cincinnati court and is sentenced to five months in prison, three months in a half-way house, 1,000 hours of community service, and a $50,000 fine. Rose will serve his time at a minimum security facility in Marion, IL. This follows Rose's lifetime ban from baseball, slapped on him in August 1989 for allegedly gambling on the game.

1994 Four ceiling tiles fall from the roof of the Seattle Kingdome postponing the Mariners game with Baltimore.

1999 Detroit RHP Jeff Weaver hits the first double by a Tigers pitcher in 27 years in a 7–6 win at Cincinnati.

20

1901 Heinie Manush b. Tuscumbia, AL.

1906 Brooklyn RHP Mal Eason no-hits the St. Louis Cardinals, 2–0.

1916 The New York Giants trade future Hall of Fame RHP Christy Mathewson to Cincinnati in a career-prolongiong move allowing him to become manager of the Reds.

1933 Chicago Cubs 2B Babe Herman hits three home runs and has eight RBIs in a regular season game.

1940 Tony Perez b. Cuba.

1941 New York Yankees CF Joe DiMaggio smacks three doubles and a home run in a 12–6, 17-inning win at Detroit.

1942 Mickey Stanley b. Grand Rapids, MI.

1958 Detroit RHP Jim Bunning hurls the first of his career two no-hitters, a 3–0 win over the Boston Red Sox.

1960 Mike Witt b. Fullerton, CA.

1965 New York Yankees RHP Mel Stottlemyre becomes the last pitcher to hit an inside-the-park grand slam home run with a blast against Boston.

1969 San Francisco RHP Gaylord Perry hits his first major league home run, 34 minutes after astronaut Neil Armstrong sets foot on the moon. Five years earlier, San Francisco manager Alvin Dark predicted that "a man will walk on the moon before Gaylord (Perry) hits a home run."

1970 Los Angeles RHP Bill Singer no-hits Philadelphia, 5–0.

1970 San Francisco trades LHP Mike McCormick to the New York Yankees for LHP John Cumberland.

1971 Charles Johnson b. Fort Pierce, FL.

1972 Texas trades 2B Ted Kubiak to Oakland for 1B Don Mincher, and INFs Marty Martinez and Vic Harris.

1973 Chicago White Sox LHP Wilbur Wood starts and loses both games of a doubleheader against the New York Yankees.

1975 Philadelphia RF Jay Johnstone, involved in a highly unusual pickoff play, is credited with a putout at first base in a game at Pittsburgh. After Pirates SS Frank Tavares reaches first base, the Phillies defense looks for the bunt. But with the infield charging and RHP Larry Christensen missing with the pitch, Philadelphia C Johnny Oates sees Johnstone charging in and throws a strike to first base. The play is scored 2–9 with Johnstone tagging out Tavares on the play for the out.

1976 Baseball's all-time home run champion, Hank Aaron, connects for his 755th and last time against California RHP Dick Drago, to help Milwaukee to a 6–2 win.

1998 St. Louis 1B Mark McGwire ties the club record for home runs in a season with his 43rd, during a 13–1 rout of San Diego. Cardinals 1B Johnny Mize hit 43 home runs in 1940.

1998 After 26 innings, 770 pitches, and nearly nine hours on the field, the New York Yankees and Detroit Tigers finish up even. Detroit wins the doubleheader opener, 4–3 in 17 innings, before the Yankees win the nightcap, by the same 4–3 score. Detroit CF Brian Hunter goes 0-for-13 in the two games.

21

1881 Johnny Evers b. Troy, NY.

1921 Cleveland and New York combine for an AL record 16 doubles as the Indians win, 17–8.

1928 Philadelphia A's 1B Jimmie Foxx becomes the first player to hit a ball over the double-decked left-field stands of Shibe Park during a game against the St. Louis Browns.

1930 St. Louis and Brooklyn combine to hit four pinch-hit homers in one game. George Puccinelli and Jim Bottomley homer for the Cardinals, while Hal Lee and Harvey Hendrick go deep for the Dodgers.

1935 Moe Drabowski b. Ozanna, Poland.

1940 Denis Menke b. Algona, IA.

1942 Mike Hegan b. Cleveland, OH.

1949 Al Hrabosky b. Oakland, CA.

1950 Mike Cubbage b. Charlottesville, VA.

1956 Cincinnati RHP Brooks Lawrence has his 13-game winning streak snapped as Roberto Clemente's three-run homer lifts Pittsburgh, 4–3.

1959 Infielder Elijah "Pumpsie" Green makes his ML debut for Boston as the Red Sox become the last franchise to integrate following the Philadelphia Phillies in 1957 and the Detroit Tigers in 1958. Green enters the game for an inning at shortstop.

1965 Mike Bordick b. Marquette, MI.

1967 Lance Painter b. Bedford, England.

1970 San Diego RHP Clay Kirby no-hits the New York Mets through eight innings, but is lifted for a pinch hitter by manager Preston Gomez as the Padres trail, 1–0. San Diego would lose the no-hitter and eventually the game, 3–0.

1973 Atlanta OF Hank Aaron belts his 700th career home run, against Philadelphia LHP Ken Brett, in the Braves' 8–4 loss to the Phillies.

1975 New York Mets 2B Felix Millan singles four straight times against the Houston Astros: Mets 3B Joe Torre, hitting next in the order, hits into four straight double plays to tie an ML record.

1986 Houston trades LHP Frank DiPino to the Chicago Cubs for 2B Davey Lopes.

1988 The New York Yankees trade OF Jay Buhner and RHP Ricky Balabon to Seattle for 3B Ken Phelps.

1995 San Francisco trades RHPs Mark Portugal and Dave Burba, and OF Darren Lewis to Cincinnati for OF Deion Sanders, 1B Dave McCarty, LHP Ricky Pickett, and RHPs Scott Service and John Roper.

1997 Chicago White Sox LHP Wilson Alvarez becomes the 28th ML pitcher to strike out four batters in one inning when he fans Detroit's Tony Clark, Phil Nevin, Melvin Nieves, and Orlando Miller.

1999 New York LF Rickey Henderson scores his 2,063rd career run, passing Willie Mays for fifth place all-time, in the Mets' 7–3 win over Montreal.

22

1876 Louisville pitcher Johnny Ryan allows 22 hits, six by Cal McVey, en route to a 30–7 beating by the Chicago White Stockings (Cubs). In his only major league appearance, Ryan doesn't walk any batters but does throw 10 wild pitches.

1893 Jesse Haines b. Clayton, OH.

1905 Philadelphia A's RHP Weldon Henley no-hits the St. Louis Browns, 6–0.

1906 Cincinnati RHP Bob Ewing defeats Philadelphia, 10–3, without a single assist registered by his team-mates.

1923 Washington RHP Walter Johnson strikes out five Cleveland batters to become the first ML pitcher to reach 3,000 career whiffs.

1926 Cincinnati collects four triples during an 11-run second inning as the Reds beat Boston, 13–1. Reds OF Curt Walker ties a NL record by getting two triples in the inning himself.

1944 Sparky Lyle b. DuBois, PA.

1947 George Lauzerique b. Cuba.

1947 Cliff Johnson b. San Antonio, TX.

1949 Tim Johnson b. Grand Forks, ND.

1954 Trying to put more power into the lineup, New York Yankees manager Casey Stengel plays Mickey Mantle at shortstop. Mantle ends the 10-inning contest against Chicago, 3–2, belting a home run.

1956 Scott Sanderson b. Dearborn, MI.

1957 Dave Steib b. Santa Ana, CA.

1962 Chicago White Sox OF Floyd Robinson hits six singles in six at-bats during a 7–3 victory over the Boston Red Sox.

1963 Mike Sweeney b. Orange, CA.

1963 Mike Thurman b. Corvallis, OR.

1967 Atlanta sets an ML record using five pitchers in the ninth inning against the St. Louis Cardinals. The Braves use RHP Ken Johnson, LHP Ramon Hernandez, RHP Claude Raymond, LHP Dick Kelley, and RHP Cecil Upshaw to close out the game.

1967 The New York Mets trade 3B Ken Boyer to the Chicago White Sox for C J.C. Martin and OF Billy Southworth.

1973 Pittsburgh OF Dave Parker hits his first of a career 339 ML home runs, this one against San Diego RHP Steve Arlin.

1986 The Chicago Cubs fire ballgirl Marla Collins after she poses for an eight-page Playboy centerfold entitled "Belle of the Ballclub."

1988 Pittsburgh trades OF Darnell Coles to Seattle for OF Glenn Wilson.

1998 The New York Yankees pound Detroit, 13–2, to push their record to a best-ever 71–25 after 96 games.

1999 New York Mets RHP Orel Hershiser becomes the 95th ML pitcher to reach the 200-win plateau with a 7–4 decision over Montreal.

1999 San Francisco RHP Jerry Spradlin becomes the 33rd pitcher in ML history to strike out four batters in one inning, during an 8–7 loss to San Diego.

23

1918 Pee Wee Reese b. Ekron, KY.

1921 The signed confessions of Chicago Black Sox scandalists "Shoeless" Joe Jackson, Eddie Cicotte, and Lefty Williams, suddenly are missing. These three players along with the rest of the "Eight Men Out" are later acquitted, but eventually banned for life from baseball for their associations with gamblers.

1922 The Boston Red Sox trade 3B Joe Dugan and OF Elmer Smith to the New York Yankees for INF/OF Chick Fewster, OF Elmer Miller, SS Johnny Mitchell, and LHP Lefty O'Doul.

1928 New York Yankees RF Babe Ruth hits his record 70th home run over a 12-month period, which began July 24, 1927. The record stands alone until St. Louis 1B Mark McGwire ties it August 8, 1998.

1936 Don Drysdale b. Van Nuys, CA.

1944 After already hitting four home runs during the second game of a doubleheader, Chicago Cubs OF Bill Nicholson receives an intentional walk with the bases loaded to force home another run against the New York Giants. Giants player/manager Mel Ott orders the intentional walk, with speculation by some that Ott doesn't want to lose the home run title to Nicholson, who wins anyway with 33. Ott finishes the year runner-up with 26 round-trippers.

1957 New York CF Mickey Mantle hits for the cycle against the Chicago White Sox, the only time he'll do it in his 18-year career.

1960 Kansas City A's RF Whitey Herzog lines into the first and only all-Cuban triple play in major league history in a game against the Washington Senators.

1964 Kansas City A's SS Bert Campaneris hits a home run on the first pitch thrown to him in the major leagues. The victim is Minnesota LHP Jim Kaat. Campaneris later homers again, tying the ML record for round-trippers in his first game.

1965 Philadelphia 1B Dick Stuart hits a home run to lift the Phillies to a 5–1 win over the Mets. Shea Stadium becomes Stuart's record–setting 23rd ballpark that he has cleared the wall on.

1969 San Francisco 1B Willie McCovey becomes only the fourth player in All-Star Game history to hit two home runs powering the NL to a 9-3 win at R.F.K. Stadium in Washington. Cincinnati 1B Lee May and Chicago White Sox pinch-hitter Carlos May become the first brothers to oppose each other in an All-Star Game.

1974 A write-in starter, Los Angeles Dodgers 1B Steve Garvey singles and doubles to lead the NL to a 7–2 win in the All-Star Game at Pittsburgh's Three Rivers Stadium.

1986 The Chicago White Sox trade OF Bobby Bonilla to Pittsburgh for RHP Jose DeLeon.

1989 Carl Yastrzemski and Johnny Bench, two players who spent their entire careers with one organization, are inducted into the Hall of Fame. During his 23 years with the Boston Red Sox, Yastrzemski belted 452 home runs and won the 1967 AL Triple Crown Award. In 17 seasons with the Cincinnati Reds, Bench clubbed 389 home runs and was a two-time NL MVP.

1994 New York Yankees 1B Don Mattingly singles to become the 197th ML player to reach 2,000 career hits, during a 7–2 win over California. Angels DH Chili Davis homers to pick up his 1,000th career RBI.

1996 Atlanta LHP Steve Avery goes on the disabled list ending an incredible streak for the Braves' starting foursome. Until now, Avery, RHP Greg Maddux, RHP John Smoltz, and LHP Tom Glavine had pitched 7,058⅔ innings without any visiting the DL.

1999 Oakland trades LHP Kenny Rogers to the New York Mets for OF Terrance Long and LHP Leo Vasquez.

24

1882 Cleveland Spiders OF Dave Rowe makes an emergency pitching appearance, allowing 29 hits, seven walks, and no strikeouts in a 35–4 drubbing by the Chicago Cubs.

1909 Brooklyn LHP Nap Rucker strikes out 16 Pittsburgh batters.

1911 A team of AL All-Stars plays the Cleveland Indians in a benefit game for the widow of the late Addie Joss. The former Indians RHP, who won 160 games in nine years for the Tribe, died suddenly on April 14, 1911 of tubercular meningitis at the age of thirty-one.

1926 In a victory over the Chicago White Sox, New York Yankees 1B Lou Gehrig steals home when he and RF Babe Ruth execute a double steal. It's the second time this season that the two sluggers have pulled off the play. Of Gehrig's career 102 steals, 15 will be swipes of home.

1931 Brooklyn OF Babe Herman becomes the first player to hit for the cycle twice in one season. He earlier did it on May 18th.

1944 St. Louis Browns RHP Nelson Potter gets ejected in a game against the New York Yankees for violating the spitball rule.

1949 Cleveland RHP Bob Lemon hits two home runs to lead his team to a 7–5 win over Washington.

1964 Barry Bonds b. Riverside, CA.

1965 Joe Oliver b. Memphis, TN.

1973 San Francisco OF Bobby Bonds hits a home run and a double to lead the NL to a 7–1 rout in the All-Star Game held at Royals Stadium in Kansas City.

1983 Kansas City 3B George Brett hits a two-run homer with two outs in the top of the ninth inning against New York RHP Goose Gossage to apparently beat the Yankees, 5–4. Yankees manager Billy Martin protests the bat which has pine tar above the legal 18-inch limit. The umpires throw out the bat, the home run, then the raging Brett. The AL President Lee MacPhail later sides with the Royals upholding their protest, and reinstates the home run.

The game resumes at a later date with Kansas City RHP Dan Quisenberry closing out the Yankees in the bottom of the ninth to preserve the win.

1989 Longtime St. Louis infielder Red Schoendienst and broadcaster Harry Caray enter the Hall of Fame together. Both broke into the major leagues on the same date in 1945. Caray's first call was a fly ball out caught by Schoendienst, the Cardinals' right fielder.

1993 New York Mets RHP Anthony Young loses his ML record 27th straight game, a string dating back to May 6, 1992.

1995 Boston trades OF Mark Whiten to Philadelphia for 1B Dave Hollins.

1996 Cleveland RHP Dennis Martinez wins his 240th career game, 10–0 over Toronto, to break Juan Marichal's record for most victories by a Latin American pitcher.

1999 New York hammers Cleveland, 21–1, for the largest Yankees scoring barrage in 46 years.

25

1907 New York Giants C Roger Bresnahan wears a Reach Pneumatic Head Protector, a half helmet, for the first time in baseball history.

1913 St. Louis Browns LHP Carl Weilman strikes out six times in a 15-inning game against the Washington Senators.

1926 Whitey Lockman b. Lowell, NC.

1930 The Philadelphia A's turn two triple plays against Cleveland.

1935 Larry Sherry b. Los Angeles, CA.

1941 Boston Red Sox LHP Lefty Grove finally gets his 300th and last career win, a 10–6 victory over Cleveland. He'll finish a 17-year career at 300–141.

1961 New York RF Roger Maris belts four home runs as the Yankees sweep the Chicago White Sox, 5–1 and 12–0. The explosion puts Maris at 40 homers for the year and 24 games ahead of Babe Ruth's 1927 pace, when the Bambino clubbed a then record 60 round-trippers.

1962 Doug Drabek b. Victoria, TX.

1967 Ed Sprague b. Castro Valley, CA.

1969 Boston Red Sox OF Tony Conigliaro hits a home run out of Seattle's Sicks Stadium, but he wrenches his back on the swing and is done for the day.

1971 Pedro J. Martinez b. Dominican Republic.

1972 Cincinnat 2B Joe Morgan singles home San Diego 1B Nate Colbert with the winning run in the bottom of the 10th inning to lift the NL to a 4–3 win in the All-Star Game at Atlanta Stadium. Braves OF Hank Aaron thrills the home crowd with a two-run home run.

1973 California RHP Nolan Ryan records eight consecutive strikeouts against Milwaukee, marking the second time in his career he has whiffed as many in succession.

1975 St. Louis trades OF Jim Dwyer to Montreal for 2B Larry Lintz.

1983 In the sixth inning at Kansas City, Cleveland records the second out and the entire team runs off the field as if the inning were over. Before the day is over, manager Mike Ferraro is fired.

1997 Texas trades 3B Dean Palmer to Kansas City for OF Tom Goodwin.

1999 New York LF Rickey Henderson reaches the 1,000 career RBI plateau with a home run in helping the Mets to a 5–1 win over the Chicago Cubs.

1999 Florida trades RHP Livan Hernandez to San Francisco for RHPs Jason Grilli and Nathan Bump.

26

1892 Sad Sam Jones b. Woodsfield, OH.
1920 Eddie Bockman b. Santa Ana, CA.
1923 Hoyt Wilhelm b. Huntersville, NC.
1928 New York Yankees OF Bob Meusel becomes the first ML player to hit for the cycle for a third time in a career.
1933 Norm Siebern b. St. Louis, MO.
1935 New York Yankees OF Jesse Hill hits a line drive at Washington RHP Ed Linke. The ball hits Linke in the forehead, ricochets back to C Jack Redmond for a 1–2 putout. Redmond then fires down to second base catching a New York baserunner off guard for an inning-ending 1–2–4 double play.
1962 Jody Reed b. Tampa, FL.
1969 Greg Colbrunn b. Fontana, CA.
1984 Cincinnati trades RHP Dan Driessen to Montreal for RHP Andy McGaffigan.
1987 Milwaukee DH Paul Molitor ties the major league record with three stolen bases in one inning.
1989 St. Louis LF Vince Coleman extends his ML record of 50 consecutive stolen bases without being caught. His streak began on September 18, 1988.
1998 San Diego RHP Trevor Hoffman has his streak of 41 straight games saved end although the Padres rally to win, 5–4, in 10 innings over Houston. Hoffman gives up a ninth inning home run to LF Moises Alou which temporarily knots the score.
1999 Seattle trades OF Butch Huskey to Boston for LHP Robert Ramsey.

27

1880 Joe Tinker b. Muscotah, KS.
1899 Rube Walberg b. Seattle, WA.

1905 Leo Durocher b. West Springfield, MA.
1912 Brooklyn Dodgers OF Casey Stengel becomes the second player of the 20th century to collect four hits in his first ML game.
1918 Brooklyn RHP Henry Heitman makes his ML debut against St. Louis facing only five hitters. Four will collect hits and score as Heitman gets only one out before leaving for a reliever. He'll later enlist in the U.S. Navy and his career will end with a 108.00 ERA.
1938 Detroit 1B Hank Greenberg hits two home runs for the second straight day. During the course of his 58-home run season, Greenberg will hit two homers in one game a record 11 times.
1946 Boston 1B Rudy York becomes only the third player in ML history to hit two grand slams in a game. York drives in 10 runs as the Red Sox beat the St. Louis Browns, 13–6.
1946 Larry Biitner b. Fort Dodge, IA.
1950 Philadelphia OF Del Ennis drives in seven runs in the seventh and eighth innings of a 13–3 victory over the Chicago Cubs. Ennis doubles with the bases loaded in the seventh, then hits a grand slam home run in the eighth.
1959 New York attorney William Shea announces the formation of a five-team Continental League with franchises in New York, Houston, Toronto, Denver, and Minneapolis-St. Paul. Branch Rickey is named league president, although the idea quickly folds.
1968 Tom Goodwin b. Fresno, CA.
1974 Los Angeles RHP Rex Hudson makes his one and only major league appearance in a two inning stint against Atlanta. Hudson allows six hits including Hank Aaron's 726th career home run.
1975 Alex Rodriguez b. New York, NY.

1982 Philadelphia 2B Manny Trillo sets an NL record by playing in his 86th consecutive errorless game.

1984 Montreal 1B Pete Rose passes Ty Cobb for most career singles hit with his 3,503rd against Philadelphia.

1986 For the second time in a season, two 300-game winners face each other as California RHP Don Sutton outpitches Boston RHP Tom Seaver, 3–0.

1988 New York LHP Tommy John sets an AL pitching record committing three errors in one inning.

1994 Detroit's Sparky Anderson moves into fourth place on the all-time managerial win list, passing Joe McCarthy, by defeating Seattle, 3–1, for his 2,126th career victory.

1996 San Diego C John Flaherty hits a go-ahead grand slam home run in a nine-run eighth inning to rally the Padres from a six-run deficit to beat Florida, 20–12. The game takes a record 4:10 the longest night game in NL history.

1997 Atlanta RHP Greg Maddux needs only 78 pitches for a complete game win over San Francisco. In the span of the same week, San Diego's pitchers needed 80 pitches during one inning against the same Giants.

1998 After starting his career with an ML record of 246 home runs without a grand slam, Chicago OF Sammy Sosa finally connects, with a 438 foot blast against Arizona LHP Alan Embree, as the Cubs win, 6–2. The grand slam is Sosa's second homer of the day and 40th of the season.

1999 St. Louis 1B Mark McGwire connects for his 494th career home run, breaking a tie with Lou Gehrig for 16th place all-time, during the Cardinals' 2–1 loss at San Francisco. McGwire (1995–99) also ties Babe Ruth (1926–30) for most home runs over a five-year span with 256.

28

1898 Louisville INF Honus Wagner hits his first career grand slam home run off New York Giants ace RHP Amos Rusie, in the Colonels' 6–4 win.

1931 Chicago OF Bob Fothergill hits a home run and a triple in an 11-run eighth inning as the White Sox edge the New York Yankees, 14–12.

1949 Vida Blue b. Mansfield, LA.

1958 For the sixth time in his career, New York Yankees OF Mickey Mantle homers from both sides of the plate in the same game. He'll do it four more times in his career.

1970 California Angels C Tom Egan collects an AL record five passed balls.

1971 Baltimore 3B Brooks Robinson, a 16-time Gold Glove winner, commits three errors in the sixth inning against Oakland, but teammate Frank Robinson's three-run homer in the ninth wins it for the Orioles.

1976 Chicago RHPs John "Blue Moon" Odom (5 IP) and Francisco Barrios (4 IP) combine on a no-hitter as the White Sox beat Oakland, 2–1.

1978 Detroit 2B Lou Whitaker hits his first ML home run against Seattle RHP Enrique Romo.

1979 Chicago OF Dave Kingman hits three home runs in a game for the second time during the year, becoming only the sixth player in ML history to do it. The Cubs, however, lose to the New York Mets, 6–4.

1983 AL President Lee MacPhail rules that George Brett's "pine tar" home run against New York on July 24th should count. The umpires had disallowed the homer because the pine tar on Brett's bat exceeded the 18-inch limit. The remainder of the game is finished August 18th with the Kansas City Royals beating the Yankees, 6–4.

1989 St. Louis LF Vince Coleman has his ML record successful stolen base streak end at 50 straight as Montreal C Nelson Santovenia guns him down. The record surpasses Los Angeles 2B Davey Lopes' 1975 mark of 38 straight steals without being thrown out.

1989 Baltimore trades LHP Brian Dubois to Detroit for OF Keith Moreland.

1990 Chicago SS Shawon Dunston ties an ML record with three triples as the Cubs beat Montreal, 10–7.

1991 Montreal Expos RHP Dennis Martinez hurls the 13th perfect game in modern baseball history and the first in the NL in 27 years, blanking Los Angeles, 2–0.

1993 Seattle CF Ken Griffey, Jr., ties an ML record by homering in his eighth consecutive game, but the Mariners lose to Minnesota, 5–1.

1993 New York Mets RHP Anthony Young snaps his ML record 27-game losing streak with a 5–4 win over Florida. The old record of 23 straight losses belonged to 1910 Boston Braves RHP Cliff Curtis.

1994 On the three-year anniversary date of Dennis Martinez' perfect game, Texas Rangers LHP Kenny Rogers throws one of his own, blanking the California Angels, 4–0. Rogers' gem is the 14th perfect game in modern history and the first by an AL left-hander.

1995 Baltimore trades OF Alex Ochoa and OF Damon Buford to the New York Mets for OF Bobby Bonilla and LHP Jimmy Williams.

1995 Chicago Cubs INF Todd Haney hits his second ML home run, exactly one year after he hit his first ML homer.

1995 Oakland trades OF Ruben Sierra and RHP Jason Beverlin to the New York Yankees for OF Danny Tartabull.

1996 New York's Darryl Strawberry hits his 300th career home run, a two-run shot to rally the Yankees past Kansas City, 3–2.

1998 After hitting his first career grand slam home run the night before, following an ML record 246 homers to start a career without one, Chicago RF Sammy Sosa becomes only the 16th player in ML history to hit a grand slam in consecutive games. His 41st homer of the season isn't enough, however, as the Cubs lose to Arizona, 7–5.

29

1908 St. Louis LHP Rube Waddell strikes out 16 of his former teammates as the Browns beat the Philadelphia A's, 5–4.

1909 National League President Harry Pulliam shocks the baseball world by fatally shooting himself at age 40.

1911 Boston Red Sox RHP Smokey Joe Wood no-hits the St. Louis Browns, 5–0, in the first game of a doubleheader. Wood collects 12 strikeouts in his gem.

1915 Pittsburgh SS Honus Wagner, age 41, belts a grand slam home run against Brooklyn.

1928 Cleveland scores eight runs in the first inning and adds nine more in the second en route to a 24–6 blowout of the New York Yankees.

1933 Pittsburgh OF Fred Lindstrom carries a 23-game hitting streak into a doubleheader against Cincinnati. Nursing a minor injury, Lindstrom can only pinch hit, which he does safely in each game to extend his streak to 25 games.

1934 Felix Mantilla b. Puerto Rico.

1935 Due to extreme heat, one NL umpire can't work, whereupon a youngster named Jocko Conlan fills in and will stay for 30 years before being elected to the Hall of Fame in 1974 for "Meritorious Service to the Game."

1951 Dan Driessen b. Hilton Head, SC.

1955 Cincinnati C Smoky Burgess hits three home runs and collects nine RBIs in a 16–5 rout of Pittsburgh.

1963 Tommy Gregg b. Boone, NC.

1965 On the eve of his 75th birthday, New York Mets manager Casey Stengel breaks his hip, forcing his retirement and ending his managerial career. "The Old Professor" completes 25 years as manager winning 1,926 games while losing 1,867. In his 12 years with the New York Yankees from 1949–60, Stengel advanced to the World Series 10 times.

1965 Luis Alicea b. Puerto Rico.

1966 San Francisco 3B Jim Davenport, a utility infielder, begins an ML record 97 consecutive errorless games streak at 3B which runs through April 28, 1968. During the span, however, Davenport commits several errors while playing other positions.

1967 Cleveland trades OF Rocky Colavito to the Chicago White Sox for 2B Marv Staehle and OF Jim King.

1968 Cincinnati RHP George Culver no-hits the Phillies, 6–1, in the second game of a doubleheader in Philadelphia.

1971 Johnny Ruffin b. Butler, AL.

1971 Milwaukee trades 2B Ted Kubiak and P Charles Loseth to St. Louis for OF Jose Cardenal, INF Dick Schofield, Sr., and RHP Bob Reynolds.

1977 Atlanta knuckleballer RHP Phil Niekro strikes out four Pittsburgh batters — Omar Moreno, Rennie Stennett, Bill Robinson, and Dave Parker — in one inning.

1983 Los Angeles 1B Steve Garvey has his consecutive games played streak end at 1,207 when he dislocates his left thumb in a home plate collision with Atlanta RHP Pascual Perez.

1986 Detroit manager Sparky Anderson wins his 600th AL game, 9–5 over Milwaukee. Having already won pennants in both the NL and AL, Anderson becomes the first manager to win 600 games in each league as well.

1988 Baltimore trades RHP Mike Boddiker to Boston for OF Brady Anderson and RHP Curt Schilling.

1989 Texas trades OF Sammy Sosa, SS Scott Fletcher, and LHP Wilson Alvarez to the Chicago White Sox for OF Harold Baines and INF Fred Manrique.

1995 Kansas City OF Vince Coleman collects five hits as the Royals set a team record with 21 singles in a 16-inning, 5–4 win over Detroit. Kansas City's only extra base hit is Jon Nunnally's game-winning home run in the 16th.

1996 Los Angeles manager Tommy Lasorda retires after 20 years at the Dodgers helm, finishing with a 1,599–1,439–2 record. Lasorda, 68, won two World Titles 1981 and 1988, four NL pennants, and eight western division titles. He joins Connie Mack, John McGraw, and Walter Alston as the only managers to last into a 20th season.

1997 Texas trades RHP Ken Hill to Anaheim for C Jim Leyritz.

1997 In a sharp contrast of starting pitching styles, Boston RHP Tim Wakefield opposes Seattle LHP Randy Johnson. The Red Sox knuckleballer's fastest pitch is clocked at 77 mph, while the flamethrowing Mariner's slowest offering is clocked at 79 mph.

1998 The Chicago White Sox trade RHP Matt Karchner to the Chicago Cubs for RHP Jon Garland, the 10th overall pick in the 1997 draft.

30

1890 Casey Stengel b. Kansas City, MO.

1928 Joe Nuxhall b. Hamilton, OH.

1937 Philadelphia Phillies 1B Dolph Camilli plays the entire 1–0 win against Cincinnati without recording a putout.

1944 Pat Kelly (OF) b. Philadelphia, PA.

1947 The New York Giants beat Cincinnati RHP Ewell Blackwell, 5–4 in 10 innings, ending Blackwell's 16-game winning streak. During the streak, Blackwell completed every game, threw five shutouts and one no-hitter.

1958 Scott Fletcher b. Fort Walton Beach, FL.

1959 San Francisco 1B Willie McCovey becomes the seventh modern player to collect four hits in his first ML game, leading the Giants to a 7–2 win over Philadelphia. San Francisco moves 1958 Rookie of the Year 1B Orlando Cepeda to LF to make room for McCovey, who will go on to win the Rookie of the Year Award for 1959.

1962 The AL gets home runs by Boston 1B Pete Runnels, Los Angeles Angels OF Leon Wagner, and Detroit OF Rocky Colavito to earn a split in the final All-Star Game series, 9–4, at Wrigley Field in Chicago. It's also the last All-Star Game the AL will win in the decade.

1962 Tom Pagnozzi b. Tucson, AZ.

1966 Washington trades RHP Diego Segui to the Kansas City A's for RHP Jim Duckworth.

1968 During the Senators' 10–1 loss to Cleveland, Washington SS Ron Hansen pulls off baseball's eighth unassisted triple play. Three days later, Hansen is traded to the Chicago White Sox for INF Tim Cullen.

1969 Houston RHP Fred Gladding, a 13-year veteran, gets his only major league hit against New York Mets' RHP Ron Taylor. Gladding's hit is part of an 11-run inning for the Astros that includes grand slams by both Denis Menke and Jimmy Wynn.

1973 Texas RHP Jim Bibby no-hits Oakland, 6–0.

1980 Houston RHP J.R.Richard collapses during a workout in the Astrodome. Stricken by a stroke, the 6-foot-8 Richard has surgery to remove blood clots from behind his right collarbone. He attempts comebacks in both 1981 and 1982 but won't win again in the major leagues, ending a 10-year career with a 107–71 record, including two NL strikeout titles with 303 in 1978 and 313 in 1979.

1982 Atlanta removes Chief Noc-A-Homa and his tepee from the left field bleachers to make room for more seats, but the Braves lose 19 of their next 21 games to blow a 10½ game lead. Atlanta brings the Chief back and recovers to regain first place.

1988 Cincinnati LHP John Franco sets an ML record with his 13th save in July as the Reds blank San Diego, 2–0.

1990 Baltimore trades OF Phil Bradley to the Chicago White Sox for OF Ron Kittle.

1990 George Steinbrenner is forced to resign as general partner of the New York Yankees by baseball Commissioner Fay Vincent. After a four month investigation by the commissioner's office, baseball found that Steinbrenner had paid admitted gambler Howard Spira $40,000 for damaging information on then-Yankees outfielder Dave Winfield. Steinbrenner had already been suspended in the 1970s by then-Commissioner Bowie Kuhn for making illegal campaign contributions to Richard Nixon.

1991 San Diego trades OF Shawn Abner to California for 3B Jack Howell.

1992 Toronto trades OF Rob Ducey and C Greg Myers to California for RHP Mark Eichhorn.

1994 Detroit C Chad Kreuter becomes the ninth player in ML history to hit three sacrifice flies in a game, during the Tigers' 14–2 win over Oakland.

1995 Chicago DH John Kruk retires with a .300 batting average after getting a hit in his final ML at-bat in the top of the first inning of an 8–3 loss at Baltimore.

1995 California scores eight times in an 8–3 win over Milwaukee, giving the Angels 201 runs in July. It's the most a team has scored in one month since the New York Yankees scored 202 in July of 1958.

1998 Seattle SS Alex Rodriguez steals his 30th base of the season to go along with his 31 home runs to become just the sixth 30–30 player in AL history.

31

1897 Brooklyn RHP William "Brickyard" Kennedy, incensed at a call by umpire Hank O'Dea, throws the ball at O'Dea while forgetting to call timeout as the winning run dashes home from third base.

1914 Elmer Riddle b. Columbus, GA.

1917 The Chicago Cubs trade RHP Al Demaree to the New York Giants for INF Pete Kilduff.

1922 Hank Bauer b. East St. Louis, IL.

1932 Philadelphia A's LHP Lefty Grove spoils the unveiling of Cleveland's new Municipal Stadium, winning 1–0 before 76,979 fans.

1939 Vic Davilillo b. Venezuela.

1954 Milwaukee Braves 1B Joe Adcock collects a record 18 total bases in a 15–7 win at Brooklyn. After smashing four home runs, Adcock just misses a fifth when the ball glances off the top of the left field wall. He settles for a double.

1959 Mike Bielecki b. Baltimore, MD.

1961 At Fenway Park in Boston, the All-Star Game ends in its only tie, 1–1, after rain halts play after nine innings. Detroit OF Rocky Colavito hits a first inning home run for the AL.

1963 Scott Bankhead b. Raleigh, NC.

1963 Los Angeles Angels RHP Paul Foytack throws an ML record four consecutive home runs against Cleveland's Woody Held, Pedro Ramos, Tito Francona, and Larry Brown during the sixth inning of the second game of a doubleheader.

1971 San Francisco 1B Dave Kingman hits the first of a career 442 major league home runs against Pittsburgh RHP Dave Giusti.

1972 Chicago White Sox 1B Richie Allen hits two inside-the-park home runs against Minnesota.

1981 Baseball's first-ever midseason strike, which began on June 12, ends when both the players' association and the owners reach a tentative agreement.

1989 Minnesota trades LHP Frank Viola to the New York Mets for RHP Rick Aguilera, LHP David West, RHP Kevin Tapani, RHP Tim Drummond, and LHP Jack Savage.

1990 Texas RHP Nolan Ryan wins his 300th career game, defeating Milwaukee, 11–3, in Milwaukee to become only the 20th ML pitcher to reach that plateau.

1994 San Francisco 3B Matt Williams hits his 40th home run of the season, setting an NL record for most home runs by the end of July.

1995 Seattle trades OF Marc Newfield and LHP Ron Villone to San Diego for

RHP Andy Benes and RHP Greg Keagle.

1996 Texas OF Juan Gonzalez ties an ML record with his 15th homer in July, a three-run shot off New York LHP Jimmy Key, in leading the Rangers to a 9–2 win over the Yankees. Gonzalez ties the mark shared by Joe DiMaggio (1937), Hank Greenberg (1938), and Joe Adcock (1956).

1996 Detroit trades 1B Cecil Fielder to the New York Yankees for OF Ruben Sierra, marking the first time in history that two players with more than 220 home runs have been traded for each other.

1996 Detroit trades RHP Greg Gohr to California for INF Damion Easley.

1997 Seattle trades OF Jose Cruz, Jr., to Toronto for LHP Paul Spoljaric and RHP Mike Timlin.

1997 Oakland trades 1B Mark McGwire to St. Louis for RHPs T.J. Mathews, Eric Ludwick, and Blake Stein.

1997 The Chicago White Sox trade LHP Wilson Alvarez, and RHPs Roberto Hernandez and Danny Darwin to San Francisco for six minor league players.

1997 Cincinnati trades LHP John Smiley and INF Jeff Branson to Cleveland for RHP Danny Graves, LHP Jim Crowell, RHP Scott Winchester, and SS Damian Jackson.

1998 Chicago LF Albert Belle breaks the ML record for home runs in July with his 16th, and 1B Frank Thomas adds a grand slam home run and five RBIs to lift the White Sox to a 10–2 win over Texas. Joe DiMaggio (1937), Hank Greenberg (1938), Joe Adcock (1956), and Juan Gonzalez (1996) all shared the previous record with 15 homers in July.

1998 Seattle trades LHP Randy Johnson to Houston for RHP Freddy Garcia and INF Carlos Guillen.

1998 Colorado trades OF Ellis Burks to San Francisco for OF Darryl Hamilton and RHP James Stoops.

1998 Los Angeles trades 2B Wilton Guerrero, OF Peter Bergeron, 1B Jonathan Tucker, and LHP Ted Lilly to Montreal for LHP Carlos Perez, SS Mark Grudzielanek, and OF Hiram Bocachica.

1998 Texas trades LHP Darren Oliver and 3B Fernando Tatis to St. Louis for RHP Todd Stottlemyre and SS Royce Clayton.

1998 Florida trades 3B Todd Zeile to Texas for 3B Jose Santo and RHP Daniel DeYoung.

1998 Toronto trades RHP Juan Guzman to Baltimore for RHP Nerio Rodriguez and OF Shannon Carter.

1998 Toronto trades OF Tony Phillips to the New York Mets for RHP Leoncio Estrella.

1998 The New York Mets trade OF Bernard Gilkey and RHP Nelson Figueroa to Arizona for RHP Willie Blair and C Jorge Fabregas.

1998 Toronto trades 3B Ed Sprague to Oakland for RHP Scott Rivette.

1998 Minnesota trades LHP Greg Swindell and 1B/OF Orlando Merced to Boston for RHP Matt Kinney, LHP Joe Thomas, and OF John Barnes.

1998 The New York Mets trade LHP Bill Pulsipher to Milwaukee for INF Mike Kinkade.

1999 Kansas City trades RHP Kevin Appier to Oakland for RHPs Blake Stein, Brad Rigby, and Jeff D'Amico.

1999 Colorado trades LHP Chuck McElroy and OF Darryl Hamilton to the New York Mets for OF Brian McRae, LHP Rigo Beltran, and OF Tom Johnson.

1999 Oakland trades RHP Billy Taylor to the New York Mets for RHPs Jason Isringhausen and Greg McMichael.

1999 The Chicago Cubs trade LHP Terry Mulholland and SS Jose Hernandez to Atlanta for LHP Micah Bowie and RHP Ruben Quevedo.

1999 St. Louis trades SS Shawon Dunston to the New York Mets for INF Craig Paquette.

1999 St. Louis 1B Mark McGwire hits his 39th home run of the season and 495th career to pass Jimmie Foxx for most lifetime homers by a first baseman during the Cardinals 6–5 win over Colorado.

AUGUST

1

1903 New York Giants RHP Joe McGinnity becomes the first hurler of the 20th century to win both games of a doubleheader.

1903 Philadelphia A's LHP Rube Waddell throws a four-hitter against the New York Highlanders with shortstop Kid Elberfeld collecting all four hits.

1906 Brooklyn RHP Harry McIntire pitches 10⅔ innings of no-hit ball before Claude Ritchie of Pittsburgh singles. McIntire weakens in the 13th inning and loses to the Pirates, 1–0, finishing with a four-hitter.

1918 Boston Braves RHP Art Nehf hurls 20 shutout innings, then loses 2–0 in the 21st inning.

1925 George Bamberger b. Stanten Island, NY.

1933 New York Giants LHP Carl Hubbell extends his NL-record scoreless innings streak to 45 in a game eventually won by the Boston Braves, 3–1.

1941 New York Yankees LHP Lefty Gomez walks 11 St. Louis batters in an 11–0 win to set an ML record for walks in a shutout.

1945 Philadelphia A's SS Irwin Hall hits a line drive at Washington RHP Dutch Leonard which results in a single as the ball hits Leonard in the stomach and trickles down into his pants.

1945 New York Giants OF Mel Ott becomes the third member of baseball's 500-homer club when he connects against Boston Braves RHP Johnny Hutchings.

1950 Milt May b. Gary, IN.

1951 Pete Mackanin b. Chicago, IL.

1952 Greg Gross b. York, PA.

1962 Boston Red Sox RHP Bill Monboquette no-hits the White Sox in Chicago, 1–0.

1967 Gregg Jefferies b. Burlingame, CA.

1968 New York RHP Stan Bahnsen sets a Yankees rookie strikeout record with 12 whiffs against the Boston Red Sox.

1970 Pittsburgh OF Willie Stargell hits three doubles and two home runs to power the Pirates past Atlanta, 20–10.

1972 San Diego 1B Nate Colbert blasts five home runs in a doubleheader sweep of Atlanta, 9–0 and 11–7. The five homers tie Stan Musial's 1954 record and the 13 RBIs give Colbert a new ML record. Ironically, Colbert was a spectator the night Musial hit his five homers.

1977 San Francisco 1B Willie McCovey blasts his 18th career grand slam.

1978 Cincinnati 3B Pete Rose goes 0-for-4 against Atlanta LHP Larry McWilliams and RHP Gene Garber to end his 44-game hitting streak, as the Braves defeat the Reds, 16–4.

1986 Minnesota RHP Bert Blyleven throws a two-hitter and becomes the 10th major league hurler with 3,000 career strikeouts in the Twins' 10–1 romp over the Oakland A's.

1993 Ewing Kauffman, who made his fortune in pharmaceuticals and who owned at least half of the Kansas City Royals since their inception in 1969, passes away at age 76.

1994 Baltimore Orioles SS Cal Ripken, Jr., plays in his 2,000th straight game, a 1–0 win at Minnesota.

1994 Toronto OF Joe Carter hits his 300th career home run in a 6–2 win over Boston.

2

1907 Washington RHP Walter Johnson makes his ML debut, losing 3–2 to Detroit. The first hit against him is a bunt single by Tigers OF Ty Cobb.

1918 Due to the U.S. involvement in World War I, AL and NL officials vote to close down the regular season by September 2nd (Labor Day) with the World Series to follow immediately.

1924 Philadelphia A's 1B Joe Hauser collects 14 total bases in a game.

1938 Brooklyn and St. Louis experiment with a "dandelion yellow" horsehide in game one of their doubleheader. Cardinals 1B Johnny Mize hits the one and only yellow home run, but the Dodgers win, 6–2. In game two, the white ball is restored and the Dodgers win again, 9–3.

1959 San Francisco 1B Willie McCovey hits the first of his 521 career ML home runs, this one against Pittsburgh RHP Ron Kline.

1961 Danny Sheaffer b. Jacksonville, FL.

1966 Tim Wakefield b. Melbourne, FL.

1968 The Chicago White Sox trade 2B Tim Cullen to Washington for SS Ron Hansen. It's the second time within a year that the two infielders are swapped for each other.

1979 New York Yankees captain Thurman Munson, age 32, is killed in a plane crash at the Canton, OH, airport. An 11-year veteran, Munson was the AL MVP in 1976 and played on two World Series winners with the Yankees in 1977–78.

1985 New York Yankees OF Rickey Henderson doubles into a double play. With Bobby Meacham on second base and Dale Berra on first, Henderson's gapper is retrieved 8–6–2 with Chicago White Sox C Carlton Fisk nailing both runners out at the plate.

1985 Pittsburgh trades LHPs John Candelaria and Al Holland, along with OF George Hendrick to California for LHPs Pat Clements and Bob Kipper, and OF Mike Brown.

1987 Kansas City 3B Kevin Seitzer goes 6-for-6 with two home runs and seven RBIs to pace a 20-hit attack in a 13–5 drubbing of the Boston Red Sox.

1987 Cincinnati OF Eric Davis leads off the bottom of the 11th inning with his 30th home run of the year to beat San Francisco, 5–4. Davis becomes the seventh major league player to reach the 30–30 plateau this early in the season.

3

1894 Harry Heilmann b. San Francisco, CA.

1913 Chicago Cubs OF Cy Williams hits his first of a career 251 ML home runs, this one against Brooklyn RHP Bull Wagner.

1914 New York Yankees C Les Nunamaker throws out three would-be Detroit base-stealers in the first inning, becoming the only catcher to accomplish the feat during the 20th century.

1921 Commissioner Kenesaw Mountain Landis bans eight Chicago White Sox players from baseball for life, even though a Chicago jury had earlier cleared them of charges that they conspired to fix the 1919 World Series.

1933 Philadelphia A's LHP Lefty Grove shuts out the New York Yankees, 7–0, ending a two-year string covering 308 games that the Bronx Bombers hadn't been blanked.

1937 St. Louis Cardinals C Mickey Owen turns an unassisted triple play.

1940 Cincinnati C Willard Hershberger, despondent over what he considers inadequate play, committs suicide in his Boston hotel room. He was batting .309 at the time of his death and had a three-year average of .316 for the Reds.

1948 Cleveland RHP Satchel Paige makes his first ML start, hurling seven innings in leading the Indians to a 5–3 win over Washington.

1952 Dan Meyer b. Hamilton, OH.

1959 In the first All-Star Game not played in July, the AL earns a split of the first time two-game series as Chicago White Sox 2B Nellie Fox singles home the deciding run in a 5–3 win at the Memorial Coliseum in Los Angeles.

1959 Jim Gott b. Hollywood, CA.

1960 Detroit and Cleveland trade managers with Jimmie Dykes going to the Indians and Joe Gordon headed to the Tigers.

1960 Sid Bream b. Carlisle, PA.

1961 Pittsburgh beats St. Louis, 19–0, for the highest scoring shutout in a NL night game.

1962 Mackey Sasser b. Gaines, GA.

1964 Kevin Elster b. San Pedro, CA.

1968 Rod Beck b. Burbank, CA.

1969 Pinch-hitter Rich Reese hits a grand slam to power the Minnesota Twins to a 5–2 win over the visiting Baltimore Orioles and end LHP Dave McNally's 17-game winning streak, which started with two decisions at the end of 1968.

1987 Minnesota Twins RHP Joe Niekro is suspended for 10 days after he is caught on the mound with an emery board.

1989 In the first inning at Houston, Cincinnati collects 16 hits, scores 14 runs, has seven players with a pair of hits each, and a dozen singles — all records in an 18–2 laugher. The first inning takes 1:38.

1989 Oakland LF Rickey Henderson steals his 50th base, giving him nine seasons with 50 or more to break the AL record he shared with Ty Cobb.

1990 Atlanta trades OF Dale Murphy and RHP Tommy Greene to Philadelphia for RHP Jeff Parrett, OF Jim Vatcher, and SS Victor Rosario.

1994 Los Angeles CF Brett Butler steals his 500th career base to become the 17th ML player to steal 500 bases, score 1,200 runs, and collect 2,000 hits.

1998 Houston LHP C.J. Nitkowski becomes only the third pitcher since 1900 to hit three straight batters, during an 11–3 loss to Florida. Pittsburgh RHP Dock Ellis (1974) and Chicago White Sox LHP Wilbur Wood (1977) were the first two. Ellis allegedly was high on LSD at the time.

1998 Oakland RHP Mike Oquist becomes the first pitcher in 21 years to give up 14 earned runs, as the New York Yankees hammer the A's, 14–1. Oquist sets a franchise record for runs allowed and gives up 16 hits in five innings. Every starter in the New York lineup has at least one hit by the fourth inning.

1890 Dolf Luque b. Havana, Cuba.

1902 Wild Bill Hallahan b. Binghamton, NY.

1908 The St. Louis Cardinals and

Brooklyn Dodgers play a nine-inning game at Brooklyn's Washington Park using only one baseball.

1910 Philadelphia A's RHP Jack Coombs and Chicago White Sox RHP Ed Walsh hook up in a 16-inning scoreless tie. Coombs strikes out 18, allowing three hits. Coombs would lead the AL in wins with 30, while Walsh would lead the league in losses with 20.

1929 Down to its last out, Cleveland erupts for nine runs in the ninth inning for a 14–6 comeback win over the New York Yankees.

1934 Dallas Green b. Newport, DE.

1939 Chicago White Sox OF Mike Kreevich ties an ML record by grounding into four double plays in a game.

1941 Brooklyn C Mickey Owen records all three outs in an inning by catching three foul pop ups.

1942 Cleon Jones b. Plateau, AL.

1945 Two rookie pitchers debut as Washington plays Boston. RHP Joe "Fire" Cleary starts for the Senators and gets shelled, retiring only one batter while allowing seven runs on five hits and three walks for a 189.00 ERA. The Red Sox win, 15–4. In relief comes LHP Bert Shepard, a World War II veteran who lost a leg when his airplane was shot down. Shepard hurls 5⅓ innings, allowing just one run. Neither pitcher will pitch in the major leagues again.

1948 Brooklyn Dodgers announcer Red Barber collapses with a bleeding ulcer in Pittsburgh. General Manager Branch Rickey wants Atlanta Crackers announcer Ernie Harwell, but has to trade minor league C Cliff Dapper for him. Harwell will eventually become the first announcer inducted into the Hall of Fame.

1948 John Grubb b. Richmond, VA.

1962 Roger Clemens b. Dayton, OH.

1962 John Farrell b. Neptune, NJ.

1963 Batting for the first time in two months after breaking his left foot, New York Yankees OF Mickey Mantle hits a ninth inning pinch-hit home run to beat Baltimore, 11–10.

1964 B.J. Surhoff b. Bronx, NY.

1969 Troy O'Leary b. Compton, CA.

1982 New York Mets OF Joel Youngblood singles off Chicago Cubs RHP Ferguson Jenkins in a 7–4 win in Chicago. After the game, Youngblood is traded to Montreal, jumps on a plane to Philadelphia, and gets into the game that night with a single against Phillies LHP Steve Carlton. Youngblood becomes the only player to get two hits for two different teams in two different cities in the same day. Both hits are against future Hall of Famers who would each surpass 3,000 strikeouts and would combine for more than 600 career wins.

1985 Chicago White Sox RHP Tom Seaver, age 40, becomes the 17th 300-game winner in ML history with a six-hitter — all singles — in a 4–1 win over the New York Yankees. Seaver walks only one and strikes out seven batters for 3,499 whiffs in his 19-year career.

1985 California 1B Rod Carew collects his 3,000th career hit against LHP Frank Viola, and the team he started his career with the Minnesota Twins. Carew becomes the first infielder to reach 3,000 hits since Chicago White Sox 2B Eddie Collins in 1925.

1989 Toronto RHP Dave Steib, who lost consecutive no-hit bids with two outs in the ninth inning the previous September, comes within one out of a perfect game before finishing with a two-hit, 2–1 win over the New York Yankees.

1994 Seattle relief RHP Rich Gossage makes his 1,000th career appearance, earning the win in a 4–2 decision over California. Gossage will finish the season, his 22nd and last, with 1,002 career appearances to rank third all-time behind only Hoyt Wilhelm (1,070) and Kent Tekulve (1,050).

1997 Minnesota RHP Brad Radke defeats Toronto, 9–3, to become only the third pitcher since 1950 to win 12 consecutive starts. St. Louis RHP Bob Gibson did it in 1968, and Baltimore RHP Pat Dobson equalled it in 1971.

1998 Baltimore RHP Mike Mussina takes a perfect game into the eighth inning before Detroit's Frank Catalanotto spoils it with a double. Mussina finishes with a two-hitter, striking out eight batters in his 4–0 gem.

5

1901 Baltimore Orioles 1B Burt Hart punches umpire John Haskell and is banned for life after playing in just 58 major league games.

1921 Pittsburgh radio station KDKA airs the Pirates 8–5 victory over Philadelphia as Harold Arlin becomes baseball's first play-by-play announcer.

1940 St. Louis Browns RHP John Whitehead pitches a rain-shortened, six inning no-hitter for a 4–0 victory over Detroit in the second game of a doubleheader.

1943 Nelson Briles b. Dorris, CA.

1953 John Hale b. Fresno, CA.

1967 Minnesota Twins RHP Dean Chance hurls five perfect innings against Boston in a rain-shortened game.

1968 John Olerud b. Seattle, WA.

1969 Pittsburgh OF Willie Stargell blasts a home run over the right field pavillion at Dodgers Stadium against Los Angeles RHP Alan Foster. Stargell's blow travels an estimated 512 feet and helps the Pirates win, 11–3.

1973 Atlanta RHP Phil Niekro pitches a 9–0 no-hitter against San Diego.

1979 Chicago Cubs announcer Jack Brickhouse broadcasts his 5,000th baseball game.

1984 Toronto's Cliff Johnson blasts his 19th career pinch-hit home run to set an ML record as the Blue Jays beat Baltimore, 4–3. He'll finish his career with 20 pinch homers.

1986 San Francisco Giants LHP Steve Carlton becomes the first left-hander and second pitcher overall in ML history to strike out 4,000 batters when he fans Cincinnati OF Eric Davis. Houston RHP Nolan Ryan reached the plateau first in 1985.

1992 Oakland RF Jose Canseco ties an ML record by receiving his seventh consecutive walk over a two-game period.

1994 Atlanta 1B Fred McGriff becomes the ninth ML player to hit 30 or more home runs in seven straight seasons.

1994 Houston 1B Jeff Bagwell sets three club records during a 12–4 win over San Francisco. Bagwell's 38 home runs, 112 RBIs, and 71 extra-base hits are all Astros records.

1999 St. Louis 1B Mark McGwire reaches 500 home runs faster than any player in ML history, then adds his 501st in a 10–3 loss to San Diego. McGwire's 500th career homer, against Padres RHP Andy Ashby, comes in his 5,487th at-bat, breaking Babe Ruth's old record of 5,801 at-bats. McGwire becomes baseball's 16th member of the 500 home run club.

1999 New York Yankees 1B Tino Martinez hits his 200th and 201st career home runs in a 7–4 win over Seattle.

6

1890 Cleveland Spiders RHP Cy Young outpitches Chicago Cubs RHP Bill Hutchinson, 8–1 on a three-hitter, to chalk up the first of his record 511 major league wins. Cleveland buys Young's contract for $300 and a new suit of clothes.

1903 Jim Turner b. Antioch, TN.

1926 Clem Labine b. Lincoln, RI.

1941 Ray Culp b. Elgin, TX.

1945 Andy Messersmith b. Toms River, NJ.

1952 St. Louis Browns RHP Satchel Paige, age 46, becomes the oldest player in ML history with either a shutout or a complete game as he beats Detroit RHP Virgil Trucks, 1–0 in 12 innings.

1966 Stan Belinda b. Huntingdon, PA.

1972 Atlanta Braves OF Hank Aaron hits two home runs, the second in the 10th inning, to beat Cincinnati, 4–3. The pair gives Aaron 661 homers as a Brave, breaking Babe Ruth's record for most with one team. Aaron will finish with 733 with the Braves, then add 22 more in two years as the Milwaukee Brewers' DH to finish with a record 755.

1986 Texas beats Baltimore, 13–11, in a record-setting battle of grand slams. The Rangers' Toby Harrah hits one in the second inning before the Orioles' Larry Sheets and Jim Dwyer connect for one each in a nine-run fourth.

1988 Oakland RF Jose Canseco becomes the 11th player in ML history to hit 30 home runs and steal 30 bases in a season when he swipes second base during the A's 5–4 win over Seattle. Canseco, who enters the contest with 31 homers, will finish the year with 42 homers and 40 steals.

1988 Chicago RHP Rich Gossage joins Rollie Fingers in the 300-save club when he preserves the Cubs' 7–4 win over Philadelphia.

1993 San Diego RF Tony Gwynn collects his 2,000th career hit, this one against Colorado LHP Bruce Ruffin.

1994 Toronto LF Joe Carter becomes the 10th ML player to collect 300 home runs and 200 stolen bases when he swipes second base in a 3–2 loss to Detroit.

1998 Colorado LF Dante Bichette hits his 200th career home run as the Rockies defeat Pittsburgh, 5–1, keeping Pirates RHP Jason Schmidt winless for a 12th consecutive start.

1998 Former sportscaster Jack Brickhouse passes away at age 82. Brickhouse announced the Cubs from 1943 to 1981, as well as the cross town White Sox, baseball New York Giants, NFL Chicago Bears and Cardinals, and NBA Chicago Bulls in a more than five decade career.

1999 San Diego RF Tony Gwynn goes 4-for-5, singling in his first at-bat, to become the 22nd player in ML history to reach 3,000 hits. In his second at-bat, Gwynn passes Roberto Clemente moving into 21st place all-time. Gwynn is the first player to reach 3,000 hits since Lou Brock in 1979. The Padres defeat Montreal, 12–10.

7

1894 Chicago Cubs INF Bill Dahlen has his 42-game hitting streak end against Cincinnati. Dahlen would be the only Chicago player to go hitless as his teammates combine for 20 safeties. Player/manager Bill Lange and Cap Anson who bat before and after Dahlen in the batting order, each get five hits. The next afternoon, Dahlen starts a 28-game streak. He'll finish the year at .362.

1903 Cincinnati SS Tommy Corcoran collects an ML record 14 assists.

1907 Washington Senators RHP Walter Johnson wins the first of his career 416 victories, 7–2 over the Cleveland Indians.

1922 St. Louis Browns OF Ken Williams hits two home runs in the sixth inning of a 16–1 victory over the Washington Senators.

1923 Cleveland 1B Frank Brower goes 6-for-6 with a double and five singles as the Indians rout Washington, 22–2.

1927 Art Houteman b. Detroit, MI.

1929 Don Larsen b. Michigan City, IN.

1931 Ray Crone b. Memphis, TN.

1943 The New York Giants loses to Philadelphia, 9–6, stranding 18 runners on base, exactly two each inning.

1955 Chicago White Sox 2B Nellie Fox begins a 798 consecutive games played streak which runs through September 3, 1960.

1967 Jason Grimsley b. Cleveland, TX.

1968 Joe Keough of the Oakland A's hits a pinch-hit home run in his first ML at-bat in the eighth inning for a 4–3 win over the New York Yankees.

1971 New York blasts Atlanta, 20–6, as 2B Ken Boswell has four hits including a grand slam against Braves LHP Mike McQueen.

1972 Daron Kirkreit b. Anaheim, CA.

1975 Edgar Renteria b. Columbia.

1985 Commissioner Peter Ueberroth announces a tentative agreement ending a two-day strike. The season resumes the next day.

1998 Houston LHP Randy Johnson, making his Astrodome debut after being traded by Seattle, throws a five-hit shutout before a record crowd of 52,071 in defeating Philadelphia, 9–0. It is Johnson's 20th career shutout.

1998 Reggie Sanders, Sean Casey, and Aaron Boone all hit bases loaded doubles during a 12-run sixth inning as the Reds bury Milwaukee, 17–0.

1999 The day after San Diego's Tony Gwynn reaches 3,000 hits, Tampa Bay 3B Wade Boggs becomes the 23rd ML player to reach the milestone, in a 15–10 loss to Cleveland. Boggs has three hits in the contest, and becomes the first member of the 3,000 club to reach the plateau on a home run when he connects against Indians LHP Chris Haney.

1999 Facing Oakland RHP Kevin Appier, Chicago 1B Frank Thomas hits his 300th career home run. The blast accounts for the White Sox' only run in an 11–1 loss to the A's.

8

1903 A week after winning both games of a doubleheader, New York Giants RHP Joe "Iron Man" McGinnity wins another doubleheader against the Brooklyn Dodgers, 6–1 and 4–3. In the second game he also steals home. For the season, McGinnity will lead the NL in wins (31), games (55), games started (48), and complete games (46).

1903 A bleacher overhang at Philadelphia's NL park collapses, killing 12 people and injuring 282.

1915 Philadelphia OF Gavvy Cravath hits four doubles and drives in eight runs as the Phillies defeat Cincinnati, 14–7.

1916 The Philadelphia A's lose their AL record 19th straight road game, which also sets the ML record for most losses in a two-week period.

1917 Ken Raffensberger b. York, PA.

1920 Detroit RHP Howard Ehmke

pitches the fastest game in AL history, 1:13, in beating the New York Yankees, 1–0.

1931 Washington LHP Bobby Burke no-hits the Boston Red Sox, 5–0.

1936 Frank Howard b. Columbus, OH.

1943 The St. Louis Browns don't record an assist in a 5–2 loss at Cleveland.

1948 Jose Cruz, Sr., b. Puerto Rico.

1952 Mike Ivie b. Atlanta, GA.

1954 The Brooklyn Dodgers score 13 runs after two outs in the eighth inning and pound Cincinnati, 20–7.

1963 Ron Karkovice b. Union, NJ.

1964 Milwaukee trades RHP Dennis Ribant to the New York Mets for RHP Frank Lary.

1966 John Hudek b. Tampa, FL.

1973 Boston DH Orlando Cepeda hits four doubles as the Red Sox beat Kansas City, 9–4.

1976 Chicago White Sox owner Bill Veeck outfits his team in navy blue bermuda shorts against Kansas City. The shorts disappear the next day.

1982 California 3B Doug DeCinces hits three home runs in a game for the second time in less than a week in powering the Angels to a 9–5 win over Seattle.

1982 The New York Yankees trade SS Bucky Dent to Texas for OF Lee Mazzilli.

1985 After a two-day walkout, baseball resumes playing with 18 games scheduled including five doubleheaders.

1988 The first night game in Wrigley Field's 74-year history is postponed with the Chicago Cubs leading Philadelphia, 3–1, after heavy rains start in the bottom of the fourth inning. Phillies LF Phil Bradley leads off the game with a home run, but everything is wiped out by rainfall.

1990 Convicted felon and baseball legend Pete Rose reports to a federal work camp at Marion, IL, to begin serving a five month sentence for tax evasion. Ironically, one of the guards on duty is the brother of former Cleveland C Ray Fosse, whom Rose bowled over to win the 1970 All-Star Game.

1990 Montreal trades LHP Zane Smith to Pittsburgh for LHP Scott Ruskin, SS Willie Greene, and OF Moises Alou.

1992 Oakland RHP Dennis Eckersley has his consecutive save record snapped at 40 by failing to protect a 2–1 lead in the ninth inning against Kansas City. Eckersley gives up a two-out, two-run single to Gregg Jefferies which gives the Royals a 3–2 lead, but the A's rally to win, 5–3 in the bottom of the ninth.

1995 Pittsburgh 3B Jeff King hits two home runs in the second inning of the Pirates' 9–5 win over San Francisco, becoming just the 16th NL player to homer twice in an inning.

1997 Seattle LHP Randy Johnson strikes out 19 batters for an ML record second time in a season and finishes with a five-hitter as the Mariners blank the Chicago White Sox, 5–0. The occasion marks the 80th time that Johnson has struck out 10 or more batters, and the 14th time that he has whiffed at least 15 batters.

1998 Minnesota DH Paul Molitor goes 5-for-5 — his sixth career five-hit game — and steals his 500th career base, making him the fifth player in major league history with at least 3,000 hits and 500 steals. The Twins, however, lose to Baltimore, 6–3, as 1B Rafael Palmeiro hits his 35th home run.

1998 St. Louis 1B Mark McGwire hits his 46th home run of the season, against Chicago Cubs RHP Mark Clark, to tie Babe Ruth's 1928 record of most homers over a 12-month period with 70.

1998 Keith Lockhart, Andres Galar-raga, Javier Lopez, Andruw Jones, and Greg Colbrunn all hit home runs as part of a season high 20-hit outburst as Atlanta buries San Francisco, 14–6.

9

1906 Chicago Cubs RHP John W. "Brakeman" Taylor hurls his record 188th consecutive complete game, a 5–3 win over Brooklyn. The string ends in his next start.

1916 The Philadelphia A's have their 20-game losing streak end with a 7–1 win over Detroit. The A's will end the season with a modern worst 36–117 (.235) record to finish 54½ games behind the Boston Red Sox.

1919 Ralph Houk b. Lawrence, KS.

1919 Fred Sanford b. Garfield, UT.

1936 Julian Javier b. Dominican Republic.

1939 Claude Osteen b. Caney Springs, TN.

1941 Paul Lindblad b. Chanute, KS.

1942 Tommie Agee b. Magnolia, AL.

1946 For the first time in ML history, all 16 teams play their games at night.

1948 Bill Campbell b. Highland Park, MI.

1949 Ted Simmons b. Highland Park, MI.

1966 Bob Scanlan b. Los Angeles, CA.

1967 Deion Sanders b. Fort Myers, FL.

1969 Troy Percival b. Fontana, CA.

1970 Pat Mahomes b. Bryan, TX.

1971 Scott Karl b. Fontana, CA.

1971 RHP Satchel Paige becomes the first player from the Negro Leagues elected to Cooperstown's National Baseball Hall of Fame.

1976 Pittsburgh LHP John Candelaria no-hits Los Angeles, 2–0.

1981 The largest crowd in All-Star Game history 72,086 watch the NL rally for a 5–4 win at Municipal Stadium in Cleveland. Philadelphia 3B Mike Schmidt's eighth inning two-run home run against Milwaukee RHP Rollie Fingers proves to be the game-winner for the NL, which has won 18 of the last 19 meetings. The game is pushed back to the latest date in history owing to the 10-week player's strike.

1988 The Chicago Cubs defeat the New York Mets, 6–4, in the first official night game at Wrigley Field. The original scheduled opener against Philadelphia the previous day was rained out after 3½ innings.

1996 San Diego LF Greg Vaughn collects his 100th RBI of the season during a 12–3 win over Pittsburgh, making him the first player in history to collect 100 RBIs in a season while playing for teams in both leagues. Vaughn had 95 RBIs with Milwaukee before being traded.

1998 Atlanta RHP Dennis Martinez becomes the winningest Latino pitcher in ML history with a 7–5 victory over San Francisco. Martinez, from Nicaragua, earns his 244th victory, passing Dominican Republic RHP Juan Marichal (243), and moving further past Cuban RHP Luis Tiant (229).

1999 Toronto sets a club record with 25 hits in a 19–4 rout over Texas.

10

1889 New York Giants RHP Mickey Welch appears as ML baseball's first pinch hitter and promptly strikes out.

1901 In a win over Washington, Philadelphia A's 2B Nap Lajoie hits two home runs for the second straight game.

1924 Detroit OF Ty Cobb steals second, third, and home in succession for an ML record sixth time.

1929 St. Louis Cardinals RHP Grover Cleveland Alexander shuts out Philadelphia in four innings of relief to gain an 11–9 victory, the 373rd and last of his 20-year career.

1933 Rocky Colavito b. Bronx, NY.

1938 The Boston Braves trade OF Vince DiMaggio, RHPs Tommy Reis and Johnny Babich, 3B Gil English, and C Johnny Riddle to Cincinnati for SS Eddie Miller.

1944 Boston Braves RHP Charles "Red" Barrett throws an ML record low 58 pitches, an average of 6½ per inning, in his 2–0 complete game shutout of Cincinnati.

1953 Tom Brookens b. Chambersburg, PA.

1963 Jerald Clark b. Crockett, TX.

1964 Andy Stankiewicz b. Inglewood, CA.

1966 Gerald Williams b. New Orleans, LA.

1968 Chuckie Carr b. San Bernardino, CA.

1971 Minnesota Twins 1B Harmon Killebrew hits his 500th and 501st career home runs against Baltimore LHP Mike Cuellar. Killebrew becomes the 10th ML player to reach the plateau.

1971 Pittsburgh trades RHP Ed Acosta and OF John Jeter to San Diego for RHP Bob Miller.

1981 The two-month, mid-season strike ends, and Philadelphia 1B Pete Rose wastes no time in breaking Stan Musial's NL career hit record with his 3,631st, against St. Louis RHP Bruce Sutter.

1987 Philadelphia Phillies RHP Kevin Gross is suspended for 10 days after getting caught with sandpaper in his glove.

1989 San Francisco LHP Dave Dravecky returns from cancer surgery and defeats Cincinnati, allowing only one hit in seven innings. Five days later, Dravecky's arm will break while pitching and he'll retire.

1994 In a 5–2 win over the Chicago Cubs, San Francisco RHP reliever Rod Beck saves his 28th consecutive game of the season and his record 40th straight dating back to August 1993. Giants 3B Matt Williams blasts his ML leading 43rd homer to move one game ahead of Roger Maris' 61-homer pace of 1961. The season will end two days later when the players strike, however, abruptly ending Williams' pursuit of the HR record.

1994 Montreal wins for the 20th time in 22 games, putting the Expos 35 games over .500 for the first time in franchise history.

1994 Mets LHP John Franco notches his 30th save for the sixth time in his career, and New York wins, 6–2, over Philadelphia.

1995 Los Angeles is forced to forfeit its home game to St. Louis, 2–1 in the ninth inning, on Baseball Night. The promotion turns ugly when fans pelt umpires and players with the souvenir balls.

1995 New York Yankees C Mike Stanley homers three times, collecting seven RBIs in a 10–9 loss to Cleveland.

1997 Atlanta RHP Greg Maddux, a four-time Cy Young Award winner, becomes baseball's highest paid player, signing a five-year contract extension that will pay him $57.5 million. Maddux, who leads the majors with 121 wins since 1991, passes San Francisco OF Barry Bonds and Chicago White Sox OF Albert Belle in the salary game.

1998 New York RHP Hideki Irabu allows only two hits over seven innings in a 7–3 win over Minnesota, as the Yankees move to 56 games above .500 (85–29) for the first time in 37 years. The last Yankees team to reach that level was the 1961 world champions, who finished 109–53.

1998 Baltimore trades of Jeff

Hammonds to Cincinnati for 3B/OF Willie Greene.

11

1907 Bobo Newsom b. Hartsville, SC.

1907 In the second game of a double-header, shortened by mutual agreement, St. Louis Cardinals LHP Ed Karger hurls a seven-inning perfect game to beat the Boston Braves, 4–0.

1926 Cleveland OF Tris Speaker collects his 700th career double, but the Indians lose to the Chicago White Sox, 7–2. Speaker will finish his 22-year Hall of Fame career as the all-time doubles leader with 793.

1929 New York RF Babe Ruth hits his 500th career home run, against Cleveland RHP Willis Hudlin, during a 6–5 Yankees loss.

1936 Bill Monbouquette b. Medford, MA.

1938 Vada Pinson b. Memphis, TN.

1949 Luis Melendez b. Puerto Rico.

1950 Boston Braves RHP Vern Bickford no-hits Brooklyn, 7–0.

1961 Milwaukee Braves LHP Warren Spahn wins his 300th career game, a 2–1 decision over the Chicago Cubs.

1970 Philadelphia RHP Jim Bunning beats Houston, 6–5, to become the first pitcher to win 100 games in both leagues since Cy Young accomplished the feat in 1904.

1972 Andrew Lorraine b. Los Angeles, CA.

1973 Edgar Alfonzo b. Venezuela.

1986 Cincinnati Reds 45-year-old player/manager Pete Rose singles four times and hits a double to set a NL record with his 10th career five-hit game. Rose also collects three RBIs, but the Reds lose to San Francisco, 13–4.

1987 Oakland A's 1B Mark McGwire

breaks Al Rosen's AL rookie home run record with his 38th in an 8–2 loss to Seattle.

1991 Chicago LHP Wilson Alvarez no-hits Baltimore, 7–0.

1994 In the last game of the season due to the baseball strike, Seattle CF Ken Griffey, Jr., hits a grand slam, his 40th home run of the season, in the Mariners' 8–1 win over Oakland.

1998 New York Yankees LHP David Wells becomes the second pitcher this century to shutout the same team in his first start following a perfect game. Wells throws a four-hitter in blanking Minnesota, 7–0, as the Yankees (86–29) move 57 games above .500 for the first time since 1939. The only other pitcher to throw a shutout after a no-hitter against the same team was Philadelphia RHP Jim Bunning against the New York Mets in 1964.

12

1880 Christy Mathewson b. Factoryville, PA.

1892 Ray Schalk b. Harvey, IL.

1919 Fred Hutchinson b. Seattle, WA.

1921 Philadelphia Phillies RHP George Smith allows 12 hits, but still throws a 4–0 shutout against the Boston Braves. Smith will win only three other games all season, while leading the NL with 20 losses.

1928 Bob Buhl b. Saginaw, MI.

1948 During the second game of a doubleheader, Cleveland beats the St. Louis Browns, 26–3, with a 29-hit barrage. The Indians set an ML record with 14 different players hitting safely.

1951 The New York Giants begin a 16-game winning streak, and will win 39 of their last 47 games to pass the Brooklyn Dodgers for the NL pennant.

1964 New York CF Mickey Mantle switch hits home runs for an ML record 10th time in his career in leading the Yankees to a 7–3 win over Chicago.

1966 Dean Hartgraves b. Bakersfield, CA.

1966 Cincinnati's Art Shamsky enters the Reds game as a pinch hitter and winds up hitting three home runs as he stays in the lineup.

1969 Jose Valentin b. Puerto Rico.

1974 California RHP Nolan Ryan strikes out 19 Boston Red Sox batters in nine innings, one short of the ML record, in the Angels' 4–2 victory.

1979 Texas trades 1B Mike Jorgensen and RHP Ed Lynch to the New York Mets for 1B Willie Montanez.

1986 Boston Red Sox DH Don Baylor is hit by a pitch for a record 25th time in a season. Kansas City LHP Bud Black is the pitcher of record as the Royals complete a doubleheader sweep with a 6–5 victory. Baylor will finish the year with a new record of 35 times being hit by a pitch, en route to his all-time mark of 255 plunks.

1987 Atlanta trades RHP Doyle Alexander to Detroit for RHP John Smoltz.

1988 The Boston Red Sox set an AL record winning their 23rd straight game at home, beating Detroit, 9–4. Boston surpasses the league mark of 22 set by the 1931 Philadelphia A's.

1994 Major league players, for the eighth time since 1972, go out on strike, which cancels the remainder of the season. The World Series, too, is lost — for the first time since 1904.

13

1893 Jim Shaw b. Pittsburgh, PA.

1910 In a unique statistical stalemate, the Brooklyn Dodgers and the Pittsburgh Pirates play to an 8–8 tie. Each team has 38 at-bats, 13 hits, 12 assists, five strikeouts, three walks, two errors, one hit batsman, and one passed ball.

1935 Jim "Mudcat" Grant b. LaCoochee, FL.

1939 The New York Yankees tie the AL record for the most lopsided shutout by drubbing the Philadelphia A's, 21–0.

1940 Tony Cloninger b. Lincoln, NC.

1947 Detroit OF Vic Wertz hits his first of a career 266 ML home runs, this one against St. Louis Browns RHP Bob Muncrief.

1948 Cleveland RHP Satchel Paige, age 42, pitches his first ML complete game, allowing only five hits in blanking the Chicago White Sox, 5–0.

1964 Jay Buhner b. Louisville, KY.

1964 Tom Prince b. Kankakee, IL.

1965 Mark Lemke b. Utica, NY.

1969 Alex Fernandez b. Miami Beach, FL.

1969 Baltimore RHP Jim Palmer no-hits Oakland, 8–0.

1972 Riding a four-game losing streak, Detroit manager Billy Martin pulls his lineup out of a hat and the Tigers go on to beat Cleveland, 3–2. Detroit will eventually win the AL East by one game.

1979 St. Louis LF Lou Brock reaches the 3,000 hit plateau with an infield single against Chicago Cubs RHP Dennis Lamp.

1995 Mickey Mantle dies of cancer, age 63.

1997 San Diego trades LF Rickey Henderson to Anaheim for RHP Ryan Hancock and LHP Stevenson Agosto.

1998 New York RHP Orlando "El Duque" Hernandez sets a Yankees rookie record, striking out 13 batters in a 2–0 win over Texas. New York improves to 88–29, 59 games above .500.

1998 San Diego LHP Mark Langston strikes out eight Atlanta batters to push his career total to 2,419 and move past Luis Tiant into sole possession of 25th place all-time. The Braves beat the Padres, however, 5–0, behind ace LHP Tom Glavine's two-hitter, which improves his record to 16–4.

14

1913 Paul Dean b. Lucas, AR.

1919 In the first game of a double-header, the Chicago Cubs beat the Brooklyn Dodgers, 2–0, in 1:10. Brooklyn wins the nightcap, 1–0, in 1:07.

1927 Don Pries b. Alameda, CA.

1930 Earl Weaver b. St. Louis, MO.

1937 Joel Horlen b. San Antonio, TX.

1937 Detroit scores an ML record 36 runs against the St. Louis Browns in a doubleheader. Tigers OF Pete Fox scores eight times.

1942 The New York Yankees turn seven double plays in a game.

1950 Jim Mason b. Mobile, AL.

1958 Cleveland Indians 1B Vic Power steals home twice against Detroit. He's just the third player in history to do it, and he'll only steal one more base all year.

1961 The Philadelphia Phillies lose their 17th consecutive game, 9–2, to the Chicago Cubs behind LHP Dick Ellsworth. Its also the 11th straight complete game thrown against Philadelphia.

1962 Mark Gubicza b. Philadelphia, PA.

1962 Milwaukee Braves OFs Tommie and Hank Aaron both hit home runs against Cincinnati, marking the third time that season the brothers connect in the same game.

1964 Mark Leonard b. Mountain View, CA.

1966 Cincinnati OF Art Shamsky hits his fourth consecutive home run in four consecutive at-bats over two games. Shamsky hit three straight homers in his previous game August 12th.

1967 Joe Grahe b. West Palm Beach, FL.

1971 St. Louis RHP Bob Gibson no-hits Pittsburgh, 11–0.

1977 Milwaukee LHP Bill Travers allows 14 earned runs in 7⅔ innings in a loss to Cleveland.

1980 The New York Yankees trade RHP Ken Clay to Texas for RHP Gaylord Perry.

1981 Philadelphia 3B Mike Schmidt hits his 300th career home run, this one against New York Mets RHP Mike Scott.

1981 Seattle DH Jeff Burroughs hits three home runs during a 13–3 rout of Minnesota.

1982 Philadelphia 1B Pete Rose, in his first at-bat of a 15–11 win over Montreal, moves into first place on the all-time at-bat list with 12,365, passing Hank Aaron.

1987 Oakland 1B Mark McGwire sets an ML rookie record with his 39th home run to help the A's to a 7–6, 12-inning victory over California.

1995 Boston trades OF Chris James to Kansas City for OF Wes Chamberlain.

15

1859 Charlie Comiskey b. Chicago, IL.

1886 Louisville RHP Guy Hecker pitches the Colonels past Baltimore, 22–6, and also has six hits, three of them homers, and scores seven runs. He'll finish the season 27–23 with a team-high .342 batting average for the American Association ballclub.

1896 Bill Sherdel b. McSherrystown, PA.

1905 Philadelphia A's LHP Rube

Waddell no-hits the St. Louis Browns, 2–0, in five innings.

1914 Brooklyn Dodgers C Jake Daubert sets a NL mark with four sacrifice bunts in a game.

1916 Boston Red Sox LHP Babe Ruth beats Washington RHP Walter Johnson, 1–0, in 13 innings at Fenway Park.

1926 Brooklyn 1B Babe Herman doubles with the bases loaded, but is credited with only one RBI and a hit into a double play as the Dodgers runners get confused and three players wind up at third base at one time.

1932 Detroit RHP Tommy Bridges shuts out Washington, 13–0, but loses a perfect game with two outs in the ninth inning on a pinch hit single by Dave Harris, the top AL pinch-hitter of the year with 14 safeties in 43 at-bats (.326).

1935 Joey Jay b. Middletown, CT.

1945 The Chicago Cubs rout Brooklyn, 20–6 at Ebbets Field as Paul Gillespie belts two homers with a single and collects six RBIs.

1945 Duffy Dyer b. Dayton, OH.

1946 Joe Lis b. Somerville, NJ.

1950 Tom Kelly b. Graceville, MN.

1955 Milwaukee Braves LHP Warren Spahn hits a home run in St. Louis against RHP Mel Wright, giving Spahn a homer in every NL ballpark.

1964 Jeff Huson b. Scottsdale, AZ.

1966 Scott Brosius b. Hillsboro, OR.

1975 Baltimore manager Earl Weaver is ejected twice by umpire Ron Luciano during a doubleheader. Weaver is tossed from the first game, then ejected again before the second game starts.

1978 Toronto trades DH Rico Carty to Oakland for DH Willie Horton and RHP Phil Huffman.

1989 San Francisco LHP Dave Dravecky breaks his arm while throwing a pitch at Montreal, ending his career.

1990 Philadelphia LHP Terry Mulholland pitches the record eighth no-hitter of the season, 6–0 over San Francisco. The previous mark of seven was set in 1908 and tied in 1917.

1990 Oakland 1B Mark McGwire hits a grand slam in the 10th inning to lift the A's to a 6–2 win over Boston. McGwire becomes the first ML player to hit 30 or more homers in his first four seasons.

1995 The funeral service for Mickey Mantle at Lovers Lane Methodist Church in Dallas, TX, attracts more than 1,500 mourners. Broadcaster Bob Costas delivers a heartfelt eulogy for the former New York Yankees great stricken by cancer. In his 18 seasons with the Yankees, Mantle played in 12 World Series, won three AL MVP Awards, including his 1956 triple crown campaign, and smashed 536 home runs, eighth best all-time.

1995 Cincinnati OF Reggie Sanders hits three home runs during an 11–3 win over Colorado.

1995 Kansas City trades OF Vince Coleman to Seattle for RHP Jim Converse.

1999 In going the distance, 12–5 over San Francisco, New York Mets LHP Kenny Rogers snaps his team's string of 139 contests without a complete game, one shy of the ML record set by the Anaheim Angels earlier in the season.

1999 Anaheim LHP Chuck Finley becomes the first pitcher in ML history to strike out four batters in one inning twice in a career, in a 10–2 win at Detroit.

16

1920 Cleveland SS Ray Chapman is hit on the head by New York Yankees RHP Carl Mays and dies the next day. It's the only on-field fatality in ML history.

1922 New York Giants RHP Phil Douglas is confronted in his Pittsburgh hotel room by manager John McGraw and Commissioner Kenesaw Mountain Landis concerning a letter written to St. Louis OF and former teammate Les Mann, in which Douglas offers to desert his team in exchange for reward money from the Cardinals players. Douglas, 11–4 at the time, is immediately banned for life. The Giants win the NL pennant without Douglas and go on to win the World Series over the New York Yankees.

1922 Gene Woodling b. Akron, OH.

1927 New York OF Babe Ruth homers over the right field roof at Chicago's Comiskey Park, an upper deck addition for which White Sox owner Charlie Comiskey paid $600,000 to contain homers.

1941 Gene Brabender b. Madison, WI.

1948 Babe Ruth, baseball's all-time home run leader at the time with 714, passes away at age 53.

1948 Mike Jorgensen b. Passaic, NJ.

1954 Milwaukee Braves 3B Eddie Mathews adorns the cover of the inaugural issue of *Sports Illustrated*. Cost is $.25.

1964 St. Louis CF Curt Flood collects eight hits in nine at-bats during a doubleheader—five singles, two doubles, and a triple.

1965 Xavier Hernandez b. Port Arthur, TX.

1966 Terry Shumpert b. Paducah, KY.

1967 Cincinnati RHP Jim Maloney mows down 19 straight Pittsburgh batters when he steps in a hole near the mound, twists his ankle, and can't finish his 4–0 victory. Maloney had thrown two no-hitters in 1965.

1967 Bret Barberie b. Long Beach, CA.

1978 The first four batters in the Minnesota order hit for a chronological cycle against Kansas City as Hosken Powell leads off with a single, Roy Smalley, III doubles, Rod Carew triples, and Glenn Adams hits a home run.

1996 San Diego beats the New York Mets, 15–10 in the opening game of a three-game series played in Monterrey, Mexico. It's the first time an ML regular season game is played outside the United States or Canada.

1998 New York CF Bernie Williams hits a solo home run into the upper deck in the bottom of the ninth inning for a 6–5 win over Texas, giving the Yankees a record-tying 90th win of the year. At 90–30, New York matches the 1944 St. Louis Cardinals for the best record after 120 games.

1998 Chicago rookie RHP Kerry Wood hurls eight strong innings with 11 strikeouts, but receives no decision in the Cubs' 2–1, 11-inning win over Houston. Wood's strikeout total pushes him to 204 for the season, making him only the fourth Cubs pitcher this century to pass 200 whiffs.

1999 Seattle SS Alex Rodriguez hits a home run in his fifth straight game in leading the Mariners to a 7–5 win over Toronto, giving the Blue Jays their fifth straight loss. Rodriguez' streak ends the next night.

17

1894 Louisville RHP Jack Wadsworth sets a NL record that still stands by allowing 28 singles in a game.

1904 Boston Red Sox LHP Jesse Tannehill no-hits the Chicago White Sox, 6–0.

1913 Rudy York b. Ragland, AL.

1933 Jim Davenport b. Siluria, AL.

1933 New York 1B Lou Gehrig plays in his 1,308th straight game, breaking Everett Scott's previous mark, during the Yankees' 7–6 loss at St. Louis.

1937 Diego Segui b. Cuba.

1937 St. Louis beats Cincinnati, 8–6, in the first game ending after midnight. The game concludes at 12:02 A.M.

1941 Boog Powell b. Lakeland, FL.

1946 Skip Lockwood b. Roslindale, MA.

1951 Butch Hobson b. Tuscaloosa, AL.

1957 Philadelphia Phillies OF Richie Ashburn hits a fan, Alice Ruth, with consecutive foul balls, the second time as she lies on a stretcher.

1965 Alex Cole b. Fayetteville, NC.

1966 San Francisco CF Willie Mays hits his 535th career home run against St. Louis RHP Ray Washburn to move into second place all-time, passing Jimmie Foxx.

1971 Jim Converse b. San Francisco, CA.

1971 Jorge Posada b. Puerto Rico.

1992 Los Angeles RHP Kevin Gross no-hits San Francisco, 2–0.

1998 A record seven major league games go into extra innings in one day.

1999 The New York Mets and Chicago Cubs announce that they will open the 2000 season in Tokyo, Japan, March 29–30, marking the first time that regular season games are played outside of North America.

1999 Baltimore LHP Jesse Orosco pitches in his major league-record 1,072nd game, helping preserve RHP Mike Mussina's 15th victory as the Orioles defeat Minnesota, 8–3. Orosco had been tied with Dennis Eckersley for most appearances lifetime.

18

1890 Buck Weaver b. Stowe, PA.

1893 Burleigh Grimes b. Clear Lake, WI.

1915 Boston opens its new NL park, Braves Field, with a 3–1 win over the St. Louis Cardinals.

1934 Roberto Clemente b. Carolina, Puerto Rico.

1943 The St. Louis Browns trade 3B Harlond Clift and RHP Johnny Niggeling to Washington for 3B Ellis Clary and RHP Ox Miller.

1955 Bruce Benedict b. Birmingham, AL.

1956 Cincinnati ties an ML record hitting eight home runs, while Milwaukee hits two to set a NL record with 10 home runs by two clubs in a nine inning night game, during a 13–4 Reds win. Cincinnati's Bob Thurman hits three homers, Ted Kluszewski and Frank Robinson get two apiece, and Wally Post adds one.

1959 Terry Blocker b. Columbia, SC.

1960 Mike LaValliere b. Charlotte, NC.

1960 Milwaukee Braves RHP Lew Burdette no-hits the Philadelphia Phillies, 1–0.

1965 Milwaukee OF Hank Aaron loses a home run against St. Louis LHP Curt Simmons when the umpire rules Aaron steps out of the batter's box. The Braves still win the contest, 6–2.

1967 At Boston's Fenway Park, California RHP Jack Hamilton hits Red Sox OF Tony Conigliaro in the face, shattering his left cheekbone and knocking him out of action until 1969.

1971 Albie Lopez b. Mesa, AZ.

1972 Philadelphia SS Larry Bowa hits his first ML home run against Houston LHP Dave Roberts. Bowa would hit only 14 more in a 8,418 career at-bats for an all-time record worst home run average of 1.069 based on 600 at-bats/season.

1972 Baltimore trades C Elrod Hendricks to the Chicago Cubs for OF Tommy Davis.

1982 Philadelphia 1B Pete Rose makes his 13,941st plate appearance in a 5–3 win over Houston to pass Hank Aaron on baseball's all-time list. Four days earlier, Rose passed Aaron for first place on baseball's all-time at-bat list as well.

1995 St. Louis RHP Tom Henke becomes the seventh ML pitcher to reach 300 saves, surviving a ninth inning rally by Atlanta and preserving a 4–3 win.

1995 Seattle 3B Mike Blowers hits a grand slam and a three-run homer in his first two at-bats, giving him seven RBIs in a 9–3 win over Boston.

1995 The Chicago Cubs pound out ML season highs of 26 runs and 27 hits, 11 for extra bases, en route to a 26–7 win over Colorado. The combined 33 runs scored are also a season high.

1998 Atlanta RHP Greg Maddux wins his 200th career game in defeating San Francisco, 8–4.

1998 New York LF Chad Curtis snaps an 0-for-15 skid with a run-scoring single in the 13th inning to lift the Yankees to a 3–2 win over Kansas City. New York, 10–0 against the Royals, blanks an opponent for the first time in a non-strike year season series outscoring Kansas City, 77–21.

1999 Seattle's Lou Piniella becomes the 18th manager in ML history to reach 1,000 victories with a 5–1 win over Toronto.

1999 St. Louis 1B Mark McGwire hits his 505th career home run to move past Eddie Murray into 15th place all-time, but the Cardinals lose to Philadelphia, 6–5.

19

1902 Baltimore OF Kip Selbach drops three fly balls and has two other hits go thru his legs for a record five outfield errors in one game.

1909 The Philadelphia Phillies are rained out for a record 10th consecutive day.

1921 Detroit OF Ty Cobb collects his 3,00th career hit, this one against Boston RHP Elmer Myers. Only 34 years old, Cobb is the youngest ever to reach this milestone.

1935 Bobby Richardson b. Sumter, SC.

1951 St. Louis Browns owner Bill Veeck sends three-foot, seven-inch, 65-pound Eddie Gaedel in to pinch hit against Detroit LHP Bob Cain. Gaedel, wearing uniform number "1/8," walks on four pitches. Major league baseball later outlaws Browns owner Bill Veeck's gimmick.

1952 Tim Blackwell b. San Diego, CA.

1957 New York Giants owner Horace Stoneham announces that the team's board of directors voted 9–1 in favor of relocating to San Francisco.

1958 Gary Gaetti b. Centralia, IL.

1960 Ron Darling b. Honolulu, HI.

1965 Cincinnati RHP Jim Maloney no-hits the Chicago Cubs, 1–0 in 10 innings, for his second no-hitter of the season. He had earlier taken a no-hitter into the 11th inning against the New York Mets, only to lose 1–0 on two hits.

1968 Woody Williams b. Houston, TX.

1969 Chicago Cubs LHP Ken Holtzman no-hits Atlanta, 3–0.

1983 Los Angeles trades RHP Dave Stewart to Texas for LHP Rick Honeycutt.

1992 Seattle 2B Bret Boone makes his ML debut, becoming the first third-generation player in baseball history. Bret follows in the footsteps of his father Bob Boone (1972–90) and grandfather Ray Boone (1948–60).

1996 Texas sets an AL record playing its 15th straight game without an error during a 10–3 win over Cleveland. The next day Rangers SS Kevin Elster commits an error during the team's 10–4 loss to Cleveland.

1998 Toronto hits for season highs with seven home runs and 21 hits, including a club record-tying 12 for extra bases, in battering Seattle, 16–2. Shawn Green and Carlos Delgado each homer twice for the Blue Jays, and teammates Jose Cruz, Jr., Darrin Fletcher, and Felipo Crespo add one each.

1998 The New York Yankees lose to Minnesota, 5–3, to match baseball's all-time best record after 123 games at 92–31, equalling the 1906 Chicago Cubs.

1999 Cincinnati RHP Pete Harnisch carries a no-hitter into the seventh inning before Mike Benjamin's single ends his bid during the Reds' 1–0 win. Harnisch, who matches his career high with 12 strikeouts, joins Reds reliever RHP Scott Williamson who hurls a hitless ninth inning for a combined one-hitter.

20

1880 Buffalo ace, five-foot, eight-inch James "Pud" Galvin no-hits Worcester, 1–0, the last no-hitter with a mound at 45 feet from home plate.

1895 Pete Schneider b. Los Angeles, CA.

1903 Pittsburgh committs a record six errors in one inning.

1908 Al Lopez b. Tampa, FL

1910 Washington RHP Jay Cashion pitches a six-inning no-hitter as the Senators beat Cleveland, 2–0.

1916 The New York Giants trade 1B Fred Merkle to Brooklyn for C Lew McCarty.

1924 George Zuverink b. Holland, MI.

1942 Fred Norman b. San Antonio, TX.

1944 Graig Nettles b. San Diego, CA.

1945 Brooklyn SS Tommy Brown becomes the youngest player in ML history to hit a home run—17 years, eight months, and four days—when he connects against Pittsburgh LHP Preacher Roe.

1957 Chicago White Sox RHP Bob Keegan no-hits Washington, 6–0.

1960 Mark Langston b. San Diego, CA.

1961 The longest losing streak in the major leagues ends at 23 games as Philadelphia defeats Milwaukee, 7–4, in the second game of a doubleheader behind RHP John Buzhardt, wearing uniform number 23. At season's end, Buzhardt (6–18) will be dealt to the Chicago White Sox.

1967 Andy Benes b. Evansville, IN.

1969 Mark Holzemer b. Littleton, CO.

1974 California RHP Nolan Ryan strikes out 19 Detroit batters, but still loses 1–0 in 11 innings to Tigers LHP Mickey Lolich. Ryan becomes the first player to exceed 100 mph with his fastball as infrared radar records him at 100.9 mph during the contest. It's also the third time during the season that Ryan whiffs 19 batters in a game.

1984 Philadelphia trades RHP Kelly Downs and LHP George Riley to San Francisco for OF Al Oliver and RHP Renie Martin.

1985 New York Mets RHP Dwight Gooden strikes out 16 batters during a 3–0 shutout of San Francisco. Gooden becomes the first NL pitcher to record more than 200 strikeouts in each of his first two seasons.

1989 Chicago Cubs OF Jerome Walton extends his NL consecutive game hitting streak to a second best ever 30 games.

1989 New York Mets 3B Howard Johnson hits his 30th home run of the year to join the 30–30 club for the second time in his career. He'll finish the season with 36 homers and 41 stolen bases.

1995 Cleveland RHP Jose Mesa collects his 37th save in 37 opportunities to set an ML record as the Indians beat Milwaukee, 8–5.

1997 Cincinnati becomes only the second NL team to complete an entire game without having a single player record an assist. The Reds collect 27 outs against Colorado on 14 fly balls, 12 strikeouts, and one unassisted groundout to first base. Nonetheless, Cincinnati loses, 5–3.

1998 St. Louis 1B Mark McGwire becomes the first ML player to hit 50 or more home runs in three consecutive seasons, during a doubleheader split with the New York Mets. McGwire connects for his 50th in the first game, a 2–0 win, then adds his 51st during the Cardinals 5–4 loss in the nightcap. Only Babe Ruth (1920–21 and 1927–28) and McGwire (1996–97) had hit 50 or more homers in prior back-to-back seasons.

1998 The New York Yankees' modern ML record of 48 consecutive games with a lead ends as Minnesota 1B Ron Coomer's second inning home run gives the Twins an early lead in an eventual 9–4 victory.

1998 Texas RF Juan Gonzalez becomes the Rangers' career hit leader when he connects for his 35th home run during an 8–2 win over Cleveland. Gonzalez' 1,181st career hit pushes him past former catcher Jim Sundberg.

1998 Baltimore 3B Cal Ripken, Jr., ties Brooks Robinson's franchise record of 2,848 hits with his 10th home run of the season, but the Orioles fall to Tampa Bay, 4–2.

1998 Oakland LHP Kenny Rogers hurls seven strong innings for his 100th career win, a 3–1 decision over the Chicago White Sox.

1999 Houston batters strike out 21 times, walk a team record-tying 17 times, strand 20 runners, blow a four-run lead, and still the Astros win, 6–4, over Florida in 16 innings.

21

1883 Owen Wilson b. Austin, TX.

1901 Baltimore RHP Joe "Iron Man" McGinnity argues with umpire Tom Connolly, finally stepping on his feet and spitting in his face. McGinnity is fined and suspended by AL President Ban Johnson for two weeks.

1916 Murry Dickson b. Tracy, MO.

1919 Philadelphia Phillies C John Adams ties a NL record for catchers with seven assists during a game.

1926 Chicago White Sox RHP Ted Lyons no-hits the Boston Red Sox, 6–0, in only 1:07.

1931 New York RF Babe Ruth hits his 600th career home run, this one against St. Louis Browns RHP George Blaeholder, during the Yankees' 11–7 win.

1943 Felix Millan b. Puerto Rico.

1945 Jerry DaVanon b. Oceanside, CA.

1963 Pittsburgh's Jerry Lynch hits his 15th career pinch-hit home run to help the Pirates to a 7–6 decision over the Chicago Cubs.

1965 Jim Bullinger b. New Orleans, LA.

1966 John Wetteland b. San Mateo, CA.

1968 Karl Rhodes b. Cincinnati, OH.

1969 Andujar Cedeno b. Dominican Republic.

1970 Craig Counsell b. South Bend, IN.

1972 Philadelphia LHP Steve Carlton has his 15-game winning streak end as Atlanta RHP Phil Niekro beats the Phillies in 11 innings, 2–1.

1973 Ismael Valdes b. Mexico.

1973 Lou Collier b. Chicago, IL.

1975 Chicago Cubs RHPs Rick and Paul Reuschel combine for a 7–0 shutout of Los Angeles. Rick starts and goes 6⅓ innings and Paul relieves for the first-ever shutout by brothers.

1982 Milwaukee RHP Rollie Fingers becomes the first hurler to record 300 saves as the Brewers beat Seattle, 3–2.

1986 Boston SS Spike Owen has four hits and becomes the first ML player in 40 years to score six runs in a game as the Red Sox rout Cleveland, 24–5, powered by a 24-hit attack.

1990 Oakland A's CF Darren Lewis begins his ML record 392 consecutive games played without an error, a streak which includes an ML record 938 consecutive errorless chances streak which lasts through June 29, 1994. The streak continues with Lewis being traded to San Francisco prior to the 1991 season.

1996 Seattle SS Alex Rodriguez becomes the fifth shortstop in ML history to hit 30 home runs in a season when he connects during the Mariners' 10–5 loss to Baltimore.

1997 Oakland hits six home runs, including a team record four in one inning, as the A's hammer Boston, 13–6.

1998 New York 1B Tino Martinez hits a pair of home runs to go over the 100 RBI mark for the third straight season. He's the first Yankees player to do so since Don Mattingly in 1984–87. Martinez goes 3-for-4 to back the six-hit pitching of LHP David Wells (16–2) in a 5–0 win over Texas.

1998 Baltimore 3B Cal Ripken, Jr.'s, seventh inning single, his 2,849th career hit, eclipses the Orioles franchise record held by Brooks Robinson. Baltimore loses to Cleveland, however, 6–3, as RHP Jaret Wright defeats them for the second time in five days.

1999 Chicago RF Sammy Sosa becomes the fourth player in ML history to post consecutive 50–home run seasons, blasting his NL-leading 50th and 51st during the Cubs' 8–6 win over Colorado. Sosa joins only Mark McGwire, Ken Griffey, Jr., and Babe Ruth in reaching the milestone.

1999 Baltimore CF Brady Anderson becomes just the third player in ML history to lead off both games of a doubleheader with a home run, but the Orioles are swept by the Chicago White Sox, 4–3 and 8–5. Anderson joins only Rickey Henderson (1993) and Harry Hooper (1913) in his feat.

22

1886 Cincinnati OF Abner Powell is brought down by the dog days of summer. Louisville OF William "Chicken" Wolf hits a deep drive which Powell takes off in pursuit of, along with a dog that has been sleeping by the fence. The dog bites Powell and won't let go of him until Wolf scores on a game-winning inside-the-park home run.

1890 Urban Shocker b. Cleveland, OH.

1891 Oscar "Hap" Felsch b. Milwaukee, WI.

1892 Chicago Cubs OF Walt Wilmot walks a NL record six times.

1934 Boston Red Sox RHP Wes Ferrell hits two home runs in a game for the second time in a season, accounting for his four homers for the year. In 15 ML seasons, Ferrell will club 38 round-trippers, 10 more than brother Rick, who hits only 28 over 18 years with nearly four times as many at-bats as a regular catcher.

1939 Carl Yastrzemski b. Southampton, NY.

1950 Ray Burris b. Idabel, OK.

1951 New York Yankees LHP Tommy Byrne walks 16 batters in a 13-inning game.

1956 Paul Molitor b. St. Paul, MN.

1961 New York OF Roger Maris, en route to his 61-homer season, becomes the first player to hit his 50th home run in August when he connects against California RHP Ken McBride. The blow puts Maris 13 games ahead of Babe Ruth's 1927 60-homer pace.

1965 Initiating an ugly brawl, San Francisco RHP Juan Marichal objects to Los Angeles C John Roseboro's throws back to LHP Sandy Koufax. Marichal, the batter, feels one whiz by his ear, then turns and clubs Roseboro with his bat. Marichal will draw a nine-game suspension and a $1,750 fine.

1989 Texas RHP Nolan Ryan, age 42, strikes out Oakland's Rickey Henderson for his 5,000th career strikeout. During Ryan's career he'll strike out more than 1,000 different hitters, 17 Hall of Famers, 42 MVPs, 10 brother combinations, and six father and son combinations.

1989 Atlanta LHP Paul Assenmacher ties an ML record by striking out four batters in one inning.

1997 Toronto RHP Roger Clemens becomes the first 20-game winner of the season and reaches the milestone for the fourth time in his career by beating Kansas City, 5–3. Clemens strikes out four batters to move past Hall of Famer Cy Young into 13th place on the career list with 2,820 whiffs.

1997 St. Louis 1B Mark McGwire hits two tape measure home runs, one an estimated 500 feet, as the Cardinals beat Florida, 7–3 in Miami.

1998 St. Louis 1B Mark McGwire hits a 477 foot home run, his 52nd of the season, during a 14–4 loss to Pittsburgh, to set an ML record with 162 over three consecutive seasons. Babe Ruth had hit 161 homers from 1926–28. McGwire also becomes the first NL player to reach 52 homers since Cincinnati LF George Foster in 1977. He also sets a Cardinals record for homers in consecutive seasons (76), and an NL record for most homers by a first baseman. New York Giants 1B Johnny Mize hit 51 in 1947.

1999 St. Louis 1B Mark McGwire hits two home runs against the New York Mets to become the first player in ML history to reach 50 homers in four consecutive seasons. McGwire hits both in the first game of a doubleheader, an 8–7 Mets win. McGwire's first inning opposite field blast measures 502 feet and leaves a dent in the scoreboard about 60 feet above the right-center–field fence.

1999 San Francisco's Barry Bonds, Jeff Kent, and Ellis Burks hit consecutive home runs in the first inning, the second time in three days that the Giants hit three in a row, in a 7–3 win at Milwaukee.

23

1901 Guy Bush b. Aberdeen, MS

1906 The Chicago White Sox have

their 19-game winning streak end against the Washington Senators.

1907 Pittsburgh RHP Howie Kamnitz pitches a five inning no-hitter in the second game of a doubleheader at New York, as the Pirates beat the Giants, 1–0.

1909 Brooklyn C Bill Bergen throws out a record seven attempted basestealers in a game.

1921 Dale Mitchell b. Colony, OK.

1924 Sherm Lollar b. Durham, AR.

1931 Philadelphia A's LHP Lefty Grove loses, 1–0, to St. Louis Browns RHP Dick Coffman, ending a 16-game winning streak. A misjudged fly ball by OF Jim Moore leads to the only run.

1936 Cleveland 17-year-old rookie RHP Bob Feller strikes out 15 St. Louis Browns in his ML debut, a 4–1 win. Feller will return home to Van Meter, IA, to finish high school later that fall.

1948 Ron Blomberg b. Atlanta, GA.

1952 At the Polo Grounds, New York Giant Bob Elliott is ejected by umpire Augie Donatelli for arguing strike two. Bobby Hofman finishes the at-bat and is also tossed for arguing the strike three call.

1957 Mike Boddiker b. Cedar Rapids, IA.

1961 During a 12-run, ninth inning against Cincinnati, San Francisco sets an ML record with five home runs in one inning. Orlando Cepeda, Ed Bailey, Jim Davenport, Willie Mays, and John Orsino all connect for the Giants.

1961 Julio Franco b. Dominican Republic.

1964 Jeff Manto b. Bristol, PA.

1970 Pittsburgh RF Roberto Clemente collects three singles, a double, and a home run in becoming the only major league player to give five hits in two straight games.

1982 Seattle RHP Gaylord Perry is ejected by home plate umpire Dave Phillips for the first time in his career for throwing a spitter against Boston. Perry will serve a 10-day suspension.

1989 Rick Dempsey's leadoff home run in the 22nd inning lifts Los Angeles to a 1–0 win over Montreal, the second longest shutout in ML history.

1993 Toronto LF Joe Carter sets an AL record with his fifth three-homer game of his career, this time victimizing his former team, the Cleveland Indians.

1995 New York Yankees Wade Boggs collects his 2,500th career hit as a pinch hitter in a 2–1 loss to Oakland.

1998 San Francisco LF Barry Bonds becomes the first player in ML history to hit 400 home runs and steal 400 bases when he connects for his 26th round-tripper of the season in a 10–5 win over Florida. In his 13-year career, Bonds has 438 stolen bases.

24

1923 New York Yankees RHP Carl Mays beats the Philadelphia A's a record 23rd straight time.

1940 Boston Red Sox OF Ted Williams makes his only ML mound appearance, hurling the final two innings against Detroit at Fenway Park. He allows one run on three hits, while striking out slugger Rudy York on three pitches. The Tigers, behind RHP Tommy Bridges, win easily, 12–1.

1943 The last-place Philadelphia A's end their record-tying 20-game losing streak with an 8–1 victory in the second game of a doubleheader at Chicago. The A's, last place finishers five of the last six years, will finish the season 49–105, 49 games behind the World Series champion New York Yankees.

1951 New York Yankees OF Gene Woodling homers against Cleveland Hall of Fame RHP Early Wynn. Woodling earlier homered against Wynn on both June 24th and July 24th in the same season.

1951 St. Louis Browns owner Bill Veeck lets fans "manage" the game for a day with "Yes" or "No" cards for certain game situations. The Browns beat the Philadelphia A's, 5–3.

1956 Tony Bernazard b. Puerto Rico.

1960 Cal Ripken, Jr., b. Havre De Grace, MD.

1968 Tim Salmon b. Long Beach, CA.

1972 Kurt Miller b. Tucson, AZ.

1975 After a record 38 straight steals, Los Angeles 2B Davey Lopes is gunned down by Montreal C Gary Carter.

1981 In his first ML game, Minnesota 1B Kent Hrbek hits a 12th inning home run to lift the Twins to a 3–2 win over the New York Yankees.

1989 Commissioner A. Bartlett Giamatti bans Pete Rose for life, for betting on baseball. The suspension prohibits Rose, baseball's all-time hit leader with 4,256, from gaining admittance to the Hall of Fame. Eight days later, Giamatti dies of a heart attack.

1991 Montreal trades RHP Richie Lewis to Baltimore for LHP Chris Myers.

1992 On his 32nd birthday, Baltimore Orioles SS Cal Ripken, Jr., receives a five-year, $30.5 million contract extention.

1997 Boston SS Nomar Garciaparra ties an AL rookie record by hitting in his 26th straight game as the Red Sox beat the Anaheim Angels, 3–2. Garciaparra collects two hits to equal Guy Cutright's 1943 record.

1997 Two teams — the Milwaukee Brewers and San Francisco Giants — score exactly one run over six straight innings.

1999 St. Louis 1B Mark McGwire hits his 51st home run of the season, but the Cardinals lose to Montreal, 8–4. McGwire's homer is his 508th lifetime and 493rd while playing first base, equalling Lou Gehrig for most at the position.

25

1887 Dick Rudolph b. New York, NY.

1921 New York Yankees LHP Harry Harper hits three Cleveland batters in the first inning.

1922 The Chicago Cubs pour across 10 runs in the second inning, and 14 more in the fourth inning, but just hang on, 26–23, as the Philadelphia Phillies leave the bases loaded in the ninth inning. It is the highest scoring game in ML history with 49 combined runs and 51 hits.

1934 Detroit RHP Schoolboy Rowe defeats Washington, 4–2, for his AL record-tying 16th consecutive victory.

1946 Rollie Fingers b. Steubenville, OH.

1952 Detroit RHP Virgil Trucks no-hits the New York Yankees, 1–0, for his second no-hitter of the year. Yankees SS Phil Rizzuto reaches base on a third inning error, which is changed to a hit, then changed back again in the sixth inning with the no-hitter still intact. It's the last win of the year for Trucks, who finishes the season with only a 5–19 record for Detroit, which loses 104 games to wind up 45 games behind the pennant winning Yankees.

1965 Moonlight Graham dies Chisholm, MN. An outfielder for the 1905 New York Giants, Graham played in only one ML game, without an at-bat. Portrayed by Burt Lancaster in the 1989 box office smash *Field of Dreams*, Graham becomes a household name.

1966 Albert Belle b. Shreveport, LA.

1967 Minnesota RHP Dean Chance becomes only the second pitcher ever to throw two no-hitters in the same month as he zips Cleveland, 2–1.

1968 New York Yankees slugger Rocky Colavito, who would hit 374 career homers, blanks Detroit on one hit over 2⅔ innings of relief and gets the win. He homers in game two for the double-header sweep. Nearly 10 years earlier to the day, while with Cleveland, he would hurl three shutout innings to finish his pitching career with a 1.000 winning percent and an ERA of 0.00.

1970 Doug Glanville b. Hackensack, NJ.

1980 Texas Rangers RHP Ferguson Jenkins becomes the first major league player arrested on a drug-related charge.

1985 New York RHP Dwight Gooden becomes the youngest pitcher to win 20 games with a 9–3 victory over San Diego. At 20 years, nine months, and nine days, Gooden is one month younger than Cleveland RHP Bob Feller who won 20 games in 1939.

1986 Oakland 1B Mark McGwire hits his first ML home run against Detroit RHP Walt Terrell.

1990 Detroit 1B Cecil Fielder becomes the first Tigers player to hit a home run over the left field roof at Tigers Stadium.

1995 Philadelphia 1B Gregg Jefferies hits for the cycle during a 17–4 win over Los Angeles.

1998 Toronto RHP Roger Clemens strikes out 18 and allows only three hits without walking a batter, as the Blue Jays blank Kansas City, 3–0. Clemens wins his 11th straight decision in improving his record to 16–6, and also records the 89th double-digit strikeout game of his career.

26

1912 The St. Louis Browns hand Washington RHP Walter Johnson a 3–2 loss, ending his AL record 16-game winning streak.

1916 Philadelphia A's RHP Joe Bush no-hits Cleveland, 5–0.

1926 Washington Senators RHP Walter Johnson (406 wins) and Chicago White Sox RHP Red Faber (197 wins) become the pitchers with the highest composite win totals to face each other, with 603 victories between them. Their record is broken in 1986 by Chicago White Sox RHP Tom Seaver (306) and California Angels RHP Don Sutton (298), with 604 victories.

1926 Pittsburgh OF Paul Waner collects six hits in as many at-bats, including two doubles and a triple. He uses six different bats in the process.

1939 In the first televised game in ML history, Cincinnati beats Brooklyn, 5–2 at Ebbets Field. Three companies each buy one commercial for the game — Mobil Oil, Wheaties, and Ivory Soap. Red Barber handles the play-by-play for experimental station W2XBS.

1947 Brooklyn boasts the first ML black pitcher, RHP Dan Bankhead, who ties a record with a home run in his first at-bat. On the mound, however, he gets creamed, allowing 10 hits in 3⅓ innings, and loses to Pittsburgh, 16–3.

1959 Chicago White Sox owner Bill Veeck has "Smith Day" at Comiskey Park with all "Smiths" admitted free. However, the day is foiled as OF Al Smith kills three rallies with strikeouts, hits into a double play and pops out in five at-bats. In the field, he drops a fly ball as Chicago loses, 7–6.

1961 Jeff Parrett b. Indianapolis, IN.

1961 New York Yankees RF Roger Maris hits his 51st home run of the season against the Kansas City A's. Maris' blast is the most ever by a player at this point in the season.

1962 Minnesota LHP Jack Kralick no-hits the Kansas City A's, 1–0.

1964 Chad Kreuter b. Greenbrae, CA.

1987 Milwaukee's Paul Molitor goes 0-for-4 ending a 39-game hitting streak as the Brewers beat Cleveland 1–0 in 10 innings on a single by Rick Manning. Molitor is waiting in the on-deck circle when Manning drives home the game winner.

1990 In his quest to be the first player since Ted Williams to hit .400, Kansas City 3B George Brett goes 5-for-5, raising his batting average to .407. Brett will finish the season at .390.

1991 Kansas City RHP Bret Saberhagen no-hits the Chicago White Sox, 7–0.

1995 San Diego ties an NL record when OF Melvin Nieves hits the club's ninth grand slam of the season. The Padres still lose to the New York Mets, however, 7–6.

1998 St. Louis 1B Mark McGwire hits a 509 foot home run, his 54th of the season, during the Cardinals' 7–6, 10-inning loss to Florida. McGwire becomes only the third NL player in history with 54 homers and the first in 49 years. Pittsburgh OF Ralph Kiner hit 54 in 1949, and Chicago Cubs OF Hack Wilson hit 56 in 1930.

1999 Arizona LHP Randy Johnson strikes out nine batters in seven innings to become the fastest pitcher to reach 300 strikeouts in a season, achieving the milestone in his 29th start, a 12–2 win at Florida. Montreal RHP Pedro Martinez held the old record of 300 whiffs in 31 starts in 1997. Johnson, who surpassed 300 strikeouts in 1993 and 1998, joins Nolan Ryan (six times) and Sandy Koufax (three times) as the only pitchers to reach the milestone at least three times.

1999 Chicago RF Sammy Sosa hits his 53rd home run of the season during the Cubs' 11–10 win over San Francisco.

27

1911 Chicago White Sox RHP Ed Walsh no-hits the Boston Red Sox, 5–0.

1918 Peanuts Lowrey b. Culver City, CA.

1927 St. Louis Browns RHP Ernie Nevers gives up Babe Ruth's 41st home run after earlier yielding Ruth's eighth homer of the season in May. By 1929, Nevers would give up baseball altogether, returning to football and earning an eventual place in the pro football Hall of Fame.

1935 Ernie Broglio b. Berkeley, CA.

1938 New York Yankees RHP Monte Pearson no-hits Cleveland, 13–0.

1946 Ed Herrmann b. San Diego, CA.

1951 Buddy Bell b. Pittsburgh, PA.

1961 Mike Maddux b. Dayton, OH.

1967 Brian McRae b. Bradenton, FL.

1970 Jim Thome b. Peoria, IL.

1974 New York LF Benny Ayala becomes the first NL player in 13 years to hit a home run in his first ML at-bat, connecting against Houston RHP Tom Griffin during the Mets' 4–2 win.

1975 Minnesota 1B Craig Kusick ties the ML record getting hit by a pitch three times. The Twins beat Milwaukee, the city where Kusick was born, 1–0 in 11 innings.

1977 Texas SS Toby Harrah and 2B Bump Wills hit back-to-back inside-the-park home runs on consecutive pitches in the seventh inning, as the Rangers beat the New York Yankees, 8–2.

1978 Cincinnati 2B Joe Morgan hits his 200th career home run to become the first ML player with both 200 homers and 500 stolen bases.

1982 Oakland's Rickey Henderson breaks Lou Brock's 1974 record of 118 steals in a season, and also swipes three more during the A's 5–4 loss at

Milwaukee. Henderson's 122 thefts happen in 127 games. He'll finish the year with a record 130 steals in 149 games.

1990 Boston OF Ellis Burks ties an ML record with two homers in the same inning.

1992 The New York Mets trade RHP David Cone to Toronto for 2B Jeff Kent and OF Ryan Thompson.

1995 Los Angeles C Mike Piazza collects a career-high seven RBIs going 4-for-4 with a grand slam home run, a two-run homer, and two doubles to carry the Dodgers to a 9–1 win over Philadelphia. Piazza also boosts his batting average to an ML tying .367. He'll finish the season at .346, second to San Diego's Tony Gwynn at .368.

1998 Minnesota DH Paul Molitor passes Willie Mays for ninth place on the all-time hit list with his 3,284th, a first inning double, but the Twins fall to Tampa Bay, 10–3.

1998 San Diego completes its first three game sweep in Philadelphia since 1969, when the Phillies played at Connie Mack Stadium, as RHP Stan Spencer wins his ML debut in an 8–1 rout.

1999 Montreal RF Vladimir Guerrero has his hitting streak end at 31 games, the longest streak in the majors in 12 years, during the Expos' 4–1 loss to Cincinnati.

28

1898 Charlie Grimm b. St. Louis, MO.

1909 Washington LHP Dolly Gray walks seven straight batters.

1913 Washington RHP Walter Johnson has his 14-game winning streak come to an end as the Senators fall to Boston, 1–0 in 11 innings.

1918 Cleveland CF Tris Speaker assaults umpire Tom Connolly drawing an immediate suspension for the remainder of the season, which is cut short by Secretary of War Newton Baker on September 2nd. The Indians finish 2½ games behind the Boston Red Sox for the AL pennant.

1926 Cleveland RHP Dutch Levsen starts and finishes both games of a doubleheader against the Boston Red Sox, winning 6–1 and 5–1, although he doesn't strike out a single batter all day. The Indians use the identical lineup for both games including catcher Harry McCurdy who has a record no chances.

1930 Chicago Cubs OF Hack Wilson collects an RBI single, scoring teammate Kiki Cuyler during the third inning of the second game of a doubleheader. The official scoresheet does not credit him with the RBI; however, it is reported by the Chicago Daily News, the Chicago Tribune, the Cincinnati Inquirer, the New York Times, and the Washington Post. Correctly totaled, the RBI gives Wilson the ML season record at 191, not the 190 recognized for decades afterward.

1936 Tony Gonzalez b. Cuba.

1938 Dick LeMay b. Cincinnati, OH.

1943 Lou Pinella b. Tampa, FL.

1946 Mike Torrez b. Topeka, KS.

1950 Ron Guidry b. Lafayette, LA.

1950 Chicago Cubs OF Hank Sauer hits three home runs against Philadelphia LHP Curt Simmons. Two years later, again at Wrigley Field, Sauer hits three more home runs against the Phillies' Simmons in a 3–2 Chicago win.

1951 Pittsburgh beats New York, 2–0, ending the Giants' 16-game winning streak. During the streak, New York cuts Brooklyn's lead from 13½ games to six.

1952 Cincinnati trades RHP Ewell Blackwell to the New York Yankees for OF Jim Greengrass, LHP Johnny

Schmitz, RHP Ernie Nevel, and OF Bob Marquis.

1967 Darren Lewis b. Berkeley, CA.

1970 Cleveland 1B Tony Horton, deeply troubled in his own pressures to succeed, is removed from the second game of a doubleheader. Later that night he attempts suicide and will never play in the major leagues again.

1971 Philadelphia RHP Rick Wise hits two home runs in helping his own cause in a 7–3 win over San Francisco.

1971 Shane Andrews b. Dallas, TX.

1977 Los Angeles 1B Steve Garvey hits three doubles and two home runs, one a grand slam, in five at-bats during an 11–0 rout of St. Louis.

1977 California RHP Nolan Ryan strikes out 11 Baltimore batters in a 6–1 win to reach the 300 whiff mark for a fifth time.

1983 Atlanta trades OF Brett Butler and 3B Brook Jacoby to Cleveland for RHP Len Barker.

1990 In a 5–2 win over Houston, the Chicago Cubs' Ryne Sandberg becomes the first second baseman in ML history with consecutive of 30 or more home run seasons.

1990 Chicago White Sox 1B Frank Thomas hits his first ML home run against Minnesota LHP Gary Wayne.

1992 The Milwaukee Brewers set an AL record with 31 hits and 26 singles during a 22–2 route of Toronto.

1996 Colorado ties a NL mark when 3B Vinny Castilla becomes the fourth Rockies player to reach the 100 RBI plateau in a season. He joins teammates Andres Galaragga, Ellis Burks, and Dante Bichette. Both the Chicago Cubs and Philadelphia Phillies had four players reach the century mark in RBIs in 1929.

1998 Chicago RF Sammy Sosa hits his 53rd home run of the season as the Cubs defeat Colorado, 10–5.

1998 Houston LHP Randy Johnson ties a franchise record for strikeouts in a game by a left-hander with 16 as the Astros blank Pittsburgh, 2–0.

29

1892 Chicago Cubs C Pop Schriver catches a baseball, recorded at more than 100 mph, from the top of the Washington Monument.

1918 The Chicago Cubs clinch the NL pennant by beating Cincinnati, 1–0.

1919 Billy Cox b. Newport, PA.

1925 New York Yankees manager Miller Huggins fines Babe Ruth $5,000 for insubordination and laziness.

1934 The Philadelphia A's end Detroit RHP Schoolboy Rowe's 16-game winning streak, 13–5.

1939 Dave Nicholson b. St. Louis, MO.

1950 Doug DeCinces b. Burbank, CA.

1965 San Francisco OF Willie Mays breaks Ralph Kiner's NL record with his 17th home run of the month during an 8–3 win over the New York Mets. Kiner had hit 16 home runs in September of 1949 playing for Pittsburgh.

1965 New York Mets manager Casey Stengel, age 75, retires 96 games into the schedule citing poor health and likelier poorer player talent. The Mets finish a franchise worst 50–112, 47 games behind the Los Angeles Dodgers. Stengel concludes his 25th year as manager and 56th year overall in baseball.

1967 Kansas City A's SS Bert Campaneris hits three triples during a 9–8, 10-inning loss to Cleveland.

1973 California RHP Nolan Ryan loses what would've been his third no-hitter of the year, when two infielder teammates allow New York Yankees C

Thurman Munson's pop-up to drop between them. Ryan settles for one of his record 12 one-hitters.

1977 St. Louis LF Lou Brock steals two bases against San Diego, raising his career total to 893, passing Ty Cobb on the all-time list.

1977 Cleveland 2B Duane Kuiper hits his only home run of a 12-year, 3,379 ML game career, against Chicago White Sox RHP Steve Stone.

1989 Montreal trades 3B Mike Blowers to the New York Yankees for LHP John Candelaria.

1990 Oakland trades OF Felix Jose, 3B Stan Royer, and RHP Daryl Green to St. Louis for OF Willie McGee.

1990 Oakland trades RHP Scott Chiamparino and RHP Joe Bitker to Texas for OF Harold Baines.

1998 Florida loses its 89th game of the season, the most ever for a defending World Series champion, as Cincinnati rallies for a 7–5 win. The 1991 Reds lost 88 games after sweeping Oakland in the 1990 World Series.

1999 Baltimore RF Albert Belle ties a team record with four doubles as the Orioles win their last game at Tiger Stadium in Detroit, 11–4.

30

1899 Kiki Cuyler b. Harrisville, MI.

1905 Detroit OF Ty Cobb makes his ML debut hitting a double off New York Highlanders RHP Jack Chesbro in the Tigers' 5–3 victory.

1906 The New York Highlanders sweep Washington, 5–0 and 9–8 in 10 innings, to begin a string of five straight doubleheader sweeps in six days. New York will outscore its opponents in that streak, 76–31.

1910 New York Highlanders RHP

Tom Hughes pitches a no-hitter against Cleveland for nine innings, but gives up one hit in the 10th inning and eventually allows seven hits in 11 innings to lose, 5–0.

1912 St. Louis LHP Earl Hamilton pitches a 5–1 no-hitter against the Tigers in Detroit.

1916 Boston Red Sox LHP Dutch Leonard pitches a 4–0 no-hitter against the St. Louis Browns, the day after the Browns pound him in the first inning and he couldn't get any outs.

1918 Ted Williams b. San Diego, CA.

1918 The New York Giants beat the Brooklyn Dodgers, 1–0, in a game that lasts only 57 minutes.

1941 St. Louis Browns RHP Lon Warneke no-hits Cincinnati, 2–0.

1944 Tug McGraw b. Martinez, CA.

1950 Dave Chalk b. Del Rio, TX.

1951 Pittsburgh OF Frank Thomas hits his first of a career 286 ML home runs against New York Giants RHP George Spencer.

1951 The Boston Braves trade RHP Johnny Sain to the New York Yankees for RHP Lew Burdette and $50,000.

1969 The Seattle Pilots trade OF Tommy Davis to Houston for OFs Danny Walton and Sandy Valdespino.

1972 Jose Herrera b. Dominican Republic.

1982 Houston trades RHP Don Sutton to Milwaukee for OF Kevin Bass, and LHPs Frank DiPino and Mike Madden.

1986 New York Yankees LHP Tommy John, 43, and RHP Joe Niekro, 41, pitch a doubleheader against Seattle to become the first 40-plus teammate combo to start a doubleheader since 1933. John loses the opener, 1–0, but Niekro hurls five innings to win the nightcap, 3–0.

1987 Texas C Geno Petralli ties an ML record with six passed balls fighting

RHP Charlie Hough's knuckleballs in Detroit. Petralli will finish the season with a record 35 passed balls.

1987 Minnesota OF Kirby Puckett has six hits in a nine inning game to tie a modern AL record, and over two contests has 10 hits, which ties another record.

1991 New York Mets RHP David Cone shares an ML record by striking out the side on nine pitches.

1995 Detroit SS Alan Trammell and 2B Lou Whitaker tie an AL record, set by Kansas City 3B George Brett and 2B Frank White, with their 1,914th game together during a 10–7 loss at Chicago.

1997 Boston Red Sox SS Nomar Garciaparra has his AL rookie record 30-game hitting streak end, going 0-for-3 in a 15–3 interleague drubbing by Atlanta. The Braves collect 19 hits and match a season high for runs.

1997 Florida RHP Alex Fernandez allows three hits in eight innings as the Marlins defeat Toronto in interleague play, 4–1, to move the franchise to a record 24 games over .500 at 79–55.

1998 For the 18th time this season, both Chicago RF Sammy Sosa and St. Louis 1B Mark McGwire hit home runs on the same day in their pursuit of Roger Maris. Sosa blasts his 54th homer in a 4–3 Cubs win over Colorado, and later that night McGwire blasts his 55th homer in an 8–7 Cardinals win over Atlanta.

1998 Toronto RHP Roger Clemens hurls a two-hitter for his third straight shutout, extending his scoreless innings streak to 29, with a 6–0 win over Minnesota. Clemens, 17–6, is unbeaten in his last 17 starts.

1998 Philadelphia RHP Curt Schilling pitches his ML leading 13th complete game, raising his NL leading strikeout total to 258, with a 5–4 win over San Francisco. The Phillies turn their first triple play since 1992 and survive Giants

LF Barry Bonds, who hits his 29th and 30th home runs of the season. It's the seventh straight year Bonds has hit 30 or more homers, and the eighth time in nine seasons he reaches 100 RBIs.

1998 Cincinnati finishes a perfect 9–0 season against Florida, winning 14–7.

1999 New York 2B Edgar Alfonso becomes the first player in Mets history to collect six hits in a game, including three home runs and a double in a 17–1 rout over Houston. Alfonso also scores six runs and has five RBIs.

31

1875 Eddie Plank b. Gettysburg, PA.

1913 Ray Dandridge b. Richmond, VA.

1915 Chicago Cubs RHP Jim Lavender no-hits the New York Giants, 2–0.

1918 Boston LHP Babe Ruth pitches the Red Sox to an AL pennant-clinching 6–1 win over the Philadelphia A's.

1935 Frank Robinson b. Beaumont, TX.

1935 Chicago White Sox RHP Vern Kennedy pitches the first no-hitter in Comiskey Park history, and adds a bases loaded triple to his own cause in a 5–0 win.

1937 Detroit C Rudy York hits two home runs against Washington, capping the biggest home run hitting month in baseball history with 18.

1937 Tracy Stallard b. Coeburn, VA.

1943 Detroit 1B Rudy York hits two home runs, giving him 17 for the month of August. It's one less than the record 18 homers he hit for a single month, also in August in 1937.

1950 Brooklyn 1B Gil Hodges becomes the first 20th-century player to hit four home runs in a game in his home park, as the Dodgers defeat the

Boston Braves, 13–9. Hodges adds a single for nine RBIs on his day at Ebbets Field.

1957 Tom Candiotti b. Walnut Creek, CA.

1958 Von Hayes b. Stockton, CA.

1959 Los Angeles LHP Sandy Koufax becomes the first modern NL pitcher to strike out 18 batters in a nine inning game, against San Francisco.

1961 Mike Hartley b. Hawthorne, CA.

1966 Jeff Frye b. Oakland, CA.

1968 Hideo Nomo b. Osaka, Japan.

1974 The New York Yankees collect 31 hits against the Chicago White Sox, the second highest total in AL history.

1980 Montreal trades INF Tony Phillips to San Diego for 1B Willie Montanez.

1985 Pittsburgh trades 3B Bill Madlock to Los Angeles for 1B Sid Bream, and OFs R.J. Reynolds and Cecil Espy.

1987 Baltimore trades LHP Mike Flanagan to Toronto for RHPs Jose Mesa and Oswald Peraza.

1988 St. Louis trades RHP Bob Forsch to Houston for OF Denny Walling.

1990 The Griffeys — 20-year-old Ken Jr. and his dad, 40-year-old Ken Sr.— make ML history leading the Seattle Mariners to a 5–2 win over Kansas City. The Griffeys become the first father and son to play together in the ML.

1990 Boston trades 1B Jeff Bagwell to Houston for RHP Larry Andersen.

1992 Oakland trades OF Jose Canseco to Texas for OF Ruben Sierra and RHPs Jeff Russell and Bobby Witt.

1993 St. Louis trades RHP Lee Smith to the New York Yankees for RHP Richard Batchelor.

1993 Los Angeles trades OF Eric Davis to Detroit for RHP John DeSilva.

1995 New York RF Paul O'Neill homers in his first three at-bats and drives in eight runs leading the Yankees to an 11–6 win against California. O'Neill's feat marks the second time this month that a Yankees player homered three times in a game as catcher Mike Stanley turned the trick August 10th.

1998 Chicago RF Sammy Sosa hits his 55th home run of the season as the Cubs beat Cincinnati, 5–4. Sosa ties Ernie Banks (1958) for second most homers at Wrigley Field with 30, and moves to within one home run of tying Hack Wilson's 68-year old club and NL record. Wilson hit 33 at Wrigley Field in 1930.

1998 Seattle trades 2B Joey Cora to Cleveland for INF David Bell.

1998 Texas DH Juan Gonzalez drives in seven runs to increase his ML leading RBI total to 143 with a home run, triple, and two doubles as the Rangers hammer Detroit, 13–2.

1998 Oakland LF Rickey Henderson scores his 2,000th career run during a 15–6 loss to Cleveland to become the sixth player in ML history to reach the milestone. The five others are Ty Cobb, Hank Aaron, Babe Ruth, Pete Rose, and Willie Mays.

1999 Cleveland 1B Richie Sexson hits a three-run home run during a 10-run eighth inning, and drives in five runs total, as the Indians rally to defeat Anaheim, 14–12. Sexson's 25th homer of the season caps the scoring for Cleveland which for the third time of the season overcomes an eight-run deficit.

1999 The Chicago Cubs trade RHP Rod Beck to Boston for LHP Mark Guthrie.

1999 San Francisco trades OF Stan Javier to Houston for RHP Joe Messman.

SEPTEMBER

1

1886 Washington RHP Ed "Cannonball" Crane walks 14 batters, throws five wild pitches, and commits an error as the Senators get trounced by Chicago, 15–2.

1890 In baseball's first tripleheader, the Brooklyn Bridegrooms sweep the Pittsburgh Innocents, 10–9, 3–2, and 8–4. Pittsburgh will finish the season in last place, 66½ games behind Brooklyn at 23–113.

1906 The Philadelphia A's score three runs in the top of the 24th inning to beat the Boston Red Sox, 4–1, in the longest game in AL history. Both Philadelphia RHP Jack Coombs and Boston RHP Joe Harris, who finishes the year 2–21, go the distance.

1906 New York beats Washington in a doubleheader, 5–4 and 5–3, the third doubleheader sweep for the Highlanders over the Senators in three days.

1912 Boston Red Sox RHP Smokey Joe Wood, on his way to a 34-win season, beats Washington RHP Walter Johnson, 1–0, in a specially arranged pitching duel in Boston. The victory is Wood's 16th straight.

1918 The Boston Red Sox win the AL pennant as Secretary of War Newton Baker ends the season to recruit for World War I. Baseball's 154-game schedule is reduced to 128 games. The Red Sox will go on to win the World Series over the Chicago Cubs behind the pitching of LHP Babe Ruth and haven't won a series since.

1920 Retired Pittsburgh SS Honus Wagner agrees to have his signature put on Louisville Slugger bats. It's believed to be the first product endorsement by a professional athlete.

1931 New York Yankees 1B Lou Gehrig, en route to an AL record 184 RBIs, becomes the third ML player to hit home runs in six straight games — a streak that includes a record three grand slams in five days.

1939 Rico Carty b. Dominican Republic.

1949 Garry Maddox b. Cincinnati, OH.

1963 St. Louis Cardinals RHP Curt Simmons allows only six hits, drives home two runs with a triple and steals home during a 7–3 win over Philadelphia. Simmons' home steal is the last by a pitcher.

1964 David West b. Memphis, TN.

1971 The Pittsburgh Pirates start the first all-minority lineup featuring black and Latin players only.

1975 New York Mets RHP Tom Seaver strikes out Pittsburgh C Manny Sanguillen in the seventh inning to become the first pitcher to whiff 200 batters in eight straight seasons. Seaver will strike out 10 Pirates in his 3–0 win, en route to his eventual NL-leading total of 243.

1978 Baltimore Orioles RHP Sammy Stewart sets a rookie record by striking out seven straight batters in a game.

1995 Detroit's Sparky Anderson manages his 4,000th ML game, a 14–4 loss to Cleveland.

1997 Pete Rose, Jr., makes his ML debut as Cincinnati's third baseman and strikes out in his first at-bat against Kansas City RHP Kevin Appier. He singles in his second at-bat, but the Reds lose to the Royals, 7–4.

1997 Minnesota 1B Paul Molitor has two hits to tie Paul Waner for 13th place on baseball's career list with 3,152, as the Twins defeat the Chicago Cubs, 7–6, in interleague play.

1998 St. Louis 1B Mark McGwire hits a pair of home runs his 56th and 57th — to set a NL record for homers in a season during a 7–1 rout of Florida. McGwire passes Hack Wilson's mark of 56 homers hit in 1930 when the Cubs outfielder also set the ML single season RBI mark of 191. With his 57th homer, McGwire also breaks Babe Ruth's record from 1927–28 with 115 round-trippers over two consecutive seasons.

1998 New York LHP David Wells, perfect against Minnesota on May 17th, almost turns the trick again taking a perfect game into the seventh inning before settling for a two-hit shutout over Oakland, 7–0. Wells, 11–0 at home this season, doesn't walk a batter and strikes out a season-high 13 batters to improve his record to an AL best 17–2. Wells loses his perfect game when A's 1B Jason Giambi singles on an 0–2 pitch with two outs. There have never been two perfect games thrown by the same pitcher in the same season.

1998 Chicago LF Albert Belle sets a club record with his 42nd home run of the season and drives in four runs as the White Sox beat Baltimore, 9–5. Belle's fourth inning homer against Orioles RHP Doug Drabek breaks 1B Frank Thomas' record set in 1993. Belle's three-run double in the ninth inning gives him 337 total bases to break the club record of 336 set by Shoeless Joe Jackson in 1920.

1999 Chicago CF Sammy Sosa hits his 56th home run of the season to provide the difference in the Cubs' 1–0 win over San Diego.

1999 St. Louis 1B Mark McGwire hits his 52nd home run of the season to lead the Cardinals to a 9–3 win over Florida.

McGwire's homer is his 509th lifetime and 494th as a first baseman, breaking Lou Gehrig's record for most at the position.

1999 New York 3B Robin Ventura hits his 200th career home run to lead the Mets to a 9–5 win over Houston.

1999 Baltimore RF Albert Belle reaches the 30 home run plateau for the eighth straight season, during the Orioles 3–1 win over Tampa Bay.

2

1850 Al Spalding b. Byron, IL.

1907 Detroit OF Ty Cobb steals second, third, and home in the same game.

1909 Monte Pearson b. Oakland, CA.

1919 Major league officials approve a best-of-nine World Series format, replacing the long-running seven-game format.

1950 Lamar Johnson b. Bessemer, AL.

1954 Rick Manning b. Niagara Falls, NY.

1957 The Milwaukee Braves set a franchise scoring record with 23 runs against the Chicago Cubs.

1958 Baltimore Orioles RHP Hoyt Wilhelm no-hits the New York Yankees, 1–0.

1960 Boston LF Ted Williams homers against Washington RHP Don Lee, marking what is believed to be the only time a player connects against a father and a son. In 1939, Williams homered against Don's father, Chicago LHP Thornton Lee.

1960 Rex Hudler b. Tempe, AZ.

1961 The estate of Hall of Fame OF Ty Cobb, who died two months earlier, is valued at $11.78 million, the majority held in Coca-Cola stock.

1961 Jeff Russell b. Cincinnati, OH.

1965 Chicago 1B Ernie Banks hits his 400th career home run against St. Louis LHP Curt Simmons as the Cubs win, 5–3.

1971 Houston CF Cesar Cedeno hits an inside-the-park grand slam home run as Los Angeles RF Bill Buckner and 2B Jim Lefebvre collide on a 200-foot pop fly. Houston wins, 9–3.

1972 Chicago Cubs RHP Milt Pappas retires 26 consecutive San Diego batters before walking pinch hitter Larry Stahl on a 3–2 pitch. Pappas then retires Garry Jestadt to complete his 8–0 no-hitter.

1973 Detroit fires manager Billy Martin after he orders a pair of pitchers to throw spitters in a game against Cleveland.

1989 Fay Vincent is appointed acting commissioner the day after Bart Giamatti passes away from a heart attack. Vincent will be formally elected as baseball's eighth commissioner on September 13, 1989, and hold the position until September 7, 1992.

1990 Toronto RHP Dave Stieb no-hits Cleveland, 3–0. It's the ninth no-hitter of the ML season and the first in Blue Jays history.

1995 During a 10–4 win over Toronto, Chicago White Sox OF Tim Raines is caught stealing, snapping his AL record of 40 straight thefts.

1996 Boston LF Mike Greenwell sets an ML record by driving in all nine runs in a 9–8, 10-inning win over Seattle. It's the most runs knocked in one game by a player responsible for all his team's runs.

1996 New York Mets C Todd Hundley sets a single-season home-run record for switch-hitters with his 39th round-tripper during a 8–5 loss to Los Angeles. He'll finish the year with 41 homers.

1998 St. Louis 1B Mark McGwire belts a pair of home runs for the second straight night against Florida — his 58th and 59th of the year — to tie Babe Ruth's 1921 mark for third most in history as the Cardinals hammer the Marlins, 14–4. McGwire surpasses his career best of 58 homers set last year (34 with Oakland and 24 with St. Louis) along with Jimmie Foxx (1932) and Hank Greenberg (1938), who also hit 58. The Cardinals have 23 games remaining for McGwire to attempt to break Roger Maris' 1961 single season record of 61 homers.

1998 Chicago RF Sammy Sosa ties Hack Wilson's 1930 club record with his 56th home run as the Cubs beat Cincinnati, 4–2.

1998 Boston SS Nomar Garciaparra hits a one-out grand slam home run in the bottom of the ninth inning to lift the Red Sox to a 7–3 win over Seattle. With his blast, Garciaparra becomes only the fifth player in ML history to hit 30 homers in each of his first two seasons, joining Mark McGwire, Rudy York, Ron Kittle, and Jose Canseco.

1998 Oakland beats New York, 2–0, to hand the Yankees — baseball's best team at 99–38 — their first shutout loss at home since September 19, 1997.

1999 Baltimore 3B Cal Ripken, Jr., hits his 400th career home run during the Orioles' 11–6 win over Tampa Bay. Ripken becomes the 29th player to reach the milestone when he connects against Devil Rays RHP Rolando Arrojo.

1999 Cleveland 2B Roberto Alomar

hits his 22nd home run and 100th RBI of the season during the Indians' 6–5 win over Anaheim. Alomar becomes the first Indians player in history to score 100 runs, hit 20 homers, drive in 100 runs, and steal 30 bases.

1999 Twenty-two ML umpires are officially jobless after their July 14, 1999, resignations are upheld during negotiations with their union and Major League Baseball in a U. S. District Court.

3

1903 Cleveland RHP Jesse Stovall becomes the first AL pitcher to throw a shutout in his first game, 1–0 over Detroit in 11 innings.

1916 Eddie Stanky b. Philadelphia, PA.

1917 Philadelphia RHP Grover Cleveland Alexander goes the distance in both games of the Phillies' 5–0 and 9–3 sweep of the Brooklyn Dodgers. Alexander will finish the season with a NL-leading 30 wins, becoming only the second ML pitcher with three consecutive 30 win seasons. New York Giants RHP Christy Mathewson won 30 or more from 1903 to 05.

1928 Philadelphia A's PH Ty Cobb strokes his 724th career double and final career hit — his 4,191st — in a game against Washington. Cobb's doubles total will be surpassed only by Tris Speaker and Stan Musial, while his hit total will be exceeded only by Pete Rose.

1947 New York collects 18 hits — all singles — in an 11–2 victory over the Boston Red Sox. Yankee OFs Joe DiMaggio and Tommy Henrich have four hits each.

1947 Philadelphia A's RHP Bill McCahan no-hits Washington, 3–0.

1951 Alan Bannister b. Buena Vista, CA.

1957 Milwaukee Braves LHP Warren Spahn records his 41st career shutout, an ML record for left-handed pitchers, with an 8–0 victory over the Chicago Cubs at Wrigley Field.

1961 Rene Gonzales b. Austin, TX.

1962 Dave Clark b. Tupelo, MS.

1963 Eric Plunk b. Wilmington, CA.

1966 Chicago Cubs RHP Robin Roberts surrenders his ML record 505th and final career home run, to Pittsburgh OF Willie Stargell.

1967 Luis Gonzalez b. Tampa, FL.

1970 Chicago Cubs LF Billy Williams takes himself out of the lineup, ending his NL record of 1,117 consecutive games played, a mark which would later be broken by Steve Garvey in 1983.

1977 Japanese basebAll-Star Sadahara Oh surpasses Hank Aaron by hitting his 756th home run.

1981 The Boston Red Sox and the Seattle Mariners play the longest game in Fenway Park history — 19 innings — before the game is suspended, tied, 7–7. The Mariners score in the first inning the next day to win, 8–7, in 20 innings.

1986 Houston OF Billy Hatcher hits a home run in the top of the 18th inning to lift the Astros to a 8–7 win over the Chicago Cubs. The two teams played 14 innings the day before, and used an ML record 53 players in the contest.

1990 Chicago White Sox RHP Bobby Thigpen sets an ML record with his 47th save in a 4–2 win over the Kansas City Royals. Thigpen breaks New York Yankees LHP Dave Righetti's previous mark of 46 from 1986, and will finish the year with a new record of 57 saves.

1995 New York Yankees SS Tony Fernandez hits for the cycle in a 10–9 loss to Oakland.

1996 St. Louis RHP Todd Stottlemyre defeats Houston, 12–3, to give him and his father Mel the record for most victories by a father-son duo. The Stottlemyres' 259 wins surpasses the old mark set by Steve and Dizzy Trout.

1997 Cleveland 3B Matt Williams and SS Omar Vizquel hit home runs to lift the Indians to a 7–3 interleague win at Pittsburgh. The Indians win twice in the three-game series, the first between the teams in their 96 years together in the major leagues. The series attendance of 126,191 is the fourth largest in Pirates history.

1997 During an interleague game against St. Louis, the Chicago White Sox collect four hits and a walk in one inning yet don't score.

1998 The Minnesota Twins, 0–65 this season when trailing after eight innings, finally snap their futility streak with a 12-inning, 5–4 win over Tampa Bay before a season-low crowd of 7,072 at the Metrodome.

1999 Chicago RF Sammy Sosa hits his 57th home run of the season during the Cubs' 8–6 loss to Los Angeles.

1999 St. Louis 1B Mark McGwire hits his 53rd and 54th home runs of the season during the Cardinals' 11-inning, 5–4 win at Milwaukee.

1999 San Francisco 2B Jeff Kent hits his eighth career grand slam home run, his 18th homer of the season, during the Giants' 12–2 win at Pittsburgh.

4

1902 Chicago Cubs LHP Alex Hardy becomes the first ML player to pitch a shutout in his first game, 1–0 over Brooklyn.

1906 The New York Yankees win their ML record fifth straight doubleheader, sweeping the Boston Red Sox, 7–0 and 1–0.

1908 Washington RHP Walter John-

son starts a four day stretch by shutting out the New York Highlanders on four hits. The next day, he'll throw a three-hit shutout against the Highlanders, and two days later Johnson will again blank New York, this time on only two hits.

1916 Cincinnati RHP Christy Mathewson and Chicago RHP Mordecai Brown pitch career finales against each other. The Reds win, 10–8, in Mathewson's only victory while not wearing the New York Giants uniform he had donned for 17 years. Eventual Hall of Famers, Mathewson would finish his career 373–188, Brown 239–129.

1919 Eddie Waitkus b. Cambridge, MA.

1923 New York Yankees RHP Sad Sam Jones no-hits the Philadelphia A's, 2–0.

1941 Ken Harrelson b. Woodruff, SC.

1941 The New York Yankees defeat the Boston Red Sox, 6–3, to clinch the AL pennant on the earliest date in history. The Yankees, 101–53, will finish 17 games ahead of the second place Boston Red Sox, 84–70.

1950 Doyle Alexander b. Cordova, AL.

1968 Mike Piazza b. Norristown, PA.

1973 At Montreal's Jarry Park, the game between the Expos and the New York Mets is delayed 11 minutes due to excessive sun brightness.

1974 Houston RHP Don Wilson is replaced by a pinch hitter after hurling eight no-hit innings against Concintini. Astros LHP Mike Cosgrove replaces Wilson and gives up a leadoff single to Tony Perez for the Reds' only hit as Cincinnati wins, 2–1.

1985 New York C Gary Carter hits two home runs to tie an ML record and singles home another run as the Mets win, 9–2, over San Diego. Carter hit three home runs the night before and becomes the 11th player in ML history to hit five home runs in two games.

1991 Major League Baseball announces that it will remove the asterisk from Roger Maris' 1961 record of 61 home runs.

1993 New York LHP Jim Abbott throws the Yankees' first no-hitter in 10 years, a 4–0 win over Cleveland.

1995 Chicago 3B Robin Ventura becomes the eighth player in ML history to hit two grand slams in the same game, leading the White Sox to a 14–3 win at Texas.

1997 Rupert Murdoch's Fox Group reaches an agreement in principle to buy the Los Angeles Dodgers from the O'Malley family for $350 million. The sale is contingent on league approval to be voted on in January 1998. The media mogul's worldwide empire includes newspapers, the Fox television network, as well as cable and satellite operations on six continents.

1998 Chicago RF Sammy Sosa breaks Hack Wilson's 68-year-old Cubs club record with his 57th of the season during a 5–2 win at Pittsburgh. Sosa, who has homered against every NL team this season, wastes little time in connecting against Pirates RHP Jason Schmidt in the first inning.

1998 The New York Yankees reach 100 victories on the earliest date in ML history as DH Bernie Williams homers twice in an 11–6 win over the Chicago White Sox. The Yankees' 100th win is reached five days earlier than both the 1906 Chicago Cubs and 1954 Cleveland Indians. The Yankees, 100–38, also set an AL record for the fewest games to reach 100 victories (138). The 1906 Cubs hold the ML record at 132 games to win 100.

5

1875 Nap Lajoie b. Woonsocket, RI.

1908 Brooklyn LHP Nap Rucker pitches a 6–0 no-hitter against Boston at Ebbets Field. Rucker strikes out 14 and walks none.

1918 Boston LHP Babe Ruth pitches a six-hitter as the Red Sox beat the Chicago Cubs, 1–0, in the opening game of the World Series. The series starts early due to World War I.

1936 Bill Mazeroski b. Wheeling, WV.

1943 Dave Morehead b. San Diego, CA.

1955 Brooklyn RHP Don Newcombe hits his NL record seventh home run of the season as the Dodgers beat Philadelphia, 11–4.

1960 Candy Maldonado b. Puerto Rico.

1963 Jeff Brantley b. Florence, AL.

1971 Houston Astros RHP J.R. Richard ties Karl Spooner's ML record by striking out 15 batters in his first ML game, against San Francisco.

1971 Chicago RHP Ferguson Jenkins gives up a home run to St. Louis OF Matty Alou, thereby completing the Alou brothers trifecta of homers against the future Cubs Hall of Famer. Jenkins had first yielded a homer against Jesus Alou (Giants) in 1967, followed by Felipe Alou (Braves) in 1968. Jesus will take Jenkins deep again in 1973 as a member of the Houston Astros.

1972 Jimmy Haynes b. La Grange, GA.

1995 Baltimore 3B Cal Ripken, Jr., ties Lou Gehrig with his 2,130th consecutive game played during the Orioles' 8–0 win over California.

1996 Minnesota's Paul Molitor collects his 200th hit of the season during a 6–2 win over California. Molitor joins Sam Rice of the 1930 Washington Senators as the only players in ML history to have a 200-hit season after their 40th birthdays.

1998 St. Louis 1B Mark McGwire hits his 60th home run of the season, against Cincinnati LHP Dennis Reyes to tie Babe Ruth's 1927 mark for second best all-time, as the Cardinals blank the Reds, 7–0. St. Louis LHP Donovan Osborn shuts out the Reds on three hits.

1999 Cincinnati hits five home runs during a 9–7 win over Philadelphia to set an ML record with 14 homers in two consecutive games.

6

1864 Oyster Burns b. Philadelphia, PA.

1883 Chicago and Detroit set both an NL and ML record having eight players collect at least three hits in a game. The record goes unequalled for 115 years until Cincinnati and Colorado match the feat on April 11, 1998.

1888 Red Faber b. Cascade, IA.

1905 Chicago White Sox RHP Frank Smith wins the most lopsided no-hitter in ML history, 15–0 over Detroit.

1912 Vince DiMaggio b. Martinez, CA.

1912 New York Giants RHP Jeff Tesreau no-hits Philadelphia, 3–0, to aid in his eventual NL lowest ERA mark of 1.96.

1924 St. Louis Browns RHP Urban Shocker pitches two complete games over the Chicago White Sox, winning both contests by the same 6–2 score.

1943 At 16 years, eight months and five days, Philadelphia A's RHP Carl Scheib becomes the youngest player to appear in an AL game.

1946 Fran Healy b. Holyoke, MA.

1950 Brooklyn RHP Don Newcombe misses pitching complete games in a doubleheader when he is relieved in the seventh inning of the second game trailing Philadelphia, 2–0. Newcombe wins the opener, 2–0.

1968 Pat Meares b. Salina, KS.

1968 Minnesota 3B Graig Nettles hits his first of a career 390 ML home runs against Detroit's 31-game winner, RHP Denny McLain.

1974 The Baltimore Orioles run their AL record consecutive shutout wins streak to five games.

1980 Montreal OF Tim Wallach hits a home run in his first ML at-bat against San Francisco LHP Phil Nastu.

1981 Los Angeles Dodgers LHP Fernando Valenzuela blanks St. Louis, 5–0, to tie an NL record of seven shutouts by a rookie pitcher.

1986 Milwaukee SS Robin Yount collects his 2,000th career hit at age 30. Only Babe Ruth and Hank Aaron reached that plateau at an earlier age.

1991 Houston RHP Pete Harnisch ties an ML record by striking out the side on nine pitches.

1995 Baltimore SS Cal Ripken, Jr., passes Lou Gehrig at 2,131 straight games played in a 4–2 win over California. Ripken goes 3-for-3 in the contest with a home run.

1996 Baltimore DH Eddie Murray becomes the 15th ML player to reach the 500 home run plateau when he connects against Detroit RHP Felipe Lira. Murray also joins Hank Aaron and Willie Mays as the only members of the 500 home run club with 3,000 base hits as well.

1997 The Colorado Rockies have their consecutive home sellout streak end at 203 games due to a scheduling change from a September 4th rainout. Rather than purchase tickets for a day/night doubleheader, more than 3,000 fans elect another date later in the season. During one of the games, the opposing St. Louis Cardinals become the first team since the 1973 Kansas City Royals to use four catchers.

1999 Chicago RF Sammy Sosa hits his 58th home run of the season, but the Cubs lose to Cincinnati, 6–3.

7

1880 Hooks Wiltse b. Hamilton, NY.

1908 Washington RHP Walter Johnson pitches his third consecutive shutout against New York in four days.

1911 Philadelphia Phillies rookie RHP Grover Cleveland Alexander posts a 1–0 victory over 44-year-old RHP Cy Young, who closes out his 22-year career with the Boston Braves.

1916 The New York Giants begin their ML record 26-game winning streak by beating Brooklyn, 4–1, at the Polo Grounds. All 26 wins are at home giving the Giants another record.

1920 Almost three weeks after SS Ray Chapman is killed by a pitch thrown by New York RHP Carl Mays, the Cleveland Indians bring up rookie SS Joe Sewell from the minor leagues to take Chapman's place. Sewell finishes the campaign with a .329 average to help the Indians win the AL pennant and the World Series. It marks a rare distinction for Sewell, who plays on his third baseball championship team in one season. In the spring he leads the U. of Alabama to a fourth straight Southern Intercollegiate Athletic Association championship, then after signing professionally, he leads the New Orleans Pelicans to a Southern Association title, prior to joining the Indians.

1923 Just three days after being no-hit by Sad Sam Jones of the New York Giants, the Philadelphia A's are again no-hit, 4–0, by Boston RHP Howard Ehmke. A's starting pitcher Slim Harriss hits an apparent double in the seventh inning, but is called out for not touching first base preserving the no-hitter.

1927 The day after he hits three home runs in a doubleheader at Boston's Fenway Park, New York Yankees RF Babe Ruth hits two more in another doubleheader to set an ML record with five homers in two days.

1945 Washington 1B Joe Kuhel hits an inside-the-park homer at home, the only home run hit at Griffith Stadium all season.

1946 Joe Rudi b. Modesto, CA.

1954 The Kansas City A's play the Washington Senators at Griffith Stadium before a reported crowd of only 460 spectators.

1962 Los Angeles SS Maury Wills steals four bases in a 10–1 loss to Pittsburgh to break the NL record with 82 thefts for the season. Wills will finish the year with a new record 104 steals.

1965 Sergio Valdez b. Dominican Republic.

1969 Darren Bragg b. Waterbury, CT.

1971 Philadelphia LF Greg Luzinski hits the first of his 307 ML home runs, this one against St. Louis RHP Reggie Cleveland.

1972 Jason Isringhausen b. Brighton, IL.

1974 New York 3B Graig Nettles' seventh inning single is disallowed as his bat shatters and several superballs come flying out. The Yankees hold on, 1–0, though, on Nettles' earlier home run.

1977 Detroit C Lance Parrish hits the first of his 324 ML home runs against Baltimore LHP Earl Stephenson, who makes his only appearance of the year.

1984 New York RHP Dwight Gooden strikes out Chicago 3B Ron Cey for his 228th whiff of the season, breaking the NL rookie record held by Grover Cleveland Alexander in 1911. The Mets defeat the Cubs, 10–0, behind Gooden's one-hitter. Gooden will finish his rookie campaign with a new record 276 strikeouts.

1992 Baseball's eighth commissioner, Fay Vincent, resigns four days after owners urge him to do so by an 18–9–1 vote.

1993 St. Louis OF Mark Whiten ties two ML records with four home runs and 12 RBIs in a 15–2 win over Cincinnati in the second game of a doubleheader. He's the only player to accomplish both feats in the same game.

1996 Philadelphia Phillies 3B Scott Rolen has his right arm broken and his season end at 130 at-bats when he is hit by a Steve Trachsel pitch during a game with the Chicago Cubs. Rolen's final plate appearance does not count as an official at-bat, thereby allowing him to stay only one below the minimum for a qualified rookie. This enables him to bounce back in 1997 to win the NL Rookie of the Year Award easily.

1997 Seattle OF Ken Griffey Jr. becomes the 15th ML player to reach the 50 home run plateau when he connects against Minnesota RHP Bob Tewksbury during the Mariners 9–6 loss to the Twins.

1998 St. Louis 1B Mark McGwire hits his 61st home run of the season to tie Roger Maris' 1961 record, victimizing RHP Mike Morgan, as the Cardinals nip the Chicago Cubs, 3–2. Cubs RF Sammy Sosa fails to homer and stays behind McGwire in the season race with 58 round-trippers.

1998 Seattle CF Ken Griffey, Jr., has four hits including two home runs — his 49th and 50th of the season — to mark the first time in ML history that three players have reached the 50-homer mark in a season. Griffey's 50th homer comes only hours after St. Louis 1B Mark McGwire belts his record-tying 61st of the season, while Chicago Cubs RF Sammy Sosa remains at 58. Griffey, who belted 56 homers last year, joins only McGwire (1996–98) and Babe Ruth (1920–21 and 1927–28) as the only players with 50 or more homers in back-to-back seasons (Sosa will join the club in 1999). The Mariners hammer Baltimore, 11–1.

1998 Houston LHP Randy Johnson records his 17th double-digit strikeout game of the season and 100th of his career in a 1–0 win over Cincinnati. The shutout is Johnson's fourth straight at home as he whiffs 14 batters while allowing only six hits and one walk in lowering his ERA to 1.00.

1998 Arizona RHP Gregg Olson earns his 200th career save as the Diamondbacks edge Los Angeles, 4–2.

8

1905 The Pittsburgh Pirates strand an NL record 18 runners on base in an 8–3 loss to Cincinnati.

1907 Buck Leonard b. Rocky Mount, NC.

1916 Philadelphia A's C Wally Schang becomes the first switch hitter to hit a home run from both sides of the plate in the same game, against the New York Yankees.

1942 Steve Hargan b. Fort Wayne, IN.

1946 Ken Forsch b. Sacramento, CA.

1955 The Brooklyn Dodgers beat Milwaukee, 10–2, to clinch the NL pennant with a 17-game lead.

1955 St. Louis trades RHP Bob Tiefenauer to Detroit for RHP Ben Flowers.

1958 Pittsburgh OF Roberto Clemente ties an ML record by hitting three triples in a 4–1 win over Cincinnati.

1963 Milwaukee Braves LHP Warren Spahn, age 42, becomes a 20-game winner for a NL-record tying 13th time, beating Philadelphia, 3–2. He'll finish the season at 23–7.

1965 Bert Campaneris of the Kansas City A's plays all nine positions, but leaves the game after a ninth inning crash with California C Ed Kirkpatrick. The Angels win, 5–3 in 13 innings.

1966 Mike Dyer b. Upland, CA.

1969 Atlanta trades OF Mickey Rivers to California for RHP Bob Priddy and LHP Clint Compton.

1972 Chicago Cubs RHP Ferguson Jenkins beats Philadelphia, 4–3, for his 20th win of the year, marking the sixth straight season that he has won at least 20 games.

1973 Bob Wolcott b. Huntington Beach, CA.

1985 Cincinnati player/manager Pete Rose ties Ty Cobb with his 4,191st career hit against the Chicago Cubs. The game is called due to darkness after nine innings, 5–5.

1988 NL President A. Bartlett Giamatti is elected to succeed Peter Ueberroth as baseball's seventh commissioner. He'll die of a heart attack less than a year later while still in office.

1990 Cincinnati LHP Randy Myers ties the NL single game record with six consecutive strikeouts by a relief pitcher.

1993 The major league owners committee meets for two days to create a new alignment and an expanded playoff format. A Central Division is added to each league, and the playoffs will include a wild-card team with the best record from among the second place finishers.

1993 Houston RHP Darryl Kile no-hits the New York Mets, winning 7–1.

1995 Cleveland ends a 41-year postseason drought by clinching the AL Central Division with a 3–2 win over Baltimore.

1995 Boston ties an ML record with four consecutive pinch hits in the eighth inning of an 8–4 loss to the New York Yankees.

1996 Florida Marlins OF Gary Sheffield homers against Montreal RHP

Pedro Martinez. It is the 4,459th home run of the season, breaking the ML season record set previously in 1987. Three weeks still remain in the season.

1998 St. Louis 1B Mark McGwire breaks Roger Maris' 37-year-old single season home run record with his 62nd of the year, victimizing Chicago RHP Steve Trachsel, as the Cardinals beat the Cubs, 6–3. The homer, McGwire's shortest of the season measuring 341 feet and just clearing the left field fence, comes on the Cardinals 144th game of the year.

1998 Philadelphia hammers New York, 16–4, setting a club record with seven home runs against four Mets pitchers. Rico Brogna, Kevin Sefcik, and Bobby Estalella each hit two homers, and pinch hitter Marlon Anderson homers in his first ML at-bat.

1999 Arizona CF Steve Finley blasts three home runs for six RBIs as the Diamondbacks rout Milwaukee, 9–1.

9

1876 Hartford RHP Candy Cummings becomes the first hurler to win two complete games in one day, beating Cincinnati, 14–4 and 8–4.

1877 Frank Chance b. Fresno, CA.

1898 Frankie Frisch b. Queens, NY.

1899 Waite Hoyt b. Brooklyn, NY.

1914 Boston Braves RHP George Davis no-hits Philadelphia, 7–0.

1918 Boston Red Sox LHP Babe Ruth has his consecutive scoreless innings streak end at 29⅔ as the Chicago Cubs score twice during World Series Game 4 at Fenway Park. The Red Sox win the game, 3–2, however, and take the series four games to two.

1922 St. Louis OF Baby Doll Jacobson hits three triples to lead the Browns to a 16–0 whitewash over the Detroit Tigers.

1928 RHP Urban Shocker, a 187-game winner with the New York Yankees and St. Louis Browns, dies of pneumonia at age 38, following his 13th and last year in the major leagues.

1936 The New York Yankees clinch their eighth AL pennant with a double-header sweep of Cleveland, 11–3 and 12–9. The Yankees finish the year in a club record, 102–51, a club record, 19½ games ahead of runner-up Detroit.

1945 Just nine days removed from his military duties, Philadelphia A's RHP Dick Fowler no-hits the St. Louis Browns, 1–0, in the second game of a doubleheader. It's Fowler's first post-war appearance and only win of the season against two losses. He had left the major leagues in 1942 to serve in World War II.

1948 Brooklyn RHP Rex Barney no-hits the New York Giants, 2–0.

1959 Tom Foley b. Columbus, GA.

1961 Jim Corsi b. Newton, MA.

1965 Los Angeles LHP Sandy Koufax throws a perfect game against Chicago, winning 1–0 for his fourth career no-hitter. The Dodgers get only one hit against Cubs LHP Bobby Hendley — a double by Lou Johnson. Los Angeles C Jeff Torborg is on the receiving end of the first of his three no-hitters caught, the others thrown by Dodgers RHP Bill Singer and California Angels RHP Nolan Ryan.

1965 Todd Zeile b. Van Nuys, CA.

1970 Joey Hamilton b. Statesboro, GA.

1988 Milwaukee SS Gary Sheffield hits his first ML home run against Seattle LHP Mark Langston.

1992 Milwaukee OF Robin Yount collects his 3,000th ML hit with a single against Cleveland RHP Jose Mesa.

Coming just a week prior to his 37th birthday, only Ty Cobb and Hank Aaron were younger than Yount when they reached that plateau.

1992 Two days after Fay Vincent resigns as baseball's eighth commissioner, the 10-member executive council names Bud Selig, longtime president and CEO of the Milwaukee Brewers, as commissioner pro tem.

1995 New York Yankees 1B Don Mattingly scores his 1,000th career run in a 9–1 win over Boston.

1997 Richie Ashburn, who spent 50 years in the sportscape of the Philadelphia Phillies, passes away at age 70. The former Hall of Fame outfielder and newspaper columnist had spent the last 35 years as a radio and television announcer.

1997 Bud Selig's reign as baseball's acting commissioner reaches its five-year anniversary. His tenure has outlasted four actual baseball commissioners.

1999 Hall of Fame RHP Jim "Catfish" Hunter dies from amyotrophic lateral sclerosis (ALS), known as Lou Gehrig's disease, at his home in Hertford, NC. Hunter, who pitched for the Kansas City and Oakland A's and New York Yankees, won 224 games in his 15 major league seasons (1965–79) including 20 or more wins five straight years (1971–75). He became baseball's first multimillionaire in 1975 when he signed a five-year, $3.5 million deal with the Yankees after being declared a free agent by an arbitrator.

1999 Chicago RF Sammy Sosa joins Babe Ruth as the only ML players to hit 59 home runs in two seasons, during the Cubs' 5–3 loss to Cincinnati. Losers of 31 of their last 39 games, the Cubs have fewer wins than Sosa's homers with 56 against 84 losses. Playing for the New York Yankees, Ruth hit 60 homers in

1927 and had 59 homers in 1921. Sosa blasted 66 round-trippers in 1998, trailing only St. Louis 1B Mark McGwire, who set an all-time record with 70.

1999 During Baltimore's 6–5 win over Minnesota, Orioles RF Albert Belle reaches the 100-RBI mark for the eighth consecutive season, while 3B Cal Ripken, Jr., grounds into the 324th double play of his career, surpassing Carl Yastrzemski for the all-time AL record. LHP Mike Riley, at 20 years and 39 days, is the youngest Orioles pitcher to make his ML debut since RHP Mike Adamson in 1967.

10

1919 Cleveland RHP Ray Caldwell no-hits the New York Yankees, 3–0.

1924 Ted Kluszewski b. Argo, IL.

1924 New York Giants 2B Frankie Frisch collects six hits in seven at-bats.

1934 Roger Maris b. Fargo, ND.

1950 New York CF Joe DiMaggio becomes the first ML player to hit three home runs in one game at Griffith Stadium, as the Yankees clobber the Washington Senators, 8–1.

1960 New York CF Mickey Mantle smashes a home run over the right field roof in Detroit, trigonometrically measured to be 643 feet.

1963 Randy Johnson b. Walnut Creek, CA.

1967 Chicago White Sox RHP Joel Horlen no-hits Detroit, 6–0.

1969 The New York Mets sweep the Montreal Expos in a doubleheader at Shea Stadium, 3–2 in 12 innings and 7–1. The victories move New York into first place in the NL East for the first time in club history. The "Amazing Mets" will win the division, defeat Atlanta in the first NL championship

series, and go on to capture the World Series over the AL champion Baltimore Orioles.

1974 St. Louis LF Lou Brock ties Maury Wills' 1962 single season stolen base record of 104 with a first inning theft against Philadelphia. In the seventh inning, Brock breaks the record and will finish the season with a new record of 118.

1976 California RHP Nolan Ryan strikes out 18 White Sox batters at Chicago's Comiskey Park.

1977 Toronto 3B Roy Howell collects nine RBIs with a single, two doubles, and two home runs as the Blue Jays hammer the New York Yankees, 19–3.

1980 Montreal RHP Bill Gullickson strikes out 18 Chicago Cubs batters, the most ever by a rookie hurler, in a 4–2 Expos win.

1989 Atlanta Falcons DB Deion Sanders returns a punt for a touchdown against the Los Angeles Rams in his first NFL game. Five days earlier he homers, doubles twice, and has four RBIs as a New York Yankees OF in a 12–2 win in Seattle to become only the second player ever (Jim Thorpe 1917 & 1919) to score an NFL touchdown and hit a homer in the same week.

1997 St. Louis 1B Mark McGwire joins Babe Ruth as the only ML players to enjoy back-to-back seasons of 50 or more home runs as he connects for a 446 foot shot against San Francisco LHP Shawn Estes. Playing for the New York Yankees, Ruth last accomplished the feat during the 1927–28 seasons. McGwire becomes the sixth player to reach 50 homers twice joining Ruth (who did it four times), Jimmie Foxx, Mickey Mantle, Willie Mays, and Ralph Kiner. McGwire also becomes the first player to reach the plateau while playing for two different teams in the same season having started the year with the Oakland A's.

1998 St. Louis 1B Mark McGwire walks twice in the Cardinals 8–7 win at Cincinnati to tie Barry Bonds' NL record with 151 walks in a season.

1999 Boston RHP Pedro Martinez pitches a one-hitter and strikes out a career high 17 batters — a record by a Yankees opponent — in beating New York, 3–1. Martinez loses both his no-hitter and shutout on Yankees DH Chili Davis' second inning home run.

1999 Arizona LHP Randy Johnson celebrates his 36th birthday by striking out seven Philadelphia batters in a 3–1 Diamondbacks win. Johnson sets a personal best for strikeouts in a season with 335, the seventh highest total in ML history.

1999 St. Louis 1B Mark McGwire hits his 55th home run of the season in an 11–5 win over Pittsburgh.

11

1918 In the earliest conclusion in the history of the World Series, Boston RHP Carl Mays stops the Chicago Cubs on three hits to lift the Red Sox to a 2–1 win in Game 6. It's the second complete game win for Mays in five days, as the series begins early due to the war effort.

1944 Dave Roberts (LHP) b. Gallipolis, OH.

1947 Larry Cox b. Bluffton, OH.

1948 Boston Braves LHP Warren Spahn hits the first of his record 35 ML homers by a pitcher against Philadelphia Phillies RHP Charlie Bicknell.

1949 The New York Yankees receive a major league record 11 walks in the third inning against Washington.

1956 Cincinnati OF Frank Robinson blasts his 38th home run of the season in the Reds' 11–5 win over San Fran-

cisco, to tie the ML record for most homers by a rookie.

1958 Don Slaught b. Long Beach, CA.

1959 Brooklyn ends Pittsburgh RHP Elroy Face's two-year, 22-game winning streak, scoring twice in the ninth inning for a 5–4 win. Face will finish the season at 18–1 for an all-time best .947 winning percentage.

1963 Chicago Cubs LF Billy Williams begins his then-NL record 117 consecutive games played streak, which runs through September 1970. His mark is eclipsed by Steve Garvey in 1983.

1964 Ellis Burks b. Vicksburg, MS.

1966 New York Mets rookie RHP Nolan Ryan makes his ML debut and gives up his first home run against Atlanta C Joe Torre.

1966 New York Yankees OF John Miller hits a home run in his first ML at-bat, against Boston RHP Lee Stange.

1969 Eduardo Perez b. Cincinnati, OH.

1985 Cincinnati player/manager Pete Rose singles against San Diego RHP Eric Show for his 4,192nd career hit to pass Ty Cobb on the all-time list.

1991 Three Atlanta pitchers — LHP Kent Mercker (6IP), RHP Mark Wohlers (2IP), and RHP Alejandro Pera (1IP) — combine to no-hit San Diego, 1–0.

1996 San Diego 3B Ken Caminiti homers from both sides of the plate for a record fourth time, breaking his own ML record set in 1995.

1997 New York 1B John Olerud hits for the cycle, driving in five runs as the Mets beat Montreal, 9–5. Olerud is the seventh Mets player to accomplish the feat, and the first to do it at Shea Stadium since Tommie Agee on July 6, 1970.

1998 Chicago RF Sammy Sosa hits his 59th home run of the season, against

Milwaukee LHP Bill Pulsipher, but the Brewers hold on to beat the Cubs, 13–11.

1998 The Florida Marlins become the first team in history to go from World Series champions to 100-game losers with a 7–2 loss at Atlanta. The Marlins, 48–100, went 92–70 a year ago to win a wild card berth before defeating San Francisco and Atlanta in the NL playoffs, and Cleveland in the World Series.

1999 Minnesota LHP Eric Milton hurls the third no-hitter of the season, 7–0 over Anaheim. Milton walks two and strikes out 13 batters against an Angels lineup stacked with late season minor league callups, as six regulars don't play.

1999 San Francisco LF Barry Bonds becomes the 210th ML player to reach 2,000 hits during the Giants' 3–2 win over Atlanta.

1999 Oakland RHP Doug Jones becomes the 11th ML relief pitcher to reach 300 saves during the A's 5–4 win over Tampa Bay.

12

1907 Spud Chandler b. Commerce, GA.

1916 Charlie Keller b. Middletown, MD.

1920 Andy Seminick b. Pierce, WV.

1926 St. Louis Browns RHP Milt Gaston shuts out the Boston Red Sox, 1–0, despite allowing 12 hits.

1930 Brooklyn C Al Lopez is credited with the last bouncing ball home run, as his drive bounds into the left field bleachers at Ebbets Field. A new rule would go into effect in 1931 which would credit such a hit as only a double.

1932 Brooklyn's Johnny Frederick hits his ML record sixth pinch homer of the season in the ninth inning to spark the Dodgers to a 4–3 win over Chicago at Ebbets Field.

1940 Mickey Lolich b. Portland, OR.

1947 Pittsburgh OF Ralph Kiner hits two home runs — his seventh and eighth in four games — for an ML record.

1952 The Boston Braves equal a franchise record for largest shutout win with a 16–0 wipeout of Pittsburgh.

1954 New York's hopes for a sixth straight pennant are dashed as Cleveland sweeps the Yankees, 4–1 and 3–2, before a record crowd of 86,563 at Municipal Stadium. The Yankees drop to 8½ games behind the eventual AL champion Indians.

1962 Washington RHP Tom Cheney strikes out 21 Baltimore batters in a 16 inning game won by the Senators, 2–1. Cheney will fan every Orioles player at least once except for 1B Boog Powell.

1967 Pat Listach b. Natchitoches, LA.

1974 At 3:13 A.M., St. Louis finally beats the New York Mets, 4–3 in 25 innings. The game takes seven hours and four minutes to play. A record 202 batters go to the plate. The Mets' Felix Millan and John Milner each have 12 plate appearances.

1976 Chicago White Sox DH Minnie Minoso, age 53, goes 1-for-3 against California LHP Sid Monge, to become the oldest player in ML history to get a hit in a regulation game.

1979 Boston's Carl Yastrzemski collects his 3,000th hit — a single off New York Yankees RHP Jim Beattie — but the Red Sox lose, 9–2.

1984 New York Mets RHP Dwight Gooden strikes out 16 Pittsburgh batters to set the record for most whiffs by a rookie with 251. Gooden breaks the record striking out Marvell Wynne in the sixth inning and finishes with six more than Herb Score's 1955 total.

1995 In a 5–4 loss to Florida, Cincinnati turns its second triple play of the season.

1996 Colorado OF Ellis Burks steals his 30th base of the year to become the 15th player in ML history to hit 30 home runs and steal 30 bases in the same year.

1996 Seattle SS Alex Rodriguez hits a first inning double during an 8–5 win against Kansas City, giving him a ML record 88 extra base hits in a season by a shortstop. The 21-year-old Rodriguez will finish the year with 91 extra base hits and a .358 batting average.

1997 Florida C Charles Johnson breaks the ML record for consecutive errorless games by a catcher reaching 160 straight. He'll finish the year without an error and only one passed ball.

1998 Chicago RF Sammy Sosa blasts his 60th home run of the season, joining Babe Ruth, Roger Maris and Mark McGwire as the only players to reach the plateau, as the Cubs rally from a 12–5 deficit to a 15–12 win over Milwaukee. Chicago PH Orlando Merced wins the game with a three-run homer in the bottom of the ninth inning. Sosa's seventh inning blast against Brewers RHP Valerio De Los Santos reaches the special number that the Cardinals' McGwire had reached only seven days earlier.

1998 St. Louis 1B Mark McGwire sets an NL record with his 152nd walk of the season, against Houston LHP Randy Johnson, but the Cardinals lose, 3–2.

1998 Seattle CF Ken Griffey, Jr., hits his 51st home run of the season, victimizing Kansas City RHP Tim Belcher, but the Mariners lose to the Royals, 5–2.

1999 Boston completes its first three-game sweep of New York at Yankee Stadium since 1986, with a 4–1 win. A sellout crowd of 56,028 helps push the Yankees' home attendance over the three

million mark for the first time in franchise history.

1999 San Francisco LF Barry Bonds hits his 442nd career home run, tying Dave Kingman for 22nd on the all-time list, as the Giants beat Atlanta, 8–4.

13

1893 Dutch Ruether b. Alameda, CA.

1897 Ed Rommel b. Baltimore, MD.

1906 Thornton Lee b. Sonoma, CA.

1925 Brooklyn RHP Dazzy Vance no-hits the Philadelphia Phillies, 10–1.

1932 The New York Yankees clinch the AL pennant as Joe McCarthy becomes the first manager to win flags in both leagues. McCarthy first won a NL pennant with the 1929 Chicago Cubs.

1933 The Chicago White Sox start two 40-plus right-handers against the Philadelphia A's as Sad Sam Jones, 41, pitches the first game, and Red Faber, 44, starts the nightcap.

1936 Cleveland RHP Bob Feller, still 17 years old, beats the Philadelphia A's, 5–2, allowing only two hits while setting a new AL strikeout record with 17 whiffs.

1942 Chicago Cubs SS Len Merullo committs four errors in one inning in a regular season game.

1945 Rick Wise b. Jackson, MS.

1946 Boston LF Ted Williams belts his only inside-the-park home run of a 521-homer career, as the Red Sox beat Cleveland, 1–0, and clinch the AL pennant for the first time since 1918.

1949 Rick Dempsey b. Fayetteville, TN.

1963 All three Alou brothers — Matty, Jesus, and Felipe — start together in the San Francisco Giants outfield.

1964 St. Louis becomes only the second team this century and the eighth all-time to score in every inning, during the Cardinals' 15–2 win over the Chicago Cubs at Wrigley Field.

1964 Greg Hibbard b. New Orleans, LA.

1965 San Francisco CF Willie Mays hits his 500th career home run, this one against Houston RHP Don Nottebart during the Giants' 5–1 win. Mays becomes the fifth player to reach the plateau.

1968 Denny Neagle b. Gambrills, MD.

1968 Bernie Williams b. Puerto Rico.

1969 Russ Davis b. Birmingham, AL.

1971 Baltimore RF Frank Robinson becomes the 11th player in ML history to reach the 500 home run plateau. Robinson follows Minnesota's Harmon Killebrew, who became the 10th player about one month earlier.

1978 The New York Yankees beat the Detroit Tigers, 7–3, to move into sole possession of first place for the first time after being 14 games out.

1990 Philadelphia trades LHP Dennis Cook to Los Angeles for C Darrin Fletcher.

1995 Detroit 2B Lou Whitaker and SS Alan Trammell play in their 1,915th game together to set a new AL record for most games as teammates.

1996 Seattle OF Mark Whiten hits the club's ML record 11th grand slam of the season, and Ken Griffey, Jr., and Dan Wilson each hit three-run homers to power the Mariners to a 13–7 win at Minnesota.

1996 Colorado OF Dante Bichette hits a record-setting 30th home run as the Rockies beat Houston, 6–3, at Denver. Bichette's blast helps the Rockies establish two NL records: Bichette, Ellis Burks (38), Andres Galarraga (43), and Vinny Castilla (37) become the first foursome with 30 or more homers in two seasons; and Bichette and Burks become only the second pair of teammates to boast 30–30 seasons.

1997 Los Angeles knuckleballer RHP Tom Candiotti becomes the second NL hurler in 23 years to hit three batters in one inning when he plunks a trio of Houston hitters.

1998 Chicago RF Sammy Sosa hits two home runs — his 61st and 62nd of the year — to tie St. Louis 1B Mark McGwire for the ML lead, as the Cubs defeat Milwaukee, 11–10 in 10 innings. Sosa ties Roger Maris' 1961 record with his 61st against Brewers RHP Bronswell Patrick, then ties McGwire with his 62nd against RHP Eric Plunk.

1998 Arizona RHP Andy Benes takes a no-hitter into the ninth inning before Cincinnati 1B Sean Casey spoils it with a single. Benes, trying to pitch the first no-hitter for an expansion team since Montreal RHP Bill Stoneman in 1969, strikes out six and walks five in his 5–0 win. Diamondbacks RHP Gregg Olson gets the last two outs for his 28th save.

1998 Texas RF Juan Gonzalez becomes the first ML player to reach 150 RBIs in a season since 1962 and the first AL player to do it since 1949, with a two-run home run in a 10–5 loss to Tampa Bay to push his total to 151 for the year. Los Angeles OF Tommy Davis drove in 153 runs for the NL Dodgers in 1962, strangely, marking the only time in his 18-year career he had more than 100. In 1949, Boston Red Sox teammates Ted Williams (LF) and Vern Stephens (SS) both drove in 159 runs to top the AL.

1999 Houston LHP Mike Hampton wins his 20th game of the season against only three losses, and the Astros set a club record with their 11th straight victory, 13–2 over Philadelphia.

14

1869 Kid Nichols b. Madison, WI.

1913 Chicago Cubs RHP Larry

Cheney shuts out the New York Giants, allowing a NL record most 14 hits during the blanking.

1936 Stan Williams b. Enfield, NH.

1951 St. Louis Browns OF Bob Nieman becomes the only ML player to hit home runs in his first two at-bats. The Boston Red Sox win the contest, however, 9–6.

1957 Tim Wallach b. Huntington Park, CA.

1963 Detroit OF Willie Horton hits the first of his 325 ML home runs, this one against Baltimore RHP Robin Roberts. It's five years to the date after another slugger, Los Angeles OF Frank Howard, hits the first of his 382 ML home runs, also against Roberts (at that time pitching for Philadelphia).

1965 New York Yankees OF Bobby Murcer hits the first of a career 268 ML home runs, this one against Washington RHP Jim Duckworth.

1968 Detroit RHP Denny McLain becomes the first ML pitcher in 34 years to win 30 games when he defeats Oakland, 4–3. McLain will finish the season at 31–6 en route to winning the AL Cy Young Award and celebrating a World Series championship. St. Louis RHP Dizzy Dean finished 30–7 for the eventual 1934 World Series champion Cardinals.

1972 David Bell b. Cincinnati, OH.

1974 Graig and Jim Nettles become the second brother combination to hit home runs against each other in the same game. Graig homers against Detroit Tigers LHP Mickey Lolich, while Jim homers against the New York Yankees RHP Pat Dobson. Rick and Wes Ferrell first turned the trick in 1933.

1975 Milwaukee SS Robin Yount breaks Mel Ott's 47-year-old record by playing in his 242nd ML game as a teenager.

1987 Toronto C Ernie Whitt hits three of the Blue Jays' ML record 10 home runs in an 18–3 slaughter of Baltimore. Orioles SS Cal Ripken, Jr., leaves the game in the eighth inning after a record 8,243 consecutive innings played dating back to June 5, 1982. His 908 consecutive games played streak remains intact, however.

1990 Ken Griffey, Sr., and his son Ken Griffey, Jr. hit back-to-back home runs in the first inning of the Seattle Mariners' 7–5 loss to California. The unprecedented father and son homers are against Angels RHP Kirk McCaskill.

1994 The baseball season, already shut down by a month-long strike, is cancelled along with the World Series in a vote by 26 of 28 teams.

1996 Oakland 1B Mark McGwire becomes the 13th ML player to hit 50 home runs in a season, but Cleveland's Albert Belle counters with his 46th homer as the Indians complete a doubleheader sweep, 9–8 at Jacobs Field. Cleveland wins the first game, 9–2, with Oakland's only runs coming off of McGwire's 49th homer.

1996 New York C Todd Hundley hits his 41st home run to set an ML record for catchers, in the Mets' 12-inning, 6–5 win over Atlanta. Brooklyn C Roy Campanella hit 40 homers in 1953.

1997 St. Louis 1B Mark McGwire hits his 51st home run of the season, a solo blast off San Diego RHP Joey Hamilton as the Cardinals beat the Padres, 10–4.

1999 Kansas City DH Mark Quinn becomes only the third player this century to hit two home runs in his ML debut, but the Royals lose to Anaheim, 6–5, in the nightcap of their doubleheader, after blowing a ninth inning lead to lose the opener as well.

1999 Colorado 3B Vinny Castilla hits his 200th career home run during the Rockies' 7–2 win over the New York Mets.

1999 The New York Yankees hits two grand slam home runs in a game for only the third time in club history to rally past Toronto, 10–6. Yankees CF Bernie Williams ties the game with an eighth inning slam, and RF Paul O'Neill follows with a ninth inning slam for the game-winner.

1999 Kansas City trades LHP Glendon Rusch to the New York Mets for RHP Dan Murray.

15

1876 Nick Altrock b. Cincinnati, OH.

1900 Harry McCurdy b. Stevens Point, WI.

1901 Detroit records the most lopsided shutout in AL history, 21–0 over Cleveland.

1902 The Chicago Cubs infielders Joe Tinker, Johnny Evers, and Frank Chance play together for the first time.

1938 Gaylord Perry b. Williamston, NC.

1938 Pittsburgh OFs Lloyd and Paul Waner hit back-to-back homers against New York Giants LHP Cliff Melton, marking the only time in ML history brothers go deep consecutively. It marks the third time that the brothers both homer in the same game and is the 28th and final round-tripper for Lloyd during his 18-year career.

1940 Frank Linzy b. Ft. Gibson, OK.

1946 The Brooklyn Dodgers beat the Chicago Cubs, 2–0, in five innings in a game halted because of gnats. The insects become such a problem for the umpires, players, and fans that the game cannot continue.

1950 New York Yankees 1B Johnny Mize hits three home runs for an ML record sixth time in his career.

1960 San Francisco CF Willie Mays

ties an ML record by hitting three triples in a game. He also hits a double and a single to lead the Giants past Philadelphia, 8–6.

1969 St. Louis LHP Steve Carlton sets an ML record with 19 strikeouts in a nine inning, 4–3 loss to the New York Mets. New York RF Ron Swoboda does the heavy damage hitting a pair of two-run homers for the difference.

1974 Boston CF Fred Lynn hits his first of a career 306 ML home runs, this one against Milwaukee RHP Jim Slaton.

1977 Atlanta C Dale Murphy hits his first of a career 398 ML home runs, this one against San Diego LHP Randy Jones.

1979 Boston Red Sox DH Bob Watson becomes the first player in ML history to hit for the cycle in both leagues, having done it for the NL Houston Astros in 1977.

1985 The New York Yankees trade LHP Jim Deshaies to Houston for RHP Joe Niekro.

1988 Montreal LHP Randy Johnson, at 6-foot-10, becomes the tallest player in ML history with this late season start.

1990 Chicago White Sox RHP Bobby Thigpen saves his 50th game of the season in a win over Boston. Thigpen will finish the year with an ML record 57 saves.

1994 Toronto and Detroit play the longest ML night game in 4:12.

1995 St. Louis SS Ozzie Smith turns an ML record 1,554th double play during a 7–6 loss to Los Angeles.

1995 Detroit 1B Cecil Fielder hits his 250th career home run in a 3–2 win over Texas.

1996 The Baltimore Orioles break the ML record for home runs in a season with 243, hitting five in pounding Detroit, 16–6. The old mark of 241 was set by the 1961 New York Yankees. Brady

Anderson begins the game with his 46th homer, marking the 10th time he has led off a game with a solo shot, breaking the previous AL record held by Rickey Henderson in 1986.

1996 Los Angeles C Mike Piazza becomes the first catcher in ML history to be leading the league in batting with as many as 500 at-bats, when he ends the day hitting a NL-best .347 with 501 at-bats. Piazza will slide to .336 at year's end, good for only third place behind San Diego's Tony Gwynn (.353) and Colorado's Ellis Burks (.344).

1997 Seattle OF Ken Griffey, Jr., hits two home runs for his 51st and 52nd of the season — to tie for the most in a season since 1961— as the Mariners beat Toronto, 7–3. Since 1961 when New York Yankee OFs Roger Maris (61) and Mickey Mantle (54) topped that mark, only San Francisco's Willie Mays (1965), Cincinnati's George Foster (1977), and Oakland's Mark McGwire (1996) had reached 52 home runs.

1997 Baltimore OF Eric Davis returns to the Orioles lineup for the first time following colon cancer surgery in June. Although he goes 0-for-3, Baltimore wins, 6–5, over Cleveland and becomes the first team in the major leagues to clinch a postseason spot.

1998 Mark McGwire adds to his single season home run record by blasting his 63rd, coming in as a pinch hitter against Pittsburgh LHP Jason Christiansen, as the Cardinals fall 8–6 in the first game of a doubleheader.

1998 Seattle CF Ken Griffey, Jr., blasts his AL-leading 52nd home run and becomes the fourth youngest player in ML history to go over 1,000 RBIs as the Mariners outslug Minnesota, 12–7. Griffey goes 4-for-6 with five RBIs to give him 132 for the season. At 28 years and 10 months, he ranks behind only Mel Ott (27 years, three months), Jim-

mie Foxx (27 years, eight months), and Lou Gehrig (28 years, 9½ months) as the fastest player to reach 1,000 RBIs.

1998 Cleveland RF Manny Ramirez clubs three home runs driving in five runs, as the Indians beat Toronto, 7–5. It's the first time Ramirez reaches 40 homers in a season.

1999 Marge Schott's stormy 15-year reign as owner of the Cincinnati Reds comes to an end as baseball owners approve the $67 million sale of her interest in the team to her limited partners, Carl Lindner, owner of the Great American Insurance Co., takes over as controlling owner.

1999 Philadelphia CF Doug Glanville has five hits as the Phillies snap their 11-game losing streak with a 10-inning, 8–6 win over Houston, ending the Astros' team record 12-game winning streak.

16

1903 The presidents of the AL Boston Somersets and NL Pittsburgh Pirates agree to a best-of-nine championship playoff— baseball's first World Series.

1919 Cincinnati defeats the New York Giants, 4–3, to clinch the Reds' first pennant of the century.

1924 St. Louis 1B Jim Bottomley collects a ML record 12 RBIs during a 17–3 thrashing of Brooklyn. In six at-bats, Bottomley hits three singles, a double, and two home runs.

1945 Ed Sprague b. Boston, MA.

1947 Gary Ross b. McKeesport, PA.

1949 Roget Moret b. Puerto Rico.

1955 Robin Yount b. Danville, IL.

1958 Orel Hershiser b. Buffalo, NY.

1959 Tim Raines b. Sanford, FL.

1960 Milwaukee Braves LHP Warren Spahn hurls the first of his two career no-hitters, a 4–0 win over Philadelphia.

1960 Mickey Tettleton b. Oklahoma City, OK.

1961 New York RF Roger Maris connects for his 57th home run of the year at Detroit, against RHP Frank Lary. It's the third time this year Maris homers against Lary, victimizing him for his 31st on July 4th, and also his 52nd on September 2nd.

1964 Washington 3B Don Zimmer's third inning hit bounces off the right field fence at Cleveland Municipal Stadium, but Indians RF Chico Salmon kicks the ball thru a hole in the wall, as the umpires rule a double for the Senators batter.

1965 Boston RHP David Morehead no-hits Cleveland, 2–0.

1967 John Ericks b. Oak Lawn, IL.

1970 Paul Shuey b. Raleigh, NC.

1972 Montreal LHP Balor Moore leads Philadelphia, 1–0, in the seventh inning, when he loses both his 25-inning scoreless streak and the lead as the Phillies score three times. Rookie Philadelphia 3B Mike Schmidt accounts for the three runs with his first ML home run. A future Hall of Famer, Schmidt will finish his career in 1989 with 548 round-trippers.

1975 Pittsburgh 2B Rennie Stennett goes 7-for-7 in a 22–0 rout of Chicago at Wrigley Field in the most lopsided shutout in ML history. Stennett collects four singles, two doubles, and a triple in becoming only the second player in history, and the only player this century with seven hits in a nine inning game.

1987 Cleveland RF Joe Carter becomes the ninth ML player to hit 30 home runs and steal 30 bases in the same season when he swipes his career high 30th base during a 5–3 loss to Seattle. Carter finishes the year with 32 homers and 31 steals.

1988 Cincinnati LHP Tom Browning hurls the 12th perfect game in modern baseball history, 1–0 over Los Angeles. It's the first perfect game by a left-hander since the Dodgers' Sandy Koufax turned the trick in 1965.

1993 Minnesota DH Dave Winfield becomes the 19th player in ML history to collect 3,000 hits with a single against Oakland RHP Dennis Eckersley. At 41, Winfield becomes the oldest player in the 20th century to reach the milestone.

1995 Atlanta RHP Greg Maddux wins an ML record 17th straight road game, 6–1 over Cincinnati.

1996 Minnesota's Paul Molitor becomes the 21st player in ML history to reach the 3,000-hit plateau when he triples in the fifth inning against Kansas City LHP Jose Rosado. Molitor becomes the first player to reach 3,000 with a hit other than a single or a double, and also becomes the first player to reach the milestone in a season in which he collects 200 hits. The triple is Molitor's 211th hit of an eventual 225 for the year.

1996 San Francisco LF Barry Bonds becomes the third player in ML history to record 40 home runs and 30 stolen bases in the same season, joining Milwaukee OF Hank Aaron (1963) and Oakland OF Jose Canseco (1988). Colorado OF Ellis Burks will join the 40–30 club later in the same month.

1997 St. Louis 1B Mark McGwire reaches the 52 home run plateau for the second straight season and becomes only the fifth ML player since 1961 to do so, when he connects against Los Angeles RHP Ramon Martinez. McGwire follows Seattle OF Ken Griffey, Jr., who reached 52 home runs only one day earlier and joins only San Francisco OF Willie Mays (1965) and Cincinnati OF George Foster (1977) with as many round-trippers during that span.

1997 Philadelphia RHP Curt Schilling becomes the 24th ML pitcher, 13th of the 20th century, to record 300 or more strikeouts in a season when he fans nine New York Mets batters for a total of 305. Schilling becomes the first NL hurler to reach the milestone since Houston RHP Mike Scott in 1986.

1998 Chicago RF Sammy Sosa blasts his 63rd home run of the season to keep pace with St. Louis 1B Mark McGwire for the all-time record. Sosa's homer — an eighth inning grand slam against San Diego RHP Brian Boehringer — gives the Cubs a 6–3 win over the Padres. Sosa also knocks in two runs with a seventh inning double to push his NL-leading RBI total to 154. He becomes the first NL player since 1962 to drive in more than 150 runs when Los Angeles OF Tommy Davis led the league with 153. Texas RF Juan Gonzalez reached the 150 RBI plateau only three days earlier in becoming the first AL player do do it since 1949.

1998 Seattle CF Ken Griffey, Jr., steals his 20th base of the season to achieve a rare milestone during the Mariners' 4–1 win at Oakland. Griffey becomes only the third player in ML history with at least 50 home runs and 20 steals, joining New York Giants CF Willie Mays (51–24) in 1955 and Baltimore Orioles RF Brady Anderson (50–21) in 1996 in the 50–20 club.

1998 Cleveland RF Manny Ramirez hits his 41st and 42nd home runs, tying the ML record with homers in four straight at-bats and five in two games, as the Indians clinch their fourth straight AL Central title by beating Minnesota, 8–6.

1998 Boston RHP Tom Gordon equals the AL single season record with his 38th consecutive save and sets a team mark with his 41st, as the Red Sox edge Baltimore, 4–3.

1998 Toronto RHP Roger Clemens wins his 14th straight decision — the longest streak in the AL since he did it with Boston in 1986 — as the Blue Jays edge Detroit, 2–1. Clemens improves his record to 19–6 and strikes out 11 batters in 7⅔ innings to push his AL leading strikeout total to 245.

1998 Chicago LF Albert Belle hits his 46th home run and sets a team record with his 139th RBI as the White Sox win 9–4 over Kansas City.

1999 Kansas City CF Carlos Beltran hits a two-run home run to become the first AL rookie to reach 100 RBIs since Mark McGwire in 1987, during the Royals' 7–1 win over Anaheim.

1999 Seattle RHP Freddy Garcia ties the ML record for victories in a season by a pitcher from Venezuela, defeating Tampa Bay, 5–3. Garcia, 15–8, ties LHP Wilson Alvarez' mark from 1993 and 1996, getting help from shortstop Alex Rodriguez, who blasts a grand slam home run, his 38th homer of the season to put him at 103 RBIs.

17

1879 Rube Foster b. Calvert, TX.

1898 Earl Webb b. Bon Air, TN.

1903 Boston defeats Cleveland to clinch the AL pennant and set up the first World Series matchup with NL champion Pittsburgh.

1910 Detroit RHP Ed Summers hits his only two ML home runs in the same game.

1912 Brooklyn CF Casey Stengel makes his ML debut with hits in his first three at-bats as the Dodgers win, 7–3 over Pittsburgh, snapping the Pirates' 12-game winning streak.

1930 Cleveland OF Earl Averill drives in eight runs with three consecutive home runs to lead the Indians to a 13–7 victory over Washington in a doubleheader opener. In the nightcap, Averill homers again during the Senators 6–4 win to set an AL record with 11 RBIs for the two games.

1937 Orlando Cepeda b. Puerto Rico.

1938 Bobby Wine b. New York, NY.

1945 Chicago Cubs OF Bill Nicholson records a major league record 10 putouts in a game.

1956 Thad Bosley b. Oceanside, CA.

1960 John Franco b. Brooklyn, NY.

1963 The Houston Colt 45's start the only all-rookie lineup in ML history in a 10–3 loss at Cincinnati. Among the starters for Houston: Aaron Pointer (RF), Jimmy Wynn (CF), Rusty Staub (1B), Joe Morgan (2B), and Jerry Grote (C).

1967 Kansas City A's RF Reggie Jackson hits the first of his ML 563 home runs against California LHP Jim Weaver.

1968 San Francisco RHP Gaylord Perry no-hits St. Louis, 1–0.

1977 Dave Kingman hits a home run for the New York Yankees, the fourth club he homers with in the same season. He had already homered for the Mets, Padres, and Angels.

1984 On the 17th anniversary of his first major league home run, California's Reggie Jackson becomes the 13th player in history to reach 500 career homers when he connects against Kansas City LHP Bud Black. In an ironic role reversal, Jackson's first homer happened while he was in a Kansas City uniform and batting against the Angels.

1984 New York rookie RHP Dwight Gooden strikes out 16 batters in a 2–1 loss to Philadelphia to tie an ML record with 32 whiffs over two consecutive games. Five days earlier, Gooden struck out 16 Pittsburgh Pirates batters as well.

1986 The New York Mets defeat the Chicago Cubs, 4–2, clinching the NL East divison behind RHP Dwight Gooden.

1988 Minnesota RHP Jeff Reardon becomes the first pitches to save 40 games in both leagues as the Twins beat the Chicago White Sox, 3–1. Reardon, who saved 42 games for Montreal in 1985, pitches the ninth inning for his 40th save in 47 opportunities.

1995 San Diego 3B Ken Caminiti sets an ML record by switch-hitting home runs for the second straight game as the Padres beat the Chicago Cubs, 11–3.

1995 Florida RHP Pat Rapp allows only one hit as the Marlins crush Colorado, 17–0.

1996 Los Angeles RHP Hideo Nomo no-hits Colorado, 9–0, for the 20th no-hitter in Dodgers history.

1997 St. Louis 1B Mark McGwire blasts his 53rd home run of the season, the most in the majors since 1961, against Chicago RHP Rodney Myers as the Cardinals beat the Cubs, 12–9.

1997 The Atlanta Braves become the first team to clinch six consecutive post-season appearances with a 10–2 rout of the New York Mets. Atlanta LF Ryan Klesko has four hits including a first inning grand slam home run which also sets a new ML record for team slams in a season with 12. Both Baltimore and Seattle hit 11 grand slams in 1996.

1998 Cleveland RF Manny Ramirez hits his 43rd home run to tie the ML record with six in three games as the Indians bury Minnesota, 9–1. Ramirez is the first player with six homers in three games since Philadelphia Phillies 3B Mike Schmidt in 1976, and the first AL player since Philadelphia A's OF Gus Zernial in 1951.

1998 Boston RHP Tom Gordon sets an AL single-season record with his 39th straight save as the Red Sox edge Baltimore, 3–2.

1998 Atlanta LHP Denny Neagle scatters four hits over six innings in a 1–0 win over Arizona. By improving to

15–11, Neagle helps the Braves become the first team since the 1930 Washington Senators with five 15-game winners. Atlanta LHP Tom Glavine leads the staff at 19–6, with RHPs Greg Maddux at 17–8, John Smoltz at 16–3, and Kevin Millwood at 16–8.

1998 Seattle CF Ken Griffey, Jr., blasts his 53rd home run of the season, against Oakland RHP Tom Candiotti, as the Mariners shut out the A's, 8–0.

1998 Chet "Red" Hoff, the oldest ex-major league player, passes away at age 107. Hoff, a LHP who pitched only four seasons with the New York Highlanders, then Yankees and St. Louis Browns from 1911–13 and 1915, struck out the first batter he ever faced — Hall of Famer Ty Cobb.

1999 Kansas City CF Carlos Beltran becomes the first rookie in 24 years to reach 100 RBS and 100 runs scored in the same season, during the Royals' 9–3 win over Oakland. Boston CF Fred Lynn was the last rookie to post the milestone numbers in 1975.

1999 St. Louis 1B Mark McGwire hits his 56th home run of the season and 513th of his career, passing both Ernie Banks and Eddie Mathews, moving into 11th place on the career list, in the Cardinals' 11–8 win over Houston.

18

1869 The Philadelphia Pythons, an all-black team rejected for membership in the National Association of Base Ball Players, play an exhibition game against an all-white team, the Philadelphia City Items. The Pythons win, 27–17.

1898 George Uhle b. Cleveland, OH.

1903 Philadelphia Phillies RHP Charles Fraser no-hits the Chicago Cubs, 10–0.

1908 Cleveland RHP Bob Rhoads no-hits the Boston Red Sox, 2–1.

1919 Chicago White Sox 1B Chick Gandil meets with Joseph "Sport" Sullivan, a small time gambler and informs him that for $100,000 the White Sox would throw the World Series.

1922 St. Louis Browns 1B George Sisler has his 41-game hitting streak end during a 3–2 loss to the New York Yankees.

1925 Harvey Haddix b. Medway, OH.

1930 New York Yankees RHP Red Ruffing hits two home runs to help his own cause in a 7–6, 10-inning win over the St. Louis Browns.

1934 St. Louis Browns RHP Bobo Newsom no-hits the Boston Red Sox, but still loses, 2–1. Newsom will lead the AL with 20 losses.

1947 Billy Champion b. Shelby, NC.

1948 Ken Brett b. Brooklyn, NY.

1954 The Cleveland Indians clinch the AL pennant with a 3–2 victory over the Detroit Tigers.

1959 Ryne Sandberg b. Spokane, WA.

1968 St. Louis RHP Ray Washburn no-hits San Francisco, 2–0, the day after Giants RHP Gaylord Perry no-hit the Cardinals, 1–0.

1971 Pittsburgh OF Richie Zisk hits the first of his 207 ML home runs, this one against New York Mets LHP Ray Sadecki.

1984 Oakland C Mickey Tettleton hits his first ML home run against Texas LHP Frank Tanana.

1984 Detroit clinches the AL East division with a 3–0 victory over the Milwaukee Brewers, making the Tigers only the fourth ML team to lead from start to finish. The other three were the 1923 New York Giants, the 1927 New York Yankees, and the 1955 Brooklyn Dodgers.

1987 Detroit's Darrell Evans becomes

the first 40-year-old player in ML history to hit 30 home runs in a season as the Tigers beat Milwaukee, 7–6.

1995 Florida OF Gary Sheffield goes 3-for-3 with two home runs and seven RBIs in a 10–3 loss to Philadelphia, giving him eight consecutive hits over two games.

1996 Boston RHP Roger Clemens ties his own ML record by striking out 20 batters in a 4–0, four-hit victory in Detroit. Clemens also ties two of Cy Young's career Red Sox records of 38 shutouts and 192 wins.

1998 St. Louis 1B Mark McGwire extends his single season home run record with his 64th against Milwaukee LHP Rafael Roque, as the Cardinals beat the Brewers, 5–2.

1998 Colorado 3B Vinny Castilla blasts his 44th and 45th home runs of the season, driving in three runs, as the Rockies beat San Diego, 4–1.

1998 Houston LHP Randy Johnson takes a no-hitter into the seventh inning before allowing four hits, but the Astros hold off Pittsburgh, 5–2. Johnson improves his record to 9–1 following his mid season trade from Seattle.

1998 Chicago DH Frank Thomas reaches 100 RBIs for the eighth straight season with a two-run home run as the White Sox beat Boston, 11–9. Thomas' homer, his 28th of the season, is one of seven in a contest that features 32 base hits.

1999 In the Cubs' 7–4 loss to Milwaukee, Chicago RF Sammy Sosa becomes the first player in ML history to hit 60 home runs twice. Sosa, who hit 66 homers for the Cubs in 1998, joins only Mark McGwire who hit 70 in 1998, Roger Maris who hit 61 in 1961, and Babe Ruth who hit 60 in 1927. Sosa's homers also continue to outpace the Cubs' wins as the defeat to the Brewers drops them to a NL second-worst 59–89.

1999 Tampa Bay calls up 35-year-old left-handed pitcher Jim Morris from Triple-A Durham. He becomes the oldest rookie in the major leagues since 36-year-old Minnesota Twins INF Minnie Mendoza in 1970. Morris, a Texas high school baseball coach, signed out of a tryout camp earlier in the year. He had retired from professional baseball 10 years earlier after pitching in both the Milwaukee Brewers and Chicago White Sox farm systems, never rising above Class A.

1999 Seattle SS Alex Rodriguez hits his 39th home run of the season to help set an ML record for combined homers by middle infielders, during the Mariners' 5–0 win over Minnesota. Rodriguez and Seattle 2B David Bell (19 homers), with 58 combined homers, break the previous mark of 57 held by 1990 Chicago Cubs SS Shawon Dunston and 2B Ryne Sandberg.

19

1890 Stuffy McInnis b. Gloucester, MA.

1901 The baseball schedule is canceled because of the funeral of President William McKinley, who was shot while on political tour in Buffalo, NY on September 6th, and died September 14th.

1914 Brooklyn RHP Ed Lafitte pitches the Federal League's first no-hitter, beating the Kansas City Packers, 6–2.

1925 Chicago RHP Ted Lyons loses his 17–0 no-hitter bid with two outs in the ninth inning when Washington pinch-hitter Bobby Veach singles. Lyons finishes with a shutout.

1926 The St. Louis Cardinals pound the Philadelphia Phillies 23–3 in the first game of a doubleheader and beat them again, 10–2 in the nightcap.

1926 Duke Snider b. Los Angeles, CA.

1930 Bob Turley b. Troy, IL.

1937 Chris Short b. Milford, DE.

1943 Joe Morgan b. Bonham, TX.

1946 Joe Ferguson b. San Francisco, CA.

1949 Pittsburgh OF Ralph Kiner becomes the first NL player to hit 50 home runs in two different seasons.

1955 Chicago Cubs SS Ernie Banks sets an ML record with his fifth grand slam home run of the season during a 12–inning, 6–5 loss to the St. Louis Cardinals.

1962 Randy Myers b. Vancouver, WA.

1967 Jim Abbott b. Flint, MI.

1968 Detroit RHP Denny McLain wins his 31st game, a 6–2 decision over New York. McLain's total is the most in the AL since since Lefty Grove's 31 wins in 1931. The Yankees' Mickey Mantle hits his 535th and next-to-last home run.

1970 Boston Red Sox OFs Billy and Tony Conigliaro both hit home runs against the Washington Senators, marking the second time in the season both went deep in the same game.

1972 Oakland manager Dick Williams and Chicago manager Chuck Tanner combine to use a record 51 players in a 15-inning, 8–7 White Sox win. The A's use 30 players, the White Sox 21.

1973 Frank Robinson hits his first home run in Texas' Arlington Stadium as a member of the California Angels. It becomes the 32nd ML ballpark that Robinson has homered in during 21 years, during which he has hit 586 round-trippers. The only parks Robinson has failed to connect in are Montreal's Jarry Park, the Houston Astrodome, St. Louis' Busch Stadium, and Seattle's Sicks Stadium.

1984 Cincinnati 1B Pete Rose reaches

the 100-hit plateau for a record 22nd consecutive year. He also ties a NL record with 725 doubles as the Reds beat Atlanta, 4–2.

1995 Cleveland LF Albert Belle hits three home runs in an 8–2 win over Chicago to tie an ML record with five homers over two consecutive games after belting two on September 18th.

1995 San Diego 3B Ken Caminiti switch hits home runs for the third time in four games, this time in a 15–4 win against Colorado.

1997 Boston SS Nomar Garciaparra breaks Ted Williams' Red Sox rookie record for total bases by belting a pair of doubles in a 5–4 loss to the Chicago White Sox. Garciaparra's two doubles push his total to 348, four more than Williams collected in 1939. Garciaparra will finish his rookie campaign with 365 total bases, only nine behind the AL rookie record of 374 set by Minnesota's Tony Oliva in 1964.

1998 In the Mariners' 5–3 loss to Anaheim, Seattle SS Alex Rodriguez hits his 40th home run of the season to become only the third player in ML history with at least 40 homers and 40 stolen bases in the same year. Rodriguez, who has 43 steals, joins Oakland A's RF Jose Canseco (42–40) in 1988 and San Francisco Giants LF Barry Bonds (42–40) in 1996 as the only members of the 40–40 club.

1998 Atlanta becomes the first team in two decades to win 100 games in consecutive seasons, beating Arizona, 5–0. LHP Tom Glavine becomes the first 20-game winner in the major leagues firing a six-hit shutout as the Braves improve to 100–56 after finishing 101–61 last season. The Philadelphia Phillies were the last team to post 100-win seasons in 1976–77, going 101–61 both years.

1998 San Francisco 3B Bill Mueller

and 2B Jeff Kent hit grand slam home runs as the Giants hammer Los Angeles, 18–4. San Francisco hits two grand slams in a game for just the second time in franchise history. Giants 1B Willie McCovey and C Dick Dietz hit slams against Montreal April 26, 1970.

1998 Texas RF Juan Gonzalez hits his 300th career home run in an 8–4 loss to Oakland. Gonzalez' homer is his 44th of the season and comes against A's RHP Jimmy Haynes.

1998 Cleveland RF Manny Ramirez hits his 44th and 45th home runs of the season, but the Indians lose, 7–6, to Kansas City. Ramirez' homers give him an ML record-tying eight in five games, equaling the mark reached twice by Washington Senators LF Frank Howard in 1968.

1999 Chicago RF Sammy Sosa hits his 61st home run of the season during the Cubs' 10-inning, 8–7 win over Milwaukee. Sosa's homers stay one ahead of the team's wins at 60–89.

20

1898 Charlie Dressen b. Decatur, IL.

1902 Chicago RHP Jim Callahan pitches the White Sox' first no-hitter, a 2–0 win over Detroit.

1907 Pittsburgh RHP Nick Maddox no-hits Brooklyn, winning 2–1.

1908 Chicago White Sox RHP Frank Smith pitches his second career no-hitter, a 1–0 victory over the Philadelphia A's.

1911 The New York Highlanders committ 12 errors in a doubleheader — seven in the first game and five in the second — but still split with Cleveland, losing the first game, 12–9, but winning the nightcap, 5–4.

1912 Boston Red Sox RHP Smokey Joe Wood has his record-tying 16-game winning streak end with a 6–4 loss to Detroit. Wood will lead the AL in wins with a 34–5 record.

1923 Detroit OF Ty Cobb collects his 3,000th hit during a 4-for-4 day against the Boston Red Sox.

1924 Chicago RHP Grover Cleveland Alexander wins his 300th game as the Cubs beat the New York Giants, 7–3, in 12 innings.

1927 Against Washington Senators LHP Tom Zachary, New York Yankees RF Babe Ruth hits his 60th home run of the season to break his own previous record of 59 homers set in 1921.

1937 Tom Tresh b. Detroit, MI.

1951 Ford Frick is elected baseball's third commissioner. He'll serve until November 16, 1965.

1953 Chicago Cubs SS Ernie Banks hits the first of his 512 ML home runs, this one against St. Louis RHP Gerry Staley.

1958 Baltimore RHP Hoyt Wilhelm hurls a 1–0 no-hitter against the New York Yankees. The Orioles' only run comes on a home run by catcher Gus Triandos.

1959 The San Francisco Giants play their last game at Seals Stadium, an 8–2 loss to the Los Angeles Dodgers before 22,923 fans. The following season, the Giants would begin play in newly constructed Candlestick Park.

1960 Dave Gallagher b. Trenton, NJ.

1967 Cincinnati C Johnny Bench hits the first of 389 career home runs, this one against Atlanta RHP Jim Britton.

1968 New York Yankees 1B Mickey Mantle hits his last home run, a solo shot against Boston RHP Jim Lonborg, to finish his career with 536 round-trippers.

1969 Pittsburgh RHP Bob Moose

no-hits the New York Mets, 4–0, at Shea Stadium.

1981 Minnesota Twins players Gary Gaetti, Tim Laudner, and Kent Hrbek all hit home runs in their first ML game. For Gaetti, it happens in his first ML at-bat.

1986 Texas RHP Kevin Brown, the team's top pick in the June 1986 draft, becomes the second Rangers pitcher of the season to register his first pro victory at the major league level when he beats Oakland, 9–5. Teammate Bobby Witt first turned the trick April 22, 1986 against Toronto. Strangely, LHP David Clyde, also with Texas, was the only other pitcher in history to turn the trick when the southpaw, barely a month out of high school, beat Minnesota on June 27, 1973.

1988 Boston 3B Wade Boggs becomes the first ML player this century to get 200 hits in six consecutive seasons as the Red Sox pound Toronto, 13–2. Boggs joins Lou Gehrig as the only players to get 200 hits and 100 walks in three straight years.

1992 Philadelphia 2B Mickey Morandini turns the first NL unassisted triple play in 65 years, the ninth in ML history, and the first ever by a second baseman, during the Phillies' 13-inning, 3–2 loss to Pittsburgh.

1995 The San Diego Padres play their 1,000th consecutive home game without a rainout. The streak began in 1983.

1997 Boston SS Nomar Garciaparra becomes the first Red Sox rookie to collect 200 hits since Johnny Pesky in 1942, but the Chicago White Sox win, 6–4.

1998 Baltimore 3B Cal Ripken, Jr., takes himself out of the Orioles lineup for the first time in 16 years, ending his consecutive games played streak at 2,632. Ripken ends the streak himself, without injury, asking manager Ray Miller not to play him in Baltimore's

final home game of the season, a 5–4 loss to the New York Yankees. The streak began on May 30, 1982.

1998 In the Cardinals 11–6 win at Milwaukee, St. Louis 1B Mark McGwire hits his 65th home run of the season but loses his apparent 66th on a disputed call which results in a ground rule double. McGwire blasts his 65th in the first inning against Brewers RHP Scott Karl, but later against rookie RHP Rod Henderson, McGwire's blast to center field is ruled a double as a fan is thought to interfere by reaching over the railing. Instant replay shows the ball actually clears the fence in what should've been called a home run.

1998 The Chicago White Sox beat Boston, 6–4, sweeping the three-game series at home for the first time since 1963.

1999 St. Louis 1B Mark McGwire hits his 59th home run of the season to break up Chicago RHP Jon Lieber's perfect game bid, as the Cardinals erupt to beat the Cubs, 7–2. Lieber retires the first 20 batters he faces, but McGwire's homer begins a string of eight straight hits which will score seven runs in the seventh inning.

21

1919 Chicago White Sox 1B Chick Gandil assembles seven teammates at the Ansonia Hotel on Broadway — LHP Lefty Williams, RHP Ed Cicotte, OF Hap Felsch, 3B Buck Weaver, SS Swede Risberg, INF Fred McMullin, and OF Shoeless Joe Jackson — as the 1919 World Series "fix" is in.

1922 St. Louis Browns 1B George Sisler, a .420 hitter who also led the AL in runs scored (134) and hits (246), becomes the first named MVP of the league since 1914, this time as recognized by the baseball writers.

1925 Philadelphia utility player Barney Friberg plays catcher for an inning against Pittsburgh, giving him the distinction of playing every position during the year.

1934 St. Louis RHPs Dizzy and Daffy Dean hurl back-to-back shutouts in a doubleheader sweep against Brooklyn. Dizzy opens with a three-hitter and Daffy follows with a 3–0 no-hitter.

1934 Jerry Zimmerman b. Omaha, NE.

1938 A hurricane wipes out an NL contest between the St. Louis Cardinals at the Boston Braves. The damage is assessed at over $3 billion and more than 600 deaths ensue.

1942 Sam McDowell b. Pittsburgh, PA.

1946 Cleveland plays its last game at League Park, a 5–3 loss to Detroit before only 2,772 fans. The 36-year-old facility will be replaced by Municipal Stadium the following season as part of new owner Bill Veeck's plan.

1956 The New York Yankees leave a record 20 men on base against the Boston Red Sox.

1959 Danny Cox b. Northampton, England.

1963 Cecil Fielder b. Los Angeles, CA.

1964 Philadelphia loses 1–0 to Cincinnati as the Reds' Chico Ruiz steals home for the game's only run. The Phillies will drop 10 straight and finish their collapse to St. Louis on the last day of the season.

1970 Oakland LHP Vida Blue no-hits Minnesota, 6–0.

1971 Baseball ends its 71-year association with the nation's capital, approving the Washington Senators' relocation to Dallas-Fort Worth for the 1972 season and the team becoming the Texas Rangers.

1981 Philadelphia LHP Steve Carlton breaks Bob Gibson's all-time NL strikeout record when he fans Montreal OF Andre Dawson for the 3,118th of his career. The Expos win, 1–0, in 17 innings.

1982 California Angels OFs Fred Lynn and Brian Downing both crash into the left center-field fence at Anaheim Stadium in pursuit of an apparent home run. Lynn makes the catch in a grassy area after knocking down an inner fence and before colliding with the outfield seats. The umpires rule an out, deciding Lynn would have made the catch and then tumbled into the seats.

1986 San Diego RHP Jimmy Jones makes his ML debut with a one-hit, 5–0 shutout victory over Houston.

1997 Los Angeles C Mike Piazza becomes only the second ML player to hit a home run completely out of Dodger Stadium, but Colorado still prevails, 10–5. Pittsburgh's Willie Stargell accomplished the feat on two earlier occasions.

1997 Philadelphia RHP Curt Schilling strikes out eight Chicago Cubs batters in a losing effort to run his season total to 313, equalling the NL strikeout record for right-handers set by Houston's J.R. Richard in 1979.

1997 New York DH Cecil Fielder celebrates his 34th birthday with his 300th career home run as the Yankees defeat Toronto, 5–4.

1998 A day after removing himself from the Baltimore for the first time in 16 years (2,632 straight games), Orioles 3B Cal Ripken, Jr., returns with two hits to move past Babe Ruth for 34th place on the all-time hit list with 2,875. The Blue Jays win, 3–1, as RHP Roger Clemens wins his 15th straight decision in becoming the AL's first 20-game winner with a 15 strikeout performance.

1998 Boston RHP Tom Gordon extends his AL record for consecutive save conversions with his 40th, in a 4–3 win over Tampa Bay in the first game of a doubleheader.

1998 San Francisco 2B Jeff Kent hits his 30th home run and drives in three runs for 122 RBIs, making him the only other second baseman in ML history besides the St. Louis Cardinals' Rogers Hornsby (1921–22) to have consecutive 120-RBI seasons. The Giants blast Pittsburgh, 8–1.

1999 Atlanta 3B Chipper Jones hits home runs from both sides of the plate to provide the difference in the Braves' 2–1 win over the New York Mets. Jones' second blast, his 43rd homer of the season, gives him 100 RBIs for the year as well.

1999 Boston RHP Pedro Martinez strikes out 12 batters, giving him a team record 300 for the season, as the Red Sox blank Toronto, 3–0. Martinez, who reached the 300-strikeout plateau with Montreal in 1997, joins LHP Randy Johnson (Seattle and Arizona) as the only pitchers to reach the plateau in each league.

1999 Seattle's Alex Rodriguez hits two home runs his 40th and 41st to become the first AL shortstop to hit 40 home runs twice in two different seasons, during the Mariners' 13–3 win over Kansas City. Rodriguez blasted 42 for Seattle in 1998. Chicago Cubs SS Ernie Banks reached the 40-homer mark five times, but in the AL, only Boston's Rico Petrocelli had done it previously, in 1969.

22

1889 Hooks Dauss b. Indianapolis, IN.

1904 New York Giants C Jim O'Rourke, at age 52, becomes the only ML player who participated in baseball's first game in 1876 to also play in a game after the turn of the century.

1911 Boston Braves RHP Cy Young, age 44, gets his last career win, 1–0 over Pittsburgh. Young will finish with an ML record 511 wins and a record 313 losses after pitching for 22 years.

1912 For the second time in 11 days, Philadelphia A's 2B Eddie Collins steals an ML record six bases in a game, during an 8–2 win over the St. Louis Browns.

1920 Bob Lemon b. San Bernardino, CA.

1926 St. Louis Cardinals SS Tommy Thevenow begins a homerless at-bat streak which will end at an ML record 3,347 through the end of the 1938 season.

1927 Tommy Lasorda b. Norristown, PA.

1935 The lowly Boston Braves lose their ML-record 110th game, en route to a 38–115 final record. The Braves finish 61½ games behind the NL pennant winning Chicago Cubs.

1936 The Detroit Tigers sweep the St. Louis Browns, 12–0 and 14–0, to record the biggest doubleheader shutout in ML history.

1946 Larry Dierker b. Hollywood, CA.

1946 New York Yankees C Yogi Berra hits the first of his 358 ML home runs, against Philadelphia A's RHP Jesse Flores.

1948 Facing the Boston Braves, St. Louis RF Stan Musial becomes the only player in ML history to collect five straight hits in a game all on the first pitch thrown to him during each at-bat in a game.

1954 Brooklyn LHP Karl Spooner becomes the first ML pitcher to strike out 15 batters in his first game, as the Dodgers blank the New York Giants, 3–0.

1959 Wally Backman b. Hillsboro, OR.

1959 The Los Angeles Dodgers collect an ML record nine pinch hits in a game.

1961 Vince Coleman b. Jacksonville, FL.

1965 Mark Guthrie b. Buffalo, NY.

1966 The Baltimore Orioles clinch their first AL pennant in 22 years with a 6–1 win over the Kansas City A's. The Orioles' last pennant came in 1944 when the franchise was known as the St. Louis Browns. The last time a pennant flew in Baltimore was in 1896 by the then NL Orioles.

1966 The smallest crowd ever to watch a game at Yankee Stadium — 413 paying customers — witness the last place Yankees fall, 4–1, to the Chicago White Sox.

1968 Minnesota's Cesar Tovar becomes only the second ML player to play one inning at each position during the Twins' 2–1 win over Oakland. The A's Bert Campaneris was the first player to play all nine positions in a nine-inning game.

1969 San Francisco CF Willie Mays becomes just the second player to reach 600 career home runs when he connects against San Diego RHP Mike Corkins in a 4–2 Giants victory.

1977 Texas RHP Bert Blyleven no-hits California, 6–0.

1984 Seattle SS Danny Tartabull hits his first ML home run against Chicago White Sox RHP Lamar Hoyt.

1986 Los Angeles LHP Fernando Valenzuela becomes the first Mexican native to win 20 games, beating Houston, 9–2, while allowing only two hits.

1987 Boston Red Sox 3B Wade Boggs reaches the 200-hit plateau for the fifth straight season during an 8–5 loss to Detroit.

1990 Chicago Cubs OF Andre Dawson steals his 300th base in an 11–5 loss to the New York Mets. Dawson becomes

only the second player in ML history besides Willie Mays to total 300 home runs, 300 steals, and 2,000 hits.

1993 Texas RHP Nolan Ryan makes an inauspicious departure from baseball, exiting a game in Seattle with a 3–1 count on batter Dave Magadan. Tearing the ulnar-collateral ligament in his elbow, Ryan ends his 27th season as baseball's all-time strikeout champion with 5,714 whiffs. His victims include 47 MVPs, 21 Hall of Famers, 10 members of the 1964 Phillies, and nine members of the 1993 Phillies. Ryan finishes his career with a 324–292 record, the third highest loss total in history.

1993 The Colorado Rockies play the final home game of their inaugural season and finish with an ML home attendance record of 4,483,350 fans.

1995 Baltimore DH Harold Baines hits his 300th career home run in a 10–3 win over Milwaukee.

1995 Los Angeles 3B Tim Wallach collects his 2,000th career hit in a 6–5 win over San Diego.

1997 Seattle CF Ken Griffey, Jr., hits his 54th and 55th home runs of the season as the Mariners beat Oakland, 4–2, to clinch at least a tie for the AL West title. The 55 homers is the most any player has hit in 36 years since Roger Maris set the standard with 61 in 1961.

1997 Atlanta becomes the first team to win six consecutive division championships, downing Montreal, 3–2, in 11 innings.

1997 Houston 1B Jeff Bagwell becomes the Astros' first 30–30 player by swiping a pair of bases during a 6–3 win at Cincinnati. Bagwell enters the contest with 42 home runs and 29 steals.

1998 Seattle CF Ken Griffey, Jr., hits his AL-leading 54th and 55th home runs in a 7–6 win over Oakland, and joins New York Yankees Babe Ruth and Lou Gehrig as the only ML players to

drive in 140 or more runs in three consecutive seasons. Gehrig accomplished
the feat from 1930–32, while Ruth did it
six straight years from 1926–31. Mariners
SS Alex Rodriguez hits his 41st homer in
the game, breaking the AL record for
most homers by a shortstop in a season
held by Boston's Rico Petrocelli in 1969.

1998 Toronto DH Jose Canseco sets
career highs with his 45th and 46th
home runs of the season as the Blue Jays
beat Baltimore, 7–3.

1998 Atlanta C Eddie Perez hits a
home run to give the Braves 208 round-
trippers for the season, breaking a 32-
year franchise record, in a 4–1 win over
Florida.

1998 Colorado 2B Mike Lansing hits
three home runs, but Arizona RF Karim
Garcia hits two homers himself as the
Diamondbacks edge the Rockies, 8–6.

1998 New York 1B John Olerud reaches
base for a NL record-tying 15th straight
time with a first inning walk, then fails in
his second at-bat, ending the streak in the
Mets' 5–3 loss to Montreal. San Francisco
LF Barry Bonds also reached base on 15
straight plate appearances this season,
while the ML record belongs to Ted
Williams who ran his streak to 16 with
the 1957 Boston Red Sox.

23

1845 Alexander Cartwright, age 25,
formally establishes the New York
Knickerbocker Base Ball Club, named
after a volunteer fire company. Formal
rules are first recorded.

1900 Lefty Stewart b. Sparta, TN.

1908 New York Giants rookie Fred
Merkle forgets to touch second base on
an apparent game-winning hit, as the
Chicago Cubs appeal for the third out.
"Merkle's boner" forces a one-game

playoff between the two teams, won by
the Cubs, who will also capture the
World Series.

1914 Cincinnati snaps a team-record
19-game losing streak with a 3–0 win
over the Boston Braves.

1941 St. Louis OF Stan Musial hits
his first of a career 475 ML home runs,
this one against Pittsburgh RHP Rip
Sewell.

1942 Woody Woodward b. Miami, FL

1942 Jim Rooker b. Lakeview, OR.

1950 Philadelphia A's reserve C Joe
Astroth knocks in a record-tying six
runs in the sixth inning during a 16–5
win over Washington. Astroth would
have only 18 RBIs all season.

1952 The Brooklyn Dodgers clinch
the NL title, marking the first time since
1948 that the pennant isn't decided in
the season's final game. The Dodgers
finish 4½ games ahead of the New York
Giants, who beat them in a one-game
playoff a year earlier.

1957 Milwaukee OF Hank Aaron
belts an 11th inning home run to give the
Braves a 4–2 win over St. Louis and
clinch the NL pennant. It's the first time
since 1950 that a New York team doesn't
finish first in the NL, and the first pennant for the Braves since the franchise
moves to Milwaukee in 1953.

1957 Boston Red Sox LF Ted
Williams has his streak of reaching base
every at-bat run to an astounding 16
straight times.

1957 The New York Yankees clinch
the AL pennant for the eighth time in
nine years.

1957 Tony Fossas b. Havana, Cuba.

1962 During a 12–2 loss to St. Louis,
Los Angeles SS Maury Wills steals his
96th and 97th bases to tie and break Ty
Cobb's 47-year-old record for thefts in a
year. Wills will finish the year with a
record 104 thefts, a mark that will stand

until 1974 when St. Louis OF Lou Brock swipes 118.

1966 Pete Harnisch b. Commack, NY.

1969 Jeff Cirillo b. Pasadena, CA.

1971 Willie Greene b. Milledgeville, GA.

1978 California OF Lyman Bostock, age 27, is fatally shot near Gary, IN. A rising star with a .311 lifetime batting average after four major league seasons, Bostock apparently falls victim to a random drive-by shooting.

1979 St. Louis LF Lou Brock steals his ML record 938th and final base, during the Cardinals' 10-inning, 7–4 win over the New York Mets.

1983 Philadelphia LHP Steve Carlton becomes the 16th pitcher in ML history to win 300 games, posting a 6–2 victory over the St. Louis Cardinals, the team he began his career with in 1965.

1984 Detroit beats the New York Yankees, 4–1, making Sparky Anderson the first manager with 100-win seasons in each league. Anderson led the NL Cincinnati Reds to 100-win seasons in 1970, 1975–76.

1986 Houston LHP Jim Deshaies sets an ML record striking out the first eight batters to start a game. He finishes with a two-hitter with 10 strikeouts as the Astros beat Los Angeles, 4–0.

1992 Cincinnati utility player Bip Roberts ties a NL record with 10 consecutive hits, covering games since September 20th.

1995 Chicago CF Lance Johnson ties an AL record with three triples in a game and goes 6-for-6 in a 14–4 win over Minnesota. Teammate Robin Ventura goes 5-for-6 with three doubles.

1997 Seattle RF Jay Buhner becomes only the tenth player in ML history to hit 40 or more home runs in three consecutive seasons as the Mariners beat Anaheim, 4–3, to clinch the AL West. Buhner's home run also gives Seattle a single season best of 258, eclipsing the previous mark set by Baltimore in 1996.

1998 Chicago RF Sammy Sosa pulls even with St. Louis 1B Mark McGwire for the all-time single season home run record with two homers — his 64th and 65th — in a heartbreaking 8–7 loss at Milwaukee. With his two solo homers, Sosa ties Hank Greenberg's 1938 ML record with 11 multi-homer games in a season, and also increases his NL-leading RBI mark to 156, passing Joe Medwick's 1937 total of 154 for fourth best all-time. The Cubs blow a 7–0 lead over the last three innings and lose in the bottom of the ninth when a two-out, bases loaded routine fly to left field is dropped by Brandt Brown, allowing three Brewers to score.

1998 Boston RHP Tom Gordon ties the ML record with his 41st straight save conversion — and his AL-leading 44th save of the year — as the Red Sox edge Tampa Bay, 5–4.

1998 The New York Yankees beat the Cleveland Indians, 8–4, to equal their 1927 franchise record of 110 victories. The 1998 Yankees, 110–48, need one more win to tie the AL record set by the 1954 Indians, who went 111–43 in a 154–game schedule.

1998 Houston 2B Craig Biggio becomes only the second player in ML history to have 50 doubles and 50 stolen bases in a season, during the Astros' 7–1 win at St. Louis. In the seventh inning, Biggio singles then steals his 50th base in 57 attempts. Biggio has 51 doubles to join Hall of Fame outfielder Tris Speaker, who had 53 doubles and 52 steals for the Boston Red Sox in 1912.

1999 Baltimore 3B Cal Ripken, Jr.'s

quest for 3,000 hits is halted nine hits short with 12 games remaining on the 1999 schedule as he undergoes back surgery.

1999 Atlanta 3B Chipper Jones hits his 45th home run of the season, as the Braves complete a three-game sweep over the New York Mets, 6–3, their nearest rivals in the NL East. Jones' homer is his fourth of the series and gives Atlanta a four game lead in the division with nine games left to play.

1999 Major League baseball announces that the 2001 All-Star Game will be played at Seattle's new Safeco Field on July 10, 2001. The 2000 All-Star Game has already been scheduled for Turner Field in Atlanta.

24

1908 National League president Harry Pulliam delcares the Cubs-Giants game from the previous day a tie. This after Giants baserunner Fred Merkle fails to touch second base on an apparent game-winning hit, which the Cubs appeal and win.

1910 Dixie Walker b. Villa Rich, GA.

1916 Cleveland utility player Marty Kavanaugh hits the AL's first pinch-hit grand slam to provide the winning margin in a 5–3 win over the Boston Red Sox.

1927 Pittsburgh OFs Paul and Lloyd Waner become the first brothers to hit home runs in the same game, and in the same inning, connecting against Cincinnati RHP Dolf Luque.

1939 After 15 years in the major leagues, Boston Braves OF Johnny Cooney hits his first home run. He'll hit another the next day. He will conclude

his 20-year career, with only those two homers to his record in 3,372 at-bats.

1940 Boston Red Sox 1B Jimmie Foxx hits his 500th career home run, off Philadelphia A's RHP George Caster, to become just the second ML player to reach the plateau and the youngest at age 32. Foxx follows LF Ted Williams' home run, and before the sixth inning is over, SS Joe Cronin and 3B Jim Tabor will also hit homers to set an AL record with four round-trippers in an inning. The Red Sox hammer the A's, 16–8.

1952 Rod Gilbreath b. Laurel, MS.

1955 Baltimore sweeps Washington in a doubleheader, giving the Senators their first 100-loss season in history. Washington finishes 53–101, 43 games behind the AL pennant-winning New York Yankees.

1956 Hubie Brooks b. Los Angeles, CA.

1964 Rafael Palmeiro b. Havana, Cuba.

1966 Bernard Gilkey b. St. Louis, MO.

1966 Cincinnati 1B Lee May hits the first of his 354 ML home runs, against New York Mets RHP Bob Shaw.

1969 New York RHP Gary Gentry pitches a four-hitter to beat St. Louis, 6–0, and clinch the NL East for the Mets in the first year of a divisional format.

1974 Detroit RF Al Kaline collects his 3,000th career hit, a double against Baltimore LHP Dave McNally, during the Tigers 5–4 loss to the Orioles.

1985 Montreal RF Andre Dawson ties the ML record for home runs in one inning with two, marking the second time in his career he accomplished the feat. Dawson hit two homers in one inning at Atlanta in 1978.

1988 Oakland RF Jose Canseco

becomes the first ML player to hit 40 home runs and steal 40 bases in one season as the A's beat Milwaukee, 9–8 in 14 innings. Canseco hits his 41st homer, and steals two bases, giving him 40 for the season.

1988 Toronto RHP Dave Steib, one strike away from a no-hitter, allows a bad hop single to Julio Franco, to settle for a one-hit, 1–0 shutout shutout against Cleveland.

1996 Boston 1B Mo Vaughn belts three home runs against Baltimore to become the first player since Red Sox OF Jim Rice in 1978 to collect 40 home runs and 200 base hits in a season. Vaughn will finish with 44 homers, 207 hits, 143 RBIs, and a .326 batting average, yet will finish a disappointing fifth in the AL MVP voting.

1997 St. Louis 1B Mark McGwire hits his 55th home run of the season during the Cardinals' 5–4 loss to Cincinnati.

1998 The New York Yankees equal the most wins in AL history with a 5–2 victory over Tampa Bay. New York (111–48) equals the 1954 Cleveland Indians (111–43) and trails only the 1906 Chicago Cubs (116–36) all-time.

1998 Boston RHP Tom Gordon sets an ML record with his 42nd consecutive save — 45th overall — as the Red Sox beat Baltimore, 9–6. Gordon shared the previous mark of 41 with Rod Beck and Trevor Hoffman.

1999 Arizona goes from expansion team to NL western division champions in one year, beating nearest rival San Francisco, 11–3. After losing 97 games in 1998, the Diamondbacks improve to 93–60 with LHP Randy Johnson striking out 11 batters to increase his ML-leading total to 353.

1999-Cleveland RF Manny Ramirez hits a grand slam home run and a three-run homer, and finishes his day with a career-high eight RBIs to lead the Indians to an 18–4 rout of Toronto.

25

1902 Pat Malone b. Altoona, PA.

1910 The scoreless streak of Philadelphia A's RHP Jack Coombs ends at 53 innings, in a darkness-shortened 5–2 loss to Chicago in the second game of a doubleheader. Coombs will lead the AL with 13 shutouts in 1910.

1917 Johnny Sain b. Havana, AR.

1918 Phil Rizzuto b. New York, NY.

1929 New York manager Miller Huggins, who led the Yankees to six pennants and three World Series championships in 12 seasons, dies suddenly of blood poisoning at age 49. Art Fletcher takes over for the remaining 11 games of the season.

1932 Philadelphia A's 1B Jimmie Foxx hits his 58th home run in the season finale against Washington.

1954 Cleveland wins its AL-record 111th game of the regular season as RHP Early Wynn throws a two-hitter at Detroit in the Indians' 11–1 win.

1955 Detroit OF Al Kaline, age 20, becomes baseball's youngest batting champion, finishing the season at .340.

1956 Brooklyn RHP Sal Maglie no-hits the Philadelphia Phillies, 5–0.

1962 Los Angeles RH reliever Ed Roebuck loses 3–2 in 10 innings against Houston for his first loss in more than two years. During the streak, Roebuck made 80 appearances and collected 12 wins.

1965 San Francisco CF Willie Mays, age 34, hits his 50th homer of the season to become the oldest player to do so. Mays was also the youngest player, at 24, in 1955 when he belted 51 homers.

1965 At an alleged 59 years of age, Kansas City A's RHP Satchel Paige becomes the oldest player to appear in the major leagues as he hurls three shutout innings against Boston. Red Sox LF Carl Yastrzemski gets the only hit against Paige.

1968 Reggie Jefferson b. Tallahassee, FL.

1984 New York Mets OF Rusty Staub joins Ty Cobb as the only major league players to hit home runs both as teenagers and past their 40th birthdays.

1986 Houston RHP Mike Scott no-hits San Francisco, 2–0, to clinch the NL western division title.

1996 San Francisco LF Barry Bonds sets a NL record with his 149th base on balls of the season, breaking the record shared by Brooklyn 2B Eddie Stanky (1945), and Houston OF Jimmy Wynn (1969).

1997 Los Angeles C Mike Piazza goes 3-for-5 during the Dodgers' 9–5 win at Colorado to give him 195 hits for the season breaking the ML record for most by a catcher. St. Louis C Ted Simmons (1975) and Milwaukee Braves C Joe Torre (1964) previously were tied at 193 hits.

1997 Montreal RHP Pedro Martinez becomes the 14th ML pitcher since 1900 and the second of the season to reach 300 strikeouts during a 3–2 win over Florida. Philadelphia RHP Curt Schilling earlier reached the 300 strike-out plateau.

1998 Chicago Cubs RF Sammy Sosa hits his 66th home run, against Houston RHP Jose Lima, but the Cubs fall, 6–2 to the Astros.

1998 St. Louis 1B Mark McGwire hits his 66th home run, against RHP Shayne Bennett, to tie Chicago RF Sammy Sosa for the ML lead as the Cardinals edge Montreal, 6–5.

1998 Seattle CF Ken Griffey, Jr., hits his 56th home run to equal a career high

set in 1997, as the Mariners crush Texas, 15–4.

1998 The New York Yankees defeat Tampa Bay, 6–1, to set an AL record for wins in a season with 112, passing Cleveland's 1954 record of 111–43. The Yankees, 112–48, improve their winning percentage to .700.

1999 Cleveland RF Manny Ramirez drives in two runs to become the first major league player in 50 years to reach 159 RBIs for a single season, during the Indians' 9–6 win over Toronto. Ramirez joins Boston Red Sox teammates Ted Williams and Vern Stephens, who each had 159 RBIs in 1949.

26

1908 Chicago Cubs RHP Ed Reulbach hurls a doubleheader shutout against Brooklyn, winning 5–0 on a five-hitter, then 3–0 on a three-hitter. Reulbach's twin wins give him nine victories against Brooklyn for the year, an ML mark for most wins against one team.

1925 Bobby Shantz b. Pottstown, PA.

1926 The St. Louis Browns and New York Yankees play an AL shortest game in 55 minutes, and then complete the shortest doubleheader in 2:07.

1945 Dave Duncan b. Dallas, TX.

1948 The Boston Braves clinch their first NL pennant since 1914 by beating the New York Giants, 3–2, on Bob Elliott's three-run home run.

1953 Detroit OF Al Kaline hits the first of his 399 ML home runs, this one against Cleveland RHP Dave Hoskins.

1954 Four days after striking out an ML record 15 New York Giants in his major league debut, Brooklyn LHP Karl Spooner strikes out 12 Pittsburgh Pirates batters.

1954 Kevin Kennedy b. Los Angeles, CA.

1961 New York Yankees RF Roger Maris ties Babe Ruth with his 60th homer of the season, against Baltimore RHP Jack Fisher.

1961 Steve Buechele b. Lancaster, CA.

1964 New York Yankees rookie RHP Mel Stottlemyre collects five hits in a game — four singles and a double.

1964 Dave Martinez b. New York, NY.

1971 Baltimore RHP Jim Palmer shuts out Cleveland, 5–0, for his 20th victory of the season to give the Orioles only the second quartet of 20-game winners in ML history. Palmer (20–9) joins RHP Pat Dobson (20–8) and LHPs Dave McNally (21–5) and Mike Cuellar (20–9) for the Baltimore foursome. The 1920 Chicago White Sox were led by RHPs Red Faber (23–13), Eddie Cicotte (21–10), and Dickie Kerr (21–9), and LHP Lefty Williams (22–14), yet finished two games behind Cleveland in the AL pennant race.

1981 Houston RHP Nolan Ryan becomes the first pitcher to hurl five no-hitters, shutting out Los Angeles, 5–0.

1983 St. Louis RHP Bob Forsch pitches the second no-hitter of his career, 3–0 over Montreal.

1993 Seattle LHP Randy Johnson strikes out 13 Oakland batters to become the 12th ML pitcher to whiff 300 batters in a season. Johnson will finish with an AL leading 308 whiffs.

1997 Philadelphia RHP Curt Schilling sets an NL record for strikeouts by a right-hander in a season by whiffing Florida's Devon White for his 314th of the season. Houston RHP J.R. Richard had 313 strikeouts in 1979.

1997 Los Angeles C Mike Piazza blasts the longest home run in Coors Field history, a 496-foot blast against RHP Darren Holmes during a 10–4 Dodgers win at Colorado.

1998 St. Louis 1B Mark McGwire blasts his 67th and 68th home runs of the season, against Montreal RHPs Dustin Hermanson and Kirk Bullinger, but the Cardinals fall to the Expos, 7-6.

1998 Philadelphia RHP Curt Schilling becomes the fifth pitcher in ML history to record consecutive 300 or more strikeout seasons with seven whiffs against Florida. Schilling hurls eight innings and receives a no decision in a 4–3, 10-inning Marlins win in the first game of a doubleheader. Schilling joins RHPs J.R. Richard and Nolan Ryan, and LHPs Sandy Koufax and Rube Waddell as the only pitchers with back-to-back 300 strikeout seasons.

1998 New York Yankees RHP David Cone defeats Tampa Bay, 3–1, for his 20th win of the season, and sets an ML record for a 10-year span between 20-win seasons. Cone (20–7) was 20–3 for the cross-town rival New York Mets in 1988.

1998 Boston RHP Dennis Eckersley sets an ML record for his 1,071st career pitching appearance, passing RHP Hoyt Wilhelm, during the Red Sox' 5–2 loss to Baltimore.

1999 St. Louis 1B Mark McGwire hits his 60th home run of the season, tying Chicago's Sammy Sosa as the only two-time members of the exclusive club, during the Cardinals' 7-5 loss at Cincinnati.

1999 Atlanta clinches its eighth straight NL East title with a 10-0 shutout win at Montreal.

27

1905 Boston Red Sox RHP Bill Dinneen throws the fourth no-hitter of the season, beating the Chicago White Sox, 2–0, in the first game of a doubleheader.

1907 Whitt Wyatt b. Kensington, GA.

1914 Cleveland 2B Napoleon Lajoie collects his 3,000th career hit, a double, as the Indians defeat the New York Yankees, 5–3.

1919 Boston Red Sox RF Babe Ruth swats his then-record 29th home run of the season in a game at Washington. Ruth's record nearly doubles the previous single-season high of 16 held by Cincinnati Reds RF Sam Crawford in 1901 and Philadelphia A's RF Sam Seybold in 1902.

1919 Johnny Pesky b. Portland, OR.

1923 New York Yankees 1B Lou Gehrig hits the first of his 493 ML home runs against Boston Red Sox RHP Bill Piercy.

1927 New York Yankees RF Babe Ruth hits his 57th home run of the season against Philadelphia A's future Hall of Fame LHP Lefty Grove.

1930 Chicago Cubs OF Hack Wilson hits his 55th and 56th home runs — an NL record — in a game against Cincinnati.

1930 Dick Hall b. St. Louis, MO.

1935 The Chicago Cubs clinch the NL pennant with their 20th straight win, a 6–2 victory over St. Louis. The streak will end at 21 games.

1936 St. Louis Cardinals 1B Walter Alston strikes out in his only ML at-bat against Chicago Cubs RHP Lon Warneke.

1940 Detroit RHP Floyd Giebell outpitches Cleveland RHP Bob Feller in the AL pennant-clinching 2–0 Tigers win. Detroit (90–64) finishes one game atop Cleveland (89–65) to advance to the World Series for the first time since winning it in 1935.

1942 The St. Louis Cardinals record a final day doubleheader sweep over the Chicago Cubs to finish with 106 victories, just two more than the Brooklyn Dodgers in an amazing NL pennant race. The Cardinals (106–48) edge the Dodgers (104–50), but run away from the rest of the league as the third place New York Giants finish 85–67, 20 games out.

1949 Mike Schmidt b. Dayton, OH.

1951 Brooklyn Dodgers rookie Bill Sharman gets kicked out of a game without ever playing. During a heated argument, umpire Frank Dascoli clears the entire Brooklyn bench, including Sharman, who'll never get another chance. A year later, Sharman gives up baseball in favor of basketball and will win four NBA titles with the Boston Celtics.

1953 The Browns lose their 100th and final game of the season to finish the franchise's final year in St. Louis with a last place 54-100 mark. Operating as the Baltimore Orioles in 1954, the team will finish with an identical 54-100 record.

1967 In their last game at Municipal Stadium, the Kansas City A's beat the Chicago White Sox, 4–0, behind RHP Jim "Catfish" Hunter. The following season, owner Charlie Finley moves the franchise to Oakland, CA. Kansas City will be without an ML team until April 8, 1969 when the AL expansion Royals begin play.

1973 California RHP Nolan Ryan strikes out 16 Minnesota batters in 11 innings, leading the Angels to a 5–4 win. Ryan's final victim, Rich Reese, is season strikeout number 383, a new ML record, breaking Sandy Koufax's 1965 mark of 382.

1992 Seattle LHP Randy Johnson strikes out 18 Texas Rangers in eight innings of work.

1996 San Francisco LF Barry Bonds becomes only the second player in ML history with 40 home runs and 40 stolen bases. Oakland RF Jose Canseco first reached the 40–40 plateau in 1988. Bonds will finish the year with 42 homers and 40 steals, the exact totals Canseco had in 1988.

1996 Baltimore Orioles 2B Roberto Alomar, incensed over a home plate strike three call by umpire John Hirschbeck, spits in the umpire's face. American League president Gene Budig suspends Alomar for five games, which becomes the first five games of the 1997 season and not during the 1996 postseason playoffs, much to the outrage of the umpires union.

1997 St. Louis 1B Mark McGwire hits his 56th and 57th home runs of the season during the Cardinals' 12–4 victory over the Chicago Cubs.

1997 Seattle OF Ken Griffey, Jr., hits his 56th home run of the season during the Mariners 9–3 win over Oakland. Seattle hits two other home runs to set an ML record with 264 for the season.

1997 New York 3B Wade Boggs collects his 2,800th career hit with an RBI triple in the Yankees' 6–1 win in Detroit.

1998 St. Louis 1B Mark McGwire hits his 69th and 70th home runs on the final day of the season, a 6–3 win against Montreal. McGwire's victims are RHPs Mike Thurman and Carl Pavano, the 66th victim of the year. In his final 11 at-bats, McGwire homers five times to extend his new ML standard.

1998 San Diego LF Greg Vaughn hits his 50th home run of the season in a 3–2 Padres win against Arizona to complete the first 50 homer foursome in ML history. Vaughn joins Mark McGwire (70), Sammy Sosa (66), and Ken Griffey, Jr. (56). San Diego RHP Trevor Hoffman earns his 53rd save to tie the NL record shared by Chicago Cubs LHP Randy Myers in 1993.

1998 The New York Yankees close out the season with their seventh straight win, 8–3 over Tampa Bay, to finish 114–48 for a .704 winning percentage. Only the 1906 Chicago Cubs, 116–36, end the regular season with more victories.

1998 In just his second ML game, Toronto RHP Roy Halladay comes within one out of a no-hitter, losing it on a pinch-hit home run by Detroit's Bob Higginson in a 2–1 Blue Jays win. Halladay strikes out eight and walks none in his first ML win.

1998 Chicago LF Albert Belle drives in three runs with a home run and two singles to lift the White Sox to a 7–6 win over Kansas City. Belle finishes the season with 201 hits, team records with home runs (49), doubles (48), RBIs (153), extra base hits (100), and total bases (401). Belle has a record 31 homers after the All-Star break, and becomes just the fifth ML player since 1950, and the first in the AL since Boston's Jim Rice in 1978, to finish with more than 400 total bases.

1998 Los Angeles beats Milwaukee, 2–1, finishing an 83–79 season with an equal number of 660 runs scored and runs allowed.

1998 Colorado defeats San Francisco, 9–8, before 48,028 fans to end the year at 3,789,347 attendance to lead the major leagues for the sixth straight season.

1998 Cincinnati sports the first all-brother infield in ML history as 1B Steve Larkin and SS Barry Larkin are joined by 2B Bret Boone and 3B Aaron Boone. The Reds defeat Pittsburgh, 4–1.

1998 Baltimore SS Jeff Rebolet commits an error during the last game of the season, a 6–4 loss to Boston, as the Orioles set an ML record with only 81 miscues in a season. Minnesota held the previous best of 84 errors during the 1988 season.

1998 Florida splits a doubleheader with Philadelphia to finish the season

54–108, the worst ever for a defending World Champion and the worst in the ML in 19 years. The Marlins finish 52 games behind NL East champions Atlanta, 106–56.

1999 In the final game played at Tiger Stadium, Detroit defeats Kansas City, 8–2, aided by DH Rob Fick's grand slam home run. Since opening as Navin Field in 1912, Detroit played 6,783 games in 88 seasons at the stadium, third most all-time behind Boston's Fenway Park and St. Louis' Sportsman Park.

1999 St. Louis 1B Mark McGwire hits his 61st home run of the season in a 9-7 loss at Cincinnati.

28

1919 In the shortest nine-inning game in ML history, the New York Giants beat the Philadelphia Phillies, 6–1, in only 51 minutes.

1920 A grand jury indicts eight Chicago White Sox players on charges of fixing the 1919 World Series in the "Black Sox Scandal." All eight players are immediately suspended by Chicago owner Charles Comiskey.

1923 The New York Yankees collect an AL record 30 hits against the Boston Red Sox.

1924 At .424 St. Louis Cardinals 2B Rogers Hornsby finishes the season with the highest batting average since Nap Lajoie hit .426 in 1901.

1930 A day after setting the NL record with 56 home runs, Chicago Cubs OF Hack Wilson drives in his ML record 189th and 190th runs in a season finale win over Cincinnati. A later recalculation reveals that Wilson actually had 191 RBIs for the season.

1930 New York Giants 1B Bill Terry finishes with a .401 batting average, and

remains the last NL hitter to reach the plateau.

1932 Connie Mack begins dismantling his powerful Philadelphia A's club, selling LF Al Simmons, CF Mule Haas, and 3B Jimmy Dykes to the Chicago White Sox for $150,000. The A's won the World Series in 1929–30, lost it in 1931 in Game 7, then finished second to New York Yankees for the AL pennant in 1932.

1938 At Wrigley Field, the Chicago Cubs and Pittsburgh Pirates are deadlocked, 5–5, in the ninth inning as umpires plan on calling the game due to darkness after player/manager Gabby Hartnett bats. The Cubs catcher saves the umpires any trouble, hitting a game-winning home run — the "Homer in the Gloamin" — to end the game, 6–5. Three days later, Chicago clinches the NL pennant.

1941 Boston Red Sox LF Ted Williams enters the last day's doubleheader against the Philadelphia A's with a .39955 batting average. Declining an opportunity to sit out, Williams goes 6-for-8 at Shibe Park to finish the year at .406. Williams remains the last ML player to reach the .400 plateau.

1942 Grant Jackson b. Fostoria, OH.

1951 New York Yankees RHP Allie Reynolds hurls his second no-hitter of the season, 8–0 over the Boston Red Sox, to clinch the AL pennant. He earlier no-hit Cleveland, 1–0, July 12th.

1957 Brooklyn LHP Danny McDevitt shuts out Pittsburgh, 3–0, in the last ML game played at Ebbets Field.

1959 Todd Worrell b. Arcadia, CA.

1960 Boston LF Ted Williams blasts a home run in his final major league at-bat, against Baltimore RHP Jack Fisher, in the Red Sox 5–4 win. Williams immediately retires with 521 career homers.

1961 Ed Vosberg b. Tucson, AZ.

1973 Milwaukee Brewers 3B Don Money begins his ML record of 261 consecutive errorless chances streak which ends on July 16, 1974. The streak helps Money achieve the highest all-time single season fielding average for his position, .989, in 1974.

1974 Montreal C Gary Carter hits the first of his 324 ML home runs against Philadelphia LHP Steve Carlton, the pitcher against whom he would connect a personal best 11 times in his career.

1975 Four Oakland pitchers combine to no-hit California, 5–0, on the final day of the season. A's LHP Vida Blue (5), RHP Glenn Abbott (1), LHP Paul Lindblad (1), and RHP Rollie Fingers (2) become the first foursome to turn the trick.

1988 Los Angeles RHP Orel Hershiser sets an ML record by pitching 59 straight shutout innings.

1997 Finishing at .372, San Diego OF Tony Gwynn ties Honus Wagner by winning his eighth NL batting title.

1997 Oakland 3B Scott Brosius goes 0-for-4 on the last day of the season to finish with a .203 batting average. Brosius becomes only the fourth ML player in history to have his batting average drop more than 100 points in consecutive seasons, after batting .304 in 1996.

1997 After 124 games, Florida C Charles Johnson completes the season without committing an error. Johnson becomes only the second ML receiver to catch more than 100 games without a miscue joining Philadelphia A's C Buddy Rosar in 1946. Johnson's last error happened June 23, 1996.

1998 Chicago wins the first NL one-game playoff in 18 years, 5–3 over San Francisco. In 1980, Houston eliminated Los Angeles in a loser out contest.

1999 Atlanta becomes the first NL team in 55 years to win 100 games three years in a row, defeating the New York Mets, 9–3. The Braves join the 1942–44 St. Louis Cardinals, and only two other AL teams — the 1969–71 Baltimore Orioles and the 1929–31 Philadelphia A's — as the only clubs to accomplish the feat this century.

29

1911 Philadelphia Phillies RHP Grover Cleveland Alexander beats Pittsburgh, 7–4, to earn his rookie record 28th win of the season which also leads the NL.

1913 Legendary international athlete Jim Thorpe, playing outfield for the New York Giants, hits his first ML home run against Boston Braves LHP Otto Hess, a Swiss native. The Olympic medal-winning Thorpe would hit seven home runs in a six-year career. Later he would be inducted into pro football's Hall of Fame.

1913 Washington RHP Walter Johnson blanks the Philadelphia A's, 1–0, to finish the season with a career high 36 wins (against only seven losses), 12 shutouts, and a 1.14 ERA — all AL highs. Johnson will later earn the Chalmers AL MVP Award.

1914 Boston clinches its first NL pennant with a 3–2 win over the Chicago Cubs. The "Miracle Braves" finish with an incredible 68–19 rush to win going away, 10½ games over the New York Giants, with a final 94–59 record. Boston would complete its amazing season with a four-game sweep over the Philadelphia A's in the World Series.

1915 Philadelphia RHP Grover Cleveland Alexander pitches a one-hitter and his NL-leading 12th shutout and 31st win as the Phillies defeat Boston, 5–0, to clinch their first pennant.

1927 New York Yankees RF Babe Ruth hits his 58th and 59th home runs of the season against Washington Senators RHPs Horace Lisenbee and Paul Hopkins, tying his 1921 season high record. Ruth will break his own record with his 60th homer the next day.

1935 Pittsburgh 2B Pep Young becomes the first non-pitcher since 1893 to strike out five times in a game.

1935 Howie Bedell b. Clearfield, PA.

1938 Mike McCormick b. Pasadena, CA.

1949 Steve Busby b. Burbank, CA.

1954 New York Giants rookie CF Willie Mays makes an impossible over-the-shoulder catch against Cleveland's Vic Wertz in Game 1 of the World Series. Mays' catch helps send the game into extra innings, which the Giants win, 5–2, on a pinch-hit three-run homer by Dusty Rhodes. New York will go on to sweep Cleveland, baseball's most successful team of the year (111 wins) in four straight games.

1956 Baltimore 3B Brooks Robinson hits his first of a career 268 ML Home runs, this one against Washington RHP Evelio Hernandez.

1957 The New York Giants play their last home game at the Polo Grounds, losing to Pittsburgh. Next season, the Giants will call San Francisco home.

1959 Brooklyn completes a two-game sweep of Milwaukee with a 12-inning, 6–5 win, to give the Dodgers their NL playoff win and the pennant.

1968 On his last at-bat of the season, Cincinnati OF Pete Rose wins his first NL batting title with a bunt single against San Francisco LHP Ray Sadecki. Rose finishes at .335, edging Pittsburgh OF Matty Alou, who finishes second at .332.

1971 Montreal 2B Ron Hunt is hit by a pitch thrown by Chicago RHP Milt Pappas, a record 50th time that Hunt

has been plunked during the season. The Expos win, 6–5.

1974 St. Louis LF Lou Brock steals his ML single-season record 118th base during the Cardinals' 7–3 win over the Chicago Cubs.

1975 Longtime player/manager Casey Stengel passes away at age 85. In 25 seasons (1934–65) with the Brooklyn Dodgers, Boston Braves, New York Yankees, and New York Mets, Stengel won 10 pennants and seven World Series titles. He was inducted into the Hall of Fame in 1966.

1976 Los Angeles manager Walter Alston, age 64, retires after 158 games into his 23rd season, all with the Dodgers. Alston wins seven NL pennants, four World Series titles, and 2,040 games with Brooklyn and Los Angeles combined.

1976 San Francisco RHP John Montefusco no-hits Atlanta, 9–0.

1985 Baltimore manager Earl Weaver gets ejected in both games of a double-header.

1986 Cleveland SS Jay Bell hits a home run on the first pitch of his first ML at-bat against Minnesota RHP Bert Blyleven. The players were traded for each other in 1985 while Bell was in the Twins' farm system. The home run allowed is a record-breaking 47th of the season for Blyleven.

1986 In the first meeting between brothers who oppose each other as starting pitchers, Chicago Cubs RHP Greg Maddux defeats the Philadelphia Phillies and RHP Mike Maddux, 8–3.

1987 New York Yankees 1B Don Mattingly hits a season-record sixth grand slam, this time against Boston LHP Bruce Hurst.

1996 Colorado 3B Vinny Castilla hits his 40th home run of the season during the Rockies' 12–3 victory at San Francisco. Castilla joins teammates Andres Galarraga (47) and Ellis Burks (40) to form the first 40-home run trio on one team since the 1973 Atlanta Braves featured Davey Johnson (43), Darrell Evans (41), and Hank Aaron (40). The Rockies also tie the NL record with their 221st home run of the season, equalling the 1947 New York Giants and 1956 Cincinnati Reds.

1996 Baltimore RF Brady Anderson sets an ML record with his 12th leadoff home run, breaking San Francisco OF Bobby Bonds' 1973 record of 11. Anderson's blast is his 50th of the year, helping the Orioles set a new single season record with 257 round-trippers.

1996 Detroit SS Alan Trammell concludes a 20-year career with a base hit in his final at-bat. He announces his retirement the next day, ending his two decades in a Tigers uniform with a lifetime .285 batting average, four Gold Glove Awards, and World Series MVP trophy for the 1984 champions.

1996 San Diego RF Tony Gwynn finishes his season with a .353 batting average to lead the NL for the seventh time.

1998 Boston 1B Mo Vaughn hits two home runs and ties an ML postseason record with seven RBIs as the Red Sox end a 13-game postseason game losing streak, 11–3 over Cleveland, in the AL divisional playoffs. Vaughn becomes the first Red Sox player since Rico Petrocelli in 1969 to have two homers in a postseason contest.

1998 San Diego RHP Kevin Brown strikes out 16 batters, allowing only two hits in eight innings as the Padres edge Houston, 2–1. Brown's 16 whiffs are the most ever in divisional series play, and fall just one short of the ML postseason record of 17 set by St. Louis RHP Bob Gibson in the 1968 World Series.

1999 St. Louis 1B Mark McGwire hits a home run in both games of a double-header sweep over San Diego, his 62nd and 63rd homers of the season.

1999 Cleveland RF Manny Ramirez collects his 161st RBI, most in the major leagues since Jimmy Foxx drove in 175 runs for the 1938 Boston Red Sox, during a 5–2 loss to Kansas City.

30

1884 Nap Rucker b. Crabapple, GA.

1910 St. Louis Browns 3B Ray Jansen goes 4-for-5 and committs three errors in his only major league game.

1915 Boston clinches the AL pennant when the St. Louis Browns hand the second place Tigers an 8–2 loss in Detroit.

1916 The New York Giants lose the second game of a doubleheader, 8–3, to the Boston Braves, for their first loss in an ML record 26 games covering 24 days. Despite an earlier 17-game winning streak, the Giants still finish in fourth place, eight games behind champion Brooklyn.

1926 Robin Roberts b. Springfield, IL.

1927 New York Yankees RF Babe Ruth breaks a 2–2 tie with an eighth inning, two-run home run against LHP Tom Zachary, his record 60th of the season, to beat Washington, 4–2.

1932 Johnny Podres b. Witherbee, NY.

1934 St. Louis RHP Dizzy Dean wins his 30th game of the season, to finish the year at 30-7 for the eventual World Series winning Cardinals. The 30-win plateau won't be reached again until 1968 when Detroit RHP Denny McLain finishes 31-6 for the eventual World Series winning Tigers.

1945 On the last day of the season, Detroit OF Hank Greenberg hits a ninth inning grand slam home run to beat the

St. Louis Browns, 6–3, and clinch the AL pennant for the Tigers.

1948 Craig Kusick b. Milwaukee, WI.

1949 Pittsburgh OF Ralph Kiner, the first NL player to reach 50 home runs twice in a career, hits his season-ending 54th in a 3–2 win over Cincinnati.

1951 On the last day of the season, The New York Giants beat the Boston Braves, 3–2, to tie the Brooklyn Dodgers for the NL pennant and force a three-game playoff. The Dodgers edge the Philadelphia Phillies, 9–8, on a dramatic 14th inning home run by Jackie Robinson. Robinson earlier prolongs the day with a game-saving catch in the 13th inning.

1956 New York CF Mickey Mantle finishes his Triple Crown year with 52 home runs, 130 RBIs, and a .353 batting average, to lead the Yankees to an eventual World Series championship.

1956 Brooklyn defeats Pittsburgh, 8–6, on the last day of the regular season to win the NL pennant by only one game over Milwaukee.

1962 In his final major league at-bat, New York Mets C Joe Pignatano hits into a triple play.

1962 Dave Magadan b. Tampa, FL.

1963 Houston OF John Paciorek, an 18-year-old rookie, makes his ML debut going 3-for-3 with two walks, scores four runs, and has three RBIs. He'll finish with a 1.000 batting average in his only game as Paciorek will later injure his back and never play again.

1967 Houston 1B Bob Watson hits the first of a career 184 ML home runs, this one against Pittsburgh LHP Jim Shellenback.

1971 With two outs in the ninth inning and the Washington Senators leading the New York Yankees, 7–5, crazed fans pour onto the field, ripping up turf and stealing bases and other sou-

venirs. The Senators' last game in the nation's capital is a forfeit loss; they become the Texas Rangers to start the 1972 season.

1972 Curtis Goodwin b. Oakland, CA.

1979 Brothers Phil and Joe Niekro both win their 21st and final games of the season to tie for the NL season high. Phil wins for Atlanta while Joe follows suit for Houston.

1980 Oakland LF Rickey Henderson passes Ty Cobb's AL record of 96 steals in a 5–1 A's win over Chicago. Henderson will finish the season with a new AL record of 100 steals, and two years later shatter that mark with a new high of 130.

1984 California RHP Mike Witt hurls the 11th perfect game in modern baseball history, 1–0 over Texas.

1990 In the last game played at old Comiskey Park, a packed house of 42,849 fans watch the Chicago White Sox beat Seattle, 2–1. In eight decades a total of 72,801,381 paying fans passed thru Comiskey Park's turnstiles.

1992 Kansas City 3B George Brett records his 59th career four-hit game during the Royals' 4–0 win over California. His last hit, against Angels LHP Tim Fortugno, is Brett's career 3,000th, making him the 18th ML player to reach that milestone. Brett follows Robin Yount who collected his 3,000th hit earlier in the month. Fittingly, both players will enter the Hall of Fame together in 1999.

1995 Cleveland LF Albert Belle belts his 50th home run in a 3–2 win over Kansas City to become the first ML player with both 50 homers and 50 doubles in the same season.

1998 Atlanta RHP John Smoltz becomes the winningest postseason pitcher in ML history, allowing five hits in 7⅔ innings, as the Braves beat the

Chicago Cubs, 7–1, in the first game of the NL Divisional Series. Smoltz, 11–3 in 21 postseason starts, passes LHP Whitey Ford and RHP Dave Stewart for career wins.

1999 During a 9-2 win over Toronto, Cleveland RF Manny Ramirez hits a three-run home run for a new team record 164 RBIs. Indians 1B Hal Trosky led the AL with 162 RBIs in 1936.

1999 A regular season record crowd of 61,389 fans see the San Francisco Giants lose their final game at Candlestick Park, 9-4 to the Los Angeles Dodgers.

OCTOBER

1

1903 Pittsburgh OF Jimmy Sebring hits the first World Series home run in Game 1 as the Pirates defeat the Boston Somersets, 7–3, with Hall of Fame RHP Cy Young taking the loss.

1904 Jimmie Reese b. Los Angeles, CA.

1922 St. Louis 2B Rogers Hornsby becomes baseball's third Triple Crown Award winner, finishing the season with a .401 batting average, 42 home runs, and 152 RBIs.

1922 New York Giants RF Mahlon Higbee hits a home run in his final major league at-bat, a day after St. Louis Cardinals 1B Del Gainer homered in his last at-bat.

1932 New York's Babe Ruth and Lou Gehrig each homer twice in World Series Game 3 as the Yankees beat the Chicago Cubs, 7–5. Ruth's second home run is the controversial "called shot" to center field against Cubs RHP Charlie Root. The Yankees will complete a four-game sweep of the Cubs the next day.

1933 Philadelphia A's 1B Jimmie Foxx (.356, 48 home runs, 163 RBIs) and Philadelphia Phillies OF Chuck Klein (.368, 28 home runs, 120 RBIs), last year's respective league MVPs, complete an unprecedented one-season double, becoming the fifth and sixth Triple Crown winners of the century.

1933 Boston OF Wally Berger leaves his sickbed to pinch-hit a grand slam home run in the seventh inning, win-ning the game and giving the Braves a fourth place finish — the first time in 12 years they have ended a season that high in the standings. Boston's 83–71 record nips the fifth place St. Louis Cardinals who finish 82–71.

1935 Chuck Hiller b. Johnsburg, IL.

1944 On the last day of the season, the St. Louis Browns win their first and only pennant, beating the New York Yankees, 5–2. Browns RHP Sig Jakucki scatters six hits and OF Chet Laabs hits two home runs.

1945 Rod Carew b. Panama.

1946 In the first postseason play-off to determine a league champion, St. Louis tops Brooklyn, 4–2, en route to sweep-ing the series and an eventual World Series title.

1948 Bill Bonham b. Glendale, CA.

1950 Philadelphia RHP Robin Roberts hurls a five-hitter and OF Dick Sisler hits a dramatic 10th inning three-run homer to give the Phillies a 4–1 win over Brooklyn and their first NL pen-nant since 1915.

1955 Jeff Reardon b. Pittsfield, MA.

1959 The Chicago White Sox blank the Los Angeles Dodgers, 11–0, in the World Series opener for the largest shutout in series history. White Sox 1B Ted Kluszewski leads the offense with two homers and five RBIs. Chicago rep-resents the AL in the World Series for the first time since the "Black Sox" scan-dal of 1919.

1960 Chicago Cubs OF Billy Williams hits his first of a career 426 ML home

227

runs, this one against Los Angeles RHP Stan Williams.

1961 New York RF Roger Maris completes his quest for Babe Ruth's home run record with his 61st against Boston RHP Tracy Stallard. Ruth hit 60 in 1927.

1961 In the last AL game played at Los Angeles' Wrigley Field, the Cleveland Indians beat the Angels, 8–5, before a meager crowd of 9,868. Steve Bilko, a longtime minor league slugger, blasts a ninth inning pinch-hit home run to give Los Angeles a record 248 round-trippers hit at one stadium for one season. The Angels hit 122, while opponents smash 126.

1963 Mark McGwire b. Pomona, CA.

1964 Roberto Kelly b. Panama City, Panama.

1970 California LF Alex Johnson has two hits on the final day of the regular season to win the AL batting title in the tightest race since 1945. Johnson finishes at .3289 to edge Boston LF Carl Yastrzemski who finishes second at .3286.

1974 Facing Cleveland RHP Steve Kline, Boston OF Jim Rice hits his first of a career 382 ML home runs.

1984 Peter Ueberroth takes office as baseball's sixth commissioner, succeeding Bowie Kuhn, who was fired by the owners November 1, 1982. As baseball's first new chief executive since 1968, Ueberroth will hold that position until March 31, 1989.

1995 Baltimore RHP Mike Mussina hurls the Orioles' fifth straight shutout, tying their own AL record, with a 4–0 win over Detroit. Baltimore first blanked five straight opponents in September 1974.

1995 The Colorado Rockies edge San Francisco, 10–9, to lock up their first-ever wildcard playoff spot. Colorado makes it to the postseason in only its third season, five years faster than any previous expansion team.

2

1908 Cleveland RHP Addie Joss hurls a perfect game against Chicago, winning 1–0. White Sox RHP Ed Walsh allows only four hits and strikes out 15 in a losing effort.

1916 Philadelphia RHP Grover Cleveland Alexander allows only three hits in throwing his ML record 16th shutout of the season as the Phillies blank the Boston Braves, 2–0.

1919 Joe Buzas b. Alpha, NJ.

1920 Bad weather earlier in the year forces Cincinnati and Pittsburgh to play the only modern tripleheader in history. The Reds win the first two games, while the Pirates win the third game, 6–0, with darkness coming in. Pittsburgh 3B Clyde Barnhart hits safely in all three games. Umpire Peter Harrison works all three contests behind the plate.

1921 New York Yankees RF Babe Ruth hits his then-record 59th home run of the season, against Boston Red Sox RHP Curt Fullerton.

1924 Bill Serena b. Alameda, CA.

1930 St. Louis OF George Watkins becomes the first NL player to hit a home run in his first World Series at-bat. It accounts for the only Cardinals run, however, as the Philadelphia A's win Game 2, 6–1, behind RHP George Earnshaw's complete game six-hitter.

1932 The New York Yankees complete a four-game sweep of the Chicago Cubs, 13–6, blasting 19 hits (including three home runs) to win their fourth World Series title.

1932 Maury Wills b. Washington D.C.

1934 Earl Wilson b. Ponchatoula, LA.

1936 The New York Yankees set a World Series record in Game 2, scoring 18 runs in defeating their crosstown rivals, the New York Giants, 18–4. Each Yankees starter has at least one hit and scores a run. Yankees 2B Tony Lazzeri belts only the second grand slam in World Series history to lead the 17-hit attack.

1938 Cleveland RHP Bob Feller, age 19, strikes out 18 Detroit batters in a 4–1 loss to the Tigers.

1946 Bob Robertson b. Frostburg, MD.

1947 The New York Yankees' Yogi Berra belts the first pinch-hit home run in the World Series, but Brooklyn rallies to win Game 3, 9–8.

1949 Both AL and NL pennant races are decided on the final day of the regular season. The New York Yankees defeat the Boston Red Sox, 5–3, to win the AL crown, while the Brooklyn Dodgers need 10 innings to defeat the Philadelphia Phillies, 9–7. Both pennant winners finish just one game ahead of their nearest rivals.

1949 The St. Louis Browns use nine pitchers in a game against the Chicago White Sox.

1951 Bobby Coluccio b. Centralia, WA.

1953 Brooklyn RHP Carl Erskine strikes out 14 New York Yankees batters en route to a 3–2 win in World Series Game 3.

1962 The longest nine-inning game is played in Los Angeles, as the San Francisco Giants beat the Dodgers, 7–2, in 4:18. The mark stands until 2000.

1963 Los Angeles LHP Sandy Koufax strikes out 15 New York Yankees batters en route to a 5–2 win in the World Series opener.

1966 Los Angeles LHP Sandy Koufax beats Philadelphia, 6–3, for his NL-leading and pennant-clinching 27th win of the season. Koufax, who later wins the Cy Young Award, helps the Dodgers to their third NL pennant in four years before retiring suddenly in November.

1968 St. Louis RHP Bob Gibson strikes out a postseason record 17 batters in the World Series opener, a 4–0 win over Detroit.

1969 Matt Walbeck b. Sacramento, CA.

1972 Montreal RHP Bill Stoneman hurls his second career no-hitter, 7–0 over the New York Mets.

1977 Cincinnati 1B Tony Perez finishes the season with 32 doubles, six triples, 19 home runs, and 91 RBIs his exact totals for the 1976 season as well.

1978 In a one game playoff for the AL East title, New York SS Bucky Dent hits a three-run home run against Boston RHP Mike Torrez to lift the Yankees to a 5–4 win over the Red Sox at Fenway Park. The Yankees complete their incredible 14-game comeback deficit, en route to an eventual World Series title.

1986 New York Yankees 1B Don Mattingly sets a team record when he collects his 232nd base hit of the season, breaking Earle Combs' mark set in 1927. Mattingly will finish the season with 238 hits and a .352 batting average.

1987 At Houston, San Diego C Benito Santiago extends his ML rookie record, hitting safely in his 34th consecutive game.

1995 Detroit manager Sparky Anderson retires as the third winningest skipper of all-time after 26 seasons nine with Cincinnati and his final 17 with the Tigers. Anderson's 2,194 victories trail only Connie Mack and John McGraw all-time. He won seven pennants and three World Series titles.

1995 Seattle defeats California, 9–1, in a one-game playoff for the AL West division title, advancing the Mariners into postseason play for the first time in their 19-year history.

1999 St. Louis 1B Mark McGwire hits his 64th home run of the season during a 6-3 loss to the Chicago Cubs.

3

1872 Fred Clarke b. Winterset, IA.

1897 Chicago Cubs 1B Cap Anson smashes two home runs against St. Louis in his last ML appearance, closing out a remarkable 27-year career begun in the National Association in 1871. Anson had homered only once previously all season and retires as the oldest player to do it at age 46.

1900 Brooklyn clinches the NL pennant with a 6–4, 5–4 doubleheader sweep at Boston, giving manager Ned Hanlon his fifth championship in seven years.

1905 The National Commission adopts the John T. Brush (New York Giants owner) rules for World Series play: a seven game format; four umpires, two from each league; and a revenue-sharing formula for the teams involved.

1907 The seventh place Boston Red Sox end their 16-game losing streak with a 1–0 win over the sixth place St. Louis Browns.

1915 Detroit OF Ty Cobb, en route to his record ninth consecutive batting title, steals an ML record 96th base in a 6–5 win over Cleveland.

1915 Chicago's season-ending victory over Pittsburgh clinches the second and final Federal League pennant by an incredible .001 over St. Louis and a half game over the Rebels. Chicago (86–66, .566) edges St. Louis (87–67, .565), and Pittsburgh (86–67, .562).

1920 St. Louis Browns 1B George Sisler collects his ML record 257th hit of the season.

1931 Bob Skinner b. LaJolla, CA.

1937 Cleveland RHP Johnny Allen, 15–0 and one win from tying the AL record for consecutive victories, drops a 1–0 final-day decision to Detroit. Allen's single-season winning percentage of .938 (15–1) is exceeded only by Pittsburgh RHP Elroy Face's .947 (18–1) in 1959.

1937 St. Louis Cardinals OF Joe Medwick wins more than an NL Triple Crown, batting .374 with 154 RBIs and tying the New York Giants' Mel Ott with 31 home runs. Medwick, later named the NL MVP, also leads the league in hits (237), doubles (56), runs scored (111), and slugging percentage (.641).

1943 St. Louis Browns C Frankie Hays begins his streak of 312 consecutive games as a catcher, which will run through April 21, 1946. During the streak, Hays will also play for the Philadelphia A's and Cleveland Indians.

1946 The St. Louis Cardinals win the NL pennant by beating Brooklyn, 8–4, and sweeping the best-of-three playoff. The Cardinals finish the season at 98–58, while the Dodgers finish 96–60.

1947 New York Yankees RHP Bill Bevens is within one out of a World Series no-hitter in Game 4 when Brooklyn PH Cookie Lavagetto doubles home two runners who had walked. Gone is the shutout, the no-hitter, and the game, 3–2. After the Series, won by the Yankees in seven games, both Bevens and Lavagetto retire.

1948 Eventual World Series champion Cleveland finishes the regular season with a record attendance of 2,620,627.

1948 For the second straight year, Pittsburgh OF Ralph Kiner and New York Giants 1B Johnny Mize finish the season sharing the NL home run title, this time with 40 round-trippers. A year ago, both belted 51 homers.

1951 Dave Winfield b. St. Paul, MN.

1951 New York Giants OF Bobby Thomson hits a three-run home run against Brooklyn reliever Ralph Branca for a dramatic two-out, bottom of the ninth inning, 5–4 win, propelling New York into the World Series. Thomson's blast is called the "shot heard 'round the world."

1954 Dennis Eckersley b. Oakland, CA.

1958 The St.Louis Cardinals trade INF Eddie Kasko, RHP Bob Mabe, and OF Del Ennis to Cincinnati for 1B George Crowe, LHP Alex Kellner, and INF Alex Grammas.

1966 Darrin Fletcher b. Elmhurst, IL.

1971 Will Cordero b. Puerto Rico.

1976 Kansas City 3B George Brett has three hits on the last day of the regular season to edge teammate Hal McRae for the AL batting title. Brett finishes at .3333 to McRae's .3326.

1978 Texas trades OF Bobby Bonds and RHP Len Barker to Cleveland for RHP Jim Kern and INF Larvell Blanks.

1982 The Milwaukee Brewers clinch their first AL pennant by beating Baltimore, 10–2, behind the pitching of RHP Don Sutton and the hitting of SS Robin Yount, who homers twice against Orioles ace RHP Jim Palmer. A capacity Memorial Stadium crowd nevertheless gives retiring Orioles manager Earl Weaver an emotional 20-minute post-game standing ovation.

1982 Oakland LF Joe Rudi homers in his final ML at-bat, a two-run shot against Kansas City LHP Larry Gura in the A's 6–3 win. Rudi becomes the only player in ML history to homer in his final World Series at-bat as well, turning the trick in Game 5 in 1974 against Los Angeles as Oakland won its third straight title.

1990 Detroit DH Cecil Fielder becomes the first ML player in 13 years to hit 50 or more home runs when he connects twice against the New York Yankees on the regular season finale to finish with 51 round-trippers. Cincinnati LF George Foster belted 52 homers in 1977.

1993 Kansas City 3B George Brett collects his 3,154th and final major league hit against Texas RHP Tom Henke.

1999 In the season finale featuring baseball's top two home run hitters, St. Louis 1B Mark McGwire hits his 65th homer and Chicago RF Sammy Sosa answers with his 64th homer, during the Cardinals' rain-shortened, 9-5 win. McGwire's blast is his 522nd lifetime, putting him in 10th place all-time, passing both Ted Williams and Willie McCovey on the career list.

4

1910 Frank Crosetti b. San Francisco, CA.

1924 New York Giants 3B Fred Lindstrom becomes the youngest to play in the World Series when at 18 he takes the field in Game 1 against the Washington Senators. Lindstrom will collect 10 hits in the Series, batting .333, but the Senators will prevail in seven games.

1925 Ty Cobb and George Sisler, two of baseball's best hitters and now player/managers, wind up the season as opposing pitchers. Sisler, with the St. Louis Browns, throws two hitless innings. Cobb, with Detroit, throws a perfect inning as the Tigers win, 11–6.

1925 St. Louis player/manager Rogers Hornsby matches his 1922 Triple Crown feat, finishing with a .403 batting average, 39 home runs, and 143 RBIs.

1944 Tony LaRussa b. Tampa, FL.

1948 Cleveland player/manager Lou

Boudreau hits two home runs to lead the Indians to an 8–3 win over the Boston Red Sox in a one-game playoff to decide the AL pennant.

1951 The Chicago Cubs trade C Smoky Burgess and OF Bob Borkowski to Cincinnati for C Johnny Pramesa and OF Bob Usher.

1955 The Brooklyn Dodgers win their only World Series, defeating the New York Yankees, 2–0, in Game 7. LHP Johnny Podres scatters eight hits and LF Sandy Amoros saves the game in the sixth inning with a running catch of Yogi Berra's drive down the left field line.

1960 Billy Hatcher b. Williams, AZ.

1961 Mike Sharperson b. Orangeburg, SC.

1962 Dennis Cook b. Lamarque, TX.

1962 Chris James b. Rusk, TX.

1963 Bruce Ruffin b. Lubbock, TX.

1964 Mark McLemore b. San Diego, CA.

1965 Boston trades RHP Bill Monbouquette to Detroit for 2B George Smith and OF George Thomas.

1972 Oakland C Gene Tenace becomes the first player in World Series history to hit home runs in his first two at-bats in leading the A's to a 3–2 win over Cincinnati in Game 1.

1986 New York Yankees LHP Dave Righetti sets an ML record for saves in a season, getting his 45th and 46th in a doubleheader sweep of the Boston Red Sox.

1986 Minnesota SS Greg Gagne ties an ML record with two inside-the-park home runs in a game, against the Chicago White Sox.

1986 Cincinnati 1B Tony Perez hits his 379th and final home run to tie Orlando Cepeda for the most lifetime homers by a Latin-American player.

1998 San Diego C Jim Leyritz hits a home run in his third straight playoff game as the Padres defeat Houston, 6–1, to wrap up the NL Divisional Series.

1999 In a one-game playoff to determine the NL wildcard entry, New York Mets LHP Al Leiter tosses a two-hitter, shutting out Cincinnati, 5-0. New York manager Bobby Valentine wins his first postseason game after 1,714 regular season contests, the longest drought by an active manager.

5

1906 New York Giants RHP Henry Mathewson, Christy's younger brother, debuts with a rookie record 14 walks.

1909 Detroit RF Ty Cobb finishes his better than Triple Crown season with a .377 batting average, nine home runs, and 107 RBIs. Cobb also leads the AL in runs scored (116), total bases (296), slugging average (.517), and stolen bases (76).

1918 New York Giants 3B Eddie Grant becomes the first of three ML fatalities during World War I as he is killed in France's Argonne Forest. Grant played 10 years in the ML with four different clubs. In all, 227 players served in the armed forces during the first World War.

1921 In the first World Series game broadcast at the Polo Grounds, sportswriter Grantland Rice handles the duties as the New York Yankees blank the New York Giants, 3–0, in the opener.

1922 The New York Giants and the New York Yankees play to a 3–3 tie in Game 2 of the World Series. After 10 innings, the game is called on account of darkness. Commissioner Kenesaw Mountain Landis, irate because the sun is still shining, donates the gate receipts to charity.

1929 On the last day of the season, Philadelphia Phillies OF Lefty O'Doul goes 6-for-8 during a doubleheader against the New York Giants to raise his NL leading batting average to .398 and set an NL record for hits in a season with 254. Phillies OF Chuck Klein sets the NL single-season home run record with his 43rd, edging Giants OF Mel Ott by one. Ott is denied an opportunity for the home run title as he receives an ML record five intentional walks in the nightcap.

1939 New York Yankees RHP Monty Pearson carries a no-hitter into the eighth inning before Cincinnati C Ernie Lombardi singles cleanly. Pearson settles for a two-hit shutout in Game 2 of the World Series as the Yankees win, 4–0, and go on to sweep the Reds in four straight.

1941 Brooklyn C Mickey Owen drops a third strike with two outs in the ninth inning, allowing New York Yankees OF Tommy Henrich to reach first base. The Yankees go on to score four times, en route to a 7–4 victory in Game 4 of the World Series. New York would wrap up the Series the next day.

1942 After dropping the World Series opener to the New York Yankees, the St. Louis Cardinals win their fourth straight game, 4–2, to wrap up the championship.

1947 Brooklyn OF Al Gionfriddo robs New York Yankee CF Joe DiMaggio of a 415-foot home run in the sixth inning to help preserve the Dodgers' 8–6 win in Game 6 of the World Series.

1949 New York 1B Tommy Henrich belts a leadoff home run in the bottom of the ninth inning to lift the Yankees to a 1–0 win over Brooklyn in Game 1 of the World Series. Until that blow, Yankees RHP Allie Reynolds had blanked the Dodgers on two hits, and Brooklyn rookie RHP Don Newcombe had

blanked New York on four hits. Henrich's blast is the first time that a World Series game ends on a home run.

1952 Umpire Art Passarella is caught on film clearly making the wrong call during the 10th inning of World Series Game 5 between the New York Yankees and Brooklyn Dodgers. Yankees RHP Johnny Sain hits a ground ball to Dodgers 2B Jackie Robinson, who throws to 1B Gil Hodges for an apparent out. However, an Associated Press photographer gets an unobstructed photo of Sain's foot, already on the base as the throw is yet to arrive. Brooklyn rallies to win the contest, 6–5 in 11 innings. Commissioner Ford Frick later declares it a blown call and Passarella is out of baseball a year later.

1953 The New York Yankees become the first and only team to win five consecutive World Series championships when they defeat Brooklyn, 4–3, in Game 6.

1954 Less than nine months after marrying Joe DiMaggio, Marilyn Monroe files for divorce.

1958 Milwaukee Braves LHP Warren Spahn throws a two-hit shutout against the New York Yankees, winning Game 4 of the World Series, 2–0. Yankees OF Hank Bauer has his record 17-game World Series streak come to an end. Bauer had hit safely during each game of the seven-game 1956 and 1957 series, and in the first three games of this year's Series.

1960 New York Yankees RF Roger Maris — the AL regular season MVP with 39 home runs and a league-leading 112 RBIs — becomes the seventh player in World Series history to homer in his first series at-bat, but the Yankees fall to Pittsburgh, 6–4 in Game 1.

1966 Baltimore tags Los Angeles starter Don Drysdale for three runs in the first inning on Brooks Robinson's solo home run and Frank Robinson's two-run shot in an eventual 5–2 win in the Series opener. The Orioles will sweep the Series in four straight games, and those three runs will be more than the Dodgers score in four games.

1967 Rey Sanchez b. Puerto Rico.

1967 Boston Red Sox RHP Jim Lonborg hurls a one-hit, 5–0 shutout over St. Louis in Game 2 of the World Series. Red Sox LF Carl Yastrzemski provides all the run support with a pair of home runs.

1970 St. Louis trades 1B Richie Allen to Los Angeles for 2B Ted Sizemore and C Bob Stinson.

1971 California trades OF Alex Johnson and C Jerry Moses to Cleveland for OFs Vada Pinson and Frank Baker, and RHP Alan Foster.

1980 The Chicago White Sox' Minnie Minoso, age 57, pinch hits in a season-ending game to become the oldest non-pitcher ever to play. Minoso is ML baseball's only five decade performer.

1980 The Los Angeles Dodgers' Manny Mota records his 150th career pinch hit.

1996 Texas OF Juan Gonzalez hits two home runs, but it's not enough as the New York Yankees bounce back to win, 5–4 in 12 innings, during the AL wildcard playoffs. New York will win the series, three games to one, despite Gonzalez tying a playoff series record with five home runs in four games.

6

1904 St. Louis RHP John "Brakeman" Taylor hurls his ML record 39th consecutive complete game in a 6–3 loss to Pittsburgh. Taylor finishes the season, 20–19.

1905 Despite losing to Washington,

10–4, the Philadelphia A's clinch the AL pennant as the last place St. Louis Browns defeat the runner-up Chicago White Sox, 6–2, on the next-to-last day of the season.

1911 Boston Braves RHP Cy Young gets knocked out in the seventh inning of a 13–3 loss to Brooklyn. Young, age 44, fails to complete only his 65th game in 815 regular season starts during his 22-year career.

1912 Pittsburgh OF Owen Wilson collects his ML record 36th triple of the season on what would've been an inside-the-park home run until he was thrown out at home plate.

1926 New York Yankees RF Babe Ruth belts three homers in World Series Game 4, a 10–5 win over St. Louis.

1929 Cleveland 3B Joe Sewell finishes the season with only four strikeouts in 578 official at-bats.

1929 After being out of the game for five years, 53-year-old Nick Altrock, a 16-year veteran pitcher, plays right field for the Chicago White Sox and singles on his only trip to the plate. Altrock becomes the oldest player in ML history to get a hit until Chicago White Sox DH Minnie Minoso ties him at age 53 in 1976.

1930 Philadelphia 1B Jimmie Foxx his a two-run, ninth inning home run against St. Louis RHP Burleigh Grimes, to lift the A's to a 2–0 win over the Cardinals in Game 3 of the World Series. Ahead a commanding 3–0 in the Series, Philadelphia will complete its four-game sweep two days later.

1936 The New York Yankees capture their first World Series title without Babe Ruth, beating the crosstown New York Giants, 13–5 in Game 6.

1942 Jerry Grote b. San Antonio, TX.

1943 Jim McGlothlin b. Los Angeles, CA.

1945 Prior to Game 4 of the World

Series between Detroit and the Chicago Cubs, local tavern owner "Billy Goat" Sianis buys a box seat for his goat. After being escorted out of Wrigley Field, Sianis places a "goat curse" over the Cubs. Chicago will lose the Series in seven games to the Tigers, marking their seventh straight World Series defeat and eighth in their last ten appearances. They have not been participants in the Fall Classic since.

1946 Gene Clines b. San Pablo, CA.

1948 Cleveland RHP Bob Feller tosses a two-hitter, but the Boston Braves win World Series Game 1, 1–0, behind the four-hit pitching of RHP Johnny Sain.

1957 Milwaukee 3B Eddie Mathews hits a two-run home run in the bottom of the tenth inning to lift the Braves to a 7–5 win over the New York Yankees in Game 4 of the World Series. Trailing 5–4 in the bottom of the inning, Braves SS Johnny Logan doubles home Nippy Jones with the tying run, setting up Mathews' game-winning blow.

1959 The Chicago White Sox set a World Series record using three pitchers in a 1–0 shutout of the Dodgers in Game 5 before a record crowd of 92,706 in Los Angeles.

1965 Ruben Sierra b. Puerto Rico.

1966 Baltimore RHP Jim Palmer, age 20, becomes the youngest pitcher to hurl a World Series shutout, blanking Los Angeles, 6–0 in Game 2. The Orioles benefit from Dodgers CF Willie Davis' three consecutive fifth inning errors.

1969 Both the NL New York Mets and the AL Baltimore Orioles wrap up their pennants with three-game sweeps in baseball's first-ever Championship Series. The Mets dispose of Atlanta, 7–2, while the Orioles eliminate Minnesota, 11–2.

1972 Benji Gil b. Tijuana, Mexico.

1985 New York Yankees RHP Phil

Niekro shuts out Toronto, 8–0, to win his 300th career game.

1991 New York Mets RHP David Cone ties the NL record with 19 strikeouts in a 7–0 shutout of Philadelphia.

1991 Baltimore loses its final game at Memorial Stadium, 7–1 to Detroit, before a sellout crowd of 50,700. Orioles Park at Camden Yards will be Baltimore's new home in 1992.

7

1857 Moses Fleetwood Walker b. Mt. Pleasant, OH.

1903 Bill Walker b. East St. Louis, IL.

1904 Chuck Klein b. Indianapolis, IN.

1904 New York Highlanders RHP Jack Chesbro beats the Boston Red Red Sox, 3–2, for his major league record 41st win of the season against 12 losses.

1914 The Indianapolis Hoosiers defeat St. Louis, 4–0, to claim the first Federal League title.

1925 Former New York Giants great RHP Christy Mathewson, age 45, dies in Saranac Lake, NY, from the aftereffects of poison gasses to which he was exposed while fighting in France during World War I.

1925 Washington OF Joe Harris becomes the first World Series participant to hit a home run in his first at-bat, leading the Senators to a 4–1 win over Pittsburgh in Game 1.

1933 The New York Giants capture their first World Series title without John McGraw at the helm, winning Game 5, 4–3, over Washington, on a tenth inning Mel Ott home run. After losing two previous World Series as a player, first baseman/manager Bill Terry wins in his last Fall Classic appearance as the team's skipper.

1935 Losers in their first four World

Series appearances, the Detroit Tigers finally win a title, scoring the game-winner in the bottom of the ninth inning to beat the Chicago Cubs, 4–3, in Game 6.

1940 Cincinnati RHP Bucky Walters hurls a five-hit shutout, and also hits a home run to lead the Reds to a 4–0 win over Detroit in Game 6 of the World Series. Cincinnati will win its first non-tainted World Series the next day, after playing in a "fixed" Series against the Chicago White Sox in 1919.

1952 With two outs and the bases loaded in the seventh inning, New York 2B Billy Martin makes a last-second catch of a short infield pop fly off the bat of Jackie Robinson to help save Game 7 of the World Series for the Yankees in their 4–2 win over Brooklyn. New York LHP Bob Kuzava retires the last eight Dodgers batters as the Yankees extend their consecutive World Championships to four straight years.

1964 New York Yankees LHP Whitey Ford starts a record eighth opening game of the World Series after having started the first games of the Fall Classic in 1955, 1956, 1957, 1958, 1961, 1962, and 1963.

1964 Rich DeLucia b. Reading, PA.

1968 Milt Cuyler b. Macon, GA.

1989 Oakland DH Jose Canseco hits the first and only fifth deck home run in ML history, an estimated 540 foot titanic blast that helps the A's to a 6–5 win over Toronto in Game 4 of the AL Championship Series played inside the Skydome.

1995 Seattle 3B Edgar Martinez hits two home runs and collects a postseason record seven RBIs in an 11–8 divisional playoff win against the New York Yankees.

8

1907 In the first World Series tie, the Cubs and the Detroit Tigers battle to a 3–3 stalemate in the opener at Chicago.

1908 The Chicago Cubs win the NL pennant as RHP Mordecai "Three Finger" Brown outduels New York Giants RHP Christy Mathewson, 4–2. The one-game playoff is necessitated after a baserunning blunder by the Giants Fred Merkle leaves the September 23rd game declared a tie. The Cubs win the pennant with a 99–55 record, followed by the Giants at 98–56 and the Pittsburgh Pirates, also at 98–56.

1917 Danny Murtaugh b. Chester, PA.

1922 The New York Giants beat the New York Yankees, 5–3, in Game 5 for a World Series sweep. Giants LHP Art Nehf hurls a complete game in closing out the Series against the Yankees for the second straight year. The Giants pitchers limit the Yankees to only 32 hits over five games, with RF Babe Ruth not connecting once in the final three. Game 2 is a declared tie, 3–3, with the sun going down after 10 innings.

1927 Babe Ruth homers as the great New York Yankees team beats Pittsburgh, 4–3, in Game 4 of the World Series, sweeping the Pirates in four straight. The Yankees' 110-win regular season is highlighted by Ruth's 60 home runs and Lou Gehrig's 175 RBIs.

1929 Philadelphia RHP Howard Ehmke strikes out 13 Chicago Cubs, and the A's win, 3–1, in the World Series opener. It's Ehmke's final win in his 15-year career.

1930 Philadelphia RHP George Earnshaw throws a five-hitter in defeating the St. Louis Cardinals, 7–1, in Game 6, as the A's become the first team to win back-to-back World Series twice.

1936 The St. Louis Cardinals trade 1B Ripper Collins and RHP Roy Parmelee to the Chicago Cubs for RHP Lon Warneke.

1939 The New York Yankees score three times on three errors in the top of the tenth inning to beat Cincinnati, 7–4, to win their fourth straight World Series and complete their second straight four-game sweep. Manager Joe McCarthy's club wins an astounding 13th time in its last 14 World Series games.

1940 Cincinnati wins its first World Series in 21 years by beating Detroit, 2–1, in Game 7. Reds RHP Paul Derringer goes the distance for his second Series win.

1946 Paul Splitorff b. Evansville, IN.

1949 Enos Cabell b. Fort Riley, KS.

1956 New York Yankees RHP Don Larsen throws a perfect game in World Series Game 5, winning 2–0 over Brooklyn. Larsen strikes out Dodgers' PH Dale Mitchell for the final out. Larsen's gem is the only no-hitter in World Series history.

1957 Brooklyn owner Walter O'Malley announces he's moving the NL Dodgers to Los Angeles.

1959 Mike Morgan b. Tulare, CA.

1960 New York Yankees 2B Bobby Richardson collects a World Series record six RBIs en route to a 10–0 shutout over Pittsburgh in Game 3.

1961 New York Yankees LHP Whitey Ford extends his World Series scoreless innings streak to 33⅔, hurling five shutout innings in a 7–0 win over Cincinnati in Game 4. Ford's mark eclipses Babe Ruth's 1918 record of 29⅔ consecutive scoreless innings.

1962 San Francisco 2B Chuck Hiller hits the first NL grand slam in World Series history. Hiller's seventh inning blast off New York Yankees LHP Marshall Bridges lifts the Giants in Game 4, 7–3.

1967 Houston trades SS Sonny Jackson and 1B Chuck Harrison to Atlanta for RHP Denny Lemaster and 3B Denis Menke.

1967 J.T. Bruett B. Milwaukee, WI.

1969 Philadelphia trades 1B Richie

Allen, RHP Jerry Johnson, and 2B Cookie Rojas to St. Louis for C Tim McCarver, LHP Joe Hoerner, OF Byron Browne, and OF Curt Flood. Flood refuses to report and the Cardinals later send 1B Willie Montanez to the Phillies to complete the trade.

1998 San Diego RHP Kevin Brown allows only three singles while striking out 11 batters in a 3–0, complete game win over Atlanta, putting the Padres up 2–0 in the NL Championship Series.

9

1889 Rube Marquard b. Cleveland, OH.

1898 Joe Sewell b. Titus, AL.

1910 Cleveland 2B Napoleon Lajoie collects eight final-day hits, seven of them on bunt singles in a doubleheader against St. Louis to finish with a .384 batting average, but still loses the batting crown to Detroit OF Ty Cobb, who's average is adjusted six days later by AL President Ban Johnson to a league-leading .385.

1916 After allowing a first inning run to Brooklyn, Boston Red Sox LHP Babe Ruth gives up only five hits over the final 13 innings in a 2–1 win in Game 2 of the World Series, played at Braves Field in Boston. Ruth's 14 innings pitched is a series record.

1919 Chicago White Sox LHP Lefty Williams gets shelled in ⅓ of an inning as underdog Cincinnati wraps up the World Series championship in Game 8. The Reds pound out 16 hits en route to a 10–5 win. A year later, Williams along with seven other White Sox players is banned from baseball for life when it is learned that this Series was fixed.

1925 Tom Giordano b. Newark, NJ.

1928 New York RF Babe Ruth homers

three times as the Yankees beat St. Louis, 7–3 to sweep the World Series in four games. Ruth bats .625 and teammate Lou Gehrig .545 with four home runs to lead New York to its second straight World Series sweep.

1934 St. Louis RHP Dizzy Dean shuts out Detroit, 11–0, on a six-hitter, as the Cardinals win Game 7 of the World Series.

1938 The New York Yankees complete a four-game sweep of the Chicago Cubs in the World Series, winning 8–3 behind RHP Red Ruffing's second complete game in four days. Yankees manager Joe McCarthy wins a record third World Series in a row.

1940 Joe Pepitone b. Brooklyn, NY.

1944 In the sixth and deciding game of the all-Sportsman Park World Series, the NL Cardinals defeat the AL Browns, 3–1.

1944 Freddie Patek b. Oklahoma City, OK.

1947 Bob Moose b. Export, PA.

1950 Brian Downing b. Los Angeles, CA.

1958 The New York Yankees beat the Milwaukee Braves, 6–2, in Game 7 of the World Series, to become the first team since the 1925 Pittsburgh Pirates to overcome a three games to one deficit to win the title.

1963 Felix Fermin b. Dominican Republic.

1966 Baltimore LHP Dave McNally shuts out Los Angeles, 1–0, as the Orioles sweep the Dodgers four straight in the World Series. Baltimore pitching allows only 17 hits in the Series and records a record 33 scoreless innings.

1970 Washington trades SS Ed Brinkman, 3B Aurelio Rodriguez, and RHPs Joe Coleman and Jim Hannan to Detroit for RHPs Denny McLain and Norm McRae, 3B Don Wert, and OF Elliott Maddox.

1973 Bill Pulsipher b. Benning, GA.

1998 Cleveland hits four home runs three in a 13-pitch fifth-inning stretch en route to a 6–1 win over the New York Yankees to take a 2–1 lead in the AL Championship Series. Indians RF Manny Ramirez, 1B Jim Thome, and LF Mark Whiten all connect in the fifth inning, and Thome will add a second round-tripper.

10

1904 The Boston Pilgrims clinch the AL pennant, 3–2, when New York Highlanders RHP Jack Chesbro uncorks a wild pitch in the top of the ninth inning allowing the winning run to score.

1904 New York Giants owner John T. Brush and manager John McGraw label the AL a "minor circuit" and refuse to meet the Boston Somersets in a second World Series.

1920 Cleveland 2B Bill Wambsganss pulls off an unassisted triple play in Game 5 of the World Series, as the Indians beat Brooklyn, 8–1. Cleveland RHP Jim Bagby, Sr., who led the AL with 31 regular season wins, picks up the complete game victory and helps his own cause by becoming the first pitcher to homer in the World Series. Teammate Elmer Smith becomes the first World Series player to hit a grand slam.

1923 New York OF Casey Stengel hits an inside-the-park home run in the top of the ninth inning to give the Giants a 5–4 win over the New York Yankees in Game 1 of the World Series. It's the first World Series contest at new Yankee Stadium.

1924 After 18 years in the major leagues, Washington RHP Walter Johnson finally celebrates a World Series championship. Hurling in relief, Johnson earns a 12th inning victory and the title in Game 7 as the Senators top the New York Giants, 4–3. In the bottom of the 12th inning, Washington's Earl McNeely hits a potential double play ground ball which hits a pebble and bounces over the head of New York 3B Fred Lindstrom, allowing the winning run to score.

1926 St. Louis RHP Grover Cleveland Alexander strikes out New York Yankees 2B Tony Lazzeri in the seventh inning with two outs and the bases loaded to help preserve the Cardinals' 3–2 win in Game 7 of the World Series. Alexander had pitched a complete game victory for the Cardinals the previous day to force a seventh game. The Series ends with the Yankees' Babe Ruth being thrown out attempting to steal. Cardinals manager Rogers Hornsby postpones his mother's funeral until after the Series is finished.

1929 Bob Tiefenauer b. Desloge, MO.

1931 The St. Louis Cardinals spoil Philadelphia's bid to win a third consecutive World Series, winning 4–2 over the A's in Game 7.

1940 Larry Maxie b. Upland, CA.

1946 Gene Tenace b. Russelton, PA.

1949 Larry Lintz b. Martinez, CA.

1950 After appearing in only one game in 1949, Brooklyn OF Chuck Connors is traded, along with 1B Dee Fondy, to the Chicago Cubs for OF Hank Edwards. Connors will appear in 66 games for Chicago in 1951, then retire to devote himself fulltime to his acting career.

1957 Milwaukee Braves RHP Lew Burdette shuts out the New York Yankees, 5–0, in Game 7 of the World Series. It is Burdette's second straight shutout and third complete game game victory in the series.

1961 In baseball's second expansion draft, the NL Houston Colt .45s select San Francisco INF Joe Amalfitano with

their first pick, while the Casey Stengelled NL New York Mets use their first pick to select St. Louis Cardinals RHP Bob Miller. Only NL teams have their rosters raided.

1964 New York CF Mickey Mantle leads off the bottom of the ninth inning with a home run to lift the Yankees to a 2–1 win over St. Louis in Game 3 of the World Series.

1967 Cincinnati trades 1B Deron Johnson to Atlanta for OF Mack Jones, 1B Jim Beauchamp and RHP Jay Ritchie.

1968 Detroit LHP Mickey Lolich defeats St. Louis RHP Bob Gibson, 4–1, in Game 7 of the World Series. It is Lolich's third complete game victory of the Series. Gibson strikes out eight Tigers in a losing cause and for the Series whiffs a record 35 batters in 27 innings in his three starts.

1970 In the first World Series game played on artificial turf, the Baltimore Orioles defeat Cincinnati, 4–3, at the Reds' Riverfront Stadium.

1972 Detroit RHP Joe Coleman strikes out a record 14 batters in a championship series, as the Tigers blank Oakland, 3–0, in Game 3. The A's will rally to win the series in five games to advance to the World Series.

1982 Milwaukee becomes the first team in the history of the League Championship Series to win the pennant after losing the first two games of the best-of-five series. The Brewers defeat California, 3–2, in the decisive fifth game to advance to the World Series against St. Louis.

1999 In the most lopsided postseason rout ever, the Boston Red Sox set a record for runs scored in trouncing Cleveland, 23–7, in Game 4 of the AL first-round playoff series. Red Sox 3B John Valentin leads the assault with four hits, including two home runs, a double, and seven RBIs. Boston sets another record with 24 hits, and scores in every inning but the sixth. The 30 combined runs by both clubs sets another record.

11

1900 Ban Johnson's new American League, claiming status as an equal to the National League, announces plans to locate franchises in Baltimore and Washington.

1906 Chicago White Sox' RHP Ed Walsh strikes out 12 Chicago Cubs batters en route to a 3–0 shutout victory in World Series Game 3.

1911 Chalmers automobile awards baseball's first MVPs: Detroit OF Ty Cobb in the AL and Chicago Cubs OF Frank Schulte in the NL.

1943 Joe McCarthy manages his seventh and final World Series champion as the New York Yankees avenge their 1942 loss to St. Louis, winning Game 5, 2–0.

1956 Philadelphia trades RHP Stu Miller to the New York Giants for RHP Jim Hearn.

1966 Gregg Olson b. Omaha, NE.

1968 St. Louis trades C John Edwards to Houston for RHP Dave Giusti and C Dave Adlesh.

1968 Cincinnati trades OF Vada Pinson to St. Louis for RHP Wayne Granger and OF Bobby Tolan.

1970 Boston trades OF Tony Conigliaro, C Jerry Moses, and RHP Ray Jarvis to California for RHP Ken Tatum, 2B Doug Griffin, and OF Jarvis Tatum.

1971 Boston trades OF Billy Conigliaro, LHP Ken Brett, RHP Jim Lonborg, 1B George Scott, OF Joe Lahoud, and C Don Pavletich to Milwaukee for RHP Lew Krausse, RHP Marty Pattin, OF Tommy Harper, and OF Pat Skrable.

1972 Pittsburgh RF Roberto Clemente plays in his last game, a 4–3 loss to Cincinnati in the fifth and final game of the NL Championship Series. Pirates RHP Bob Moose wild pitches George Foster home in the bottom of the ninth inning for the deciding run.

1973 Dmitri Young b. Vicksburg, MS.

1997 Cleveland CF Marquis Grissom steals home on a botched suicide squeeze attempt by teammate Omar Vizquel to give the Indians a dramatic 12th inning, 2–1 win over Baltimore. Orioles C Lenny Webster contends that Vizquel foul tipped the pitch from LHP Randy Myers but is overruled as the game ends, giving the Indians a 2–1 lead in the AL Championship Series. The ending overshadows an outstanding pitching performance by Baltimore starter Mike Mussina, who sets a new championship series record with 15 strikeouts in seven innings.

1999 Boston RHP Pedro Martinez comes out of the Red Sox bullpen to hurl six hitless innings to lead his team to a 12-8 win over Cleveland in the fifth and deciding game of the AL first-round playoffs. Martinez, the AL's top winner (23-4) and strikeout king (313) enters a wild 8-8 game in the fourth inning and strikes out eight Indians batters to close out the series.

12

1905 Rick Ferrell b. Durham, NC.

1906 Joe Cronin b. San Francisco, CA.

1907 The Chicago Cubs complete the first World Series sweep, winning 2–0 over the Detroit Tigers, and capturing four straight games after Game 1 was called because of darkness in Chicago, tied 3–3.

1920 In the seventh and deciding game of the World Series, Cleveland RHP Stan Coveleski wins his third complete game on a five-hitter in blanking Brooklyn, 3–0. The Indians win their first world title defeating the Dodgers five games to two. Coveleski allows only two runs and 15 hits in 27 innings.

1929 The Chicago Cubs blow an eight-run, seventh inning lead against the Philadelphia A's in World Series Game 4. The A's score 10 times in the inning, hammering four pitchers for an eventual 10–8 win. The eight-run deficit represents the most runs a team has overcome to win a World Series game.

1936 Tony Kubek b. Milwaukee, WI.

1940 Glen Beckert b. Pittsburgh, PA.

1962 Sid Fernandez b. Honolulu, HI.

1967 In the seventh and deciding game of the World Series, St. Louis RHP Bob Gibson strikes out 10 batters and hits a home run to lead the Cardinals to a 7–2 win over the Boston Red Sox. In picking up his third complete game Series victory, Gibson allows only three earned runs and strikes out 26 Boston batters in 27 innings.

1971 Pittsburgh RHP Steve Blass hurls a three-hitter in beating Baltimore, 5–1, in World Series Game 3. It's the first World Series night game, and it attracts a record Pittsburgh crowd of 50,403.

1986 Boston OF Dave Henderson hits a two-out, two-run home run in the top of the ninth inning, with his team only one strike away from elimination. His hit rallies the Red Sox to a 6–5 lead and an eventual 7–6 win over California in Game 5 of the AL Championship Series. Boston will turn the series around, winning the final three games, including the deciding seventh game.

1997 Florida RHP Livan Hernandez strikes out a NL championship record 15 batters and allows three hits as the Mar-lins defeat Atlanta, 2–1, to take a 3–2 series lead.

13

1876 Wild Bill Donovan b. Lawrence, MA.

1876 Rube Waddell b. Bradford, PA.

1894 Swede Risberg b. San Francisco, CA.

1903 Boston RHP Bill Dinneen shuts out Pittsburgh, 3–0, in Game 8 to lead the Red Sox to the first World Series championship. It is Dinneen's second shutout and third win of the Series.

1914 Boston wraps up an improbable four-game World Series sweep over the Philadelphia A's, winning 3–1 in Game 4. The "Miracle Braves" had won 68 of their final 87 regular season games to get to the World Series.

1915 Boston RF Harry Hooper, who hit only two home runs during the regular season, hits two more in Game 5 of the World Series, including a ninth inning game-winner against Philadelphia LHP Eppa Rixey which wins the championship for the Red Sox, 5–4 over the Phillies.

1921 New York Yankees RHP Waite Hoyt loses Game 8 of the World Series, 1–0, to the New York Giants. In three starts, Hoyt does not allow an earned run in 27 innings.

1926 Cleveland 1B George Burns, who hits .358 with a record 64 doubles, captures the AL MVP Award, even though New York Yankees RF Babe Ruth hits .372 with a league-leading 47 home runs and 146 RBIs.

1926 Eddie Yost b. Brooklyn, NY.

1931 Eddie Mathews b. Texarkana, TX.

1960 Pittsburgh 2B Bill Mazeroski's bottom of the ninth inning home run against New York Yankees RHP Ralph Terry wins the World Series for the Pirates, 10–9, in Game 7. It's the first time a World Series is decided by a final home run, and the final World Series game ever played at Forbes Field in Pittsburgh.

1964 Chris Gwynn b. Los Angeles, CA.

1967 Scott Cooper b. St. Louis, MO.

1967 Trevor Hoffman b. Bellflower, CA.

1970 Baltimore LHP Dave McNally belts a grand slam home run to support his own cause in a 9–3 win over Cincinnati in Game 3 of the World Series.

1970 Kansas City trades OF Pat Kelly and RHP Don O'Riley to the Chicago White Sox for 1B Gail Hopkins and OF John Matias.

1970 The Chicago Cubs trade SS Roger Metzger to Houston for SS Hector Torres.

1971 In the second night game in World Series history, Pittsburgh defeats Baltimore, 4–3, in Game 4. Pirates rookie RHP Bruce Kison picks up the win throwing one-hit relief for 6⅓ innings.

1971 The New York Yankees trade OF Jim Lyttle to the Chicago White Sox for LHP Rich Hinton.

1974 Oakland PR Herb Washington gets picked off by Los Angeles reliever Mike Marshall as the A's lose, 3–2, in Game 2 of the World Series. It's the only game of the Series that Oakland would lose en route to a championship. Washington never bats but appears in 91 regular season games with 28 stolen bases and 29 runs scored.

1974 St. Louis trades 1B Joe Torre to the New York Mets for LHP Ray Sadecki and RHP Tommy Moore.

14

1862 Brooklyn Niagaras RHP James Creighton, baseball's first star, homers against the Unions of Morrisiana and collapses on the bases with a ruptured spleen. He dies four days later.

1896 Oscar Charleston b. Indianapolis, IN.

1905 New York Giants RHP Christy Mathewson hurls his third World Series shutout in six days, blanking the Philadelphia A's, 2–0, in Game 5 to wrap up the championship. Mathewson's performance includes only 14 hits and one walk allowed in 27 innings, while striking out 18. The Giants do not allow the A's an earned run in the Series. Athletics LHP Rube Waddell misses the Series, excused by a shoulder hurt while he was roughousing on a train. Some believe gamblers promised to make it worth his while for not playing.

1911 The World Series opens at the Polo Grounds in New York as Giants RHP Christy Mathewson outduels Philadelphia A's RHP Chief Bender, 2–1.

1929 In the fifth and deciding game of the World Series, the Philadelphia A's trail the Chicago Cubs, 2–0, in the bottom of the ninth inning when OF Mule Haas hits a two-run homer to tie the score. Before the inning ends, Philadelphia scores the winning run to end the game and the Series, four games to one.

1940 Tommy Harper b. Oak Grove, IL.

1946 Al Oliver b. Portsmouth, OH.

1946 Frank Duffy b. Oakland, CA.

1948 Ed Figueroa b. Puerto Rico.

1954 Willie Mays Aikens b. Seneca, SC.

1964 Joe Girardi b. Peoria, IL.

1965 In the seventh and deciding game of the World Series, Los Angeles LHP Sandy Koufax hurls a three-hitter striking out 10 batters, as the Dodgers beat Minnesota, 2–0. For Koufax, it's his second shutout win of the Series, both times defeating Twins LHP Jim Kaat.

1967 Pat Kelly (2B) b. Philadelphia, PA.

1968 In baseball's third expansion draft, the NL Montreal Expos select Pittsburgh OF Manny Mota with their first pick, while the NL San Diego Padres select San Francisco OF Ollie Brown with their first pick. Only NL teams have their rosters raided.

1971 Midre Cummings b. St. Croix, Virgin Islands.

1972 Prior to the World Series opener between Oakland at Cincinnati, Jackie Robinson throws out the first ball. Robinson passes away 10 days later at age 53.

1973 In the longest game in World Series history, 4:13, the New York Mets top Oakland, 10–7, in 12 innings in Game 2.

1974 St. Louis trades C Marc Hill to San Francisco for C Ken Rudolph and RHP Elias Sosa.

1997 Florida RHP Kevin Brown goes the distance, scattering 11 hits over nine innings as the Marlins win the NL pennant, 7–4, over Atlanta in Game 6 of the Championship Series. In only their fifth year of existence, the Marlins become the fastest team to reach the World Series.

1999 The New York Yankees win their record-tying 12th consecutive postseason game in beating Boston, 3-2, to take a 2-0 lead in the AL Championship Series. The victories tie the great Yankees teams of Babe Ruth and Lou Gehrig that swept World Series titles in 1927, 1928, and 1932.

15

1892 In his only appearance of the season, Cincinnati RHP Charles "Bumpus" Jones no-hits Pittsburgh, 7–1. It's the latest date on the calendar for a no-hitter and the last one thrown from a 50-foot distance.

1909 Mel Harder b. Beemer, NE.

1925 Pittsburgh OF Kiki Cuyler hits a tie-breaking two-run double in the eighth inning to lift the Pirates to a 9–7 win and world championship over Washington in Game 7 of the World Series. The Pirates become the first team to erase a 3–1 deficit to win a World Series. Senators SS Roger Peckinpaugh, the AL regular season MVP, commits two errors, giving him a record eight for the Series.

1945 Jim Palmer b. New York, NY.

1946 St. Louis OF Enos Slaughter races home from first base on an eighth-inning double by Harry Walker to win Game 7 of the World Series, 4–3, over Boston. Red Sox SS Johnny Pesky holds the relay from left field allowing the winning run to score.

1964 St. Louis RHP Bob Gibson pitches his third complete game striking out nine New York Yankees batters in winning Game 7 of the World Series, 7–5. Gibson tallies 31 strikeouts in his 27 innings of work.

1967 Carlos Garcia b. Venezuela.

1968 A day after the NL holds its expansion draft for Montreal and San Diego, the AL holds its own expansion draft for new members Kansas City and Seattle. The Royals take Baltimore RHP Roger Nelson with their first pick, while the Pilots take California 1B Don Mincher. Only AL teams have their rosters raided.

1971 Chad Mottola b. Augusta, GA.

1972 Oakland LF Joe Rudi homers and makes a game-saving catch in the bottom of the ninth inning to preserve a 2–1 win over Cincinnati in Game 2 of the World Series. Rudi's catch against the wall robs Denis Menke of a certain extra base hit.

1986 In the sixth and deciding game of the NL Championship Series, the New York Mets beat the Houston Astros, 7–6 in 16 innings to win the longest postseason game in history.

1988 Los Angeles PH Kirk Gibson's two-out, two-run home run in the bottom of the ninth inning lifts the Dodgers to a stunning 5–4 win over Oakland in Game 1 of the World Series.

1997 Cleveland 2B Tony Fernandez, a last minute lineup addition, homers with two outs in the top of the 11th inning to give the Indians a 1–0 win at Baltimore in Game 6 of the AL Championship Series and propels them into the World Series for the second time in three years.

16

1900 Goose Goslin b. Salem, NJ.

1912 A dropped fly ball by New York Giants OF Fred Snodgrass and a dropped pop foul by 1B Fred Merkle gives Boston new life in the bottom of the 10th inning in Game 7 of the World Series. The Red Sox rally to win, 3–2.

1940 Dave DeBusschere b. Detroit, MI.

1941 Tim McCarver b. Memphis, TN.

1959 Brian Harper b. Los Angeles, CA.

1962 San Francisco slugger Willie McCovey lines out to New York Yankees 2B Bobby Richardson with two outs in the bottom of the ninth inning to end Game 7 of the World Series. Yankees RHP Ralph Terry escapes with a 1–0 win as he leaves runners on second and third base.

1964 The day after the Cardinals defeat the Yankees in the World Series,

St. Louis manager Johnny Keane resigns, and New York skipper Yogi Berra is fired.

1969 Juan Gonzalez b. Puerto Rico.

1975 Cincinnati wins Game 5 of the World Series, 6–2 over Boston. Tony Perez, mired in a 0-for-15 slump, breaks loose with two home runs to lead the Reds to a 3–2 lead in the Series. During one stay at second base, Cincinnati's Joe Morgan, draws 16 pickoff throws.

1983 Baltimore LHP Scott McGregor hurls a five-hitter, and teammate Eddie Murray hits two home runs as the Orioles close out the World Series in five games with a 5–0 win over Philadelphia. Baltimore SS Cal Ripken, Jr., the AL Most Valuable Player, becomes the first player in history to play in every inning of every game, including regular season, League Championship Series, and World Series — 171 total games.

1999 Two days after equalling a record with 12 consecutive postseason wins, the New York Yankees suffer their worst ever postseason loss, 13-1, at Boston in Game 3 of the AL Championship Series. Red Sox RHP Pedro Martinez dominates New York with 12 strikeouts in seven shutout innings of work.

17

1848 Candy Cummings b. Ware, MA.

1927 AL founder and 28-year president Ban Johnson retires, three days after 416-game winner Walter Johnson calls it quits after 21 seasons with the Washington Senators.

1928 Jim Gilliam b. Nashville, TN.

1960 The New York Mets are born when the city is awarded an NL franchise to begin play in 1962.

1962 St. Louis trades C Jimmie Schaffer, RHPs Lindy McDaniel and

Larry Jackson to the Chicago Cubs for RHP Don Cardwell, OF George Altman, and C Moe Thacker.

1962 Glenn Braggs b. San Bernardino, CA.

1976 In the coldest game to date in the World Series, the Reds defeat the New York Yankees, 4–3, in Game 2 at Cincinnati amid 39 degree temperatures. Four days later, Cincinnati will complete a four-game sweep.

1989 Prior to Game 3 of the World Series, an earthquake measuring 7.1 on the Richter scale rocks San Francisco's Candlestick Park. The Series between the Giants and Oakland A's is delayed for 10 days.

1996 Atlanta completes its NL championship rally against St. Louis by bombing the Cardinals, 15–0, in Game 7. The Braves win the most lopsided victory in 92 years of postseason play, and in turn become the first NL club to rally from a three games to one deficit in the Championship Series. Over the final three games, Atlanta outscores St. Louis, 32–1.

1998 New York 2B Chuck Knoblauch hits a three-run home run and 1B Tino Martinez follows with a grand slam homer in the seventh inning, as the Yankees rally to beat San Diego, 9–6, in Game 1 of the World Series. Martinez' slam is the Yankees' first in the World Series since Joe Pepitone's 34 years earlier — October 14, 1964 — in Game 6 at St. Louis.

1999 In the longest postseason game in ML history, the New York Mets edge Atlanta, 4–3, in 15 innings, in Game 5 of the NL Championship Series. Mets 3B Robin Ventura hits an apparent game-winning grand slam home run, but he's mobbed by teammates after touching first base and is credited with only a single. A postseason record 45 players are used in the lengthy 5:46 marathon.

18

1942 Willie Horton b. Arno, VA.

1949 George Hendrick b. Los Angeles, CA.

1950 After 50 years as manager of the Philadelphia A's and 53 years total, Connie Mack retires from baseball at age 88. His managerial career produced 3,776 victories and 4,025 defeats in 7,878 games (all all-time highs), as well as nine AL pennants and five World Series championships. In 1953, Philadelphia's Shibe Park is renamed Connie Mack Stadium in his honor.

1966 Alan Mills b. Lakeland, FL.

1971 St. Louis trades RHPs Chuck Taylor and Harry Parker, 1B Jim Beauchamp, and INF Tom Coulter to the New York Mets for LHPs Rich Folkers and Charles Hudson, RHP Jim Bibby, and OF Art Shamsky.

1973 Pittsburgh trades 2B Dave Cash to Philadelphia for LHP Ken Brett.

1977 New York Yankees RF Reggie Jackson homers three times in consecutive at-bats in World Series Game 6 to beat Los Angeles, 8–4, and wrap up the Series. Jackson's homers come against RHPs Burt Hooton, Elias Sosa, and Charlie Hough.

1988 Oakland 1B Mark McGwire hits a home run in the bottom of the ninth inning to lift the A's to a 2–1 win over Los Angeles in Game 3 of the World Series. McGwire's blast marks the first time in World Series play that two games are decided by a final at-bat homer, following the Dodgers' Kirk Gibson who won Game 1 with a pinch-hit two-run blast.

1992 Atlanta LF Deion Sanders plays in his first World Series game, a 5–4 loss to Toronto in Game 2. Sanders will become the first athlete to play in a

World Series and also a Super Bowl with the NFL San Francisco 49ers (1994) and Dallas Cowboys (1995).

1997 Florida wins Game 1 of the World Series, 7–4, over Cleveland, as Indians starting RHP Orel Hershiser ties an ML record with seven earned runs allowed. Marlins RHP Rob Nen, with a fastball clocked at 102 mph, closes out the contest by striking out Jim Thome and Sandy Alomar, Jr., to record the save. The Miami crowd of 67,245 is the largest turnout for a World Series contest since October 2, 1963 when 69,000 fans turned out at Yankee Stadium for Game 1 between New York and the Los Angeles Dodgers.

19

1876 Mordecai Brown b. Nyesville, IN.

1932 The Baseball Writers' Association of America selects its league MVPs, with each playing in Philadelphia: 1B Jimmie Foxx of the AL A's and OF Chuck Klein of the NL Phillies. Foxx leads the AL in home runs (58), RBIs (169), runs scored (151), total bases (438), and slugging percentage (.749). Klein leads the NL in hits (226), runs scored (152), stolen bases (20), total bases (420), and ties the Giants' Mel Ott in home runs (38).

1946 The New York Yankees trade 2B Joe Gordon and 3B Eddie Bockman to Cleveland for RHP Allie Reynolds.

1949 The Philadelphia A's trade 2B Nellie Fox to the Chicago White Sox for C Joe Tipton.

1961 Tim Belcher b. Sparta, OH.

1965 Mike Gardiner b. Sarnia, Ontario.

1966 Dave Veras b. Montgomery, AL.

1972 Marc Newfield b. Sacramento, CA.

1972 Cleveland trades INF Eddie Leon to the Chicago White Sox for OF Walt Williams.

1985 St. Louis defeats Kansas City, 3-1, in Game 1 of the World Series, marking the first Fall Classic in which all seven games are scheduled at night. The Series needs all seven games before the Royals earn their first championship in the all-Missouri final.

1998 Atlanta RHP Greg Maddux wins his ninth Gold Glove Award, tying St. Louis RHP Bob Gibson for most in NL history. Texas C Ivan Rodriguez wins his seventh Gold Glove, surpassing the AL record held by former Rangers C Jim Sundberg. Cincinnati 2B Bret Boone wins his first Gold Glove, marking just the second time in history for a father-son combination. Boone's father, Bob, won seven Gold Gloves as a catcher. The first father-son combination was OFs Bobby and Barry Bonds, who this year earns his eighth Gold Gloves honor.

1999 Atlanta beats the New York Mets, 10-9, in 11 innings, to wrap up the NL pennant in Game 6 of the NL Championship Series. Mets LHP Kenny Rogers walks Braves OF Andruw Jones with the bases loaded to force home the deciding run.

20

1901 Seven members of the St. Louis Cardinals, including NL batting champion OF Jesse Burkett, jump to the AL's new St. Louis Browns franchise.

1931 The Baseball Writers Association of America names its first NL MVP: St. Louis 2B Frankie Frisch, who bats .311 and leads the league with 28 stolen bases for the World Series champion Cardinals.

1931 Mickey Mantle b. Spavinaw, OK.

1952 Dave Collins b. Rapid City, SD.

1953 Keith Hernandez b. San Francisco, CA.

1965 St. Louis trades 3B Ken Boyer to the New York Mets for LHP Al Jackson and 3B Charley Smith.

1967 Harvey Pulliam b. San Francisco, CA.

1976 San Francisco trades LHP Mike Caldwell, RHP John D'Acquisto, and C Dave Rader to St. Louis for OF Willie Crawford, INF Vic Harris, and LHP John Curtis.

1990 Cincinnati scores twice in the top of the eighth inning to rally and win, 2–1, over Oakland to sweep the World Series in four games and extend the Reds' record of consecutive World Series games won to nine. After winning the decisive seventh game of the 1975 World Series over Boston, Cincinnati swept the New York Yankees four straight in 1976 before also sweeping Oakland in this Series.

1993 Toronto defeats Philadelphia, 15–14, in Game 4 of the World Series to set a record for most combined runs (29), and also for the longest nine-inning contest in series history at 4:14.

1996 Atlanta rookie LF Andruw Jones has three hits, including two home runs in his first two at-bats. His five RBIs lead the Braves to a 12–1 romp over the New York Yankees in the World Series opener. At 19 years old, Jones becomes the youngest player to start a World Series game after 18-year-old New York Giants 3B Fred Lindrom in 1924.

1998 New York 3B Scott Brosius hits two home runs, including a deciding three-run blast in the eighth inning, as the Yankees rally to defeat San Diego, 5–4, in Game 3 of the World Series. New York takes a commanding 3–0 lead

over the Padres in the Series, and will complete a four-game sweep the next day.

21

1921 Baseball commissioner Kenesaw Mountain Landis suspends New York Yankees Babe Ruth, Bob Meusel, and Bill Piercy for their illegal barnstorming after the 1921 World Series.

1928 Whitey Ford b. New York, NY.

1935 Detroit 1B Hank Greenberg is unanimously selected AL MVP after batting .328 with 203 hits, 46 doubles, 16 triples, and a league-leading 36 homers and 170 RBIs en route to carrying the Tigers to their second world title

1940 Ted Uhlaender b. Chicago Heights, IL.

1948 Bill Russell b. Pittsburg, KS.

1959 George Bell b. Dominican Republic.

1960 Franklin Stubbs b. Laurinburg, NC.

1967 John Flaherty b. New York, NY.

1975 Boston C Carlton Fisk homers in the bottom of the 12th inning to lift the Red Sox over Cincinnati, 7–6, in Game 6 of the World Series.

1976 Cincinnati C Johnny Bench hits two homers to power the Reds to a 7–2 win over New York to complete a four-game sweep of the Yankees in the World Series. Cincinnati's World Series sweep is baseball's first since the Baltimore Orioles blanked the Los Angeles Dodgers in four straight in the 1966 classic.

1996 RHP Greg Maddux continues Atlanta's pitching dominance in Game 2 of the World Series. Maddux scatters six hits, walks none, and induces 20 groundball outs in his eight innings of work as the Braves blank the New York Yankees, 4–0. Atlanta closer Mark

Wohlers strikes out the side in the ninth inning for the save. Braves 1B Fred McGriff knocks in three runs to break the postseason RBI record with 15.

1997 Florida edges Cleveland, 14–11, in Game 3 of the World Series to record the second highest combined run production in Series history with 25. Marlins RF Gary Sheffield has three hits — including a home run — drives in five runs, and also prevents an Indians home run with a leaping catch over the right field wall. Florida ties the 1936 New York Yankees with a seven-run ninth inning, then hangs on as Cleveland scores four times in its last at-bat.

1998 The New York Yankees complete their four game World Series sweep over the San Diego Padres, winning 3–0 in San Diego. The Yankees finish as baseball's all-time winningest team at 125–50 (.714) and with 24 titles become the all-time leader in professional sports, besting the NHL's Montreal Canadians. New York also completes its first World Series sweep since 1950 when it blanked the Philadelphia Phillies in four games. Yankees 3B Scott Brosius, who bats .471 with two home runs and six RBIs, is named unanimous MVP.

22

1895 Johnny Morrison b. Pelleville, KY.

1907 Jimmie Foxx b. Sudlersville, MD.

1918 Harry Walker b. Pascagoula, MS.

1927 New York Giants OF Ross Youngs, a 10-year veteran with a .322 lifetime batting average, dies of Bright's diesease at age 30.

1932 Gib Bodet b. New Orleans, LA.

1941 Wilbur Wood b. Cambridge, MA.

1943 Bobby Mitchell b. Norristown, PA.

1970 Milwaukee trades C Gerry McNertney, RHP George Lauzerique, and P Jesse Huggins to St. Louis for OF Carl Taylor and LHP Jim Ellis.

1971 Philadelphia trades OF Larry Hisle to Los Angeles for 1B Tom Hutton.

1972 Oakland RHP Jim "Catfish" Hunter earns a 3–2 victory in relief as the A's win Game 7 of the World Series over the Cincinnati Reds. It is the A's first title since 1930 when the franchise was in Philadelphia.

1973 Milwaukee trades OFs Ollie Brown and Joe Lahoud, RHP Skip Lockwood, LHP Gary Ryerson, and C Ellie Rodriguez to California for OF Ken Berry, C Art Kusner, and LHPs Steve Barber and Clyde Wright.

1974 San Francisco trades OF Bobby Bonds to the New York Yankees for OF Bobby Murcer.

1974 Pittsburgh trades OF Gene Clines to the New York Mets for C Duffy Dyer.

1992 Longtime baseball broadcaster Red Barber passes away at age 84. A broadcaster from 1934 thru 1966 for Cincinnati, Brooklyn, and the New York Yankees, Barber did the first ML night game in 1935 and the first televised baseball game in 1939. In 1978, he and former New York Yankees announcer Mel Allen received the first Ford Frick Award for excellence in broadcasting.

1997 Cleveland defeats Florida, 10–3, in Game 4 to even the World Series at two wins apiece amid the coldest playing conditions the 1975 season. At game time it is 38 degrees, and before its conclusion, snow falls. Indians 3B Matt Williams leads the offense, going 3-for-3 with a home run, two walks, two RBIs, and three runs scored.

23

1910 Philadelphia RHP — Jack Coombs who led the AL in wins with 30 during the regular season — hurls his third complete game victory in just six days in beating the Chicago Cubs, 7–2, leading the A's to their title in only five games.

1920 Vern Stephens b. McAlister, NM.

1922 Ewell Blackwell b. Fresno, CA.

1931 Jim Bunning b. Southgate, KY.

1945 Brooklyn general manager Branch Rickey announces that the Dodgers have signed Jackie Robinson to a minor league contract to play for the AAA Montreal Royals next season. Robinson is hand picked by Rickey to lead the integration of blacks in the major leagues.

1965 Al Leiter b. Toms River, NJ.

1993 Toronto LF Joe Carter hits a three-run home run in the bottom of the ninth inning to lift the Blue Jays to an 8–6 win over Philadelphia in Game 6 of the World Series. Carter's blast gives Toronto back-to-back titles and also marks just the second time in World Series play that a home run ends it. Pittsburgh's Bill Mazeroski was the first to do it when his round-tripper ended the 1960 Series.

1996 New York scores two in the top of the 10th inning to beat Atlanta, 8–6, in Game 4 of the World Series in a record 4:17. The Yankees overcome an early 6–0 deficit, rallying with Jim Leyritz's three-run homer to force extra innings.

1997 Florida defeats Cleveland, 8–7, in Game 5 of the World Series to take a 3–2 lead. Marlins RHP Livan Hernandez, age 22, becomes the first rookie starter since 1947, matching the New York Yankees RHP Spec Shea to win two

Series games. Losing Indians RHP Orel Hershiser, age 39, falls to 0–2 in the Series. The age difference between the two starting pitchers — 16 years, five months, and five days — is the greatest in World Series history.

24

1905 Jack Russell b. Paris, TX.

1911 The longest rain delay in World Series history ends at six days as Philadelphia A's RHP Chief Bender beats New York Giants' RHP Christy Mathewson, 4–2, in Game 4.

1937 Juan Marichal b. Dominican Republic.

1950 Rawly Eastwick b. Camden, NJ.

1961 Rafael Belliard b. Dominican Republic.

1969 Arthur Rhodes b. Waco, TX.

1972 Jackie Robinson, who broke baseball's color barrier in 1947, passes away at age 53. In his 10 seasons with the Brooklyn Dodgers, Robinson played in six World Series. He was elected to the Hall of Fame in 1962.

1973 Kansas City trades RHP Dick Drago to Boston for RHP Marty Pattin.

1978 San Diego RHP Gaylord Perry becomes the first pitcher to win the Cy Young Award in both leagues, after posting an NL-best 21–6 mark for the Padres. Perry won the 1972 AL Cy Young Award after posting a 24–16 record with Cleveland.

1988 The New York Yankees trade 1B Jack Clark and LHP Pat Clements to San Diego for RHPs Lance McCullers and Jimmy Jones, and OF Stan Jefferson.

1992 The Toronto Blue Jays, the first Canadian team to play in the World Series, become the first to win it, besting Atlanta 4–3 in 11 innings in Game 6. In his 19th season, 41-year-old Dave

Winfield strokes a two-run double for the margin of victory.

1994 Atlanta RHP Greg Maddux becomes the first pitcher to win three straight Cy Young Awards, his unanimous selection after posting a 16–6 record with a 1.56 ERA during a strike-shortened season.

1996 The New York Yankees continue their perfect postseason play winning Game 5 of the World Series, 1–0, in Atlanta. LHP Andy Pettitte pitches into the ninth to earn the win as New York extends its postseason road record to 8–0. The Yankees sweep all three games in Atlanta's Fulton County Stadium, which will be replaced next season by the new Turner Field.

1998 New York Mets C Mike Piazza signs the richest sports contract to date — $91 million over seven years — a record for total dollars and average per season ($13.5).

25

1889 Smokey Joe Wood b. Kansas City, MO.

1923 Bobby Thomson b. Glasgow, Scotland.

1951 Al Cowens b. Los Angeles, CA.

1952 Roy Smalley III b. Los Angeles, CA.

1955 Danny Darwin b. Bonham, TX.

1955 Cleveland trades OF Larry Doby to the Chicago White Sox for OF Jim Busby and SS Chico Carrasquel.

1965 Steve Decker b. Rock Island, IL.

1966 Mike Harkey b. San Diego, CA.

1973 San Francisco trades 1B Willie McCovey and OF Bernie Williams to San Diego for LHP Mike Caldwell.

1977 New York Yankees LHP Sparky Lyle becomes the first AL reliever to win the Cy Young Award. Lyle leads the AL

with 72 appearances and has a 13–5 record with 26 saves and a 2.17 ERA.

1978 Texas trades 1B Mike Hargrove, 3B Kurt Bevacqua, and C Bill Fahey to San Diego for OF Oscar Gamble and INF Dave Roberts.

1997 Cleveland defeats Florida, 4–1, in Game 6 of the World Series to knot the Fall Classic at three games apiece. Indians RHP Chad Ogea defeats Marlins ace RHP Kevin Brown for the second time in the series. Ogea also becomes the first Cleveland pitcher to drive in a run in 25 years, helping his own cause, going 2-for-2 with a double, two RBIs and a run scored.

26

1866 Kid Gleason b. Camden, NJ.

1899 Judy Johnson b. Snow Hill, MD.

1917 New York owner Jacob Rupert signs former St. Louis Cardinals manager Miller Huggins to manage the Yankees.

1931 Charles Comiskey, one of the AL's founding fathers and longtime owner of the Chicago White Sox, dies at age 72.

1934 Washington trades SS/Manager Joe Cronin to the Boston Red Sox for SS Lyn Lary and $225,000. Bucky Harris, who managed Boston in 1934, takes over for the Senators in 1935.

1948 Toby Harrah b. Sissonville, WV.

1949 Mike Hargrove b. Perryton, TX.

1949 Steve Rogers b. Jefferson City, MO.

1960 The AL announces that the Washington Senators will relocate to Minneapolis–St. Paul, yet award 1961 expansion franchises to Los Angeles and Washington, again.

1965 Gil Heredia b. Nogales, AZ.

1973 St. Louis trades OF Bernie Carbo and RHP Rick Wise to Boston for OF Reggie Smith and RHP Ken Tatum.

1973 The Chicago Cubs trade RHP Ferguson Jenkins to Texas for 3B Bill Madlock and INF Vic Harris.

1982 Philadelphia Phillies LHP Steve Carlton wins his record fourth NL Cy Young Award after going 23–11 with a league-leading 286 strikeouts and six shutouts.

1985 The Kansas City Royals blank St. Louis, 11–0, in World Series Game 7 and leave the Cardinals with a composite .185 batting average, lowest ever in World Series play for a seven game Series.

1991 Minnesota CF Kirby Puckett hits an 11th inning home run to lift the Twins to a 4–3 win over Atlanta in Game 6 of the World Series. The Twins would wrap up the title the next night, 1–0 in 12 innings.

1996 The New York Yankees complete their amazing comeback in the World Series, defeating Atlanta, 3–2, in Game 6. New York captures its record 23rd championship by overcoming an 0–2 deficit to win four straight games. Yankees closer, RHP John Wetteland, records his fourth save in as many games to earn MVP honors.

1997 The Florida Marlins become the fastest expansion team to win the World Series, defeating Cleveland 3–2 in 11 innings in Game 7. In only their fifth year of existence, the Marlins record their first winning record, aided by billionaire owner H. Wayne Huizenga, who spends nearly $100 million in the free agent market to build the club.

27

1922 Ralph Kiner b. Santa Rita, NM.
1922 Del Rice b. Portsmouth,OH.
1945 Mike Lum b. Honolulu, HI.
1952 Pete Vukovich b. Johnstown, PA.

1953 Barry Bonnell b. Clermont County, OH.

1961 Bill Swift b. South Portland, ME.

1963 Bip Roberts b. Berkeley, CA.

1964 Luis Polonia b. Dominican Republic.

1965 Philadelphia trades C Pat Corrales, RHP Art Mahaffey, and OF Alex Johnson to St. Louis for C Bob Uecker, 1B Bill White, and SS Dick Groat.

1972 Brad Radke b. Eau Claire, WI.

1972 Atlanta trades OF Rico Carty to Texas for RHP Jim Panther.

1972 Minnesota trades C Rick Dempsey to the New York Yankees for OF Danny Walton.

1991 Minnesota PH Gene Larkin's 12th inning single scores Dan Gladden with the game's only run as the Twins defeat Atlanta, 1–0, in Game 7 of the World Series.

1992 The New York Mets trade OF D.J. Dozier and RHP Wally Whitehurst to San Diego for SS Tony Fernandez.

1999 The New York Yankees complete their second straight World Series sweep, defeating Atlanta, 4–1, in Game 4 at New York. The sweep gives the Yankees a 12-game World Series winning streak, equalling the record started by the 1927 Yankees. The Yankees' World Championship is their 25th of the century, more than any other organization including the NFL, NBA, NHL, or the major leagues.

28

1917 Joe Page b. Cherry Valley, PA.
1931 The Baseball Writers' Association of America names its first AL MVP: Philadelphia LHP Lefty Grove, who leads the league in wins (31), winning percentage (.886), complete games (27),

and strikeouts (175) for the pennant-winning A's.

1935 Bob Veale b. Birmingham, AL.

1954 Gary Rajsich b. Youngstown, OH.

1964 Lenny Harris b. Miami, FL.

1965 Larry Casian b. Lynwood, CA.

1966 Juan Guzman b. Dominican Republic.

1972 San Diego trades OF John Jeter to the Chicago White Sox for RHP Vicente Romo.

1975 The Chicago Cubs trade SS Don Kessinger to St. Louis for RHP Mike Garman.

1979 New York Yankees manager Billy Martin punches a salesman in Minneapolis and is again fired by owner George Steinbrenner.

1988 San Diego trades 3B Chris Brown and C Keith Moreland to Detroit for RHP Walt Terrell.

1995 Atlanta wins its first World Series since the franchise moved from Milwaukee in 1966. The Braves blank Cleveland, 1–0, in Game 6 as LHP Tom Glavine and RHP Mark Wohlers hurl the first combined one-hitter in World Series play.

29

1939 Pete Richert b. Floral Park, NY.

1959 Jesse Barfield b. Joliet, IL.

1967 Greg Gohr b. Santa Clara, CA.

1974 The New York Mets trade 2B Ken Boswell to Houston for OF Bob Gallagher.

30

1867 Ed Delahanty b. Cleveland, OH.

1898 Bill Terry b. Atlanta, GA.

1922 The Boston Red Sox trade RHP Rip Collins and 2B Del Pratt to Detroit for RHPs Carl Holling and Howard Ehmke, 2B Danny Clark, OF Babe Herman.

1927 Joe Adcock b. Coushatta, LA.

1936 Jim Perry b. Williamston, NC.

1941 Jim Ray Hart b. Hookerton, NC.

1960 Gerald Perry b. Savannah, GA.

1960 Dave Valle b. Bayside, NY.

1962 Danny Tartabull b. Miami, FL.

1962 Mark Portugal b. Los Angeles, CA.

1972 Oakland trades OF Brant Alyea and OF Bill McNulty to Texas for LHP Paul Lindblad.

1986 Baltimore trades RHP Storm Davis to San Diego for C Terry Kennedy and RHP Mark Williamson.

1999 Colorado trades OF Dante Bichette to Cincinnati for OF Jeffrey Hammonds and RHP Stan Belinda.

31

1916 Ken Keltner b. Milwaukee, WI.

1942 Dave McNally b. Billings, MT.

1948 Mickey Rivers b. Miami, FL.

1960 Mike Gallego b. Whittier, CA.

1963 Fred McGriff b. Tampa, FL.

1963 Matt Nokes b. San Diego, CA.

1968 Eddie Taubensee b. Beeville, TX.

1970 Steve Trachsel b. Oxnard, CA.

1972 Philadelphia trades 3B Don Money, RHP Billy Champion, and INF John Vukovich to Milwaukee for RHPs Jim Lonborg and Ken Sanders and LHPs Ken Brett and Earl Stephenson.

1973 Pittsburgh trades C Milt May to Houston for LHP Jerry Reuss.

1977 The Chicago Cubs trade RHP Bill Bonham to Cincinnati for RHP Bill Caudill and LHP Woodie Fryman.

NOVEMBER

1

1914 After being swept in the World Series four straight by the Boston Braves, Philadelphia manager Connie Mack begins dismantling his powerful A's ballclub by asking waivers for RHPs Chief Bender and Jack Coombs and LHP Eddie Plank. The same day, Bender (Baltimore) and Plank (St. Louis) will sign contracts with the new Federal League.

1916 Harry Frazee, a New York theatre owner and producer, purchases the Boston Red Sox for $675,000.

1960 Fernando Valenzuela b. Mexico.

1964 Eddie Williams b. Shreveport. LA.

1966 Bob Wells b. Yakima, WA.

1982 Unhappy with Commissioner Bowie Kuhn, baseball's chief executive for the past 14 years, the owners fire him and begin a two-year search for a replacement.

2

1913 The outlaw Federal League begins its challenge as a third major league when the Kansas City Packers entice St. Louis Browns manager George Stovall to jump leagues.

1914 Johnny Vander Meer b. Prospect Park, NJ.

1916 Al Campanis b. Greece.

1920 Dick Sisler b. St. Louis, MO.

1942 Ron Reed b. LaPorte, IN.

1955 Greg A. Harris b. Lynwood, CA.

1958 Willie McGee b. San Francisco, CA.

1963 Sam Horn b. Dallas, TX.

1966 Orlando Merced b. Puerto Rico.

1972 Philadelphia LHP Steve Carlton, who finishes 27–10 for the last place 59–97 Phillies, is a runaway winner for the NL Cy Young Award.

1972 Kansas City trades RHP Mike Hedlund to Cleveland for INF Kurt Bevacqua.

1972 Atlanta trades 2B Felix Millan and LHP George Stone to the New York Mets for RHPs Danny Frisella and Gary Gentry.

1972 The last surviving member of the first World Series game, Freddy Parent, passes away at age 96. Parent was the starting shortstop for the 1903 World Champion Boston Somersets.

1974 Atlanta trades home run king Hank Aaron to the Milwaukee Brewers for OF Dave May and RHP Roger Alexander. Aaron returns to the city where he began his major league career in 1954, and will hit 22 more home runs, pushing his all-time record to 755.

1993 Cincinnati trades C Dan Wilson and RHP Bobby Ayala to Seattle for 2B Bret Boone and RHP Erik Hanson.

1993 Philadelphia trades OF Ruben Amaro, Jr., to Cleveland for RHP Heathcliff Slocumb.

1999 Texas trades two-time AL MVP

(1996 & 1998) OF Juan Gonzalez, RHP Danny Patterson, and C Greg Zaun to Detroit for LHPs Justin Thompson and Alan Webb, RHP Francisco Cordero, OF Gabe Kapler, INF Frank Catalanotto, and C Bill Haselman.

3

1918 Bob Feller b. Van Meter, IA.

1945 Ken Holtzman b. St. Louis, MO.

1951 Dwight Evans b. Santa Monica, CA.

1956 Bob Welch b. Detroit, MI.

1968 Paul Quantrill b. London, Ontario.

1970 St. Louis trades disgruntled OF Curt Flood to Washington for RHP Jeff Terpko, 1B Greg Goossen, and OF Gene Martin.

1971 St. Louis trades 2B Ted Kubiak to Texas for LHP Joe Grzenda.

1971 Houston trades INF Marty Martinez to St. Louis for C Bob Stinson.

1980 The New York Yankees trade 2B Brian Doyle and SS Fred Stanley to Oakland for RHP Mike Morgan.

1992 The New York Yankees trade OF Roberto Kelly to Cincinnati for OF Paul O'Neill and 1B Joe DeBerry.

1997 Boston SS Nomar Garciaparra becomes the fifth unanimous winner of the AL Rookie of the Year Award, receiving all 28 first place votes by the Baseball Writers' Association of America. Garciaparra, 24, batted .306 with 30 home runs, 98 RBIs, 122 runs scored, and 22 stolen bases. He set ML records for most RBIs by a leadoff hitter, and most home runs by a rookie shortstop. The four previous unanimous winners were Boston C Carlton Fisk (1972), Oakland 1B Mark McGwire (1987), Cleveland C Sandy Alomar, Jr. (1990), and California RF Tim Salmon (1993).

4

1922 Eddie Basinski b. Buffalo, NY.

1930 Dick Groat b. Wilkinsburg, PA.

1942 New York Yankees 2B Joe Gordon edges out Boston Triple Crown winner Ted Williams by 21 votes for AL MVP honors. Gordon bats .322 for the pennant-winning Yankees, while Williams is denied the top honor despite leading the AL in batting (.356), home runs (36), RBIs (137) as well as total bases (338), walks (145), and slugging percentage (.648).

1963 The New York Mets trade RHP Roger Craig, who topped the NL in losses for each of the two previous seasons with 22 and 24, to St. Louis for OF George Altman and RHP Bill Wakefield.

1967 Eric Karros b. Hackensack, NJ.

1968 Carlos Baerga b. Puerto Rico.

1997 Philadelphia 3B Scott Rolen is unanimously voted the NL Rookie of the Year, ending the Los Angeles Dodgers' five-year hold on the award. The Phillies' 22-year-old becomes the youngest NL player to reach 90 RBIs since New York RF Darryl Strawberry in 1984. Rolen led all NL rookies in batting average (.283), runs scored (93), hits (159), doubles (35), home runs (21), and RBIs (92). He receives all 28 first place votes in balloting by the Baseball Writers' Association of America.

1998 St. Louis 1B Mark McGwire is named The Associated Press Major League Baseball Player of the Year. The Cardinals slugger, who hit a record 70 home runs, beats Sammy Sosa of the Chicago Cubs 103–80 in voting by AP newspaper and broadcast members.

5

1891 Alfred "Greasy" Neale b. Parkersburg, WV.

1913 Jim Tabor b. Owens Crossroads, AL.

1942 Richie Scheinblum b. New York, NY.

1959 Craig McMurtry b. Temple, TX.

1970 Javier Lopez b. Puerto Rico.

1973 Johnny Damon b. Fort Riley, KS.

1976 In baseball's fifth expansion draft, the AL Seattle Mariners take Kansas City OF Ruppert Jones with their first pick, while the AL Toronto Blue Jays take Baltimore INF-OF Bob Bailor with their first pick. Only AL teams have their rosters raided.

1976 Oakland A's owner Charlie Finley trades manager Chuck Tanner to Pittsburgh for C Manny Sanguillen and $100,000.

1997 On the day he is voted the AL Manager of the Year, Baltimore skipper Davey Johnson resigns, ending an ongoing feud with owner Peter Angelos. Johnson led the Orioles to an AL-best 98–64 record before bowing to Cleveland in the AL Championship Series.

1997 The Milwaukee Brewers become the first ML baseball team to switch leagues this century, announcing they will play in the NL Central Division in 1998. The switch is necessitated with the additions of the expansion Tampa Bay Devil Rays and Arizona Diamondbacks who will begin play in 1998. Tampa Bay joins the AL East, moving the Detroit Tigers from the AL East to the AL Central. Kansas City is given the first choice to move, but the Royals opt to stay in the AL Central.

6

1887 Walter Johnson b. Humboldt, KS.

1922 Buddy Kerr b. Astoria, NY.

1953 John Candelaria b. Brooklyn, NY.

1968 Chad Curtis b. Marion, IN.

1970 Hector Fajardo b. Mexico.

1972 St. Louis trades OF Jorge Roque to Montreal for C Tim McCarver.

1974 Los Angeles RHP Mike Marshall, who appears in an ML record 106 games and leads the NL with 21 saves, becomes the first relief pitcher to win the Cy Young Award.

1996 Los Angeles OF Todd Hollandsworth wins the NL Rookie of the Year Award, becoming the record 5th straight Dodgers player to win the award. The previous winners were RHP Hideo Nomo (1995), OF Raul Mondesi (1994), C Mike Piazza (1993), and 1B Eric Karros (1992). Hollandsworth, 23, led all rookies in hits, doubles, home runs, RBIs, stolen bases and fewest errors. He batted .291 with 12 homers and 59 RBIs.

1997 Boston trades RHP Aaron Sele, RHP Mark Brandenberg, and C Bill Haselman to Texas for C Jim Leyritz and OF Damon Buford.

7

1928 The Boston Braves trade NL batting champion 2B Rogers Hornsby (.387) to the Chicago Cubs for five players: RHP Bruce Cunningham, RHP Socks Seibold, LHP Percy Jones, C Lou Legett, and 2B Freddie Maguire.

1932 Dick Stuart b. San Francisco, CA.

1933 A referendum is passed by Pennsylvania voters legalizing Sunday baseball for Pittsburgh and Philadelphia — the only major league cities still observing the blue law.

1938 Jim Kaat b. Zeeland, MI.

1944 Joe Niekro b. Martins Ferry, OH.

1948 Buck Martinez b. Redding, CA.

1963 New York Yankees C Elston Howard becomes the first black MVP in AL history. Howard batted .287 with 28 home runs for the pennant winning Yankees.

1964 NL owners grant permission for the Braves to relocate from Milwaukee to Atlanta after the 1965 season.

1969 Dave Fleming b. Queens, NY.

1997 The New York Yankees trade LHP Kenny Rogers and $5 million to Oakland for 3B Scott Brosius.

1999 Cleveland signs Cuban defector RHP Danyso Baez to a four-year contract worth $14.5 million. The deal is worth more than double what the New York Yankees gave fellow Cuban defector RHP Orlando Hernandez in 1998.

8

1896 Bucky Harris b. Port Jervis, NY.

1944 Ed Kranepool b. New York, NY.

1952 John Denny b. Prescott, AZ.

1963 Dwight Smith b. Tallahassee, FL.

1965 Jeff Blauser b. Los Gatos, CA.

1966 Baltimore RF Frank Robinson, baseball's 13th Triple Crown winner with 49 home runs, 122 RBIs, and a .316 batting average, becomes the first player to win MVP honors in both leagues. Robinson won the 1961 NL MVP with the Cincinnati Reds.

1967 Eric Anthony b. San Diego, CA.

1967 Henry Rodriguez b. Dominican Republic.

1968 Jose Offerman b. Dominican Republic.

1974 San Diego trades OF Clarence Gaston to Atlanta for RHP Danny Frisella.

1999 Toronto trades OF Shawn Green and 2B Jorge Nunez to Los Angeles for OF Raul Mondesi and LHP Pedro Borbon.

9

1879 Archibald "Moonlight" Graham b. Fayetteville, NC.

1931 Whitey Herzog b. New Athens, IL.

1934 NL officials select Ford Frick as league president, six days after John Heydler resigns for health reasons.

1935 Bob Gibson b. Omaha, NE.

1953 In a case charging baseball with operating illegally in interstate commerce, the U.S. Supreme Court votes 7–2 to reaffirm Justice Oliver Wendell Holmes' 1922 decision that baseball is a sport rather than an interstate business as defined by federal antitrust laws.

1962 Dion James b. Philadelphia, PA.

1969 Angel Miranda b. Puerto Rico.

1970 Chad Ogea b. Lake Charles, LA.

1993 San Francisco LF Barry Bonds is voted the NL MVP for the third time in four years after reaching career highs with a .336 batting average, 46 home runs, 129 runs scored, and 123 RBIs. Bonds joins Stan Musial, Roy Campanella, and Mike Schmidt as the NL's only three-time MVPs.

1998 Chicago RHP Kerry Wood is voted NL Rookie of the Year, edging Colorado 1B Todd Helton for the award. Wood, who tied an ML record with a 20-strikeout game against Houston, was 13–6 with a 3.40 ERA and 233 strikeouts in 166⅔ innings in helping the

Cubs into the postseason for the first time since 1989. Helton hit .315 for the Rockies with 25 home runs and 97 RBIs.

1998 Seattle trades LHP Paul Spoljaric to Philadelphia for RHP Mark Leiter.

10

1896 Jimmy Dykes b. Philadelphia, PA.

1930 Gene Conley b. Muskogee, OK.

1934 Norm Cash b. Justiceburg, TX.

1953 Larry Christensen b. Everett, WA.

1955 Jack Clark b. New Brighton, PA.

1964 Kenny Rogers b. Savannah, GA.

1971 Butch Huskey b. Anadarko, OK.

1972 Shawn Green b. Des Plaines, IL.

1978 Texas trades LHPs Dave Righetti and Paul Mirabella, RHP Mike Griffin, and OF Juan Beniquez to the New York Yankees for LHPs Sparky Lyle and Dave Rajsich, RHP Larry McCall, INF Domingo Ramos, and C Mike Heath.

1997 Cincinnati trades RHP Jeff Brantley to St. Louis for 1B Dmitri Young.

1997 Toronto RHP Roger Clemens becomes the first AL pitcher to win four Cy Young Awards. In his first season with the Blue Jays, Clemens led the AL in wins (21), ERA (2.05), and strikeouts (292). He finished 21–7 and received 25 of the 28 first place votes by the Baseball Writers' Association of America. Clemens also won the award with the Boston Red Sox in 1986, 1987, and 1991. The only other pitchers to win four Cy Youngs were in the NL: LHP Steve Carlton and RHP Greg Maddux.

1998 Oakland LF Ben Grieve wins the AL Rookie of the Year Award, collecting 23 of a possible 28 first place votes from the Baseball Writers' Association of America. Grieve, whose father Tom Grieve played nine years in the major leagues and is a former general manager of the Texas Rangers, led AL rookies with 168 hits, 18 home runs, 94 runs, 41 doubles and 89 RBIs.

1998 Cincinnati trades 2B Bret Boone and LHP Mike Remlinger to Atlanta for LHP Denny Neagle, OF Michael Tucker, and RHP Rob Bell.

1998 Arizona trades LHP Alan Embree to San Francisco for OF Dante Powell.

1999 San Diego trades RHP Andy Ashby to Philadelphia for RHPs Carlton Loewer, Steve Montgomery, and Adam Eaton.

11

1891 Walter "Rabbitt" Maranville b. Springfield, MA.

1899 Harold "Pie" Traynor b. Framingham, MA.

1964 Roberto Hernandez b. Puerto Rico.

1969 Damion Easley b. New York, NY.

1981 Los Angeles LHP Fernando Valenzuela becomes the first rookie to win a Cy Young Award. Valenzuela, the NL Rookie of the Year as well, paces the strike-shortened season in strikeouts with 180, shutouts with eight, and finishes 13–7 with a 2.48 ERA.

1996 Atlanta RHP John Smoltz, 24–8 with a 2.94 ERA, wins the NL Cy Young Award. It marks a record fourth consecutive Cy Young Award winner and the fifth in six years for the Braves.

1997 Barely a month after winning the World Series, the Florida Marlins begin their payroll downsizing by trading LF Moises Alou to Houston for RHPs Oscar Henriquez and Manuel Barrios.

1997 Montreal RHP Pedro Martinez ends the Atlanta Braves' string of four straight NL Cy Young Awards at four, capturing his first and the first for the Expos organization. Martinez went 17–8 and led the ML with a 1.90 ERA, becoming the first ERA leader with 300 strikeouts since Philadelphia LHP Steve Carlton in 1972. His 305 strikeouts ranked second in the majors behind Philadelphia RHP Curt Schilling's 314.

1998 Los Angeles trades OF Bobby Bonilla to the New York Mets for RHP Mel Rojas.

1998 Larry Dierker, Houston's broadcaster-turned-manager, wins the NL Manager of the Year Award after leading the Astros to a team record 102 wins and their second straight Central Division title.

1999 Toronto trades RHP Pat Hentgen and LHP Paul Spoljaric to St. Louis for LHP Lance Painter, RHP Matt DeWitt, and C Alberto Castillo.

12

1891 Carl Mays b. Liberty, KY.

1920 Kenesaw Mountain Landis is elected baseball's first commissioner.

1923 The New York Giants trade OF Casey Stengel, OF Bill Cunningham, and SS Dave Bancroft who becomes a player/manager to the Boston Braves for OF Billy Southworth and RHP Joe Oeschger.

1936 Joe Hoerner b. Dubuque, IA.

1947 Brooklyn 1B Jackie Robinson caps his historic season by winning baseball's first Rookie of the Year Award. Robinson, who broke the color barrier in April, batted .297 with a NL-leading 29 stolen bases for the pennant winning Dodgers.

1947 Ron Bryant b. Redlands, CA.

1950 Bruce Bochte b. Pasadena, CA.

1961 Greg Gagne b. Fall River, MA.

1962 Jeff Reed b. Joliet, IL.

1968 Sammy Sosa b. Dominican Republic.

1987 The Chicago White Sox trade RHPs Richard Dotson and Scott Nielsen to the New York Yankees for OF Dan Pasqua, C Mark Salas, and LHP Steve Rosenberg.

1998 New York Yankees manager Joe Torre is a runaway winner for the AL Manager of the Year Award, garnering 23 of 28 first place votes by the Baseball Writers' Association of America. Torre's Yankees won a baseball record 125 games concluding a memorable season by sweeping the San Diego Padres four straight games in the World Series.

1999 Los Angeles trades RHP Ismael Valdes and 2B Eric Young to the Chicago Cubs for RHPs Terry Adams and Chad Ricketts.

1999 Baltimore trades LHP Jesse Orosco to the New York Mets for LHP Chuck McElroy.

1999 Philadelphia trades C Bobby Estalella to San Francisco for RHP Chris Brock.

13

1911 John Jordan "Buck" O'Neil b. Carrabelle, FL.

1915 Ted Wilks b. Fulton, NY.

1939 Wes Parker b. Evanston, IL.

1941 Mel Stottlemyre b. Hazelton, MO.

1968 Pat Hentgen b. Detroit, MI.

1968 Mark Kiefer b. Orange, CA.

1979 For the first time in ML history, two players share the MVP Award. The NL co-winners are St. Louis 1B Keith Hernandez and Pittsburgh 1B Willie Stargell. Hernandez led the NL in hitting at .344, runs scored with 116, and doubles with 48. Stargell is the inspirational leader of the Pirates, blasting 32 home runs during the regular season, and five more during the postseason playoffs including the World Series to lead his team to a world championship.

1995 Atlanta RHP Greg Maddux wins his unprecedented fourth consecutive NL Cy Young Award after a league best 19–2 record and 1.63 ERA.

1996 San Francisco trades 3B Matt Williams to Cleveland for SS Jose Vizciano, 2B Jeff Kent and RHP Julian Tavares.

1997 Colorado OF Larry Walker becomes the first Canadian b. player to win an MVP Award, capturing the NL trophy. Walker led the NL with 49 home runs, slugging percentage (.720), extra base hits (99), and on base percentage (.452). His 409 total bases represent the most in the major leagues since Stan Musial's 429 in 1948.

1998 Cleveland trades RHP Chad Ogea to Philadelphia for RHP Jerry Spradlin.

1999 In the first four-team trade since 1985, nine players are dealt involving Tampa Bay, Colorado, Milwaukee, and Oakland. The Devil Rays get 3B Vinny Castilla from the Rockies. The Rockies get 3B Jeff Cirillo and LHP Scott Karl from the Brewers and RHP Rolando Arrojo and INF Aaron Ledesma from the Devil Rays. The Brewers get RHP Jamey Wright and C Henry Blanco from the Rockies and RHP Jimmy Haynes from the A's. The A's get RHP Justin Miller from the Rockies.

14

1900 The National League rejects the American League as an equal, declaring it an "outlaw league" outside the National Agreement.

1929 Jimmy Piersall b. Waterbury, CT.

1937 Jim Brewer b. Merced, CA.

1966 Curt Schilling b. Anchorage, AK.

1967 Paul Wagner b. Milwaukee, WI.

1973 Ruben Rivera b. Panama.

1999 Boston trades OF Jon Nunnally to the New York Mets for OF Jermaine Allensworth.

1999 Houston trades OF Carl Everett to Boston for SS Adam Everett.

15

1928 Gus Bell b. Louisville, KY.

1991 Cleveland trades LHP Greg Swindell to Cincinati for RHPs Jack Armstrong, Scott Scudder, and Joe Turek.

1999 Arizona LHP Randy Johnson becomes only the second pitcher to win the Cy Young Award in each league, capturing the NL trophy after compiling a 17–9 record with a 2.48 ERA. Johnson, who won the AL Cy Young Award with Seattle in 1995, led the major leagues with 12 complete games, and his 364 strikeouts represented the fourth highest total all-time. Johnson joins only RHP Gaylord Perry as the only winners in each league.

1999 San Diego trades RHP Dan Miceli to Florida for RHP Brian Meadows.

16

1964 Dwight Gooden b. Tampa, FL.

1966 Tim Scott b. Hanford, CA.

1968 Chris Haney b. Baltimore, MD.

1998 Toronto RHP Roger Clemens

wins an unprecidented fifth Cy Young Award, and unanimously for the second time, receiving all 28 first place votes by the Baseball Writers' Association of America. Clemens finished the season 20–6 with a 2.65 ERA, striking out 271 batters in 234⅔ innings. He was unbeaten in his last 22 starts, winning 15 decisions after starting 5–6. Clemens becomes only the third unanimous Cy Young award winner in the AL following Detroit RHP Denny McLain (1968) and New York Yankees LHP Ron Guidry (1978). His fifth Cy Young also breaks a tie with Steve Carlton and Greg Maddux.

1999 Boston RHP Pedro Martinez becomes only the fourth unanimous AL Cy Young Award winner, and joins RHP Gaylord Perry and LHP Randy Johnson (who did it the day before) as the only pitchers to win the honor in each league. Martinez, who led the league with a 23–4 record, 2.07 ERA, and 313 strikeouts, received all 28 first place votes by the Baseball Writers' Association of America. The only previous unanimous AL winners were RHP Denny McLain (1968), LHP Ron Guidry (1978), and RHP Roger Clemens (1986 and 1998). Martinez won his NL Cy Young Award with the 1997 Montreal Expos.

1999 Colorado trades RHPs Darryl Kile, Dave Veres, and Luther Hackman to St. Louis for RHPs Jose Jimenez, Manny Aybar, and Rick Croushore, and INF Brent Butler.

17

1923 Mike Garcia b. San Gabriel, CA.
1936 Gary Bell b. San Antonio, TX.
1944 Tom Seaver b. Fresno, CA.
1953 St. Louis Browns owner Bill Veeck sells his financially strapped franchise to a syndicate headed by Clarence W. Miles, who gets league approval to shift the franchise to Baltimore, bringing major league baseball to that city for the first time since 1902. The new Orioles will play in Memorial Stadium, a multipurpose sports facility built in 1950.

1964 Mitch Williams b. Santa Ana, CA.

1965 Paul Sorrento b. Somerville, MA.

1965 General William Eckert is elected as baseball's fourth commissioner, replacing Ford Frick. He'll serve until December 20, 1968.

1966 Jeff Nelson b. Baltimore, MD.

1969 Philadelphia trades OF Johnny Callison to the Chicago Cubs for OF Oscar Gamble and RHP Dick Selma.

1975 Atlanta trades OF Dusty Baker and INF Ed Goodson to Los Angeles for OF Jimmy Wynn, 2B Lee Lacy, 1B Tom Paciorek, and INF Jerry Royster.

1975 Texas trades RHP Ferguson Jenkins to Boston for OF Juan Beniquez and LHP Steve Barr.

1992 The Chicago Cubs trade SS Alex Arias and 3B Gary Scott to Florida for LHP Greg Hibbard.

1992 Cincinnati trades LHP Norm Charlton to Seattle for OF Kevin Mitchell.

1992 The NL Colorado Rockies and NL Florida Marlins hold baseball's first expansion draft in 16 years. Picking first, the Rockies select RHP David Nied from Atlanta, and the Marlins make Toronto OF Nigel Wilson their first selection. For the first time, the expansion draft includes teams from both the AL and the NL.

1998 Atlanta LHP Tom Glavine narrowly wins the NL Cy Young Award, edging San Diego RHP Trevor Hoffman, who actually received more first place votes by the Baseball Writers' Association of America. Glavine, who led the NL with 20 wins and tied for third in ERA at 2.47, edged Hoffman by only 11 points in bringing the Cy Young Award back to an Atlanta hurler for the sixth time in eight years. Glavine also won the award in 1991.

1999 Atlanta 3B Chipper Jones, who hit .319 with 45 home runs, 110 RBIs, and 116 runs scored, becomes a runaway winner for the NL MVP Award. Jones, who helped the Braves to their eighth straight NL East title, becomes the franchise's fifth MVP, joining Bob Elliott (1947), Hank Aaron (1957), Dale Murphy (1982 and 1983) and Terry Pendleton (1991).

18

1882 Jack Coombs b. LeGrande, IA.

1925 Gene Mauch b. Salina, KS.

1926 Roy Sievers b. St. Louis, MO.

1936 Jay Hook b. Waukegan, IL.

1947 The Boston Braves trade 2B Danny Murtaugh and OF Johnny Hopp to Pittsburgh for OF Jim Russell, C Bill Salkeld, and RHP Al Lyons.

1952 Dan Briggs b. Scotia, CA.

1954 Baltimore and the New York Yankees agree on the first part of the biggest trade in ML history—17 players at completion. The Orioles send RHPs Bob Turley and Don Larsen, and SS Billy Hunter to the Yankees for RHPs Harry Byrd and Jim McDonald, OF Gene Woodling, SS Willie Miranda, and catchers Hal Smith and Gus Triandos. The deal is finalized December 1, 1954.

1962 Jamie Moyer b. Sellersville, PA.

1963 Dante Bichette b. West Palm Beach, FL.

1963 The Kansas City A's trade RHP David Wickersham, RHP Ed Rakow, and 2B Jerry Lumpe to Detroit for OF

Rocky Colavito and RHP Bob Anderson.

1965 Scott Hemond b. Taunton, MA.

1965 Mark Petkovsek b. Beaumont, TX.

1967 Tom Gordon b. Sebring, FL.

1968 Gary Sheffield b. Tampa, FL.

1970 Allen Watson b. Jamaica, NY.

1974 Detroit SS Eddie Brinkman is traded twice in the same day. First, he goes to San Diego along with OF Dick Sharon, and P Bob Strampe for 1B Nate Colbert. The Padres then trade Brinkman to St. Louis for RHPs Alan Foster and Sonny Siebert, and LHP Rich Folkers.

1976 Baltimore trades C Dave Duncan to the Chicago White Sox for OF Pat Kelly.

1980 Kansas City 3B George Brett, who's .390 batting average is the highest in the major leagues since 1941, is a runaway selection for AL MVP.

1987 Toronto LF George Bell becomes the first Dominican to win the AL Most Valuable Player Award. Bell leads the AL with 134 RBIs, while smacking 47 home runs, scoring 111 runs, and batting .308 during the regular season.

1994 Cleveland trades RHPs Jerry DiPoto, Paul Byrd, and Dave Mlicki to the New York Mets for OF Jeromy Burnitz and RHP Joe Roa.

1997 ML baseball holds its expansion draft to stock the new Arizona Diamondbacks and Tampa Bay Devil Rays franchises, who will begin play in 1998. Selecting first, Tampa Bay takes Florida LHP Tony Saunders, while Arizona follows by taking Cleveland LHP Brian Anderson with its first pick.

1997 Detroit trades 3B Travis Fryman to Arizona for three players just taken in the expansion draft—3B Joe Randa, 3B Gabe Alvarez, and RHP Matt Drews, whom the Tigers lost just hours earlier.

1997 Atlanta trades 1B Fred McGriff to Tampa Bay for a player to be named later.

1997 Two of the three Martinez brothers are traded on the same day. Montreal RHP Pedro Martinez, the NL Cy Young Award winner, is sent to Boston for RHPs Carl Pavano and Tony Armas, Jr. Los Angeles LHP Jesus Martinez is selected in the expansion draft by Arizona, then is traded to Florida for CF Devon White.

1997 Florida trades RHP Robb Nen to San Francisco for RHPs Mike Villano, Joe Fontenot, and Mike Pageler.

1997 Montreal trades 2B Mike Lansing to Colorado for RHPs Jake Westbrook and John Nicholson, and OF Mark Hamelin.

1997 Philadelphia trades SS Kevin Stocker to Tampa Bay for OF Bob Abreau, who earlier is selected from Houston in the expansion draft.

1997 San Diego trades C John Flaherty to Tampa Bay for two players just selected in the expansion draft: RHP Brian Boehringer (Yankees) and SS Andy Sheets (Mariners).

1998 Texas RF Juan Gonzalez wins his second AL MVP Award in three years, easily outdistancing Boston SS Nomar Garciaparra, the runner-up, 357 votes to 232 as cast by the Baseball Writers' Association of America. Gonzalez, who collected 157 RBIs in the season, most in the AL since 1949, also batted .318 with 45 home runs as the Rangers won the AL West title for the second time in three years.

1999 Texas C Ivan Rodriguez, who batted .332 with 35 home runs and 113 RBIs, wins the AL MVP Award despite becoming only the fourth winner in history without the most first place votes. Boston RHP Pedro Martinez, who earlier captured the AL Cy Young Award, had eight first place votes and finished with 239 points. Rodriguez, who had seven first place votes, finished with 252 points in the closest MVP vote since 1996 when Texas OF Juan Gonzalez edged Seattle SS Alex Rodriguez, 290–287.

19

1921 Roy Campanella b. Philadelphia, PA.

1942 Larry Haney b. Charlottesville, VA.

1945 Bobby Tolan b. Los Angeles, CA.

1947 Bob Boone b. San Diego, CA.

1962 St. Louis trades RHP Don Cardwell and INF Julio Gotay to Pittsburgh for SS Dick Groat and LHP Diomedes Olivo.

1966 Los Angeles LHP Sandy Koufax, age 30, retires from baseball due to an arthritic elbow. In his last five years with the Dodgers, Koufax is a dominating 111–34. He'll join the Hall of Fame in 1972.

1967 Gary DiSarcina b. Malden, MA.

1993 Montreal trades 2B Delino DeShields to Los Angeles for RHP Pedro Martinez.

1996 Abandoning the Cleveland Indians, free agent LF Albert Belle gets an early Thanksgiving present, signing the largest contract in baseball history—$55 million for five years with the Chicago White Sox.

1997 A day after being traded from Montreal to Boston, RHP Pedro Martinez signs the richest contract to date—six years for $75 million. In 1997, Martinez became the first right-hander since Walter Johnson in 1910 to strike out more than 300 batters (305) and have an ERA under 2.00 (1.90).

1998 Chicago Cubs RF Sammy Sosa,

who battled Mark McGwire for the home run race all season, wins his first NL MVP Award, edging the Cardinals' first baseman for top honors. Sosa, who batted .308 with 66 home runs and a major league-leading 158 RBIs, helped the Cubs into the postseason for the first time since 1989. McGwire finished second in the voting despite hitting an ML record 70 home runs during the regular season.

20

1869 Clark Griffith b. Stringtown, MO.
1945 Rick Monday b. Batesville, AR.
1945 Jay Johnstone b. Manchester, CT.
1967 Alex Arias b. New York, NY.
1968 Chuck Ricci b. Abington, PA.
1972 The Chicago Cubs trade OF Bill North to Oakland for RHP Bob Locker.
1997 Detroit trades 3B Phil Nevin and C Matt Walbeck to Anaheim for RHP Nick Skuse.
1997 Florida's last original expansion player, 1B Jeff Conine, is traded back to his original team, Kansas City for RHP Blaine Mull. The Marlins continue dismantling their world championship team by also trading LHP Ed Vosberg to San Diego for RHP Chris Clark.

21

1908 Paul Richards b. Waxahachie, TX.
1920 Stan Musial b. Donora, PA.
1941 Tom McCraw b. Malvern, AR.
1952 Billy Almon b. Providence, RI.
1962 Dick Schofield, Jr., b. Springfield, IL.
1962 Pittsburgh trades 1B Dick Stuart

and RHP Jack Lamabe to Boston for C Jim Pagliaroni and RHP Don Schwall.
1964 San Francisco trades OF Jose Cardenal to the Los Angeles Angels for C Jack Hiatt.
1967 Tripp Cromer b. Lake City, SC.
1967 Cincinnati trades OF Tommy Harper to Cleveland for RHP George Culver and 1B Fred Whitfield.
1968 Cincinnati trades SS Leo Cardenas to Minnesota for LHP Jim Merritt.
1969 Ken Griffey, Jr., b. Donora, PA.
1969 Cleveland trades OF Jose Cardenal to St. Louis for OF Vada Pinson.
1971 John Roper b. Southern Pines, NC.

22

1926 Lew Burdette b. Nitro, WV.
1934 The Chicago Cubs trade RHPs Guy Bush and Jim Weaver, and OF Babe Herman to Pittsburgh for LHP Larry French and OF Fred Lindstrom.
1943 Wade Blasingame b. Deming, NM.
1950 Greg Luzinski b. Chicago, IL.
1950 Lyman Bostock b. Birmingham, AL.
1958 Lee Guetterman b. Chattanooga, TN.
1965 Mike Benjamin b. Euclid, OH.
1967 Houston trades 3B Eddie Mathews to Detroit for RHP Fred Gladding.
1975 Cleveland trades OF Oscar Gamble to the New York Yankees for RHP Pat Dobson.

23

1910 Hal Schumacher b. Hinckley, NY.
1940 Luis Tiant b. Cuba.

1947 Tom Hall b. Thomasville, NC.
1969 Dave McCarty b. Houston, TX.
1976 Houston trades RHP Larry Dierker and INF Jerry DaVanon to St. Louis for C Joe Ferguson and OF Bob Detherage.

24

1911 Joe Medwick b. Carteret, NJ.
1930 Bob Friend b. Lafayette, IN.
1939 Jim Northrup b. Breckenridge, MI.
1948 Steve Yeager b. Huntington, WV.
1953 Walter Alston signs a one-year contract to manage the Brooklyn Dodgers. It's the first of 23 one-year contracts Alston will sign for the Dodgers, both in Brooklyn or Los Angeles. Alston will win seven pennants and four World Series titles in his term from 1954–76.
1962 Randy Velarde b. Midland, TX.
1967 Cal Eldred b. Cedar Rapids, IA.
1967 Al Martin b. West Covina, CA.
1967 Ben McDonald b. Baton Rouge, LA.
1968 Dave Hansen b. Long Beach, CA.
1993 Minnesota trades RHP Willie Banks to the Chicago Cubs for C Matt Walbeck and RHP Dave Stevens.

25

1914 Joe DiMaggio b. Martinez, CA.
1928 Ray Narleski b. Camden,NJ.
1944 Baseball commissioner Kenesaw Mountain Landis dies while in office at age 77. He had served as commissioner since being elected November 12, 1920.
1951 Bucky Dent b. Savannah, GA.
1966 Mark Whiten b. Pensacola, FL.

1972 Oakland trades OF Matty Alou to the New York Yankees for LHP Rob Gardner and INF Rich McKinney.
1981 Milwaukee Brewers RHP Rollie Fingers, already named the AL Cy Young Award winner, becomes the first relief pitcher to win the AL MVP as well. Fingers leads the AL in saves with 28, posting a 6–3 record with a paltry 1.04 ERA in 47 games.
1996 The Tampa Bay Devil Rays make Pennsylvania high school RHP Matt White the richest free agent signing in baseball history, agreeing to a reported $10.2 million contract. A first round draft pick of San Francisco in June, White was declared a free agent after the Giants failed to tender him a contract offer within the required 15 days.
1998 First baseman Mo Vaughn becomes the newest highest paid player in baseball, agreeing to a 6-year, $80 million deal with the Anaheim Angels. Vaughn, who batted .337 with 40 home runs and had 115 RBIs for the Boston Red Sox this season, averages $13.3 million per season with his new contract to put him ahead of the Mets' Mike Piazza.
1998 New York CF Bernie Williams, the AL batting champion at .339, agrees to stay with the Yankees, signing a seven-year, $87.5 million contract.

26

1866 Hugh Duffy b. Cranston, RI.
1909 Lefty Gomez b. Rodeo, CA.
1922 Ben Wade b. Morehead City, NC.
1938 Minnie Rojas b. Cuba.
1947 Richie Hebner b. Brighton, MA.
1947 Larry Gura b. Joliet, IL.

1948 Three days after passing away, unclaimed Hall of Fame OF Hack Wilson is finally given a funeral as NL President Ford Frick pays $350 for the coffin and arrangements.

1959 Mike Moore b. Eakly, OK.

1962 Los Angeles trades RHP Stan Williams to the New York Yankees for 1B Bill Skowron.

1962 Houston trades OF Roman Mejias to the Boston Red Sox for INF Pete Runnels.

1962 Baltimore trades C Gus Triandos and OF Whitey Herzog to Detroit for C Dick Brown.

1962 Chuck Finley b. Monroe, LA.

1963 The Kansas City A's trade 1B Norm Siebern to Baltimore for 1B Jim Gentile.

1969 Cincinnati trades OF Alex Johnson and SS Chico Ruiz to California for RHPs Pedro Borbon, Jim McGlothlin, and Vern Geishert.

1975 Boston Red Sox CF Fred Lynn becomes the first rookie MVP in baseball history. Lynn leads the AL in doubles (47), runs scored (103), and slugging average (.566), while also batting .331 with 21 home runs and 105 RBIs.

1986 The New York Yankees trade RHPs Doug Drabek, Logan Easley, and Brian Fisher to Pittsburgh for RHPs Rick Rhoden and Cecilio Guante, and LHP Pat Clements.

1996 Seattle trades LHP Sterling Hitchcock to San Diego for RHP Scott Sanders.

1996 Major league baseball owners ratify a collective bargaining agreement with the player's union, essentially ending four years of labor strife which included a 232-day strike that wiped out the last 7½ weeks of the 1994 season — including the World Series — and the first 3½ weeks of the 1995 season.

27

1884 Jack Kading b. Waukesha, WI.

1892 Joe Bush b. Brainerd, MN.

1939 Dave Giusti b. Senaca Falls, NY.

1941 New York Yankees CF Joe DiMaggio wins his second AL MVP Award by a slim 37-point margin over Boston Red Sox LF Ted Williams. DiMaggio led the league in RBIs with 125 and socked 30 home runs while batting .357 for the world champion Yankees, while Williams led the league in home runs with 37 and batted .406, the last player to reach the .400 hitter in history.

1947 New York Yankees CF Joe DiMaggio wins his third AL MVP award in the closest ballot in history — one vote over Boston Red Sox LF Ted Williams. Williams led the AL in home runs, runs scored, RBIs, walks, batting average, and slugging average, while DiMaggio only led the league in fielding percentage for the pennant winning Yankees. The occasion marks the second time that Williams captures the AL Triple Crown (1942 earlier) and fails to win the league MVP.

1951 The Chicago White Sox trade SS Joe DeMaestri, LHP Dick Littlefield, C Gus Niarhos, 1B Gordon Goldsberry, and OF Jim Rivera to the St. Louis Browns for RHP Al Widmar, C Sherm Lollar, and SS Tom Upton.

1958 Mike Scioscia b. Upper Darby, PA.

1961 Cleveland trades RHP Bobby Locke to the Chicago Cubs for INF Jerry Kindall.

1961 The Chicago White Sox trade OF Minnie Minoso to St. Louis for OF/1B Joe Cunningham.

1962 Cincinnati trades 2B Cookie Rojas to Philadelphia for RHP Jim Owens.

1962 Cleveland trades OF Ty Cline, OF Don Dillard, and RHP Frank Funk to Milwaukee for 1B Joe Adcock and LHP Jack Curtis.

1972 The New York Mets trade OF Tommie Agee to Houston for OF Rich Chiles and RHP Buddy Harris.

1972 The New York Yankees trade C John Ellis, OFs Rusty Torres and Charlie Spikes, and INF Jerry Kinney to Cleveland for 3B Graig Nettles and C Jerry Moses.

1974 Commissioner Bowie Kuhn suspends New York Yankees owner George Steinbrenner after he is convicted of illegal political campaign contributions.

1979 Montreal trades 2B Dave Cash to San Diego for SS Bill Almon and 1B/OF Dan Briggs.

1981 Detroit trades OF Steve Kemp to the Chicago White Sox for OF Chet Lemon.

1991 Cincinnati trades OF Eric Davis and RHP Kip Gross to Los Angeles for RHP Tim Belcher and RHP John Wetteland.

1996 The Anaheim Angels trade 1B J.T. Snow to San Francisco for LHP Allen Watson.

1997 Negro League star Walter Fenner "Buck" Leonard passes away at age 90.

28

1927 Pittsburgh trades OF Kiki Cuyler to the Chicago Cubs for 2B Sparky Adams and OF Pete Scott.

1953 Sixto Lezcano b. Puerto Rico.

1956 Brooklyn RHP Don Newcombe is named baseball's first Cy Young Award winner. Newcombe leads the Dodgers to the NL pennant after going a league best 27–7 during the regular season.

1958 Dave Righetti b. San Jose, CA.

1961 Philadelphia trades RHP John Buzhardt and INF Charley Smith to the Chicago White Sox for 1B Roy Sievers.

1962 Philadelphia trades OF Ted Savage and 1B Pancho Herrera to Pittsburgh for 3B Don Hoak.

1963 Walt Weiss b. Tuxedo, NY.

1964 John Burkett b. New Brighton, PA.

1965 Matt Williams b. Bishop, CA.

1967 Los Angeles trades C John Roseboro, RHP Bob Miller, and LHP Ron Perranoski to Minnesota for SS Zoilo Versailes and RHP Jim "Mudcat" Grant.

1967 Baltimore trades RHP Eddie Fisher to Cleveland for LHP John O'Donoghue.

1969 Pedro Astacio b. Dominican Republic.

1972 Los Angeles trades RHPs Bill Singer and Mike Strahler, INFs Bobby Valentine and Billy Grabarkewitz, and OF Frank Robinson to California for RHP Andy Messersmith and 3B Ken McMullen.

29

1922 Minnie Minosa b. Havana, Cuba.

1939 Dick McAuliffe b. Hartfort, CT.

1941 Bill Freehan b. Detroit, MI.

1950 Mike Easler b. Cleveland, OH.

1960 Howard Johnson b. Clearwater, FL.

1965 Philadelphia trades INF Ruben Amaro, Sr., to the New York Yankees for INF Phil Linz.

1966 The New York Yankees trade 3B Clete Boyer to Atlanta for OF Bill Robinson and RHP Chi Chi Olivo.

1966 Los Angeles trades OFs Tommy Davis and Derrell Griffith to the New York Mets for INF Ron Hunt and OF Jim Hickman.

1967 Bob Hamelin b. Elizabeth, NJ.

1967 California trades OF Jose Cardenal to Cleveland for INF-OF Chuck Hinton.

1967 Baltimore trades SS Luis Aparicio, OF Russ Snyder, and 1B John Matias to the Chicago White Sox for RHPs Bruce Howard and Roger Nelson, and INF Don Buford.

1969 Mariano Rivera b. Panama City, Panama.

1971 San Francisco trades RHP Gaylord Perry and SS Frank Duffy to Cleveland for LHP Sam McDowell.

1971 Houston trades OFs Cesar Geronimo and Ed Armbrister, 2B Joe Morgan, 3B Denis Menke, and RHP Jack Billingham to Cincinnati for 1B Lee May, 2B Tommy Helms, and INF Jim Stewart.

1971 Oakland trades OF Rick Monday to the Chicago Cubs for LHP Ken Holtzman.

1972 San Francisco trades OF Ken Henderson to the Chicago White Sox for RHPs Steve Stone and Tom Bradley.

1972 St. Louis trades OF Larry Hisle to Minnesota for RHP Wayne Granger and LHP John Cumberland.

30

1960 Bob Tewksbury b. Concord, NH.

1961 San Francisco trades RHPs Eddie Fisher, Dom Zanni, and Verle Tiefenthelir and 1B Bob Farley to the Chicago White Sox for LHP Billy Pierce and RHP Don Larsen.

1962 Bo Jackson b. Bessemer, AL.

1962 San Francisco trades OF Manny Mota and LHP Dick LeMay to Houston for INF Joey Amalfitano.

1964 Philadelphia trades INF-OF Danny Cater and SS Lee Elia to the Chicago White Sox for RHP Ray Herbert and 1B Jeoff Long.

1964 Cleveland trades 1B Bob Chance and INF Woody Held to Washington for INF-OF Chuck Hinton.

1966 Washinton trades OF Don Lock to Philadelphia for LHP Darold Knowles.

1967 Cincinnati trades RHP Sammy Ellis to California for RHPs Bill Kelso and Jorge Rubio.

1967 The Chicago Cubs trade INF Paul Popovich and OF Jim Williams to Los Angeles for OF Lou Johnson.

1969 Mark Lewis b. Hamilton, OH.

1970 The Chicago White Sox trade OF Ken Berry, RHP Billy Wynne, and INF Syd O'Brien to California for OF Jay Johnstone, RHP Tom Bradley, and C Tom Egan.

1970 The Chicago Cubs trade RHP Hoyt Wilhelm to Atlanta for 1B Hal Breeden.

1970 Baltimore trades RHP Moe Drabowski to St. Louis for SS Jerry DaVanon.

1971 Ray Durham b. Charlotte, NC.

1971 Minnesota trades SS Leo Cardenas to California for LHP Dave LaRoche.

1971 Ivan Rodriguez b. Puerto Rico.

1972 Baltimore trades 2B Davey Johnson, RHP Pat Dobson, RHP Roric Harrison, and C Johnny Oates to Atlanta for C Earl Williams and INF Duncan Taylor.

1972 Minnesota trades OF Cesar Tovar to Philadelphia for RHP Ken Sanders, LHP Ken Reynolds, and 1B Joe Lis.

1972 The Chicago Cubs trade RHP Bill Hands, RHP Joe Decker, and P Bob Maneeley to Minnesota for LHP Dave LaRoche.

1998 The Arizona Diamondbacks make LHP Randy Johnson baseball's highest paid pitcher and the game's second highest paid player, inking the 6'10" strikeout leader to a four-year, $52.4

million contract. Johnson's $13.1 average salary is exceeded only by new Anaheim Angels 1B Mo Vaughn, who averages $13.3 million in a recently signed six-year, $80 million deal. Between Seattle and Houston in 1998, Johnson led the major leagues with 329 strikeouts.

1999 Major league umpires overwhelmingly vote to oust union leader Richie Phillips, ending his 21-year reign, and form a new union that includes dissident umpires that lost their jobs in September.

1999 The first merger of a baseball and basketball team wins final approval, clearing the way for the New York Yankees and New Jersey Nets to join business operations. Baseball owners unanimously approve the deal, which has already been approved by the NBA.

DECEMBER

1

1882 Ed Reulbach b. Detroit, MI.
1911 Walter Alston b. Venice, OH.
1912 Cookie Lavagetto b. Oakland, CA.
1917 Marty Marion b. Richburg, SC.
1925 Cal McLish b. Anadarko, OK.
1948 George Foster b. Tuscaloosa, AL.
1954 The Baltimore Orioles and the New York Yankees complete the biggest trade in major league history—17 players—as 10 players go to Baltimore and seven head to New York. The trade begins November 18th with RHPs Don Larsen and Bob Turley being the principal Yankees acquisitions.
1963 Greg W. Harris b. Greensboro, NC.
1965 San Francisco trades OF Matty Alou to Pittsburgh for LHP Joe Gibbon and C Ozzie Virgil.
1965 Cleveland trades C Phil Roof to the Kansas City A's for OF Jim Landis.
1966 Pittsburgh trades 3B Bob Bailey and SS Gene Michael to Los Angeles for SS Maury Wills.
1966 Greg McMichael b. Knoxville, TN.
1966 Larry Walker b. Maple Ridge, British Columbia.
1967 Reggie Sanders b. Florence, SC.
1970 Boston trades SS Luis Alvarado and 2B Mike Andrews to the Chicago White Sox for SS Luis Aparicio.
1970 Atlanta trades 3B Bob Aspromonte to the New York Mets for RHP Ron Herbel.

1970 Baltimore trades SS Enzo Hernandez, RHP Tom Phoebus, RHP Fred Beene, and RHP Al Severinsen to San Diego for RHP Pat Dobson and RHP Tom Dukes.
1972 Oakland trades 1B Mike Epstein to Texas for RHP Horacio Pena.
1972 Philadelphia trades OF Roger Freed and Oscar Gamble to Cleveland for OF Del Unser and INF Terry Wedgewood.
1972 Cincinnati trades OF Hal McRae and RHP Wayne Simpson to Kansas City for RHP Roger Nelson and OF Richie Scheinblum.
1997 Cleveland trades 3B Matt Williams to Arizona for 3B Travis Fryman and LHP Tom Martin.
1998 In a three-team trade, the New York Mets trade C Todd Hundley and RHP Arnold Gooch to Los Angeles for C Charles Johnson and OF Roger Cedeno. The Mets then trade Johnson to Baltimore for RHP Armando Benitez.
1998 The Baltimore Orioles make OF Albert Belle the highest paid player in club history, signing the former Chicago White Sox free agent to a five-year, $65 million deal.

2

1946 Pedro Borbon b. Dominican Republic.
1948 Wayne Simpson b. Los Angeles, CA.

1958 Cleveland trades 1B Vic Wertz and OF Gary Geiger to Boston for OF Jimmy Piersall.

1963 The Los Angeles Angels trade OF Leon Wagner to Cleveland for 1B Joe Adcock and RHP Barry Latman.

1965 San Francisco trades C Randy Hundley and RHP Bill Hands to the Chicago Cubs for RHP Lindy McDaniel and OF Don Landrum.

1966 Minnesota trades OF Jimmie Hall, 1B Don Mincher, and RHP Pete Cimino to California for RHP Dean Chance and SS Jackie Hernandez.

1968 Darryl Kile b. Garden Grove, CA.

1970 Kansas City trades SS Jackie Hernandez, RHP Bob Johnson, and C Jim Campanis to Pittsburgh for RHP Bruce Dal Canton, C Jerry May, and SS Freddie Patek.

1971 Los Angeles trades 1B Richie Allen to the Chicago White Sox for LHP Tommy John and INF Steve Huntz.

1971 Texas trades C Paul Casanova to Atlanta for C Hal King.

1971 Cleveland trades OF Roy Foster, C Ken Suarez, RHP Rich Hand, and LHP Mike Paul to Texas for OF Del Unser, and LHPs Gary Jones, Dennis Riddleberger, and Terry Ley.

1971 Houston trades 1B John Mayberry to Kansas City for LHP Lance Clemons and RHP Jim York.

1971 The Chicago White Sox trade INF Rich McKinney to the New York Yankees for RHP Stan Bahnsen.

1971 Baltimore trades OF Frank Robinson and LHP Pete Richert to Los Angeles for RHP Doyle Alexander, LHP Bob O'Brien, C Sergio Robles, and 1B Royle Stillman.

1974 Boston trades OF Tommy Harper to California for INF Bob Heise.

1990 Toronto trades INF Luis Sojo and OF Junior Felix to California for OF Devon White and RHP Willie Fraser.

1993 Houston trades RHP Jeff Juden and RHP Doug Jones to Philadelphia for LHP Mitch Williams.

3

1912 Charlie Wagner b. Reading, PA.

1942 New York Yankees CF Joe DiMaggio enlists in the United States Army Air Corps. He'll serve three years before returning to the Yankees in 1946.

1947 Wayne Garrett b. Brooksville, FL.

1957 The Chicago White Sox trade OF Larry Doby, LHP Jack Harshman, RHP Russ Heman, and 1B Jim Marshall to the Baltimore Orioles for OF Tito Francona, RHP Ray Moore, and INF Billy Goodman.

1960 San Francisco trades LHP Johnny Antonelli and OF Willie Kirkland to Cleveland for OF Harvey Kuenn.

1963 Damon Berryhill b. South Laguna, CA.

1963 San Francisco trades OF Felipe Alou, C Ed Bailey, LHP Billy Hoeft, and INF Ernie Bowman to Milwaukee for C Del Crandall, LHP Bob Hendley, and RHP Bob Shaw.

1964 Darryl Hamilton b. Baton Rouge, LA.

1964 The Los Angeles Angels trade LHP Bo Belinsky to Philadelphia for LHP Rudy May and 1B Costen Shockley.

1966 Minnesota trades 2B Bernie Allen and RHP Camilo Pascual to Washington for RHP Ron Kline.

1969 Atlanta trades OF Felipe Alou to Oakland for RHP Jim Nash.

1969 Kansas City trades 3B Joe Foy to the New York Mets for OF Amos Otis and RHP Bob Johnson.

1971 Milwaukee trades OF Jose Cardenal to the Chicago Cubs for OF Brock Davis, RHP Jim Colborn, and LHP Earl Stephenson.

1971 San Diego trades LHP Dave Roberts to Houston for INF Derrel Thomas, RHP Bill Grief, and LHP Mark Schaeffer.

1971 Cincinnati trades RHP Wayne Granger to Minnesota for LHP Tom Hall.

1974 The Chicago White Sox trade 1B Richie Allen to Atlanta for C Jim Essian.

1974 Baltimore trades 1B Enos Cabell and 2B Rob Andrews to Houston for 1B Lee May and OF Jay Schlueter.

4

1868 Jesse Burkett b. Wheeling, WV.

1890 Bob Shawkey b. Brookville, PA.

1930 Harvey Kuenn b. Milwaukee, WI.

1936 Pittsburgh trades INF Cookie Lavagetto and LHP Ralph Birkofer to Brooklyn for LHP Ed Brandt.

1957 The Chicago White Sox trade OF Minnie Minoso and 3B Fred Hatfield to Cleveland for RHP Early Wynn and OF Al Smith.

1957 Lee Smith b. Jamestown, LA.

1958 Los Angeles trades OF Gino Cimoli to St. Louis for OF Wally Moon and RHP Phil Paine.

1963 Philadelphia trades OF Don Demeter and RHP Jack Hamilton to Detroit for RHP Jim Bunning and C Gus Triandos.

1964 Los Angeles trades OF Frank Howard, 3B Ken McMullen, RHP Phil Ortega, and RHP Pete Richert to Washington for LHP Claude Osteen and INF John Kennedy.

1968 Houston trades 3B Bob Aspromonte to Atlanta for INF Marty Martinez.

1968 Baltimore trades OF Curt Blefary and INF John Mason to Houston for LHP Mike Cuellar, SS Enzo Hernandez, and INF Elijah Johnson.

1968 The New York Yankees trade OF Andy Kosco to Los Angeles for LHP Mike Kekich.

1969 Houston trades OF Curt Blefary to the New York Yankees for 1B Joe Pepitone.

1969 Detroit trades RHP Pat Dobson and INF David Campbell to San Diego for RHP Joe Niekro.

1969 The Seattle Pilots trade LHP George Brunet to Washington for RHP David Baldwin.

1974 Baltimore trades LHP Dave McNally, OF Rich Coggins, and P Bill Kirkpatrick to Montreal for OF Ken Singleton and RHP Mike Torrez.

1984 The Chicago Cubs trade OF Henry Cotto, C Ron Hassey, RHP Rich Bordi, and RHP Porfi Altamirano to the New York Yankees for LHP Ray Fontenot and OF Brian Dayett.

1988 Baltimore trades 1B Eddie Murray to Los Angeles for RHP Brian Holton, RHP Ken Howell, and SS Juan Bell.

5

1856 The *New York Mercury* refers to baseball for the first time as "the National Pastime."

1941 Detroit 1B Hank Greenberg is released by the U.S Army because at 30 he is beyond draft age. Two days later, the Japanese bomb Pearl Harbor and Greenberg reenlists in the Army Air

Corps. He'll miss 3½ seasons before coming back to Detroit in 1945. In 1946, he'll club 44 homers to lead the AL for a fourth time.

1951 Shoeless Joe Jackson dies in Greenville, SC., age 62, 10 days before he was supposed to appear on the Ed Sullivan Show. Banned from baseball for his involvement in the 1919 Black Sox scandal, Jackson left the game after the 1920 season with the third highest lifetime batting average, .356.

1957 Cincinnati trades OF Curt Flood and OF Joe Taylor to St. Louis for RHPs Willard Schmidt, Marty Kutyna, and Ted Wieand.

1964 Gene Harris b. Sebring, FL.

1964 Cincinnati trades INF Cesar Tovar to Minnesota for LHP Gerry Arrigo.

1969 San Francisco trades C Bob Barton, RHP Ron Herbel, and 3B Bobby Etheridge to San Diego for RHP Frank Reberger.

1969 Oakland trades 1B Danny Cater and INF Ossie Chavarria to the New York Yankees for LHP Al Downing and C Frank Fernandez.

1972 Cliff Floyd b. Chicago, IL.

1973 Kansas City trades INF Kurt Bevacqua, C Ed Kirkpatrick, and 1B Winston Cole to Pittsburgh for RHP Nelson Briles and INF Fernando Gonzalez.

1973 Los Angeles trades OF Willie Davis to Montreal for RHP Mike Marshall.

1973 St. Louis trades OF Tommie Agee to Los Angeles for LHP Pete Richert.

1973 When the Chicago Cubs try to trade 3B Ron Santo to the California Angels, he becomes the first ML player to veto a trade based on a new baseball rule that allows a 10-year veteran who has spent the last five years with the same team to nix a deal. The following week, Santo agrees to a trade to Chicago's South Side, where he will play his final season with the White Sox.

1974 Montreal trades OF Willie Davis to Texas for INF Pete Mackanin and RHP Don Stanhouse.

1974 Milwaukee trades LHP Clyde Wright to Texas for RHP Pete Broberg.

1977 California trades OFs Bobby Bonds and Thad Bosley and RHP Richard Dotson to the Chicago White Sox for RHPs Chris Knapp and Dave Frost and OF Brian Downing.

1984 Oakland trades LF Rickey Henderson and RHP Bert Bradley to the New York Yankees for RHPs Jay Howell, Jose Rijo, Eric Plunk, and Tim Birtsas, and OF Stan Javier.

1988 The Chicago Cubs trade 1B Rafael Palmeiro, and LHPs Jamie Moyer and Drew Hall to Texas for LHPs Mitch Williams, Paul Kilgus, and Steve Wilson, INFs Curtis Wilkerson and Luis Benitez, and OF Pablo Delgado.

1990 San Diego trades LF Joe Carter and 2B Roberto Alomar to Toronto for 1B Fred McGriff and SS Tony Fernandez.

6

1899 Jocko Conlan b. Chicago, IL.

1903 Tony Lazzeri b. San Francisco, CA.

1945 Larry Bowa b. Sacramento, CA.

1946 Baseball owners decide to return the All-Star vote for the starting lineups to the fans.

1957 Steve Bedrosian b. Methevn, MA.

1959 The Chicago White Sox trade 1B Norm Cash, C John Romano and 3B John Phillips to Cleveland for OF Minnie Minoso, C Dick Brown, LHP Don Ferrarese, and P Wilbur Striker.

1959 The Chicago Cubs trade OFs Lou Jackson and Lee Walls and LHP Bill Henry to Cincinnati for INF Frank Thomas.

1960 Baseball's first expansion teams — the AL Los Angeles Angels and the AL Washington Senators — select their rosters for the 1961 season during the first-ever expansion draft. The Angels first select New York Yankees RHP Eli Grba, while the Senators select New York Yankees LHP Bobby Shantz with their first pick. Only AL teams have their rosters raided.

1963 Lance Blankenship b. Portland, OR.

1964 Kevin Campbell b. Marianna, AR.

1965 Baltimore trades LHP Darold Knowles and OF Jackie Brandt to Philadelphia for RHP Jack Baldschun.

1967 Kevin Appier b. Lancaster, CA.

1968 Commissioner William Eckert is fired by the owners at the conclusion of the season and replaced by Wall Street lawyer Bowie Kuhn.

1968 Cincinnati trades C Don Pavletich and LHP Don Secrist to the Chicago White Sox for RHP Jack Fisher.

1969 Oakland trades 2B Ted Kubiak and RHP George Lauzerique to Milwaukee for RHP Diego Segui and SS Ray Oyler.

1971 Cleveland trades OF Ted Uhlaender to Cincinnati for RHP Milt Wilcox.

1973 The Chicago Cubs trade C Randy Hundley to Minnesota for C George Mitterwald.

1974 San Francisco trades 2B Tito Fuentes to San Diego for RHP Butch Metzger and INF Derrel Thomas.

1976 Milwaukee trades OF Bernie Carbo and 1B George Scott to Boston for 1B Cecil Cooper.

1976 Milwaukee trades RHP Jim Colborn and C Darrell Porter to Kansas City for OF Jim Wohlford, C Jamie Quirk, and LHP Bob McClure.

1976 Toronto trades DH Rico Carty to Cleveland for OF John Lowenstein and C Rick Cerone.

1979 Kansas City trades OF Al Cowens, INF Todd Cruz, and RHP Craig Eaton to California for 1B Willie Aikens and INF Rance Mulliniks.

1979 Atlanta trades RHP Adrian Devine and INF Pepe Frias to Texas for RHP Doyle Alexander, INF Larvell Blanks, and $50,000.

1988 Texas trades OF Oddibe McDowell, 1B Pete O'Brien, and INF Jerry Browne to Cleveland for INF Julio Franco.

1989 San Diego trades C Sandy Alomar, Jr., OF Chris James, and 3B Carlos Baerga to Cleveland for OF Joe Carter.

1992 California trades LHP Jim Abbott to the New York Yankees for 1B J.T. Snow, RHP Russ Springer and LHP Jerry Nielsen.

1995 Seattle trades 1B Tino Martinez, RHP Jeff Nelson, and RHP Jim Mercir to the New York Yankees for LHP Sterling Hitchcock and 3B Russ Davis.

7

1935 Don Cardwell b. Winston-Salem, NC.

1942 Alex Johnson b. Helena, AR.

1947 Johnny Bench b. Oklahoma City, OK.

1950 Rich Coggins b. Indianapolis, IN.

1951 Paul Dade b. Seattle, WA.

1960 The Milwaukee Braves trade OF Billy Bruton, C Dick Brown, 2B Chuck Cottier, and RHP Terry Fox to Detroit for 2B Frank Bolling and OF Neil Chrisley.

1966 Philadelphia trades RHP Ray Culp to the Chicago Cubs for LHP Dick Ellsworth.

1967 Tino Martinez b. Tampa, FL.

1967 Atlanta trades C Bobby Cox to the New York Yankees for C Bob Tillman and LHP Dale Roberts.

1973 Kansas City trades OF Lou Piniella and RHP Ken Wright to the New York Yankees for RHP Lindy McDaniel.

1973 Boston trades RHPs Lynn McGlothen and Mike Garman, and LHP John Curtis to St. Louis for RHPs Reggie Cleveland and Diego Segui and 3B Terry Hughes.

1979 Cleveland trades OF Bobby Bonds to St. Louis for OF Jerry Mumphrey and RHP John Denny.

1979 Detroit trades OF Ron LeFlore to Montreal for LHP Dan Schatzeder.

1983 Cleveland trades OF Gorman Thomas and 2B Jack Perconte to Seattle for 2B Tony Bernazard.

1984 The Detroit Tigers trade 3B Howard Johnson to the New York Mets for RHP Walt Terrell.

8

1914 Philadelphia A's manager Connie Mack continues his housecleaning, selling All-Star 2B Eddie Collins to the Chicago White Sox for $50,000.

1941 Ed Brinkman b. Cincinnati, OH.

1941 The day after the Japanese bomb Pearl Harbor, Cleveland RHP Bob Feller enlists in the Navy to head the list of 340 ML players and over 3,000 minor leaguers to go to war.

1947 Pittsburgh trades SS Billy Cox, LHP Preacher Roe, and 2B Gene Mauch to Brooklyn for OF Dixie Walker, RHP Hal Gregg, and LHP Vic Lombardi.

1950 Tim Foli b. Culver City, CA.

1966 The New York Yankees trade OF Roger Maris to St. Louis for 3B Charley Smith.

1968 Mike Mussina b. Williamsport, PA.

1975 San Francisco trades LHP Pete Falcone to St. Louis for 3B Ken Reitz.

1977 Boston trades RHP Don Aase to California for 2B Jerry Remy.

1977 St. Louis trades OF Hector Cruz and C Dave Rader to the Chicago Cubs for OF Jerry Morales and C Steve Swisher.

1978 Cleveland trades 3B Buddy Bell to Texas for 3B Toby Harrah.

1987 Cincinnati trades OF Dave Parker to Oakland for RHP Jose Rijo.

1987 The Chicago Cubs trade RHP Lee Smith to Boston for RHPs Al Nipper and Calvin Schiraldi.

1991 San Diego trades 2B Bip Roberts and OF Craig Pueschner to Cincinnati for LHP Randy Myers.

1991 California trades LHP Kyle Abbott and OF Ruben Amaro, Jr., to Philadelphia for OF Von Hayes.

1992 California trades INF Luis Sojo to Toronto for 3B Kelly Gruber.

1997 Cleveland trades OF Marquis Grissom and RHP Jeff Juden to Milwaukee for RHP Ben McDonald, RHP Mike Fetters, and LHP Ron Villone. The Indians then trade Fetters to Oakland for RHP Steve Karsay.

9

1902 The AL announces plans to locate a franchise in New York — the Highlanders — for the 1903 season.

1936 AL owners grant the Browns permission to play night baseball in St. Louis, and also rule that players must have at least 400 at-bats to qualify for a batting championship.

1941 Darold Knowles b. Brunswick, MO.

1943 Jim Merritt b. Altadena, CA.

1948 George "Doc" Medich b. Aliquippa, PA.

1952 Jim Riggleman b. Fort Dix, NJ.

1959 Pittsburgh trades RHP Dick Hall to the Kansas City A's for INF Ken Hamlin and C Hal Smith.

1959 The Chicago White Sox trade OF Johnny Callison to Philadelphia for 3B Gene Freese.

1960 Juan Samuel b. Dominican Republic.

1965 Branch Rickey passes away, at age 83, in Columbia, MO.

1965 Cincinnati trades OF Frank Robinson to Baltimore for OF Dick Simpson, and RHPs Milt Pappas and Jack Baldschun.

1971 Todd Van Poppel b. Hinsdale, IL.

1976 Texas trades OF Jeff Burroughs to Atlanta for OF Ken Henderson, OF Davey May, RHP Carl Morton, LHP Roger Moret, RHP Adrian Devine, and $250,000.

1977 Seattle trades OF Dave Collins to Cincinnati for LHP Shane Rawley.

1980 St. Louis trades 1B Leon Durham, 3B Ken Reitz, and OF Ty Waller to the Chicago Cubs for RHP Bruce Sutter.

1982 The New York Yankees trade 1B Fred McGriff, OF Dave Collins, RHP Mike Morgan and cash to Toronto for OF Tom Dodd and RHP Dale Murray.

1982 Cleveland trades OF Von Hayes to Philadelphia for RHP Jay Baller, 2B Manny Trillo, OF George Vukovich, SS Julio Franco, and C Jerry Willard.

1982 Seattle trades RHP Rich Bordi to the Chicago Cubs for OF Steve Henderson.

1987 Baltimore trades RHP Ken Dixon to Seattle for RHP Mike Morgan.

1992 Boston trades OF Phil Plantier to San Diego for RHP Jose Melendez.

1994 Boston trades OF Otis Nixon and 3B Luis Ortiz to Texas for OF Jose Canseco.

10

1935 The Philadelphia A's trade 1B Jimmie Foxx to the Boston Red Sox for two players and $150,000. Philadelphia owner/manager Connie Mack continues to sell off his stars from his 1929-31 pennant-winning teams.

1944 Steve Renko b. Kansas City, KS.

1951 Cincinnati trades C Smoky Burgess, RHP Howie Fox, and 2B Connie Ryan to Philadelphia for C Andy Seminick, INF Eddie Pellagrini, 1B Dick Sisler, and LHP Niles Jordan.

1960 Paul Assenmacher b. Allen Park, MI.

1963 Doug Henry b. Sacramento, CA.

1965 The New York Yankees trade RHP Pete Mikkelsen to Pittsburgh for RHP Bob Friend.

1966 Norberto Martin b. Dominican Republic.

1966 Mel Rojas b. Dominican Republic.

1971 California trades SS Jim Fregosi to the New York Mets for RHP Nolan Ryan, RHP Don Rose, OF Lee Stanton, and C Francisco Estrada.

1972 The AL votes unanimously to adopt the Designated Hitter for a three-year experimental basis. The NL decides against the rule.

1975 Philadelphia trades OF Mike Anderson to St. Louis for RHP Ron Reed.

1975 Phiadelphia trades OF Alan Bannister, RHP Dick Ruthven, and RHP Roy Thomas to the Chicago White Sox for LHP Jim Kaat and INF Mike Buskey.

1976 The Chicago White Sox trade RHP Rich Gossage and LHP Terry Forster to Pittsburgh for OF Richie Zisk and RHP Silvio Martinez.

1980 The Boston Red Sox trade SS Rick Burleson and 3B Butch Hobson to California for 3B Carney Lansford, OF Rick Miller, and RHP Mark Clear.

1984 Montreal trades C Gary Carter to the New York Mets for C Mike Fitzgerald, OF Herm Winningham, 3B Hubie Brooks, and RHP Floyd Youmans.

1985 Atlanta trades OF Milt Thompson and RHP Steve Bedrosian to Philadelphia for C Ozzie Virgil and RHP Pete Smith.

1986 Los Angeles trades 1B Greg Brock to Milwaukee for RHPs Tim Leary and Tim Crews.

1991 Houston trades CF Kenny Lofton and INF Dave Rhode to Cleveland for C Ed Taubensee and RHP Willie Blair.

1991 The New York Mets trade 3B Hubie Brooks to California for OF Dave Gallagher.

1997 Boston RHP Pedro Martinez signs the largest contract to date, agreeing to a $75 million, six-year deal.

11

1854 Charles "Old Hoss" Radbourn b. Rochester, NY.

1887 Fred Toney b. Nashville, TN.

1914 Bill Nicholson b. Chestertown, MD.

1917 The Philadelphia Phillies trade RHP Grover Cleveland Alexander and C Bill Killefer to the Chicago Cubs for RHP Mike Prendergast and C Pickles Dillhoefer.

1930 Major league officials grant the Baseball Writers' Association of America permission to conduct future MVP balloting — a practice that will continue without interruption.

1951 New York Yankees CF Joe DiMaggio retires after 13 years — 10 of which ended in a World Series — and a career .325 batting average. He'll enter the Hall of Fame in 1955.

1952 Rob Andrews b. Santa Monica, CA.

1959 The Kansas City A's trade OF Roger Maris, 1B Kent Hadley, and SS Joe DeMaestri to the New York Yankees for RHP Don Larsen, 1B Marv Throneberry, OF Norm Siebern, and OF Hank Bauer.

1961 Mike Henneman b. St. Charles, MO.

1964 Thomas Howard b. Middletown, OH.

1965 Jay Bell b. Eglin AFB, FL.

1968 Derek Bell b. Tampa, FL.

1968 California trades C Ed Kirkpatrick and C Dennis Paepke to Kansas City for RHP Hoyt Wilhelm.

1969 Minnesota trades 3B Graig Nettles, RHP Dean Chance, RHP Bob Miller, and OF Ted Uhlaender to Cleveland for RHP Luis Tiant and RHP Stan Williams.

1970 Cleveland trades C Duke Sims to Los Angeles for RHP Alan Foster and RHP Ray Lamb.

1972 Frank Rodriguez b. Brooklyn, NY.

1973 The Chicago Cubs trade 3B Ron Santo to the Chicago White Sox for RHP Steve Stone, LHPs Ken Frailing and Jim Kremmel, and C Steve Swisher.

1975 The Chicago White Sox trade 3B Bill Melton and RHP Steve Dunning to California for OF Morris Nettles and 1B Jim Spencer.

1975 The New York Yankees trade OF Bobby Bonds to California for OF Mickey Rivers and RHP Ed Figueroa.

1975 The New York Yankees trade RHP Doc Medich to Pittsburgh for 2B Willie Randolph, LHP Ken Brett, and RHP Dock Ellis.

1975 Cleveland trades C John Ellis to Texas for RHP Stan Thomas and C Ron Pruitt.

1981 Pittsburgh trades 1B Dorian Boyland to San Francisco for RHP Tom Griffin.

1987 In a three team, eight player trade, the New York Mets send LHP Jesse Orosco to Oakland. The A's then trade Orosco, SS Alfredo Griffin, and RHP Jay Howell to Los Angeles for RHP Bob Welch, LHP Matt Young, and LHP Jack Savage. Oakland then trades Savage, RHP Wally Whitehurst, and RHP Kevin Tapani to the Mets.

1991 The New York Mets trade INF Gregg Jefferies, 2B Keith Miller, and OF Kevin McReynolds to Kansas City for RHP Bret Saberhagen and INF Bill Pecota.

1991 San Francisco trades OF Kevin Mitchell and LHP Mike Remlinger to Seattle for RHP Mike Jackson, RHP Bill Swift, and RHP Dave Burba.

1991 Cincinnati trades RHP John Wetteland and RHP Bill Risley to Montreal for OF Dave Martinez, SS Willie Greene, and LHP Scott Ruskin.

1991 Kansas City trades RHP Storm Davis to Baltimore for C Bob Melvin.

1999 Boston trades OF Damon Buford to the Chicago Cubs for SS Manny Alexander.

12

1908 The New York Giants trade C Roger Bresnahan to the St. Louis Cardinals for C Admiral Schlei, RHP Bugs Raymond, and OF Red Murray.

1930 Baseball changes two rules: the sacrifice fly is eliminated, and balls bouncing into the stands are classified as ground-rule doubles instead of home runs.

1933 The Philadelphia A's trade C Mickey Cochrane to Detroit for C Johnny Pasek and $100,000.

1940 Tom Brown b. Laureldale, PA.

1945 Ralph Garr b. Ruston, LA.

1950 Gorman Thomas b. Charleston, SC.

1969 The New York Mets trade OF Jim Gosger and INF Bob Heise to San Francisco for LHP Ray Sadecki and OF Dave Marshall.

1969 The Chicago White Sox trade C Don Pavletich and LHP Gary Peters to Boston for P Billy Farmer and INF Syd O'Brien.

1969 Boston trades INF Dalton Jones to Detroit for SS Tom Matchick.

1975 Houston trades 2B Tommy Helms to Pittsburgh for 3B Art Howe.

1975 The New York Mets trade OF Gene Clines to Texas for OF Joe Lovitto.

1975 Cincinnati trades SS Darrel Chaney to Atlanta for OF Mike Lum.

1975 St. Louis trades OF Buddy Bradford and RHP Greg Terlecky to the Chicago White Sox for INF Lee Richard.

1975 Montreal trades 3B Bob Bailey to Cincinnati for RHP Clay Kirby.

1975 Detroit trades OF Bob Baldwin and LHP Mickey Lolich to the New York Mets for OF Rusty Staub and LHP Bill Laxton.

1975 Atlanta INF Larvell Blanks is traded twice in the same day. The Braves send him and OF Ralph Garr to the Chicago White Sox for OF Ken Henderson, RHP Dick Ruthven, and P Dan Osborn. Blanks is then traded from Chicago to Cleveland for 2B Jack Brohamer.

1980 St. Louis trades RHPs Rollie

Fingers and Pete Vukovich and C Ted Simmons to Milwaukee for OFs Sixto Lezcano and David Green, RHP Lary Sorensen, and LHP Dave LaPoint.

1980 Seattle trades LHP Rick Honeycutt, C Larry Cox, OF Willie Horton, OF Leon Roberts, and SS Mario Mendoza to Texas for OF Richie Zisk, SS Rick Auerbach, RHP Brian Allard, RHP Ken Clay, LHP Jerry Don Gleaton, and RHP Steve Finch.

1990 Texas trades 3B Scott Coolbaugh to San Diego for C Mark Parent.

1997 The New York Mets trade OF Alex Ochoa to Minnesota for OF Richie Becker.

1997 Montreal trades OF Henry Rodriguez to the Chicago Cubs for RHP Miguel Batista.

1998 The Los Angeles Dodgers make RHP Kevin Brown baseball's first $100 million player, inking the former San Diego Padres star to a whopping $105 million contract over seven years, an average of $15 million per season.

13

1923 Larry Doby b. Camden, SC.

1926 Carl Erskine b. Anderson, IN.

1928 NL president John Heydler, contending fans are tired of watching weak-hitting pitchers try to bat, proposes a designated hitter rule that is voted down at the annual winter meetings. Forty-five years later, in 1973, the DH becomes a reality in the AL.

1932 Six months after being traded by St. Louis to Washington, the Senators return RHP Dick Coffman to the Browns for the same player they had earlier dealt away, LHP Carl Fischer.

1935 Lindy McDaniel b. Hollis, OK.

1956 Brooklyn trades INF Jackie Robinson to the rival New York Giants for LHP Dick Littlefield, but the trade is cancelled when Robinson opts to retire instead.

1956 Dale Berra b. Ridgewood, NJ.

1943 Ferguson Jenkins b. Ontario, Canada.

1963 The Chicago Cubs trade LHP Jim Brewer and C Cuno Barrigan to Los Angeles for LHP Dick Scott.

1966 Washington trades LHP Mike McCormick to San Francisco for RHP Bob Priddy and OF Cap Peterson.

14

1889 Lefty Tyler b. Derry, NH.

1925 Sam "Toothpick" Jones b. Stewartsville, OH.

1938 The NL grants Cincinnati, baseball's first professional team, permission to follow tradition by hosting the new season's opening contest.

1948 Washington trades RHP Early Wynn and 1B Mickey Vernon to Cleveland for RHPs Joe Haynes and Eddie Klieman, and 1B Eddie Robinson.

1948 The Philadelphia Phillies trade RHP Monk Dubiel and RHP Dutch Leonard to the Chicago Cubs for 1B Eddie Waitkus and RHP Hank Borowy. Waitkus is shot in a Chicago hotel room by an infatuated teenager when the Phillies return to Wrigley Field the next summer.

1949 Bill Buckner b. Vallejo, CA.

1949 The Boston Braves trade SS Alvin Dark and 2B Eddie Stanky to the New York Giants for OF Sid Gordon, SS Buddy Kerr, OF Willard Marshall and RHP Red Webb.

1965 Craig Biggio b. Smithtown, NY.

1965 Ken Hill b. Lynn, MA.

1966 San Francisco trades OF Len Gabrielson to California for 1B Norm Siebern.

1969 Scott Hatteberg b. Salem, OR.

1969 Dave Nilsson b. Brisbane, Queensland, Australia.

1982 Philadelphia trades LHP Mark Davis, RHP Mike Krukow, and OF Charles Penigar to San Francisco for 2B Joe Morgan and LHP Al Holland.

1994 The Chicago White Sox trade RHP Jack McDowell to the New York Yankees for LHP Keith Heberling and LF Lyle Mouton.

1994 Cincinnati trades INF-OF Tim Costo to Cleveland for SS Mark Lewis.

1995 San Francisco trades SS Royce Clayton and 2B Chris Wimmer to St. Louis for LHP Allen Watson, LHP Doug Creek, and RHP Rich DeLucia.

15

1900 The New York Giants trade RHP Amos Rusie to Cincinnati for RHP Christy Mathewson. Rusie will will lose his only decision in 1901 after 243 wins over a 10-year career, while Mathewson will win 372 of his career 373 victories (third best all-time) with the Giants over the next 17 years before returning to the Reds in 1916.

1920 Brooklyn trades LHP Rube Marquardt to Cincinnati for LHP Dutch Ruether.

1929 Ray Herbert b. Detroit, MI.

1944 Stan Bahnsen b. Council Bluffs, IA.

1944 Jim Leyland b. Toledo, OH.

1946 Art Howe b. Pittsburgh, PA.

1948 Doug Rau b. Columbus, TX.

1959 San Francisco trades OF Leon Wagner and INF Daryl Spencer to St. Louis for 2B Don Blasingame.

1960 Milwaukee trades LHP Juan Pizzaro and RHP Joey Jay to Cincinnati for SS Roy McMillan. The Reds then trade Pizzaro to the Chicago White Sox with RHP Cal McLish for 3B Gene Freese.

1961 William "Dummy" Hoy, the 14-year ML outfielder with a hearing deficiency which forced umpires to create hand signals, dies at age 99.

1962 Baltimore trades RHP Jack Fisher, LHP Billy Hoeft, and C Jimmie Coker to San Francisco for LHP Mike McCormick, RHP Stu Miller, and C John Orsino.

1965 Los Angeles trades INF Dick Tracewski to Detroit for RHP Phil Regan.

1966 The Chicago White Sox trade OF Floyd Robinson to Cincinnati for LHP Jim O'Toole.

1967 Mo Vaughn b. Norwalk, CT.

1967 Boston trades C Mike Ryan to Philadelphia for LHP Dick Ellsworth and C Gene Oliver.

1967 The New York Mets trade OF Tommy Davis, RHP Jack Fisher, RHP Billy Wynne, and C Buddy Booker to the Chicago White Sox for OF Tommie Agee and INF Al Weis.

1969 The Chicago White Sox trade OF Angel Bravo to Cincinnati for LHP Jerry Arrigo.

1970 Rick Helling b. Devils Lake, ND.

1970 Cincinnati trades RHP Jim Maloney to California for LHP Greg Garrett.

1974 Oakland RHP Jim "Catfish" Hunter is ruled a free agent by an arbitrator since A's owner Charlie Finley had violated an agreement to pay $50,000 on Hunter's life insurance policy.

1978 Texas trades RHP Reggie Cleveland to Milwaukee for RHP Ed Farmer and 1B Gary Holle.

1980 Dave Winfield becomes the highest paid player in team sports when the New York Yankees sign him to a $16 million contract.

1990 Los Angeles trades 3B Hubie Brooks to the New York Mets for LHP Bob Ojeda and RHP Greg Hansell.

1997 Florida trades RHP Kevin Brown to San Diego for 1B Derrick Lee, RHP Rafael Medina, and LHP Steve Hoff.

1999 Arizona trades OF Dante Powell to St. Louis for INF Luis Ordaz.

1999 Florida trades OF Todd Dunwoody to Kansas City for INF Sean McNally.

16

1926 Baseball commissioner Kenesaw Mountain Landis is elected to a second seven-year term.

1951 Mike Flanagan b. Manchester, NH.

1957 Cincinnati trades OF Wally Post to Philadelphia for LHP Harvey Haddix.

1964 Billy Ripken b. Havre de Grace, MD.

1967 Philadelphia trades RHP Jim Bunning to Pittsburgh for LHP Woodie Fryman, LHP Bill Laxton, P Harold Clem, and SS Don Money.

1970 Baltimore trades OF Roger Freed to Philadelphia for LHP Grant Jackson, INF Jim Hutto, and OF Sam Parilla.

1971 Jeff Granger b. San Pedro, CA.

1976 Cincinnati trades 1B Tony Perez and LHP Will McEnaney to Montreal for LHP Woodie Fryman and RHP Dale Murray.

1988 Philadelphia trades OF Milt Thompson to St. Louis for C Steve Lake and OF Curt Ford.

17

1924 The New York Yankees trade RHPs Joe Bush and Milt Gaston, and LHP Joe Giard to the St. Louis Browns for RHP Urban Shocker, the pitcher the Yankees dealt away six years earlier and who enjoyed four straight 20-win seasons with St. Louis.

1932 The St. Louis Cardinals trade 1B Jim Bottomley to Cincinnati for OF Estel Crabtree and RHP Ownie Carroll.

1935 Cal Ripken, Sr., b. Aberdeen, MD.

1960 Charlie Finley receives approval to buy the hapless Kansas City A's. Perrenial losers throughout their years in Kansas City, Finley finds immediate success once he relocates the franchise to Oakland for the 1968 season.

1967 Steve Parris b. Joliet, IL.

18

1886 Ty Cobb b. Narrows, GA.

1930 Bill Skowron b. Chicago, IL.

1940 Zoilo Versalles b. Havana, Cuba.

1953 Roy Howell b. Lompoc, CA.

1969 The Chicago White Sox trade 1B Pete Ward to the New York Yankees for LHP Mickey Scott.

1981 Cincinnati trades 3B Ray Knight to Houston for OF Cesar Cedeno.

1999 Milwaukee trades 2B Fernando Vina to St. Louis for RHP Juan Acevedo.

19

1934 Al Kaline b. Baltimore, MD.

1935 Tony Taylor b. Cuba.

1962 Bill Wegman b. Cincinnati, OH.

1964 Mike Fetters b. Van Nuys, CA.

1966 Joe Slusarski b. Indianapolis, IN.

1997 Florida trades LHP Dennis Cook to the New York Mets for LHP Scott Comer and OF Fletcher Bates.

20

1881 Branch Rickey b. Stockdale, OH.

1888 Fred Merkle b. Watertown, WI.

1900 Gabby Hartnett b. Woonsocket, RI.

1921 The New York Yankees trade RHP Rip Collins, SS Roger Peckinpaugh, RHP Jack Quinn, and RHP Bill Piercy to the Boston Red Sox for SS Everett Scott, RHP Joe Bush, and RHP Sad Sam Jones.

1926 The St. Louis Cardinals trade 2B Rogers Hornsby to the New York Giants for 2B Frankie Frisch and RHP Jimmy Ring.

1949 Cecil Cooper b. Brenham, TX.

1949 Oscar Gamble b. Ramer, AL.

1960 Jose DeLeon b. Dominican Republic.

1983 California trades OF Bobby Clark to Milwaukee for RHP Jim Slaton.

1984 Pittsburgh trades INF Dale Berra and OF Jay Buhner to the New York Yankees for OF Steve Kemp and SS Tim Foli.

1989 Los Angeles trades OF Mike Marshall and RHP Alejandro Pena to the New York Mets for OF Juan Samuel.

1999 Major league owners unanimously approve the $815 million, six-year television contract with ESPN that was agreed to earlier in the month.

1999 Baseball commissioner Bud Selig denies Los Angeles 3B Adrian Beltre his plea to become a free agent. Contending that he was illegally signed by the Dodgers at age 15 in 1994, Beltre was ruled to have participated in the scheme, and his claim for free agency had come too late in accordance with baseball Rule 22. Selig fines the Dodgers $50,000 and also prohibits them from scouting or signing any Dominican Republic players for one year.

21

1911 Josh Gibson b. Buena Vista, GA.

1920 Bill Werle b. Oakland, CA.

1925 Bob Rush b. Battle Creek, MI.

1947 Elliott Maddox b. East Orange, NJ.

1948 Dave Kingman b. Pendleton, OR.

1957 Tom Henke b. Kansas City, MO.

1960 Andy Van Slyke b. Utica, NY.

1960 Roger McDowell b. Cincinnati, OH.

1972 LaTroy Hawkins b. Gary, IN.

22

1915 The Federal League officially disbands after a two-year existence. It debuted in 1914 as a third major league.

1926 Baseball greats Ty Cobb and Tris Speaker deny accusations by former Detroit LHP Dutch Leonard that they had conspired to throw 1919 Tigers-Indians games and had bet on their outcome. The charges would be investigated by commissioner Kenesaw Mountain Landis and later dropped for lack of evidence.

1938 Matty Alou b. Dominican Republic.

1940 Elrod Hendricks b. St. Thomas, Virgin Islands.

1944 Steve Carlton b. Miami, FL.

1948 Steve Garvey b. Tampa, FL.

1961 Andy Allanson b. Richmond, VA.

1964 Mike Jackson b. Houston, TX.

1968 David Nied b. Dallas, TX.

1987 The New York Yankees trade OF Henry Cotto and LHP Steve Trout to Seattle for LHP Lee Guetterman, RHP Clay Parker, and RHP Wade Taylor.

1997 The New York Mets trade OF Carl Everett to Houston for RHP John Hudek.

1999 Atlanta trades 2B Bret Boone, 1B/OF Ryan Klesko, and RHP Jason Shiell to San Diego for 1B Wally Joyner, 2B Quilvio Veras, and OF Reggie Sanders.

1999 The New York Yankees trade RHP Hideki Irabu to Montreal for RHP Jake Westbrook.

23

1871 Sam Leever b. Goshen, OH.
1899 Tommy Thomas b. Baltimore, MD.
1928 Tony Roig b. New Orleans, LA.
1941 Ken Hubbs b. Riverside, CA.
1943 Dave May b. New Castle, DE.
1943 Jerry Koosman b. Appleton, MN.
1975 Arbitrator Peter Seitz rules that Los Angeles RHP Andy Messersmith and Montreal LHP Dave McNally, who had played the 1975 seasons without contracts, are free agents because the reserve clause binds a player to his team for only one year after his contract expires. The clause is not automatically renewed as the owners contended.
1990 Montreal trades OF Tim Raines, RHP Jeff Carter, and RHP Mario Brito to the Chicago White Sox for OF Ivan Calderon and RHP Barry Jones.
1997 Philadelphia trades 2B Mickey Morandini to the Chicago Cubs for OF Doug Glanville.

24

1966 Mo Sanford b. Americus, GA.

25

1855 James "Pud" Galvin b. St. Louis, MO.
1888 At Philadelphia's State Fairgrounds Building, the first indoor baseball game is played as the Downtowners defeat the Uptowners, 6-1, under Cartwright rules.
1925 Ned Garver b. Ney, OH.
1927 Nellie Fox b. St. Thomas, PA.
1935 Al Jackson b. Waco, TX.

1958 Rickey Henderson b. Chicago, IL.
1989 Former New York Yankee player and manager Billy Martin is killed in an automobile accident near his home in Johnson City, NY. The 61-year-old Martin played 11 years in the major leagues, winning three World titles with the Yankees in the 1950s. He later managed five different AL clubs, and in 1977 guided the Yankees to their first World Series victory in 15 years. Martin was hired and fired by New York owner George Steinbrenner five times as the feud between the two men became legendary.

26

1927 Stu Miller b. Northampton, MA.
1940 Ray Sadecki b. Kansas City, KS.
1947 Carlton Fisk b. Bellows Falls, VT.
1948 Chris Chambliss b. Dayton, OH.
1950 Mario Mendoza b. Mexico.
1951 Mark Helminiak b. Stevens Point, WI.
1954 Ozzie Smith b. Mobile, AL.
1964 Jeff King b. Marion, IN.
1967 Esteban Beltre b. Dominican Republic.
1971 Brien Taylor b. Beaufort, NC.

27

1912 Jim Tobin b. Oakland, CA.
1943 Roy White b. Los Angeles, CA.
1963 Jim Leyritz b. Lakewood, OH.
1968 Dean Palmer b. Tallahasee, FL.

28

1900 Ted Lyons b. Lake Charles, LA.
1906 Tommy Bridges b. Gordonsville, TN.
1946 Bill Lee b. Burbank, CA.

1947 Aurelio Rodriguez b. Mexico.
1949 John Milner b. Atlanta, GA.
1952 Ray Knight b. Albany, GA.
1960 Zane Smith b. Madison, WI.
1971 Melvin Nieves b. Puerto Rico.
1994 San Diego trades SS Ricky Gutierrez, OF Phil Plantier, OF Derek Bell, LHP Pedro Martinez, RHP Doug Brocail, and INF Craig Shipley to Houston for 3B Ken Caminiti, OF Steve Finley, SS Andujar Cedeno, 1B Robert Petagine, and RHP Brian Williams.

29

1962 Devon White b. Kingston, Jamaica.
1964 Craig Grebeck b. Johnstown, PA.
1964 Rod Nichols b. Burlington, IA.
1968 James Mouton b. Denver, CO.
1969 Scott Ruffcorn b. New Braunfels, TX.

30

1907 The Mills Commission, assembled by sporting goods magnate Albert G. Spalding to determine the origin of baseball and chaired by former NL president Abraham G. Mills, reveals that the game was invented by Abner Doubleday in 1839 at Cooperstown, NY.
1935 Sandy Koufax b. Brooklyn, NY.
1945 Jose Morales b. St. Croix, Virgin Islands.

31

1900 Syl Johnson b. Portland, OR.
1961 Rick Aguilera b. San Gabriel, CA.
1965 Sil Campusano b. Dominican Republic.
1966 Atlanta trades 3B Eddie Mathews, INF Sandy Alomar, Sr., and RHP Arnie Umbach to Houston for OF Dave Nicholson and RHP Bob Bruce.
1972 Pittsburgh OF Roberto Clemente is killed in a plane crash in Puerto Rico. After 18 years with the Pirates and a .317 lifetime batting average, Clemente will be instantly inducted into the Hall of Fame in 1973. He becomes the first Latin player enshrined.
1974 After being declared a free agent less than two weeks earlier by arbitrator Peter Seitz, Oakland RHP Jim "Catfish" Hunter signs a five-year, $3.75 million contract with the New York Yankees.

Index